JOLLY JACK'S CASTLE

JOLLY JACK'S CASTLE

M2 Easy Publishing

www.m2easypublishing.com
Let us publish your book for free

Copyright 2011 by **Ken Dunn**

Kindle edition November 2011 available from
www.m2easypublishing.com

Paperback edition available from
www.m2easypublishing.com

Acknowledgements

There two people and one institution I have to thank without whom this tale of educational nonsense would never seen the light of day. First, Malcolm Channing who has applied several levels of expertise and advice which have been invaluable towards the organisation of this book. Second is my wife Wendy who, painstakingly, has not only proofed the text but suggested several 'tweaks' to the text as well as correcting my grammar and punctuation which have never been my strengths.

Lastly I have to thank the actual school I was unlucky enough to be part of for several years and particularly the individual I have named as 'Jolly Jack'. Without him, the others in 'management', many of the staff at the time and the idiotic situations which unfolded, none of this would ever have been able to come to print. 95% of it has been recorded as it actually happened, albeit truncated into one year, with only a few fictional additions from me to help the narrative 'flow'. Such a rich source of mindless stupidity would have been difficult to invent.

About the Author

For 5 years, between 1959 and 1964 Ken Dunn trained as an Industrial Designer and then took a PGCE, Post Graduate Certificate in Education – a one year teacher training course. Not wanting to enter education then he worked in Local Government and Museums as a Graphic and Exhibition Designer and after that for several years as a freelance designer. In 1983 he entered secondary education and eventually retired in 2005. He and his wife Wendy now live in Somerset.

THE MANAGEMENT

Wooden The Prick Fat Controller

Jolly Jack

'Anyone who has been to an English
public school will always feel
comparatively at home in prison.'

Evelyn Waugh 1903-66

MICHAELMAS
TERM

1

She drove along savouring the relative peace and tranquillity of the West Country. It was mid May, brilliant sunshine and the journey from London had only taken three hours. Almost there. Going down now around a gentle bend and there was the Cathedral below and the little town of Braumston surrounding all. Entering the town she slowed down and after a couple of minutes found the entrance to her destination. Sliding through huge cast iron gates she parked carefully and stepped up the short flight of stone steps to the entrance of a building of undetermined age. Once inside she found an interior resplendent with ceramic floor tiles, regency wall decoration and the smell of recent floor polish. Passing through two massive oak double doors to a reception area, and brooding behind an old and slightly battered utilitarian desk, sat a 'sporty' looking woman of fifty plus, Maisie Hatter, secretary to the Headmaster, who dragged herself up, coughed painfully and fixed her with a steely eye.

Maggie Thornton introduced herself, was silently ushered into an adjacent drawing room and onto an elaborately carved corner chair. Maggie was an attractive woman in her late twenties, dressed in a sober, charcoal grey two piece, with long dark hair which she found herself fiddling with as she waited. Minutes crawled by as she surveyed the heavily panelled room containing a grotesque grand piano, two lumpy settees, a low table covered in Independent School propaganda and several rubber plants in various states of desiccation.

Her mood was shattered by the sudden reappearance of the secretary who propelled her into the inner sanctum, the Headmaster's study, and to a very low chair in front of an imposing mahogany tree masquerading as a desk. From behind this emerged an intense figure uttering a single, 'Hi!' and extending an arm. This was the Headmaster, Mr H E Roales, known to more than a few on the teaching staff as 'Jolly Jack'. In his late 50's, with thick greying hair and bushy dark eyebrows, he gave the impression of being rather avuncular, family friend, but then everyone made that mistake at the first meeting.

She shook the slightly damp, limp hand which extended from his dark blue, grey, baggy suit and then waited until he made his way back to his perch behind the desk. The noise of flicking paper reached her ears and then, 'Ahh! Yessss… err… Ms… ahh, good, excellent, excellent!'

A few short mumbles later and he appeared again, slightly agitated, walking sideways with a fixed and manic grin saying, 'I'll only be a moment,' and was gone. Seconds later Maisie Hatter, his secretary, reappeared.

'Sorry 'bout that, dear,' she leered. 'He's got a slight, err… problem y'know…? If y'see what I mean.'

This was followed with a knowing wink which obviously presumed an understanding of Jolly Jack's 'condition' but then she grasped Maggie's arm and marched her out to the reception area and to the care of a 6th form pupil, all spots, no chin and about seven feet tall.

'Now we have the tour,' Maisie said, grinning. 'Tarquin will take you to our Admin centre first, won't you Tarky?' Maisie grinned darkly as 'Tarky' nodded silently, without a flicker of emotion.

Following this silent beanpole into the maze of the school, the 'Admin Centre' turned out to be a rather ancient pair of badly converted stables. Maggie caught glimpses of tiny darkened rooms with a few folk hunched over huge volumes, reminiscent of Dickensian counting houses, and then she was upstairs facing the Bursar, Group Captain Wilfred O'Rourke, RAF, retired. He was an officious little man and better known as the 'Prick', because he was. Standing next to him was a rather chubby, but fragile and pained, individual. The Prick introduced her to this obvious invalid, a creature with the name of Michael F Hunt, the 'Financial (Fat) Controller', although it appeared that he was having great difficulty controlling his bowel movements let alone anything else.

With initial introductions over Maggie wondered what was coming next. A rapid stream of questions followed from both of them…. Experience?…. Track record?…. Commitment?…., all of which she felt she answered badly but then she was all too quickly on her way again following the walking dead, Tarky, to another unknown venue.

A few staring, uniformed pupils passed them as they wound their way through the site to a huge 17th century manor house, tucked behind enormous cedar trees. She was greeted by a rotund, gaitered and balding scowl of a man, the Dean, Chairman of Governors. Another small chair and huge desk prevailed with questions which were bizarre to say the least.

Homosexuality?…. Women in the Church?…. Smoking?…. Again miserable with her answers she was taken back to Jolly Jack's study. The Head's secretary, Maisie Hatter, was in mid-mouthful from a messy plate of evil looking spaghetti.

'Back already, dear?' she spluttered. This was not a welcome or encouraging statement.

Wiping her chin with a, 'Thank you, Tarky,' Maisie led Maggie back onto the low chair in front of Jolly's desk. Maggie sat there wondering why she had bothered to apply for this job in the first place. Then Jolly burst in, slightly red-faced and surreptitiously pulling up his trouser zip.

'Sorry 'bout that,' he panted. 'Had a parent to see. Rather urgent.'

She didn't dare think about misunderstanding that but then Jolly was speaking again.

'Do you have any questions, hmm?'

She couldn't think of one.

'Good, good, excellent, excellent!' was his reply and that was the interview over. Maggie drove back to London, quite bemused about the last two hours, resigned to grazing through the papers for something else. Braumstate Cathedral School had proved to be very, very bizarre.

For almost eight hundred years Braumstate Cathedral School had educated the cream of the gentry but now it was down to the skimmed milk and that was rapidly drying up. It desperately needed an increase in revenue via pupil numbers as well as a major TLC operation before any more bits fell off its crumbling buildings.

The school, nestling in its own extensive grounds and tucked in below the rolling Quantock Hills in Somerset, sits at the north eastern edge of Braumston, a small, confused little place with the surprisingly massive edifice of a Cathedral, built in the 12th century as a direct result of the behaviour of a rather obscure but very randy Baron Bathdere.

He had, according to historians, heavily compromised several female members of the aristocracy, including one of the ladies within the Royal household of Henry II. Never slow to anger at the best of times Henry was spectacularly apoplectic at having a member of his entourage 'up the duff'. Some kind of punishment, short of disembowelling, was needed. But, as he'd already had several 'administrative' punch-ups across the land, in between rows with

Thomas Becket, and the Baron just happened to have a large private army, all of whom were as nuts as he was, an 'understanding' was established to prevent more blood being spilled. Henry handed down a cold ultimatum to the Baron to placate the situation and, he hoped, pacify any further wranglings with Becket. A Cathedral would be built.

The Baron, realising that his monarch was intent on this happening lest he vented his bloodlust upon him, duly ordered his followers to flog the local population into the construction of a vast guilt box, as he saw it, a new Cathedral, and continued with this endeavour for the better part of forty years. During that time he ran out of all likely female company, the word had somehow leaked out about his little ways, but, always the one to take advantage of any situation, he developed an unnatural taste for the clergy who flocked to the site as the Cathedral began to rise, as he did, if you see what I mean. Anyway, as a result of his exertions, at least in the building sense, the prospect of an earlier and rather messy Civil War was diffused. The whole thing wasn't finished until well after he died, completely knackered and still unsatiated, in 1213.

Then some bright spark at the time decided it would be a good idea to found a chorister's school to feed the clergy's 'needs' in perpetuity. Over the centuries the school grew to its present size of 650 pupils, from 5 to 18, and still serving the Cathedral with its requisite quantity of large mouthed, evil, bone idle little bastards ever to be found in any school. Still rooted in the feudal past, and boys only, it had survived the worst that time could throw at it. That included the Black Death, the later Civil War, the Labour Party and, worst of all, Margaret Thatcher but not without the odd hic-cup.

One unforgettable event had happened in the late 1950's when horrified staff and clergy alike shuddered at the introduction of a *female* (!) to the teaching body. This happened to be a rather blowsy, very loud Domestic Science teacher appointed on the rather grey basis of an indiscreet liaison with the then Deputy Head during the summer hols in Penrith. 'Cooking' had arrived to both bemuse and confuse both the boys and staff. Others had arrived after her, all highly asexual but with the standard 'sticky-out-bits' to aid identification but they did, at least, soften the overall persona of the school which was seen as a rugby playing, stiff upper lipped, *'don't be such a pansy boy and get back out there in the snow and finish your push-ups!'* kind of a place. Then in the 60's, as if what had happened wasn't enough, co-education arrived. *Girls*!!! The sound of emotional nails being scraped down the blackboard of education could be heard for quite some time after that.

Ten years later the Music School was established as a result of a fairly hairy 'fling' the senior master of the time had experienced with a spectacularly, large bosomed, base clarinet player in Brighton. Specialist musicians, and others, from all over the country began to arrive due to an intriguing entry in the advertising columns of the Times. It had read, '*Wanted. Musicians to handle small things. Girls and boys available.*' This had been placed by a more than angry senior master, furious at the way the base clarinet player had quickly ditched him for the Headmaster. But eventually 'musical' children arrived in coach loads, their parents desperate for them to exercise their 'art' and pick up the three 'R's' at the same time.

The School had now received its final quota of teaching staff, mostly completely nuts, which it has maintained, with a few additions here and there, to the present day. Many of them have been there for almost 40 years and one of them, and this has to be a record for any school, Mr Chips or not, had clocked up 53 years! No wonder he was such a bent, bald and backbiting little shit. What has kept them there is beyond all reason but there they were in this remote outpost of academia, probably happy to continue with their blinkered little lives until they had to be put down.

In any case by the end of the 70's the school was well and truly on the educational map. Punters rolled up in their hundreds, paid their entrance fees, uniform fees, equipment fees, book fees, term fees, extras and so on, all delighted to have their little darlings established in this presumed pinnacle of educational excellence. The 'Education Reform Act 1988' arrived and slid by without causing a ripple. State education might have had to grapple with that but here? Some independent schools are still suffering from ignoring that. But then the 90's arrived and things began to tighten and tighten... A wave of panic, far higher than anything that had happened before, struck the school. Not even good old Baron Bathdere in his most staunch and randiest stance could have gripped the school in as ice-like a grip as the fear of ... *losing income and customers*!

A plan was needed and quickly. Now 'quickly' is a word which has rarely been used, applied or understood by many in this establishment and a few well-deserved heart attacks ensued amongst the Governing body when it popped up. The Headmaster and those who remained were faced with having to do something, anything, before the previous flood of punters they had enjoyed rapidly reduced to less than a trickle. A few silly old buggers suggested 'Sponsored sheep dipping' and 'Own a Stone' for a tenner but the most radical thought, rumoured to have been spawned by a pupil in the remedial class was…*advertising*! They agonised over this for weeks without knowing or understanding what to do until a glimmer of hope came from an unexpected source.

Julian Jolyonn Johnson was a 'geeky' 6th form boarding pupil who spent far too much of his evenings reading the business columns of the Times instead of getting on with revision for his final examinations. His particular interest was in property as he fancied himself as an estate agent. After all, he thought, what's the point in working for a living when you can bull-shit your way through life and earn a lot of money. He confided this to a fellow geek one evening but the conversation was overheard by his housemaster who just 'happened' to be listening at the dormitory door…

'What do you mean, loads of dough?'

'Easy. Just introduce yourself as being in estate management, give 'em loads of crap about using technology to sell stuff and bingo!'

'Bingo?'

'Yeah! Look at this!'

He held up a page from the ad section of the Times and read out loud.

'Development Officer required for Estate Management with skills in Information Technology and Marketing.'

'What the hell does that mean?'

'It means, talk a load of bollocks about organising buildings and stuff, use a friggin' computer to flog things at the same time and persuade the plebs to join in and pay up. Can't be any harder than selling dodgy cars or double glazing!'

'But what do you get out of that?'

'A starting salary of at least 35 grand!'

The housemaster straightened up like a released spring, his eyes wide. Could this be an answer to the School's problems? He scuttled off immediately to phone the Headmaster.

Two days later the Dean of the Cathedral as Chairman of Governors, with the Headmaster in attendance, presided over an extraordinary meeting of the Governing body to discuss this totally new idea given to them by that prying, spying housemaster who, not surprisingly, had claimed the idea as his own after 'many hours of thought given to such a pressing problem'.

Most of the Governors, and particularly the Headmaster, were very unsure about the whole idea. The difficulty for most of them lay in the terminology. 'Development', 'Information Technology' and 'Marketing'. More than a few struggled to understand how a house builder (Development Officer), who could read a dictionary or mend the video (Information Technology) and do the shopping (Marketing) could ever help the school at all.

The Dean, however, thought this might be worth trying however distasteful it may have seemed, particularly the factor of demeaning the tradition of the School through having to *advertise*. After all, they had wasted weeks and weeks over this and here, now, was the only solid contribution that had arrived from anyone which had the remotest chance of gaining new pupils and tackling the alarming erosion of the very fabric of the School. In late April a momentous advertisement appeared in the Times after having been carefully written and checked several times.

BRAUMSTATE CATHEDRAL SCHOOL......
FOR THE BEGINNING OF THE ACADEMIC YEAR...
A DEVELOPMENT OFFICER WITH PARTICULAR SKILLS IN INFORMATION TECHNOLOGY AND MARKETING.....

Dozens of applications arrived within a couple of days of this appearing. Most of them should have been 'binned' immediately but the School's secretary had the onerous task, prior to handing them over to the Headmaster, of organising them alphabetically, listing skills - according to the outline given in the advertisement - age and, lastly, gender. Significantly, only one woman had applied. Maggie Thornton.

Three days after her 'interview' Maggie sat in her flat staring at the outline of the job which had arrived with the application forms. None of this had been fully explained during the so-called interview she'd gone through. So why did they want a Development Officer and what was actually required for the job? There were references to the introduction of Information Technology, Marketing the School to the whole universe and a rather vague and brief statement about the reorganisation of ground staff with regard to the 'fabric', whatever that meant. Pushing the papers away she sat back and sighed, resigned to forgetting about the place which had been… well, 'weird' didn't really cover it. Then she heard the letterbox flap and a single letter lay there with a West Country postmark on it. Puzzled, she opened it and, to her great astonishment, it was from the Headmaster of Braumstate Cathedral School offering her the job!

This was ridiculous! Did she really want this job? Damned right she did! Anything was better than her role with the venerable, London based, Greville, Boman and Hunt, an old quasi-government agency specialising in development schemes. After eighteen months of making the tea, delivering memo's and answering the bloody phone she'd had enough. She phoned the school immediately, was connected to Jolly who was delighted to hear her accept, and followed that brief conversation with a formal letter of acceptance as well as another resigning from her 'executive' roll with G. B. H. There was no going back now!

By the end of July she had sold her flat, giving her a modest profit, and she concentrated on finding somewhere in or around Braumston. She ended up with a first floor, two bedroomed place in the older part of the town and within easy walking distance to the School. On a late August afternoon she made her way to a pre-arranged appointment with Jolly Jack and was again ushered into his office by the Head's secretary, Maisie Hatter. Jolly came bounding in behind them gushing a welcome.

'Hi, Hi! So good to see you, so good! Tea?'

Maisie brought it in on a trolley and left them to it.

'I'll be mother,' Jolly grinned.

With the tea poured they sat on the large sofa opposite his desk and discussed her new responsibilities. Maggie thought she managed to sound reasonably knowledgeable, in the circumstances. The circumstances, in fact, were very simple. With only a thin outline of what she would be doing, little did she know that there was nothing to beat, nothing to prove and nothing to worry about. She would be dealing with a bunch of complete numbskulls who knew far, far less than she did but she wouldn't find that out until later.

'I thought it might be useful if you were to meet the ground staff today,' Jolly then remarked.

They made their way from the main building, round a large, wide lawn to where the ground staff hung out. This was an untidy strip of single storey, brick outhouses, tucked away to one side and screened by a tall, thick hedge of shrubs. They were all in there, sitting round a battered old table all wrapped up in a tense game of five-card brag when Jolly breezed in.

'Good afternoon, gentlemen!' he said, grinning from ear to ear.

They shot to attention trying to hide the cards. Six individuals in various states of boiler-suited dress, fidgeting, looking at each other and then Jolly, all waiting for the bollocking they thought he was about to deliver. But Jolly had missed the cards. He was too involved in being host to this new addition to the school.

'I would like you all to meet Ms Thornton, your new head of department,'

A line of stubbled jaws almost hit the ground. None of them could speak. A woman as their boss! But Jolly missed that reaction and continued.

'I know you will give your support and expertise for the many tasks ahead of us.'

None of them understood what the hell he was talking about but nodded and grinned inanely.

'Now,' Jolly continued. 'I'll introduce you, one by one, so that Ms Thornton can get to know you and your responsibilities.'

The first three looked after the games pitches and the gardens. Kevin Monkton, 'Monkey' to the rest of them, Fred McBride, 'Big Mac', a huge barrel-chested individual and Craig Combe, another huge red-faced character known as 'CC', which had more to do with his capacity for the local ale than anything else. Then there was Harry Jackson, 'Maintenance Engineer' but actually no more than a ham fisted electrician and plumber. He was known as 'Rick O'Shea' because he always had to come back to sort out the cock-ups he'd already committed. Desmond Aston was next, known to all as 'Des Aster', a self-explanatory reference to his 'skill' as a general builder. Last of all was Henry Atterton, pebble glasses, cap, very small and the general handyman. The others had held out there sausage-like hands for Maggie to shake but Henry, bless him, gave a little curtsy! Maggie smiled and they all melted into little boys, looking at their boots, embarrassed and feeling silly.

'Well,' Jolly said. 'That's excellent, excellent! Thank you gentlemen. I'm sure you'll get along splendidly!'

Maggie and he left them, all standing in line, and walked back to Jolly's study. She hoped that the rest of the staff would be a little more 'erudite'.

2

In early September, on the morning of the first day of term for the staff, Jolly, complete in his Headmaster's 'batman' gown, was walking through the School deep in conversation with the Bursar, Group Captain Wilfred O'Rourke, RAF, retired, the Prick. They picked their way along occasionally stepping over an odd lump of stone or broken tile which had recently fallen from the ancient roofs above.

'…so, as you can see, Wilfred,' Jolly was saying urgently, 'I'm very concerned about the fabric.'

The Prick quickly checked his fly then closely inspected Jolly's trousers, clearly puzzled by this odd statement.

'No, no, no!' Jolly spat at him, smacking away the Prick's prying fingers. 'I'm talking about the fabric of the buildings, you silly man!'

Crestfallen, the Prick simply said, 'Oh.'

The Prick was always deferential to Jolly but with everyone else he expected the respect of his rank. He rarely got it. Besides, his only active service had been 'flying' from desk to desk throughout his whole air force career. He was typical of many ex-service parasites who infest independent schools. Jolly walked on waving his hands around.

'Just look at the place! It's falling down! We must do something to organise some kind of refurbishment before major works become inevitable.'

'But we do have the ground staff, Headmaster,' the Prick said, limply.

'Yes, yes,' said Jolly, 'I know we do but they need someone to pull them together! I know you have overall responsibility for them but we need someone *under* you and *above* them to control things. That's exactly where Ms Thornton will be able to help us.'

The Prick was struggling to work out the physiological possibility of that when a pigeon took off from the roof above them, dislodging a piece of the stone capping. It grated down over the roof tiles, shot off the edge and down to smash on the ground in front of them. Both ducked instinctively.

'You see! You see!' Jolly squeaked. 'That's happening all the time! We have to get Ms Thornton onto all of this and very quickly before the whole place falls down around our ears!'

A resounding crash from behind froze both of them. Turning slowly they saw the crumbled ruin of an ancient wooden door lying flat on the ground, dust slowly settling around it. In the doorway stood a small boy still holding the door handle with a few splintered remains of the door around it.

'It wasn't me, sir!' he squeaked. 'It just came off in me hand!'

Then came the sound of breaking glass from somewhere ahead diverting the impending explosion from Jolly and he, followed hotly by the Prick, stumbled round the corner to discover one of the ground staff with a ladder over his shoulder, the rear part of which had just demolished a rather fine example of an ancient, leaded, library window. Henry Atterton, the handyman, cap twisted to one side, squinted through his pebble glasses looking very confused.

'Wahwuzzat?' he mumbled to himself as Jolly and the Prick galloped up to him.

'Henry!' Jolly screeched. 'You've done it again!'

'Hoozddatt?' Henry spat out, sticking his neck out and screwing up what remained of his near useless eyes.

'It's me you stupid old fool!' Jolly exploded.

Two staff heads appeared at a window overlooking the courtyard.

'Henry's done it again,' said one. 'That's four this week.'

'Five,' said the other.

Across the courtyard, in a first floor boarding house window, a small cherub displayed an agitated 'moonie'. Sadly, it went unseen but he scampered off giggling hysterically anyway. The staff continue to watch the furore below as Sid, the caretaker, a 'Tommy Cooper' look-alike, ambled up pulling a bent metal trolley loaded high with pink toilet rolls. Sid surveyed all before him with a poker face. Nothing could phase Sid. He'd seen it all. Two World Wars, the Beatles, Jeremy Beadle, Neighbours, nothing could shake his outlook on the world. He leaned against the trolley waiting to ask a question. By this time Jolly was puce with rage, the Prick limp with frustration and Henry just stood there like a startled owl, gaping and occasionally blinking. More staff gathered at the upper window watching the performance.

'This does not bode well for the morning meeting,' muttered one of them.

'When does anything?' returned another.

Sid, fed up with waiting, asked his question, unheard by the ranting going on in front of him. Jolly stopped in full flood and mouthed, 'Wha...?'

Sid asked his question again, ignoring Jolly completely, fixing his lugubrious gaze on the Prick.

'I said, where d'y want these 'ere bog rolls?'

Jolly smacked his own forehead and stomped off, leaving the Prick, Henry and Sid to sort themselves out. From the window above the staff scattered, as one warned, 'Look out! Jolly's on his way!'

Another wondrous Braumstate educational day was about to begin.

It began. Jolly's worried, furry brow moved in great agitation, twitching spectacularly, reacting to the mixed conversation from the packed room. His expression became further animated and his furtive eyes flicked nervously right, left and then down to a loose collection of notes which he shuffled around in a manilla file. A last flick upwards of the eyes and he spoke.

'Good morning everyone.'

It was an attempt at a rising sonorous wedge to cut through the lack lustre mumblings of those assembled. It failed. He testily cleared his throat and tried again, a little louder this time.

'Good... Morning... Everyone.'

Conversation reluctantly faded as he scanned the faces in front of him and waited for silence from sixty people, all crammed into a room which could barely hold thirty. The local fire officer would have had apoplexy if he'd known about it. Most of them subsided into self-induced hypnosis, as there would be no escape until this mindless ritual of the first staff meeting of the new academic year, usually lasting for an hour and a half, was over. Jolly always delivered a stream of puerile minutia and allowed others to do the same. The Prick, followed by the Financial Controller then droned on about the prospect of a potentially dire financial future. Just the thing to generate and ensure enthusiasm from the whole teaching body. After fifty five minutes the meeting was showing no sign of drawing to a close. One particularly disaffected member of the teaching body glanced at his watch, muttering, 'How much more of this bloody crap can there be?'

'The same amount of crap as last time,' came a muted reply.

Other mumbles began to rise from the less sycophantic members of staff as Jolly gave the floor to his Deputy, known to all as 'Wooden' due to his propensity to seem almost comatose during any conversation. Jolly treated him very badly, as all bullies do, and this had taken its toll. He was a broken man and it didn't help that he was Irish with all the jokes his countrymen had to endure. The mutterings from the staff increased and Wooden wilted then simply sat down in slow mid-sentence. A few toadies stuck up their hands, in the hope of impressing 'sir' with their usual ineffectual crap, much to the disgust of a few hard liners but, unusually, Jolly ignored them bringing the meeting to a sudden halt with a clipped, 'I will see you all in the morning!'

'Bursting for a piss again then?' one of the staff mumbled with obvious satisfaction at the sudden end to their collective ordeal.

Jolly's little problem had indeed intervened but had also prevented him giving them all the important news that they now had an addition to management, Maggie Thornton.

Maggie just sat there wondering what to do next. Her 'office' was more of an open cupboard than anything else, stuck outside the secretary's office at the end of the careers corridor, exposed to all and sundry and adjacent to the Deputy's room, where Wooden lived. Not exactly a useful or welcoming working atmosphere. She'd arrived first thing in the morning ready to begin her new role within the school and she was still sitting there. Apart from a brief welcome from Jolly, before he'd disappeared for the staff meeting, she hadn't see anyone at all save for Maisie Hatter who, sympathetically, made her a cup of coffee and then left her to it. This was not the vibrant start she had expected. Almost an hour slid by then Maisie shuffled out of her office, came over to her and perched on the edge of Maggie's desk.

'So, how's it going?'

'Oh, fine,' Maggie answered sitting back and sighing. 'I haven't been able to talk to the Headmaster, I don't know what he wants me to do, I haven't met any of the staff, I don't know my way around, I have no idea if I have any kind of a budget to work with, there isn't a job description that I'm aware of and my coffee's gone cold.'

Maisie cackled out loud.

'Hah, hah! Join the club. We're all in the same boat, kiddo. Come on, let's have another coffee.'

Maggie joined Maisie over the kettle and shook her head.

'Is it always like this?'

'Oh, no,' Maisie answered calmly, handing her a steaming cup. 'Sometimes it's worse! Joll... that is our esteemed Headmaster, Mr Roales, has been here for about ten years and I can't remember him ever making the simplest of decisions about anything, until you arrived. And that wasn't really anything to do with him. No. It was the Dean who insisted we needed someone to help.'

'So what on earth am I supposed to be doing?' Maggie stated, rather than asked.

'Well...' Maisie said slowly. 'The best thing to do is just wait for a little while. In the meantime get to know the place and the staff if you can. 'Things' tend to happen by themselves around here. It's a case of trying to control them when they happen... and they will.'

Maggie could only give another sigh at the prospect of that.

Maisie grinned and sipped her coffee, gave Maggie a wink and said, 'You won't have to wait that long.'

'How do you know that?'

'Because in about...', she looked at the clock on the wall, '...30 seconds, Jolly will rush through here to, well, service his little problem, then scuttle into his office, then, later may well scamper out with his latest 'idea'.

As the second hand of the clock flicked away the seconds Maggie slowly set her cup down, not realising she was holding her breath. Her cup touched the surface of the desk as the last of the thirty seconds clicked on the clock and Jolly suddenly appeared, rushing passed them in a direct line to the management WC next to his office.

Maisie winked again but then said, ' You'd better brace yourself for Jolly's next 'big idea' which is certainly coming your way!'

Two hours later nothing had happened but then Maggie's phone rang. It was Betty Gordon who ran the School library. The word was beginning to leak out about the new Development Officer.

'Oh, hello,' said a little squeaky voice. 'Is that Ms Thornton?'

'Yes, that's right,' Maggie replied. 'Can I help you?'

'I understand you're looking after the buildings now,' Betty said.

'Well, yes I am,' Maggie answered, but not really sure that she was and wondering what was coming next. 'Anything I can do?'

'Oh, I do hope so. It's Betty Gordon here. I run the library and I have a little problem.'

'You're not the only one,' Maggie thought, but then said, 'Oh, right. So what is the problem?'

'Well,' Betty continued. 'I wondered if you could come up. It's a bit difficult to explain.'

Maggie was intrigued. What could this be?

'OK,' she answered, 'I'll be right there.'

Taking a map of the school site Maggie wound her way through the maze of buildings and found the library. As she walked through the door a strange smell hung in the air. It was not a pleasant one. Betty Gordon came over to her, a little spindle of a woman who darted rather than walked. She was known as 'Flash' to the kids.

'Ms Thornton?' she asked, brightly.

They shook hands and Betty took her into the small office behind a large paper and book strewn desk. The smell was far worse in there.

'What *is* that smell?' Maggie asked.

'That's my little problem,' Betty said, a worried look on her face. 'I don't know. It's been getting worse for days now and nobody seems to know what it is. I don't know what to do about it and thought, with you being the Development Officer, you might, perhaps, be able to do something.'

Maggie didn't have a clue where to start 'doing something' but didn't want to admit that. They stood there sniffing, trying to identify a more precise source for the smell as Sid the caretaker came in carrying two large brown paper packages. He dumped them on the desk and then sniffed.

'Cor, bloody hell!' he grunted. 'Who's dropped one?'

The few kids who were sitting around flicking through the pages of various books sniggered as he said it. Betty came out and gave a loud 'Shhhhh!' in their direction. Sid still stood there, his nose wrinkling up at the smell.

'What have you done then?' he asked.

'I haven't 'done' anything! Betty said haughtily. 'It's in there!' she said, pointing to the office.

Maggie came out still looking puzzled.

'What's she done then?' Sid asked, his face returning to its normal deadpan expression.

'Nobody's '*done*' anything!' Betty snapped. 'It's the room! Just the room!'

'Oh,' Sid replied. 'The room, is it?'

The Prick came in on some errand and hit the smell. With the office door now wide open it was even thicker than before. Some of the kids were now looking quite ill. They left hurriedly, holding their mouths.

'I say,' said the Prick. 'What's that smell?'

'It's coming from the office,' Maggie told him.

'The office?' he queried, sticking his head round the door but pulling it back from the stench. 'It wouldn't be a dead rat, would it? He asked. 'We have had the odd infestation now and again, you know.'

He then prattled on and on about mice, beetles, bats, hedgehogs, cats, dogs, owls, starlings, spiders, bees, wasps, snails, slugs and practically every species of wild life which had been discovered in the school over the years. Fascinating stuff, for him. Everyone else was quickly bored rigid. Sid stood impassively, as ever, behind them all. Before the Prick had stopped talking Sid casually interrupted with two simple words. 'The bog.'

They all turned to him, surprise on every face.

'I beg your pardon?' Betty asked.

'The bog!' he said again, a little louder, but giving nothing away.

'What do you mean by 'the b...', what you just said,' Maggie asked.

'The office. That room,' Sid answered. 'Used to be a bog.'

The Prick was totally confused by this. The others were not exactly in tune either.

'You'll have to explain that, Sid,' Maggie said.

Sid just looked at them all, not a flicker of care on his face. Then he spoke.

'Bout forty or more year ago,' he said, 'that room used to be a bog, a toilet. This place hasn't always been a library. No. Used to be the old laundry. Had to move it 'cos o'the drains. Drains couldn't take the pressure. Happens now and again. Last time were nearly twenty year ago. Had to rip up the whole courtyard to fix it. Hell of a mess that were. Didn't do it properly though. Must be blocked up again. Big job that. Old sewer still runs under there. The old bog.'

The history lesson was over. Sid walked off leaving them standing there.

'Well,' said Maggie brightly, breaking the silence. 'Now we know what the problem is. I'll get the ground staff onto it. I'll be in touch Betty.'

She left the library with the Prick wittering on about something as mindless as his last offering and made straight for the ground staff base. Having explained the problem to them they nodded and began to gather some rather heavy-duty equipment together, loading it into the school truck.

'It's OK, boss,' Big Mac told her, a huge grin on his face just before they drove off. 'We'll get it sorted, never fear.'

Maggie walked back to her desk and slumped into her chair.

'Day one,' she thought, and my first task has been to sort out the old 'bog'. Great!'

Maisie came out of her office with a fresh cup of coffee, placed it in front of her and with a wide grin on her face said, 'Bit different round here,' she said, 'don't you think?'

3

The School was now coming back to life after the summer holiday Boarders had returned and the new kids were being shown the 'ropes' by house staff and some of the senior pupils Day pupils began to arrive, huddling against the cold wind of an early Saturday morning

With the full staff meeting now behind them the first 'normal' morning meeting for the staff, prior to the beginning of the first day of teaching, was about to begin. Jolly arrived in the staff room followed closely by Wooden, the Deputy Head, for the standard morning 'briefing'. All the teaching staff were waiting for them, all jammed together again, ready for another round of useless, purile, verbal nonsense. It would not be truly riveting stuff. A few odd remarks floated up as Jolly and Wooden squeezed their way through to the front.

'Hey, watch it!'

'Who did that?'

'Oohh! That was nice!'

With Jolly now in position in front of them the various mutterings from the staff gradually faded away after his statutory, 'Good morning everyone,' had been delivered. He then ground on with his usual trivia list. Paranoia about money, or the lack of it. Numbers of pupils, or the lack of them. 'Do's' and 'Don'ts' for the year ahead. The importance of arriving on time for lessons. Ensure the delivery of highest quality of education. Be aware of important notices on the staff room notice board. Shut the windows after school. Switch off the lights after lessons. Be on guard against graffiti.... And numerous other 'valuable' pieces of advice, all of which increased the collective depression of everyone. The P.E. Oaf, standard to every school, was already asleep in the corner. Next to him sat the bulk of the Wide Mouthed Frog, Second Deputy and House Mistress, on row three of some vile woollen thing she'd been knitting for weeks. So much for attentive attitudes.

But then all of Jolly's advice was always instantly forgotten by anyone with half a brain. Unfortunately that only covered a very small number of the teaching body. All the sycophants could be easily spotted during Jolly's 'majesterial' announcements by their nodding heads, not unlike those bloody awful things which can be found on the rear shelf window of some cars. Jolly then handed over to Wooden. Good old Wooden. Nervous as hell he began his own rote-like reminders. Shirt tails to be tucked in... Advance information regarding requests for out of school visits... Check notices for the week ahead... and so on, and on, and on...

A soft snoring wafted up from the P.E. Oaf but that was quickly rectified by a deft elbow job from the Head of Science. Conversation grew as Wooden continued to spew out more verbal garbage but Jolly rescued him by asking for any comments or notices for the day. Sheamus Gilpin, the Head of Middle School for kids between 11 and 14, took the opportunity to bark out his own reminders to all and sundry. This was his standard routine for the beginning of every academic year. He was another Irishman who was difficult to understand due to his loud, halted and extremely garbled delivery. Not unlike a certain well known, elderly, now retired former Irish MP. He stopped speaking as suddenly as he had started but no one was any the wiser. But at least he was happy. He'd done his duty, whatever it had been about and whatever it had meant. A few toadies stuck up their hands, were ignored, and the meeting came to an end with Jolly urgently requesting that they should all rush off to assembly. A scrum for the door took place before Jolly was able to button-hole anyone with mindless questions. A few languished in the staff room as the rest scuttled away. The usual comments were muttered to no one in particular.

'Christ! What a fucking way to start the day!'

'What the hell was he talking about this time?'

'Who?'

'Well, I usually like to add just a smidge of lemon juice to the mixture to give it that...'

Others, after the chore of calling out registers, trudged with their charges to the only large building capable of holding the whole School, the Sports Hall. The smell of mouldering sweat pervaded everything. A wonderful test of keeping your breakfast intact for ten minutes. Another day, the first day of the new academic year, had begun in Braumstate Cathedral School....but Jolly still hadn't told them about Maggie Thornton.

With the first teaching day over three of the more 'normal' of the staff were sitting in the staff room. It was well after 5.00pm but they hadn't been able to get away due to the mountain of paper they were obliged to wade through at the beginning of every term. Apart from the obvious garbage which invaded the pigeon hole of every teacher, most of it came from Jolly who used paper as a machine gun fires bullets. His love affair with the stuff was nothing short of obscene. If 'it' wasn't on paper 'it' didn't exist as far as he was concerned. Most of it missed the vital point that communication on the simplest of levels, *talking*, could be extremely valuable. Consequently, all of his memo's, reminders, warnings, queries and copious copies of governmental recommendations ended up in the bin. The only stuff worth keeping were pupil lists, timetables and a diary for the whole year. Many of the staff had been in before the beginning of term to sift through all this 'valuable' information but some of them, these three for sure, refused to waste their own precious time doing that. They had, however, rooted out their own timetable before they began to teach that morning. Knowing when and who they would be teaching was, in fact, fairly important to know. The rest of the stuff now resided in the staff room waste bin which was crammed full and overflowing. That process had, in truth, taken less than 5 minutes and since then they had spent the time swapping notes about the holidays or offering raucous suggestions for the year ahead.

All three of them had been trying to get away from the place for a number of years and had come together as an unofficial 'Escape Committee', resolute in maintaining their sanity against the mindlessness of their so called 'management team'. The conversation, inevitably, settled once again on the dire prospect of yet another term of stupidity from Jolly and his toadies.

'Oh, fuck it!' one of them eventually said. 'I'm fed up with this bloody place!'

'Cor! We've only been back here a few hours. That's a record!' said another.

'Fuck off!' returned the first.

'Go forth and procreate might be better,' Gerald Price offered, smiling. He was known simply as 'Vic'. Gerald was the Chaplain and teacher of R.E., a man of singular directness with a bad habit of telling the truth whether he was asked or not. 'Management' couldn't cope with that. At the same time he was not averse to using language in a surprising way, for a vicar. He was reading one of the national newspapers.

'Have you two seen this new league table?' he asked.

Harry, sitting next to him, he of the 'F off' repost, shook his head. Harry Fulton was the Careers Officer but mostly performed as Head of History. Vic straightened the paper and read out, 'Braumstate Cathedral School. Number one for arseholes!'

'Speak for yourself,' Harry grunted.

The other of the trio stood grinning and made his way to a louver-doored wall cupboard which held a collection of spirit bottles, complete with optics, but now rather low in volume. He decanted three more scotches and brought them over. This was Richard Gates, Head of English with a non-de-plume of 'Rusty', something to do with a combination of his name and hair colour.

'Did either of you see that rather tasty piece walking around with Jolly the other day?' he asked sitting down.

'What tasty piece?' Harry asked, sitting up.

'Don't know who she is. Saw them disappearing round the back of the ground staff's place, that's all.'

'The dirty old bugger!' Vic grinned. 'Didn't think Jolly was like that!'

'He isn't,' Harry said flatly.

As they sat there wondering about this new arrival the door opened and in walked 'Chewbacca', Head of Design and Technology, more normally known as Arthur Chambers. Hirsute and well over six feet tall there was little to figure out concerning his nick-name.

'Hello, you drunken bastards!' was his immediate greeting. Never a shy one was old Arthur.

Grunts were offered in response. He helped himself to a drink and joined them.

'Good to be back, eh?' he said, grinning.

'Piss off!' was the collective reply.

'Oh, good,' he said. 'For one horrible moment I thought you'd forgotten where we are!'

Another Escape Committee member arrived. Amy Scott, Head of Languages, lighting a cigarette as she came in. 'Fag-ash Lill' or just 'Lill' to the others.

'Christ!' she vented. 'Pissed already?'

'YES!' four voices as one.

Lill sat down then looked at Chewy with a puzzled expression.

'What the hell happened to you?' she asked him.

Chewy looked as though he'd been out in the rain, his shoulders and hair quite damp and his jacket had a few scorch marks on it. He sighed and told them his tale of woe. As he ended it Harry couldn't help guffawing and then said, 'Bloody hell! Day one and disaster has already struck!'

Chewy wasn't amused and deliberately changed the subject. At the same time two 5th form scruffs, or year 11's in current educational parlance, were having a chat and sharing a fag in the bushes at the back of the Sports Hall. They were talking animatedly about the same event which Chewy had just told the others of the Escape Committee.

'I tell you, that's what happened!'

'Bollocks!'

'You ask Smudga if you don't believe me!'

'Nah!'

'It's true I tell you and Chewy really wasn't happy about it,' the first one countered, flicking the remains of their illicit fag-end behind him. The other grinned as he imagined the scene.

During the summer holidays Harry Jackson, or 'Rick-O'Shea' –he who always had to return to re-repair his repairs – and so-called maintenance engineer, had installed a creaking central heating system through the Design and Technology building, a Grade One listed, 14th century converted coach house. Chewy had been complaining for years about having to work in freezing conditions every autumn and winter and, at last, the management had scraped a meagre amount of money together to do something about it. It wasn't quite finished by the time the new term arrived and Rick was still in the building on that first teaching day seeing to the last few connections. With the last joint in place he had wandered off. Chewy, always wary of anything Rick was involved with and particularly apprehensive at having him doing anything in his department, was too busy to check as he had a 5th form mob to cope with. He was right to be concerned. The last disaster Rick had committed centred on a repair to a water heater in the Science block. He had rewired the thing but had missed the fundamental fact that it was gas fired. The hole in the wall left after the unit had exploded was quite a sight. Chewy, with some relief, noticed Rick leaving and, unfortunately, thought no more about it.

Five minutes later an increasing hissing noise throughout the building distracted everyone inside it. Without a gas supply in the place Chewy couldn't figure out what the hell was going on when, suddenly, all the pipes Rick had just finished fitting erupted scalding water throughout the two floors of the building. The place was quickly awash, water cascading down the stairs and out through the entrance door.

Sprayed with hot water the kids ran in all directions but Chewy eventually managed to get them outside where he and they stood, dripping. At that moment Rick ambled round the corner whistling to himself. Chewy ran over and pinned him against the wall shouting an assortment of 'anglo-saxon' 'questions'. Before Rick could answer a violent explosion ripped through the building. Windows shattered followed by a billowing, black poisonous cloud. The phase three electrical system had given up to the deluge of hot water, sparks showering down onto and igniting a faulty, half empty gas bottle Rick had brought to use for soldering the pipes. Another, and more than just a small, refurbishment was going to be needed.

The cleaners, bless them, Bessie and Sharon, turned up at the building at 5.30pm. Bessie was in her late 50's, plump and short while Sharon, a mere 28 years old was something of a stick insect. They stood at the main door, brooms and black plastic waste bags in hand, gawping at the mess.

'Buggermee!' Bessie said to herself.

Sharon blinked a few times then summed up the devastation perfectly. 'Don't think 'Mr Sheen' will have much effect 'ere.'

The damage to the department was the latest structural 'problem' the School could easily have done without. But it wasn't so much the 'ancientness' of the original buildings which provided the main problem. No. It was the other less ancient, but no less dilapidated, structures which needed a great deal of attention. As the school numbers had increased over the years the problem of having enough classrooms became critical. That was partially solved by bringing in a few, cheap, easily erected, pre-fabricated, temporary wooden units. Previous Headmasters, recognising a good thing when they saw it, kept on doing it.

The British Army had been another main source for these shacks and in the late 50's an enterprising Bursar, another ex-forces twerp, had pulled what he thought was an amazing deal. He bought seven wooden barrack huts for a whole fiver each. They had been classified by the Army as, *'Personnel, Accommodation for the use of, Redundant.'* Now, when the Army have the sense to get shot of stuff like that there really isn't much point in having them. Not so the School. Almost forty years later all these corrugated metal roofed huts were still on the site but the only thing holding them together were the thousands of layers of paint, creosote and varnish which had been liberally smeared over them every year since they had arrived.

The area which they covered, smack in the middle of the School site, was known, not quite affectionately, as 'Shanty Town'. Jacked up on short piles of bricks they did nothing for open days when the parents flooded the place. Prefects were carefully briefed to divert the punters well away from them. This deflection technique needed rigorous control as some visitors to the site had almost been decapitated on a few occasions from rusting roof sections sliding off when least expected. A couple of the staff, smokers, had been known to deliberately flick a near dead fag under the open bases in the hope of an 'accidental' fire which might sweep the whole lot away. This, sadly, had never worked. On the rare occasion when a small flame had actually taken there had always been some helpful idiot who raised the alarm and managed to put the damned thing out.

In the ten years Jolly had been Headmaster he had succeeded in doing absolutely nothing to improve any of this, apart from anything else, hoping that someone else might deal with it but, of course, they didn't. With Ms Thornton on the staff he now hoped that something could be done before any embarrassing questions were asked... of him.

Maggie Horton asked the question again.

'Headmaster. When will we be able to organise the ground staff properly?'

Jolly blinked and tried to side step the question completely.

'But the ground staff are doing a sterling job, as you know. My only concern is that they should, with your help, co-ordinate themselves to the tasks ahead of them.'

Maggie took a deep breath and tried again.

'They *are* co-ordinated, Headmaster. What they really need is someone to direct them on a daily basis which I don't have the time to do.'

To anyone else that would have been blindingly obvious. Introducing computerisation to the school as well as implementing a strategy for marketing the place to the wide world wasn't exactly a part-time occupation. If she was to make any kind of headway with either of these areas someone else would have to look after the day to day repair or refurbishment of the buildings on the site. Days had gone by before she was able to arrange this appointment to talk to Jolly. He'd been too 'busy', fretting about how the beginning of term had been going but Maggie was in no mood to be fobbed off any more.

'But,' Jolly then said, weakly, 'surely Mr Aston could provide the necessary expertise, couldn't he?'

'Headmaster,' Maggie said calmly, 'Mr Aston, Desmond Aston, although a very nice chap, is known to all as 'Des Aster'. Doesn't that tell you something?'

Maggie had done her homework as far as the ground staff were concerned.

'Oh, really?' Jolly asked, a puzzled expression on his face. 'Then what do you suggest?'

'Well.' She began slowly. 'Why don't we try to find a… Development Manager… a Works Manager… a Manager of the Works…'

'Or..', Jolly said brightly, 'a *Clerk* of the Works!'

In his little head this new, to him, term combined his love for paper and the immediate problem before him. It would be yet another way of perpetuating his love of the paper chase to everything around him.

'Fine,' Maggie sighed, hoping she'd made her point. 'That will do nicely. Would you like me to write out the advertisement?'

'Yes, yes, excellent, excellent!' Jolly enthused. 'That would be a very good idea. Thank you, thank you!'

Relieved, Maggie walked back to her desk to pass Maisie who was standing, grinning, leaning against the doorframe of her office. She followed Maggie over to her desk and perched on the end, the wide grin still on her face.

'So,' Maggie said. 'you were listening through the intercom, eh?'

'Yup!' Maisie said. 'But well done. You actually managed to get a decision out of him. Not an easy task.'

'Well, I had to do something. A works manager will make a big difference.'

'A *Clerk* of the Works.' Reminded Maisie. 'But you do realise that this will now be *his* idea, the '*big idea*' I warned you about and God only knows what he'll do with it!'

The following day, Friday, and Jolly had wound himself up, at last, for a major announcement. Taking a deep breath he opened the staff room door followed by Wooden, the Prick and the Fat Controller. As they pushed their way through the throng Chewy sank into his seat with a groan.

'Oh, shit!' he grunted. 'It's the four horsemen of the bloody Apoplectic!'

He had good reason to say this. Apart from the beginning of term staff meeting the only other times the Prick and FC arrived was when something serious was in the wind. Jolly cleared his throat loudly and spoke the magic words. 'Good morning everyone.'

'Oh, God. Now what?' grumbled Vic.

An audible, collective sigh oozed out and several hardened individuals, mostly the Escape Committee, braced themselves for what they thought would be a verbal onslaught of dire proportions. Was this to be the beginning of job cuts or worse?

'Refurbishment!' Jolly said suddenly. 'Refurbishment!' he snapped again and sixty pairs of eyes widened.

'I have been aware,' Jolly continued without a pause, 'as no doubt you are, that there are serious problems developing within the school.'

'Is he talking about himself?' murmured Lill.

Jolly continued. 'Today, I have to inform you that, with the Governors approval, we will be appointing a full-time Clerk of the Works to control this situation. This position will be overseen by our new Development Officer. She will be with us in a few moments.'

Seconds of stunned silence ticked by, the relief of still having a job mixed with the revelation of a new, female, Development Officer! The hiss of 'She?!' punctuated the void, uttered by several misogynists.

'What Development Officer?' grumbled Rusty. 'It's the first I've heard of this!'

A general rumble bubbled up which Jolly quietened down with some difficulty. He began again, obviously flustered by the general reaction his statement had made.

'We.., we will now be able,' he said, 'to apply a professional approach to a problem which has been concerning me for some time.'

'Now that's a bloody first!' Chewy hissed sideways to the others who couldn't help a muffled chortle.

'I will be grateful if you will help the Develoment Officer in all her needs,' Jolly then said.

'Happy to oblige!' Rusty said, lasciviously.

The Prick and FC hadn't said a word and Wooden, after a gesture from Jolly, took over the meeting having the effect of switching everyone off completely. The meeting crumbled into a growing mumble, a collective fascination revolving around these two new additions to the 'work force'. Intense speculation grew about whoever the poor sod was who'd been appointed Development Officer and then who they would wind up with as Clerk of the Works. Wooden gave up and fell silent. Jolly didn't even notice this as he was engaged in an intense, whispered conversation with the Prick and the FC.

Maggie Thornton took a deep breath and climbed the stairs to the staff room. She approached the door and could hear the low rumble of conversation from the other side. This was it. Hand on the door knob… and it was yanked away from her as Jolly hurtled passed her in a state of great agitation, desperate to service his 'little problem', again. The Prick and Wooden pushed their way through to her.

'He'll be back in a minute,' Wooden monotoned to her. 'He's just popped out to… err…'

The Prick interrupted with, 'To see someone.' A sickly smile slid across his face, his hands in 'Uriah Heap' mode. Then he backed away, an open palm indicating where she should go, which was next to the FC. He just stood there with a blank expression, staring directly ahead. Then Jolly was back, pushing through and taking her arm.

'Forgive me, my dear,' he panted. 'An urgent, err… telephone call. Now…' and he turned with her to the rest of the staff.

'May I introduce you to the staff, Ms Thornton.' He waved a hand expansively in their direction, which was everywhere. 'Ms Thornton is our new Development Officer.'

Maggie met sixty pairs of eyes and total silence. She could feel herself going bright red with embarrassment which was not helped when Jolly moved back and left her standing by herself. She nodded at them, then turned, wanting to run away but simply stepped back next to Jolly and hoped this wouldn't last much longer. The silence continued but Jolly suddenly said, 'Right! Good! Excellent, excellent! Let's all cut along to assembly now!'

A low rumble from the staff floated up as they broke ranks for the door, Jolly holding Maggie back to have a few words.

'Well, now,' he said, 'I'd like to introduce you to the whole School after our assembly, if you don't mind. I do like everyone to know who the staff are and what they do.'

The School had gathered in the large and squat brick box of the Sports Hall and a lull settled over all of them as Jolly arrived with an ashen Development Officer. After the brief, legal requirement of a religious nature, several notices were given, mere repetitions of previous sycophantic statements, and then came the moment of introduction. Maggie could only summon a sickly grimace as she felt as if the hundreds of kids and staff were almost dissecting her with their eyes…in total silence.

Later, in the staff room, during morning break…

'She had a lovely…' Chewy was saying.

'Behave yourself!' Lill warned.

'Smile! – I was about to say!' he retorted.

'Oh, yeah, I'll bet you were!' Rusty chipped in.

'Poor cow,' sighed Vic. 'She probably doesn't☐realise what she's taking on. Can you imagine what Jolly might be wittering on about right now? *'Well, my dear, I think we should examine all the possibilities, be aware of the potential, weigh up the situation and be cautious how the implementation of any progress should be handled.'* After a few minutes of that kind of crap she won't know where the hell to start!'

'Oh, I don't know,' smirked Chewy. 'She could, *'Hear what he says,'* *'Take it all on board,'* *'Run some ideas up the flag pole,'* and, *'Prepare a thorough assessment for the future.'* In short, end up doing sod all, just like the rest of our esteemed management.'

'If all she does is sack some of the plonkers amongst the ancilliary staff,' added Rusty, 'and find someone who isn't a demolition expert she'll be well ahead.'

'Well, let's at least give her a chance,' Lill said. 'She can't be as bloody useless as the rest of them.'

Harvey Sheasby, Head of Geography and Senior Master, scowled in their direction.

'Appalling!' he thought. 'Never a good word from any of them!'

Harvey was a 'company man', a complete creep and a direct line to Jolly on any slight criticism of the School. Most of the staff were careful what they said, either directly to him or within his hearing. Whatever he heard it always went straight to Jolly. Chewy noticed Harvey's attention and nudged Lill, who signalled to Vic, who passed it on to Rusty. Harvey flicked his eyes away and back to his crossword puzzle, obviously bridling inside. He would have to pass this information to the Headmaster as soon as possible.

-4-

Some days later Maggie Thornton was sifting through a pile of applications which had arrived for the post of Clerk of the Works She'd written out a serviceable advertisement for this, attempting to cover all the areas of expertise she thought were necessary, showed it to Jolly who was happy to allow her to place it as quickly as possible Maisie was impressed

'That was quick,' she said. 'It usually takes a week or more to get him to even begin to think about agreeing to do anything.'

'I did wonder about that,' Maggie admitted. 'But at least we're moving in the right direction.'

'That's because *you* are handling *his* 'big idea' and if it goes wrong, guess who'll get the blame?'

'Oh, thanks a lot,' was all Maggie could say.

Lunch beckoned and she decided to try out the School Dining Room. Up till now she hadn't found the time. Over-seeing the ground staff working on the 'drain' problem, familiarising herself with the school and thinking about 'marketing' had kept her fairly busy. Sandwiches and a couple of cups of coffee with Maisie had been the norm until now. She still hadn't met any of the teaching staff and this might be an opportunity to make some kind of contact with them.

She arrived, fortunately, after the initial melee had been and gone. A scattering of kids were still there but no staff. As she sat down, with an unidentifiable piece of pie surrounded by a few limp vegetables, a few of the staff drifted in who then flanked and surrounded her, all members of the Escape Committee. They were intrigued by this new face and a couple of them had the vague notion that she might even be recruited to their cause, the confusion of the management. Not difficult. With friendly introductions over Chewy opened the conversation.

'How's it going, then?'

'Oh, not so bad.'

'That's good,' Lill said with a smile. 'I wish I could say that.'

'Anything interesting in the pipeline?' Chewy asked.

'Ah, yes,' Maggie said brightly. 'Your place for a start. The ground staff are close to completing the drain problem and they should be with you tomorrow.'

'Oh, that's so good to hear,' Chewy beamed. 'It's been a bit tricky trying to teach on a bomb site!'

Maggie grinned. 'I'm just sorry I haven't been able to get the lads over before now, but I promise you they'll be there tomorrow.'

'That's great!' Chewy said. 'Looking forward to that.'

Rusty couldn't help asking the next question.

'Can you tell us anything about this 'Clerk of the Works' job?'

'Ah, that,' Maggie replied. 'I'm trying to sort out the applications for that right now.'

'Really?' Chewy mused. 'How do they look?'

'Not sure,' she answered, slightly hesitantly, but then relaxed and thought, 'Ah, what the hell!'

'To be quite honest,' she admitted, 'it's not an area of work I'm completely familiar with.'

This was becoming very interesting. Chewy and Rusty exchanged discrete but knowing looks. Harry noticed that but didn't say anything.

'Want a hand?' Chewy asked, an innocent look on his face.

'If you wouldn't mind!' Maggie beamed at him.

Vic, Harry, and Lill looked on. They could almost smell the whiff of potential sabotage.

'O.K.,' Chewy said. 'What about after school today?'

'Great! Where?' she asked.

'Come over to the office,' Chewy said. 'The D&T block is just behind the courtyard from the Library. You can't miss it. It's the one with the broken windows and scorch marks!'

After School had ended for the day Chewy sat in the D&T office, ignoring the devastation immediately outside it, looking out of the window. Sitting with him was his number two, Howard Stokes, an absolute whiz-kid on computers, and Eddie Domple, technician, known as the 'Dumpling'.

Some time ago Chewy had decided to cover the inside of the window surfaces with a thin, transparent, plastic security film. The building was at the junction to the main road and a small one-way street which cut right through the School. The whole point of this addition to the windows was to keep prying eyes out while still allowing light to come through. He then realised it gave the distinct advantage of seeing out while not being seen. Many a few minutes had been spent by all of them, gazing through the windows while the kids and staff passed by, all of them totally unaware of being watched.

This was such a day. As they looked out to the main road the Poisoned Dwarf, the diminutive Art Mistress, reversed out of the car park from the left, in her normal fashion, at about thirty miles an hour. She just missed three kids, almost connected with a Post Office van but rammed the base of an extension ladder which Henry the handyman happened to be up at the time. As she drove off, oblivious to all of this, Henry grimly clung on while the ladder teetered about then fell with a terrible crash, landing him across the bows of a saloon car which had just entered the narrow one-way street. The car stopped with a fiendish screech of brakes and a loud argument broke out between a rather winded and myopic Henry and the occupants of the car.

'Bloody tourists!' Chewy growled, sipping his coffee.

The episode had ended by the time Maggie turned up to see him. Howard had sloped off to fiddle with his electronic 'rams' and 'roms' and Eddie had decided to go and join the ground staff for their late afternoon card game. She picked her way through the heavily charred entrance, found the office, settled herself into a chair offered by Chewy and accepted a cup of coffee. Rusty turned up grinning widely.

'Now,' Chewy said. 'How can we help?'

Maggie pulled out the applications for the Clerk of the Works job from a shoulder bag and slapped them on the table.

'Well,' she said. 'There they are.'

Chewy flicked through them with Rusty looking over his shoulder.

'Oh, I think we can find you someone from this lot,' Chewy grinned.

This was a truly golden opportunity for the Escape Committee. The applications ranged from totally incompetent DIY buffoons to desperate ex-forces nut cases. The temptation of advising for either complete disaster or something akin to common sense was now, literally, in their hands. It didn't take too long to make the decision. Whatever they suggested would almost certainly be cocked up by Jolly so, without giving another thought, they randomly pulled out six applications.

'There we are!' beamed Chewy. 'That should do it!'

Maggie was delighted. 'Thanks. You really have saved me a great deal of time. But which of these do you think should get the job?'

'Ah,' Rusty said. 'Now that needs a little more thought.'

Chewy and he poured over the six applications, organised them into a kind of rank order and handed them over again. She took them, quickly scanned through each one, packed them back into her bag and thanked them again.

'Pleasure,' said Chewy. Both Rusty and he gave her a huge grin as she left the building.

The following morning Jolly Jack was impressed. On his desk were the six applications for the Clerk of the Works job with a covering memorandum from Maggie. She had quickly cottoned on to the love affair he had with paper communications. As far as he was concerned she had executed this first step in an exemplary manner. Sifting through them for an hour or so gave him no more of an idea of what he really wanted or what a Clerk of the Works actually did. Then his intercom buzzed.

'Yes?' he enquired.

'I have Mr Quentin Braumsley waiting for his 10.30 appointment,' Maisie said, sounding bored rigid. She probably was. Braumsley could send anyone to sleep with his endless drivel.

'Oh, fine, fine,' Jolly answered. 'Do send him in.'

Quentin flounced in, plopped onto the chair in front of Jolly's huge desk and began to prattle on. He was a complete buffoon. His mother, Lady Braumsley, owned most of the town and surrounding area as well as large tracts of the School's land and buildings. The Braumsley ancestors had been toadies to the infamous Baron Bathdere of old and, as a result of their endless arse licking, as well as even more unsavoury acts, he gave them a vast chunk of land in recognition of their 'services'. Even the town, Braumston, had been named after the family.

Over the centuries they had interbred like rabbits and now they were not only very wealthy people, due to the income from their estate, but they were all either half crackers or absolutely bloody mad. Quentin was roughly between these two states and had never worked in his life. He spent most of his time talking and dreaming up ridiculous schemes. Whether there was anyone listening to him or taking notice of his 'ideas' didn't really seem to matter to him. His 'hobby' was the School which he couldn't keep away from and he regularly saw Jolly to discuss mindless notions about how the place could be 'improved'. Jolly endured these visits to keep Lady Braumsley off his back. She was not the easiest of people to get on with and as 'landlord' of the School he had to be careful. On this occasion Quentin was very anxious about potted plants. There didn't seem to be enough of them around the School.

'So you see,' Quentin was saying, 'if we had a grand plan where they could be 'woven' into the very fabric of the whole site it would make such a difference, don't you think?'

Jolly picked him up on that.

'A grand plan you say?'

'Yes.' Quentin continued, enthusiastically. 'I see the need for a more organised 'routine', if you get my drift, which will make this kind of thing easy to implement. After all, it would really make a difference to the general 'ambience' of the whole School, if you see what I mean.'

Jolly did. He became quite animated by this and it suddenly gave him an idea and a new direction to go in. He was no longer concerned about which of the candidates he might appoint to the Clerk of the Works job. Picking up the applications he stuffed them into a drawer and leaned across his desk, smiling sweetly.

'Quentin,' he began. 'Have you ever been involved in the practical side of running a School?'

'He's done *WHAT*?!' they all said at once.

Maggie Thornton said it again, slowly.

'The Headmaster… has appointed… Mr Quentin Braumsley… as Clerk of the Works.'

The Escape Committee couldn't believe their ears. Anyone was better qualified than that bumbling, barmy, buffoon Braumsley!

'Christ!' Rusty said in despair. 'He wasn't even amongst the applications! We'd be better off with Bugs bloody Bunny or Tom and Jerry than that stupid bastard!'

Chewy slapped his hands over his ears and closed his eyes with a grimace of pure frustration.

'And we spent all that time trying to screw up the management with a random collection,' he said. 'One of them might have been able to do the job, however badly, but now Jolly does this instead!'

Harry slumped further into his chair. 'Give me the Time Ed,' he said desperately. 'There has to be another bloody job somewhere else.'

Lill just sat there, dumbfounded. Vic rubbed his chin and then said, very slowly, to nobody in particular, 'Well, we now have not only a Headmaster who doesn't know his elbow from his arse, a Deputy who forgot where he left his brains thirty years ago, a Bursar who expects to be saluted all the time, a Financial Controller who can't add up, a Maintenance Engineer who uses the plans of the Titanic as a guide to plumbing… but now we have a Clerk of the Works who wouldn't know a brick from a lump of shit even if it crawled up his leg and bit his bum. With management like this how can we lose?'

The louvre doored wall cupboard was duly opened and much needed anaesthetic was ceremoniously and liberally dispensed to all. Another blow had been struck against all reason or was that the sound of yet one more nail being hammered into the educational coffin of the School? Time alone would tell.

5

Quentin sat in the great drawing room of the Braumsley home, a rambling and ancient country house, set in the middle of extensive park land and a couple of miles outside the town Scattered around him were numerous copies of 'House and Garden', 'Country Life', 'Good Houskeeping' and several other 'up-market' magazines He was flicking through one of them, whistling and chattering away to himself, occasionally stopping to cut out a picture, advertisement or article On the table next to him lay a large scrapbook which he was slowly filling He'd been sitting like this for hours muttering the odd, 'Oohh! That's nice!' and 'Ahh! That's lovely!' as he assessed the contents of these guides to 'style' The floor around him was covered in shredded paper The fact that what he was amassing had nothing whatsoever to do with the actual duties of a Clerk of the Works hadn't entered his little head at all He was working on a plan he'd been fretting about for some time and this was going to be the introduction of potted plants to the whole School site The Headmaster had seemed very interested in this and now, with his new role as Clerk of the Works, he was determined to make sure that his scheme would enrich and enhance the whole School… and how *pretty* it would be! He could almost hear the parents now, congratulating him on having such sensitivity, such good taste, such…

'*QUENTINNN!*'

The door had opened and there stood his mother, eighty nine years old, propped on a walking stick, grossly over-weight, slightly cross eyed and dripping with pearls. Lady Agatha, Hortense, Daisy – her father had a 'thing' about cows – Braumsley. She was a poisonous old bat and hated her son who she regarded as a stupid, idle 'poof', and said so, often.

'*Quentin!*' she barked again. 'What the hell are you doing, you little sod!'

The little sod jumped up, quivering. Although he was in his sixties he still had a healthy respect for 'Mummy'.

'Oh, hello, Mummy!' he squeaked. 'I… I didn't hear you come in!'

'Course you didn't hear me,' she snapped, hobbling over to him. 'Too busy sticking silly pictures into another stupid book again! What is it this time? Save the slugs? Home rule for pussycats? A campaign for off the shoulder buckets? What?'

'Well,' he began, 'I was just putting the finishing touches to…'

'No. no, *no*! Don't tell me!' she snapped, waving her free hand in his face. 'I really don't want to know!'

'But…' he tried to say.

'No! That's enough!' she snarled.

He sat down, completely deflated, and began to sulk.

'Don't just sit there, you silly boy!' she growled at him, impatiently. 'We have to be at the Town Hall tonight in less than an hour! Had you forgotten? We are the guests of the Council. They want to talk to me about some sort of 'proposals'. Get along and sort yourself out. The car will be ready for us at seven. *So move yourself!*'

Quentin crept off leaving his cuttings and the surrounding mess he'd made behind him. 'Mummy' poked at the stuff with her stick, gave a great 'Harrumph!' and stomped off, leaving it all for the domestic staff to clean up.

The Braumsley Rolls slid to a halt outside the Town Hall. Quentin opened the door on his side and began trotting off towards the pub on the other side of the square. Before the chauffeur opened the other door for her Ladyship she bellowed through the open window at her son.

'QUENTINNNNN!'

He stopped dead in his tracks, turned, shoulders drooping and shuffled back, a hangdog expression on his face. The chauffeur helped Lady B from the car and stepped back as Quentin took her arm. Supporting her great bulk he walked slowly by her side, up the steps to the double doored entrance of the Town Hall. They were met by the Town Clerk, George Mossop, a slight, little man of wizened features and of the hand-wringing variety.

'A very good evening to you, Lady Braumsley,' he said, grinning inanely.

She merely grunted in reply and swept past him across the foyer to the steps leading to the Council Chamber with Quentin hanging on. The steps took some time to negotiate, without a great deal of help from her son, but she eventually made it to the top, stomped through the open doors and into the Chamber. Settling herself into a large chair by the side of the Town Clerk's lectern she scanned the faces of the Council members who were already there, all standing politely and now sitting down, one by one, in ranks on either side of her, ascending row by row.

With his mother in place Quentin dithered around not knowing where to sit. He fiddled about for a few seconds, much to Lady B's great irritation, until one of the ushers escorted him to a chair behind her. Now that the pair of them were settled the formal meeting could begin. George Mossop, standing behind the lectern, unrolled a parchment-like scroll and began to read.

'Let it be stated here that this is a formal statement of renewal and refurbishment…'

At this last word Quentin perked up. That was just what he was trying to do at the School! He went sailing off into his own little world, thinking of all the new additions he would be making to the School environment. The Roses, the Lupins, the Hollyhocks and the Dephiniums! It was going to be so… so pretty!

'… and in so far that the afore mentioned Lady Braumsley has agreed to the schemes, in principle, I now put it to the vote.'

George Mossop slowly sat down, placing the scroll across the lectern. Quentin had heard nothing of this. He'd been totally wrapped up in his own pot-planting scheme for the last fifteen minutes but then wondered why all the Council members were holding their hands up. Quentin stuck his own hand up, just in case this was the 'thing' to do. You could never tell with this kind of event. The Town Clerk gave him an odd look but then turned away to look at the ranks of Council members on either side.

'I recognise the wishes of the Council,' he said gravely. 'The motion is carried.'

Quentin shrugged, wondering what all that had been about but then jumped off his chair as his mother barked at him to help her. He hung onto her all the way back to the Rolls and then they were on their way home.

The following day the local newspaper had given over its front page, and many of the others, to the previous evenings meeting at the Town Hall. Jolly Jack spread the thing across his desk and sat there with his head in his hands. This was terrible news. He couldn't understand why he hadn't been forewarned or informed much earlier. The mystifying thing was that Quentin had been there! Why hadn't he told him what was going on? Jolly turned the pages again which were full of George Mossop's speech, statements from other Council members and maps about the new proposals for the town. He flicked them back in disgust leaving the main banner headline staring up at him.

NEW BY-PASS AT LAST!
Braumsley Estate agrees to sell land for major by-pass for the town!

'Maisie!' Jolly spat into his intercom. 'Get me Mr Quentin Braumsley as soon as you can!'

'Yes, sir!' Maisie answered immediately.

'Oh, God!' she thought. 'What the hell's going on now?'

She could always tell when Jolly was in one of his 'states' and this one seemed to be fairly frantic. Twenty minutes later after several phone calls she still hadn't tracked Quentin down and just as she was wondering where he might be and who else she could contact he turned up, mincing into her office.

'Hi!' he greeted her, a stupid grin on his face and holding an enormous pot spewing a thick bush of long, lank, dark green leaves. 'Is the man available?'

'Oh, yes,' Maisie said darkly. 'That he is.'

Jolly Jack glared across his desk as Quentin entered his study and settled himself in front of it, still holding the pot plant, the same silly grin on his face.

'Quentin,' Jolly said quietly but through clenched teeth. 'What were you doing last night?'

'Last night?' Quentin asked brightly, missing the expression of fury on Jolly's face. 'Last night... Oh, yes, I was with Mummy at a Council meeting.'

'Yes,' Jolly replied, barely keeping his temper. 'I know you were with... 'Mummy' at a Council meeting. I want you to tell me... *why*?'

'Because she insisted I should go, that's 'why',' Quentin said, crumpling slightly under this sudden interrogation. He fumbled with the pot plant and then plopped it onto Jolly's desk so that he could get his hankie out. Jolly had to move his chair to see across the desk instead of being faced with an enormous amount of foliage which had been dumped in front of him.

'You do realise what actually happened last night, don't you?' Jolly asked him.

Quentin was busy blowing his nose.

'Your mother,' Jolly continued not waiting for an answer, his voice rising, 'has agreed to hand over to the Council an extensive, wide strip of land *which cuts right through the middle of the School for a new by-pass for the town!*'

Quentin stopped blowing his nose, wiped it and slowly put away his hankie.

'Has she? Did she?' he answered quietly.

'*You were there!*' Jolly almost shouted, standing up and leaning over the desk, his hands spread wide.

'Oh, dear! That's awful!' Quentin mewed, sagging into the chair below the venomous glare from the not so jolly Jolly Jack.

The staff room common room was buzzing with the news before Jolly arrived for the morning meeting. A hush settled over everyone as he came in, pushing his way through to the front. Today was different. No trivia. No nonsense. No bullshit. Not even 'Good morning everyone'. He came straight to the point.

'Many of you may be aware of the statements in the local press about the events which took place last night at the Council meeting in the Town Hall.'

There wasn't a sound. He had their full attention. Even the P.E. Oaf was wide awake and listening intently. The Escape Committee, in particular, were fascinated as to what he was going to say next. Jolly took a deep breath and began again.

'Although it seems we might lose a major area of land and several buildings for a new road system, this so-called agreement is in 'principle' only, so there may be the opportunity to amend, if not change, the proposals as they presently exist.'

A rumble of conversation rippled around the staff room at this but Jolly was on his way out, leaving Wooden to deliver the trivia for the day. He began to speak but the staff were too busy talking about the road proposals to take any notice of him. He gave up and sat down, staring emptily into space.

Maggie Thornton wandered back to her desk as the others reluctantly made their way to assembly. She now had a larger and dual disaster. She not only had a complete idiot as a Clerk of the Works but a major problem in the shape of this revelation of a new by-pass through the land used by the school. She had known nothing about this and realised that all of the staff, including Jolly, hadn't known about it either. How the hell was she going to put a 'Development Plan' together with this kind of thing happening out of the blue and totally beyond her control? A meeting with Jolly was now a top priority.

In the staff room, after lessons that day, Lill, Chewy and Rusty were deep in conversation about the by-pass proposal.

'But if it goes ahead,' Chewy was saying, 'It'll chop the whole bloody place up!'

'We don't know that,' Rusty said. 'They've been talking about a by-pass for years and years and every time it comes up there's a storm of protest from all sorts of folk.'

'Yes,' Lill chipped in, 'but this time that old bat Braumsley is allowing her land to be used. She's always refused before. That's what makes this quite different from all the other schemes of the past. Anyone living or working on her land, like us, haven't got a chance.'

She had summed the whole thing up in a nut-shell. There seemed to be no way out.

'What I can't figure out,' Chewy said, 'is why the old battleaxe has actually changed her mind. There must be something else going on we don't know about.'

'Not necessarily,' said Rusty. 'I think she's just a greedy old bitch and has probably noticed how land prices are beginning to rocket.'

As it turned out that wasn't so far from the truth.

Vic came in and sat down. 'Looking a bit glum, aren't we?'

'Too bloody right we are,' Chewy answered.

'Oh, the road,' Vic grinned.

'What the hell are you so happy about?' Rusty asked.

'Oh, I wouldn't say 'happy' exactly,' Vic replied. 'It's just that there's always a way around things. After all, life is never that black or white.'

'Hey!' Chewy said. 'Pack it in, Vic. We can do without one of your bloody sermons. Just what the hell do you mean by, 'there's always a way *around* things?'

Vic smiled and leaned back, his hands coming up to cradle the back of his head.

'Blackmail,' he said, and then very slowly, 'black…mail.'

For a vicar he was certainly 'unconventional' in his dealings with people and situations. The others sat in silence waiting to hear what the hell he was talking about. Vic looked from face to face, his smile breaking into a wide grin.

'Well?' Chewy asked.

'Well,' Vic began, leaning forward and savouring every word, 'there is an old rumour that a certain old bat had a fling with someone on her estate a long, long time ago and… there is an 'addition' to her family… somewhere.'

Not one of them said a word, their eyes wide with surprise.

'How do you know that?' Lill then asked.

'Gossip,' Vic replied. 'Good old gossip. But if a little research could be done… well, that could be, in the circumstances, an interesting 'tit-bit' to… shall we say… use, couldn't it?'

He sat back watching all of them as the thought he'd planted quickly grew in all of them. Then they all burst out laughing at the prospect of proving the rumour was true.

'Do you know who this 'addition' to her family might be?' Lill asked when she had calmed down.

'No,' Vic replied, 'but it's something which has been talked about for years. If it's true, and we can find out who it is…'

Without any of them knowing, Harvey Sheasby, chief toady to Jolly, had waddled in and was faffing about in the small side office where the pigeon holes for all the staff were mounted. He heard the others talking followed by gales of laughter. Crouching down he tried to listen to what was going on. He had missed Vic's revelation but knew in his water that they were planning something.

'Where the hell do we start looking,' Chewy was saying.

'And who the hell do we approach first?' Rusty added. 'You know what this place is like. Finding someone to talk isn't going to be easy.'

'We need to track down anyone who used to, or still does, work on the estate,' Lill suggested.

'What about the list of ancillary staff for the School? Rusty asked. 'Doesn't that include estate workers? Some of them might have worked on the place years ago.'

'I'll check,' Chewy offered, ambling over to the notice board.

Just as he began leafing through the layers of crap notices he caught sight of Harvey Sheasby on his hands and knees, peeping round from the side office, his ears obviously straining to hear what they were saying.

'Lost the contact lenses again, eh, Harv?' Chewy said calmly, not even looking at him as he continued to search for the list of ancillary staff.

Harvey coloured up and shot unsteadily to his feet, trying desperately to regain his dignity.

'Paper clip', he said pathetically. 'Dropped a paper clip, that's all.' He scuttled out as fast as his pomposity would allow.

'How long has that little shit been there?' Rusty wondered.

'Who the hell cares,' said Chewy, rejoining the rest of them. 'Even if he heard something, which I doubt, it doesn't really matter. What would Jolly say to us? What could he say? All we'd have to do is deny it. That would drop 'Harve' right in the brown sticky stuff, especially if we made a formal complaint about the Senior Master who we actually caught spying on us!'

'Hells teeth!' Rusty said, grinning. 'We could take that right up to the Governors!'

'Exactly!' Chewy agreed. 'Anyway, I can't find that list so we'll need to check with the Mad Hatter. She's bound to have one and then we'll need to tread as quickly but as carefully as possible. We've only got another week before the Governors meeting where they'll obviously be discussing the whole proposal. The old Braumsley cow will almost certainly be there as well as some of the Council members. There's not a lot of time left so... who's for another drink?'

Harvey was still lurking outside the staff room door. His little hands clenched into hard blobs as he realised he couldn't take what he'd overheard any further. He walked stiffly away but was now intent on one thing. One of these days he would get them all, every one of them. It was only a matter of time.

Maggie sat with Jolly in his study trying to discuss the new road proposals. She'd been there for almost an hour but all she had been able to get from him was a stream of worries about the whole thing.

'So, what *can* we do?' she asked in exasperation.

Jolly was pacing up and down, hands behind his back and shaking his head. He stopped as she asked the question.

'I just don't know,' he said miserably. 'With the Braumsley Estate owning most of the land around here we don't have a great deal of room to manoeuvre. Lady Braumsley is not exactly the easiset person to get on with either.'

'Then what about a straightforward planning objection?' Maggie suggested.

That sent Jolly off into one of his 'turns'.

'Oh, no!' he gasped. 'We couldn't do that! She would be very cross if we did that! Just think of how many of our buildings she owns, quite apart from the land. She could make life very difficult for us!'

There seemed to be no way out. No matter what they did they were firmly caught in the Braumsley grip. At the same time Maggie didn't want to just lie down and let the old bat trample all over them. There had to be a way out, somehow. She left Jolly fretting and walked out back to her desk, feeling very depressed. With no conclusions, and even less in the way of any kind of a decision from Jolly, she still had that cretin Quentin to deal with although she wondered whether she should even bother.

Quentin sat quietly while Ralph, the butler, ladled soup into a bowl in front of him. His mother sat at the other end of the long mahogany table. A large, silver candelabra sat in the middle of the table, its candles flickering in the slight draught coming through the expansive, wood panelled dining room. Neither mother or son could see each other. Ralph withdrew, as if on wheels. Quentin dipped his spoon into the liquid before him and brought it up to his mouth.

'Quentin,' his mother suddenly said.

He dropped his spoon, splashing soup all over the place.

'Quentin!' the call came again.

Ralph was already mopping up the mess as Quentin, flustered as usual under his mother's dominance, stuttered an answer.

'Y,y,y,yes, Mummy?'

'What have you been doing today?'

His immediate reaction was guilt. What was he supposed to be doing? What hadn't he done? Why was she asking? What should he say?

'Well? She snapped. 'Are you going to answer me?'

'S,s,sorry, Mummy,' he answered nervously. 'Nothing much.'

'Nothing much?' she asked. 'I thought you were supposed to be 'Clerking' or something with the School?'

'Oh, that... yes,' he said, relieved at the question. 'I've been finalising placing a few pot plants around the School.'

'Pot plants?'

'Yes, Mummy. Pot plants.'

Silence fell again and Ralph slid back in to take away his, now empty, bowl. Quentin then steeled himself for the question he wanted to ask.

'Mummy?'

'What?'

He cleared his throat quietly, took a deep breath and began the difficult route towards the question.

'The Headmaster asked me something about roads today.'

'Did he now?' came the reply.

'Yes. He seemed to be a bit upset about it,' he said carefully.

'Was he now?' was the response.

'I wasn't much help, I'm afraid,' Quentin continued, wondering what she was thinking. 'I couldn't answer some of the questions he was asking. I just thought you might be able to clear things up for me.'

'Really?'

He screwed up his eyes imagining that she might throw the table at him and asked 'the' question.

'What are the road proposals?'

'Proposals?' she snarled. 'Why do YOU want to know about the proposals?'

'Well,' he said, gritting his teeth, 'the Headmaster seemed to think that large areas of the School might be swept away because of them, that's all.'

'Stupid boy!' she snapped. 'What do you think is happening around here? How do you think the Estate runs? By itself? With elastic bands? Clockwork? No! It runs on *money*. Money! The one thing we haven't got a lot of these days!'

Quentin just sat there while she went off into one of her manic deliveries of what she understood to be the truth. Even Ralph had the good sense to hang back while her words echoed around the room.

'By selling off the land for this half-arsed road system of theirs,' she thundered on, 'we can make a great deal of money! Enough to set the Estate back on its feet! This bloody Government have been bleeding us dry for years! This is an opportunity to stick two fingers up at them and sit back for the next thirty years counting the profit!'

Quentin shuddered. Would she really be around for another thirty years? The last sixty of his life had been a torment. He couldn't face another three decades of this. He needn't have worried. She was talking nonsense. It boiled down to the fact that she was a very greedy woman. The Estate was in fairly good 'nick'. There was plenty of money coming in from rent alone. All the land she'd agreed to sell was, as far as she was concerned, of no real value being common pasture in most cases. There were a few School buildings involved but they were ancient decrepit rubbish anyway. She'd be happy to see them go in the face of 'progress'. In truth the old cow didn't give a stuff for anyone but herself. She just liked the thought of checking monthly interest figures rather as an old miser would finger every coin he possessed, knowing each one on an almost personal basis.

'In any case,' Lady B continued, a little calmer now, 'next Friday and the job will be done. I've asked for a formal dinner at the Town Hall and after that we can finalise the deal. I can't face another of those bloody awful Governors meetings. There'll be representatives from the School and the Council as well as myself... *and you!* After that we can expect a very healthy bank balance.'

Quentin was very unhappy. He didn't really believe they needed to sell the land or compromise the School. He certainly wasn't looking forward to the formal dinner next Friday. His mother relaxed and sat back in her chair. Ralph moved silently forward to deliver the next course but Quentin had lost his appetite.

6

Saturday dawned and the day rolled along. Three days had passed since Vic had made his 'suggestion' to the others of the Escape Committee but they were no further forward with their research. Maisie had given Chewy a list of ancillary workers but not one of them had worked on the Braumsley estate. Lill and Chewy sat in the staff room as depression settled around them. As with many independent schools this was just another teaching morning until midday. After that the day was usually filled with games matches of one sort or another with the more urgent on the staff parading around in their games kit looking like refugees from a holiday camp. The less involved, such as Lill and Chewy, now watched a few of their colleagues through the staff room window performing on the games pitch on the other side of the School.

'Just look at that stupid sod,' Chewy was saying, a cup of coffee in his hand, watching 'Goosy' blowing his little whistle to no effect whatsoever. Goosy was Cyril Braithwaite, Head of Mathematics, a degree from Oxford and a train spotter. What a combination. He always appeared to be startled, his eyes wide, his expression surprised, hence his nick-name. Although he was well over forty years old he was still a child of the world, unknowing, completely 'unstreetwise' and a spectacular bore. As Chewy would have said, and often did, 'What a fucking and absolute pain in the arse!'

'Don't do that,' Lill said. 'Come and sit down. You'll only upset yourself.'

Rusty came in. 'Hi fans!' he said, helping himself to a cup of coffee. 'How's it hanging?'

'As large and helpless as ever,' Chewy replied, settling himself once again into one of the chairs.

'Oh, good,' Rusty said, joining them. 'Glad to hear it.'

'Why are you so bloody happy?' Lill asked.

'No particular reason,' he answered, raising an eyebrow.

'Oh, yeah,' Chewy countered. 'So what's the actual reason?'

'Well,' Rusty began, 'as you know I usually have a very hectic Saturday morning but today I was able to set aside some time and discovered something rather important, if not vital, for the big 'do' on Friday.'

'Hang on,' Chewy interrupted. 'In the first place you don't bloody teach on a Saturday and…'

'And in the second place,' Lill cut in, 'what's this *important of not vital* stuff all about?'

'Patience children,' Rusty said, 'all will be revealed.'

'So reveal!' they both demanded.

'O.K. On Friday evening, as we all know, the dinner and the meeting takes place where Lady Bitch will try to sell us down the river, yes?'

'Yes.'

Rusty leaned forward and continued in a more conspiratorial fashion. 'I've just found us a life raft!'

'Typical bloody English teacher!' Chewy moaned. 'What the fuck are you talking about?'

Rusty explained. Having taken an early lunch he'd been on his way back to his office when, turning a corner, he bumped straight into Bernie who was taking out a bin full of rubbish to the skip. Bernie Haskins was the School 'Refuse Disposal Officer', better known as 'Bernie the Bin'. He was a minute, chubby, balding character with hardly any teeth and when he smiled it was quite a sight to see. Very few of the staff ever talked to Bernie or even gave him the time of day. Rusty and a few others always did, having an occasional quick 'crack' with him out of simple courtesy. He was harmless and enjoyed the odd quip now and again. Consequently he would do anything for the few staff who bothered to talk to him. But Bernie had a problem that morning.

'It's me box,' said Bernie. 'It won't work.'

Rusty had a bit of trouble with that.

'Your box?' he asked.

'Yeh, me box. Plugged me lectric banklin in last night,' Bernie said, very seriously, 'an me box went bang!'

'Bang?'

'Yeh, bang it went, bang!' Bernie said again. 'Had to use candles after that.'

'Come on then,' Rusty said, realizing what had happened. 'It's probably just a fuse. Let's go and have a look.'

Bernie lived just a short distance from the School in a little lodge, all by itself, which at one time had been the gate keeper's house on the edge of the Braumsley Estate. He'd lived there as long as anyone could remember. Single storeyed, stone built and four rooms was all it comprised. It had a small living room, a little dining room next to this and a kitchen at the back. Across a narrow hall lay his bedroom. At the far end of the hall, above the back door, was an ancient fuse box. Standing on a chair Rusty pushed the metal lever to cut the power and opened it up. There was only one fuse inside. All the power came through that and a scorched surround showed that the thing had blown and not for the first time. Rusty pulled it out and stepped down.

Bernie scrabbled around inside a few drawers in the kitchen and found some fuse wire and a screwdriver. Within a minute or so Rusty had the fuse in place and the power back on. Bernie bustled about and made a pot of tea to celebrate. Rusty was in the living room looking at a few of the pictures when Bernie came in, grinning from ear to ear, with a teapot and a couple of his best cups and saucers.

'That's the old Estate and a few of me mates,' he said, nodding at one of the framed photographs on the wall.

Rusty peered at the one Bernie was looking at. It was a dark, sepia photograph and he could just make out a very young Bernie, with the same grin, and a few other characters standing in a line. The handwritten date in the bottom right hand corner was 1938.

'I were only four year old then,' Bernie said, grinning.

'Who are the others,' Rusty asked.

'That's me Dad on the end,' Bernie said proudly. 'He was the Land Agent and the rest were the gardeners. There were a lot of staff in them days,'

They both sat down and sipped their tea,

'How did you end up in this house, Bernie?'

'Oh, it's a long story. When the war was over things changed. It was difficult to get staff. As things went the Estate was taken over by a company who ran it for the family an' people like the gate keeper, an' a few others, weren't needed no more. Dad took the place over an' he an' me just stayed on, like.'

'What about your Mum?'

'Don't know,' Bernie said, looking down into his cup. 'Never knew her. Dad said she died givin' birth t'me. Sad really.'

'And you've lived here ever since?'

'Ever since.' Bernie looked across at the photograph, sniffing. 'Dad died 'bout twelve year ago. Lady B was very kind. Cried a lot at the funeral. Couldn't understand that. She hardly ever came down here. But she let me stay on. Always remembers me birthday, an' Christmas. I don't pay any rent either. Don't know why.'

As Rusty listened to this *he* realised why. Vic had been right! He left Bernie, happy to have his 'banklin' working again, as well as everything else, and made straight for the staff room where he found Lill and Chewy.

Lill was dabbing her eyes by the time Rusty finished his story but Chewy was ecstatic.

'That's brilliant!' he said, standing up and marching to the door.

'Where are you off to?' Rusty called after him.

'To see the Mad Hatter!' Chewy replied over his shoulder.

'It's Saturday, you silly sod!' Rusty yelled. 'She probably won't be there!'

'Yes she bloody will!' Chewy shouted back.

She was.

Chewy phoned all of the Escape Committee later that afternoon requesting a special meeting that evening at his place, a 'safe' venue. They duly arrived, one after the other, and he told them what he'd managed to organise with the help of the Mad Hatter. Half an hour later and they'd finalised a plan of action which they hoped would work.

'So, now that we have the seating arrangements for the dinner on Friday, compliments of Maisie, and with a few 'adjustments' already organised, we can set our plan in motion. It's just a matter of who we decide should guide the conversation on the night.'

'I'll do it!' Rusty offered. 'I'd love to see the look on the old faggots face!'

'No,' Vic said. 'I don't think any of us should. There's only one person who could make this work.'

'Who's that?' Lill asked.

'Maggie Thornton,' Vic said. 'Our new Development Officer.'

'Fantastic!' Rusty said. 'New to the School, obviously pissed off with Jolly and the whole place and, unlike us, completely beyond suspicion!'

'D'you think she'll go for it?' Chewy wondered.

'Don't see why not,' Vic said. 'If it works it'll make life a lot easier for her without having to deal with the problems of a by-pass through the School!'

'O.K.,' Chewy nodded. 'Let's get her on the blower. We need to start this off as soon as we can.

Rusty reached for the phone and dialled but there was no reply.

'I'll stick a note in her pigeon hole on Monday,' Chewy said, 'and I'll try to talk to her before lunch, if I can.'

On Monday morning, as Chewy made his unenthusiastic way to the staff meeting, Jolly nobbled him just outside the staff room. Chewy braced himself expecting the worst. Harvey must have spilled his guts about what he'd overheard on Saturday. But no, it had nothing to do with that.

'Arthur,' Jolly began, 'I wonder if you could help me out?'

Chewy was very suspicious. Jolly rarely asked him for anything.

'Well,' Chewy began, 'if I can Joll... err... Headmaster. What's the problem?'

'Not really a problem. More of a service, as it were.'

This left Chewy totally mystified. What was the silly old bugger on about?

'Oh, really?' he said, waiting for an explanation.

Other staff were arriving on their way for the morning meeting so Jolly pushed the staff room door open and took Chewy into the pigeon hole area.

'Could you take Ms Thornton around the School?' Jolly asked quietly. 'You know it as well as any. It would be useful for her to ☐familiarise herself with the layout and the, err, 'detail' of the place.'

This was probably code language for how the place was falling down.

'Fine,' Chewy said, 'but there's only one problem.'

'What's that?' Jolly asked, worriedly.

'Lessons. What about my lessons today?'

'Oh, don't worry about that,' Jolly said. 'I'll have other staff cover for you.'

With that he scuttled off into the staff room. Chewy now had a golden opportunity to talk to Maggie Thornton about the 'plan' and he remembered to slip a note into her pigeonhole before joining the unavoidable morning meeting. As soon as it was over he told the rest of the Escape Committee.

'That's great! Rusty said. 'Wonderful timing! Make sure you get your facts right.'

'Nice to see your confidence overflowing,' Chewy commented dryly.

When all the staff had shuffled off to assembly Chewy took his time over a cup of coffee and scanned some of the newspapers. With the whole day ahead of him there seemed to be no point in rushing around. Half an hour later, when he knew the rest of the staff would be fully engaged with the educational process, he ambled over to see Maggie and found her pouring over old plans and layouts for previous road proposals.

'You can chuck that lot straight in the bin,' he said, sitting on the edge of her desk.

Maggie sat back in her chair. 'Well, I had to start somewhere. Oh, I've just picked up your note from my pigeon hole. It's a bit mysterious. *'Must talk, road plans, see you around 9.30am.'* What are you plotting?'

Chewy smiled. 'Now, what makes you think that?'

'Just a thought,' she said.

'Fine,' Chewy replied, still smiling widely, 'but first things first. Jolly wants me to take you on the grand tour.'

'Oh, yes. He did say something about that on Saturday.'

'Hasn't the Head organised this for you before now,' Chewy asked.

Maggie shook her head. 'No. But I've been able to get around, when I've had the time, with this map of the school site and Maisie's been very helpful.'

Chewy wasn't surprised. Basic 'nounce' wasn't Jolly's strong point. Jolly probably hadn't thought about it nor had any of the 'maagement'. Looking at the map he sighed. It was at least ten years out of date.

'Well,' he grinned. 'Let's put that right now and do it properly, eh?'

As they walked around the whole site Chewy gave a Maggie a thorough historical commentary as well as a series of very frank statements on every aspect of the School. She asked the odd question from time to time but began to realise just how much effort and money would be needed for 'refurbishment', especially in the Shanty Town area. The gloom which could have descended over her was successfully dispersed by a few 'visits' to particular venues. The first one of note was the Geography Department, affectionately known as 'The Old Cow Shed' and, apart from a few others, was primarily Harvey Sheasby's domain.

'Hi, Harve!' Chewy said cheerily as they walked in. 'This is Maggie Thornton, our Development Officer. The Head asked me to show her around.'

Harvey managed to nod in Maggie's direction, reasonably content that 'his' Headmaster had allowed this invasion. Kids began to push into the room for the next lesson, shuffling quietly into position and waiting for a signal from Harvey to sit.

'Excuse me,' Harvey said, ' I'd better get on.'

Maggie followed Chewy to the back of the room while the kids were given permission to sit, in silence, Harvey raising a hand and indicating when each one could move to their desk. Then, when they were seated, he pulled out a very dog-eared folder and called out their names. The kids answered like robots and it became clear that he had them sitting alphabetically, front to back. How quaint. Maggie found a couple of books at the back of the room one of which had the title of 'The Development of Science.' She flipped through the first few pages and found the beginning of a chapter which stated, 'The modern computer is now small enough to fit into a normal family living room.' The publication date was 1956. Next to that were a pile of pristine maps of the region but there was something odd about them. Looking closer she realised there wasn't a single motorway but there were railways, everywhere! The map was dated 1948. Harvey was in full flood by this time, quacking on about 'sedimentary levels' and 'strata'.

Pointing at the book and the maps Maggie whispered to Chewy, 'Does he really use this stuff to teach with?'

'The Empire still lives,' Chewy hissed back.

He had to lead her sedately out, as she was near to bursting out into giggles, not helped by Harvey coming out, in heavy Victorian tones, with one of his classic pieces of advice to the kids. That was, 'I want you all to read… learn… and inwardly digest.'

It took them a minute or so to calm down but they walked on and arrived outside the 6th form study centre. This was another stone built conversion from a previous past, probably a former shelter for animals but with a second storey. In any case its function hadn't really changed in that most of the 6th form, instead of using it for study, had other, more creative activities in mind.

Maggie noticed a scattering of fag ends as they walked in and a sudden scurrying sound from above. A single head popped up from the top of the staircase, looked down and disappeared. She distinctly heard a muffled, 'Oh, shit! It's Chewy!'

Chewy was half way up the stairs when the Head Boy and one of the 6th form girls appeared at the top, both of them looking slightly dishevelled.

'Getting on top of your work?' Chewy asked as they rushed past him and out.

A few minutes later they were walking past 'Parrots' room when the sound of machine gun fire flew out of the window.

'What the hell was that?' Maggie asked.

'Ah, that's Derek Matthews's place, our tame historian but known as 'Parrot'. He's a great mimic. Probably demonstrating something about the last war. Take a look.'

Matthews was standing on top of one of the tables, as if he was holding a huge sub-machine gun, the sound coming from his mouth, kids staring open mouthed.

'Colourful,' Chewy commented, 'isn't he?'

'Are there any more like him?' Maggie asked.

'Oh, no,' Chewy answered. 'Some are worse! Let's see.' He checked his watch. 'O.K. It's time for P.S.E. This should be good.'

'P.S.E.?' Maggie asked. 'What's that?'

'Well, I'm told that it means 'Personal and Social Education' but... it tends to end up as 'Pretty Stupid Education'. But you can decide for yourself. Here we are. Just take a peek through there.'

He motioned to a window where inside the room the Wide Mouthed Frog, Second Deputy, was opening a large book with the whole class around her.

'Now,' she said. 'We've talked about the human body and this part is very important.'

She opened the book and up popped a huge, pink, cardboard penis. Her eyes lit up but some of the kids stepped back in horror, terrified.

'I think I've seen enough,' Maggie said, walking on.

Morning break had arrived but instead of going up to the staff room Chewy thought it might be better to scrounge a cup of coffee in the Dining room where it would be quiet and he'd be able to talk to Maggie about 'the plan'. She didn't object and after Chewy had a word with one of the catering staff they were soon sitting with a fresh pot of coffee and two cups.

'So, what do you really want to talk to me about, Arthur?' she asked.

'O.K., ' Chewy said with a grin. 'It's like this...'

He explained the whole thing in detail, holding nothing back. She said nothing to begin with and Chewy began to think he might have made a very big mistake but then... she smiled and laughed out loud. Rusty, on his way to the staff room, spotted them sitting there and came in looking expectantly at Chewy.

'So far, so good!' Chewy said.

'Ahh!' Rusty said, relieved, then looked at Maggie. 'That's.... all right then?'

'Well, I'll do it but I'm not looking forward to sitting next to Lady B, that's for sure!'

'At-a-girl!' Rusty said. 'There's no danger at all. Even that twerp of a son of hers could do it, if he had any brains, which of course he hasn't.'

'I'm not sure that's the kind of encouragement I need,' Maggie said, 'especially as I have to see Quentin as soon as possible to attempt something else which might prove to be totally impossible.'

'What's that?' they both asked.

'Refurbishment!'

7

By the late afternoon of Monday Maggie eventually managed to track Quentin down He was fussing around in the dining room with a large, two-tiered trolley stuffed full of pot plants, much to the general irritation of the catering staff who were trying to organise the place for tea He'd been wandering around for the better part of an hour and a half, carefully positioning a plant here and a plant there. Occasionally he would stand in the middle of the room and look around at his efforts. A rash of plants were now in position on windowsills and the odd shelf. He seemed satisfied with the general effect That's when Maggie walked in.

'Quentin,' she called down the room. 'Can we talk?'

Quentin looked up brightly and said, 'Oh, hello. What do you think?'

Maggie looked around and simply said, 'Very nice. Now can we talk?'

'Yes, certainly,' he said, pushing the trolley in front of him. 'Glad you like them. They add a certain something don't you think?'

She nodded, unconvinced. As they left the Dining room a few of the catering staff stood, arms folded, looking around at all the foliage he'd inflicted on them, wondering how long they would last after the kids came in. Anything that wasn't screwed down was fair game for some of the little sods.

Quentin parked his trolley next to Maggie's desk and sat down. Maggie leaned forward wondering how this conversation would go.

'We have a lot to do,' she began.

'Oh, yes,' he said. 'There are lots of places which need brightening up. Now that I've done the dining room I want to have a look at all the classrooms. I've got the whole thing mapped out here and...'

He leaned over to the trolley and pulled over a large, rolled up plan of the School which was covered in coloured stickers.

'That's not what I was talking about,' Maggie interrupted him. 'I was more concerned about the buildings themselves.'

'Do you know,' Quentin started, putting his master sheet down, 'I do so see what you mean! They're so dowdy! A good lick of paint here and there will do them the world of good.'

Maggie leaned back, unable to prevent a sigh escaping. This was going to be much more difficult than she had first thought.

'I think they need more than just a lick of paint,' she said.

'We could get the window cleaners in,' he said. 'That would help as well. Nothing like clean, sparkly windows, I always say!'

'Quentin,' she said slowly. 'Do you know anything at all about refurbishment, rebuilding, structural repairs, building maintenance, electrical work, plumbing, gas appliances or general cleaning up?'

He thought this list through and latched onto the last item.

'We could start by tidying the place up! A good old spring clean, lots of dusters of course!' he said, sitting up very straight with a single finger pointing up. 'It is looking a bit grubby! The ground staff could give it a good sweep! That would make a big difference!'

Maggie gave up. She was by herself. This twerp would be of no use whatsoever.

'Thank you Quentin,' she said, folding her arms. 'You've been a great help.'

'Happy to oblige,' he said, getting up. 'Now I must run along! Lots to do!'

With his rolled up plan tucked under his arm he trundled off with his pot plant trolley. Maggie watched him go and just sighed.

The first week of term was always a hectic round of administration, administration and more administration. This was known to all as the 'Jolly effect'. The amount of paper he generated was spectacular to say the least. One of the most irritating manifestations of this paper chase was the number of memos he dispatched to all staff with the consequent proliferation of many more from others on the staff, especially the creeps. Very few staff actually talked to each other but hid behind this blizzard of paper messages to one another. A day could not go by without several memos appearing in everyone's pigeonhole. It drove the Escape Committee up the wall but they were unable to stop the insidious flow. Dumping them immediately into waste baskets only generated more, several of them enquiring why there had been no reply!

Some of the more earnest amongst the staff checked the staff notice board in the staff room every day but there was little point to that. Anything there had already appeared in their pigeon holes. So, during one morning break, as Chewy walked in to have a quick look at the newspapers, he was amused to see one female member of staff craning her scrawny neck to read some inconsequential rubbish at the top of the notice board. At just under five feet tall and skinny with it, she was on her tip-toes, eyes screwed up, trying to read whatever it was.

As he walked past her, grinning, he asked, 'Want a bunk-up, then?'

Her reaction was instantaneous. She flopped back down, spun round, and almost spat out, 'Certainly not!'

Chewy cheerily related this to the Escape Committee later on.

'It was extraordinary,' he told them. 'I couldn't have had a worse reply even if I'd asked her for a shag!'

'Perhaps you should have done,' Rusty mused. 'She might have said 'yes'!'

Chewy closed his eyes at the thought of that and shuddered.

In amongst all of this paper 'information' were the dates and times for the various parents' evenings. The first was now due, the second Monday of the first term of the new academic year, for parents who had kids of eleven years old who were new to the school. All of the staff were obliged to turn up, 'to be seen'. It was usually a fairly painful affair but this time it turned out to be slightly different.

The Escape Committee was up in the staff room as parents began to arrive in the Dining room, the only place more comfortable than the Sports Hall. All the creeps on the staff were busily seeing the punters to their seats before the meeting began which was due to start at 7.00pm. Harvey was there, rushing around and making sure Jolly would notice his 'caring' attitude. He really was the chief of creeps.

Chewy, now on his third double scotch, leaned back in his chair and held up his glass.

'Here's to parents!' he said. 'May they forever pay my salary!' and drained the glass.

Harry was sitting next to Vic. 'I can really do without these bloody meetings,' he said.

'What's up, Harry?' Vic asked. 'Got a snot on?'

'No,' Harry replied. 'It's just that you never know what to say to the buggers this early in the term. We've only been back a few days and been in contact with this new bunch for a few hours and they think we can virtually foresee which friggin university they'll be going to. I ask you. How the hell can anyone say anything sensible about a snotty nosed eleven year old after such a short time. It's bloody madness!'

Lill, Rusty and Vic giggled and even Chewy had to smile.

'Well,' he said. 'You know exactly what I mean.'

They all did. Chewy stood up and then, sticking his hands into his pockets said, 'We should handle these events the way old Seedpod does.'

'Seedpod' was the nickname for the head of Braumstate Juniors, the 'feeder' School to the Senior part of the whole organisation. Seedpod, or Mr Runner, ruled his staff very autocratically and didn't mess about the way Jolly did. His parent's evenings were a straightforward lecture from him and him alone. He always harangued parents for the better part of an hour and a half telling them in detail what would happen over the year ahead and rarely allowed questions.

'Chance would be a fine thing,' Rusty muttered. 'I'd rather be bored rigid by Seedpod than go through the bloody torture that Jolly allows.'

'Time's up!' Lill said, looking at her watch. 'Show time!'

They trouped down the stairs and negotiated their way through the crowd of parents still arriving and stood as far back in the dining room as they could. The room had been cleared of tables for the evening and set out with row upon row of plastic chairs. The punters were all fussing around, buzzing with conversation and after a few more minutes they eventually settled themselves for the meeting. Chewy and Rusty stood next to each other, both of them hoping, together with most of the teaching staff, that they wouldn't be asked to speak.

At just after seven o'clock Jolly got to his feet and launched into his standard welcoming speech. He was flanked by Wooden on one side and the Wide Mouthed Frog, Mrs Hilda Broadstead, on the other, the statutory female she would always say, although there were few to agree to the accuracy of that. Next to her sat Sheamus Gilpin, Head of Middle School and then Harry as Careers Officer, who was dreading the inevitable 'university' advice.

As Jolly came to the end of his sycophantic speech he introduced the Wide Mouthed Frog to the parental body who proceeded to bore everyone rigid for a few minutes wading up to her emotional neck in the importance of the Children's Act and how understanding they all were about the children, especially those who were boarding. As a 'House Mistress' she knew about these things. A few of the parents wondered about the 'Mistress' part but then dismissed that very quickly. Then she started banging on about preventing 'gender polarisation', whatever that meant, and by the time she'd finished a few of the parents had actually nodded off, the P.E. oaf leading as usual.

Then it was Sheamus Gilpin's turn. He launched into an incomprehensible tirade about Middle School procedure. That woke up the sleeping few and with the parents who were still awake sat glumly during this whole performance, quite bemused and not understanding a single word of what he was talking about but too polite to even ask each other. Jolly took over again from the silence which settled amongst them all and asked if anyone had a question. A few seconds dragged by but then a mother stuck her hand up, was recognised by Jolly and she stood up and asked him, rather loudly, about games.

'Why are there not more games on the weekly timetable?' She almost yelled this out. Jolly was quite taken aback at the venom in her voice and it had the effect of waking up some who had drifted off again, including the P.E. oaf.

'We really should have more games!' she continued just as loudly. 'The children would really benefit from more games!' Then she sat down, smugly, to wait for the reply.

Jolly fumbled with his papers as he gave his answer. 'I'm not sure what you mean by needing more games,' he said. 'We do have a fairly intensive programme organised for all year groups.'

'Not enough!' shouted the same parent. 'Not nearly enough!'

Jolly tried to cover his discomfort at a parent confronting him with such a direct challenge but deftly handed the problem over to the Head of P.E. The 'Oaf' himself.

Duane Hedley, Head of P.E., known to his immediate colleagues as 'DH', but to everyone else as 'Dick Head', stood up in the middle of the hall and blinked several times, wondering what to say. Jolly tried to rescue the situation by putting the question again, this time a little more slowly so that Duane could understand it.

'The question was,' he said, enunciating every word very carefully, 'Why don't we have more games?'

Duane slowly absorbed this, the parents looking on, fascinated by the slow motion of his response. Then he brightened as an answer swirled to his consciousness.

'We can only provide the time for games in accordance with the timetable!' Then he sat down again, grinning inanely, leaving the problem squarely back with Jolly. Jolly moved on quickly, hoping for another question just in case the same parent stood up again and asked another question about games. A hand snaked up from the other side of the hall. With obvious relief Jolly invited the question. Chewy sagged in a state of great and instantaneous depression as the question was asked.

'Can you give us an explanation of what exactly 'Design and Technology' means?'

Jolly beamed widely at this. Here was an opportunity to show the parents how much the School was in touch with the present even though he didn't actually understand it himself. He motioned to Chewy and then introduced him.

'Mr Chambers, our Head of Design and Technology, can best answer that question for you.'

Chewy walked slowly down to the front and turned to the parents. He looked at them, sighed and then pulled himself up to his full six feet plus height and began a long and detailed lecture. Trying to explain his subject area was never easy at the best of times. But he shrugged mentally and thought, 'Bollocks! Might as well give them the full works!' And so he started. He'd been looking forward to giving this particular 'explanation' for some time but hadn't expected to do it so early in this academic year. With the full compliment of staff and all the parents of the new intake this was just as good an opportunity as any other.

'There was a time,' he began, 'When there was Woodwork, Metalwork and Technical Drawing and the world was all right.'

Harry covered his mouth to hide the huge grin which had rapidly spread across his face.

'We had the Empire,' Chewy continued, 'red blotches all over the globe, Mrs Dale's Diary, Muffin the Mule and the Flower Pot Men. My colleagues and I, up and down the country, spent a great deal of time churning out useless tea pot stands, match box holders and tenon joints. Everybody was happy. We walked about in our brown, scruffy workshop coats. We would arrive in the staff room and anyone could spot the Woodwork or Metalwork teacher. They were the ones talking to the Tech. Drawing teacher or the Domestic Science staff, fags hanging out of their mouths as they talked about, 'four b'two's', or 'swarf'.'

Jolly began to wilt, raising a hand to his forehead. Was this a migraine coming on? He could see that Chewy was about to climb onto a large hobby horse of his. The Wide Mouthed Frog looked like thunder. She thought this was a disgraceful performance. Several other staff were transfixed. How could he be talking to parents in this way? Chewy didn't care. This was a once and for all opportunity to get things straight. He ploughed on.

'Then, with the advent of GCSE, all that had to change. Now we were supposed to be 'analysing', 'developing' and 'realising' things. That is code language for 'looking', 'thinking' and 'making'."

Rusty, at the back of the hall, recognised the same beginnings of the Chewy bandwagon and mumbled to himself, 'Oh, shit! He's pissed!' But there was no stopping Chewy now.

'We rose to the challenge. Organised and resolute we prepared our ground. As the National Curriculum advanced towards us we were ready, computerised, our pneumatics at the ready, our electronics waiting to be connected, our hydraulics primed with control systems quivering and mechanisms clicking for the word to go. Now we'd all come 'up market'. We now smoked pipes, the fellas that is. The brown scruffy coats have gone and instead of just old workshops there are also studios, databases and multi-media work rooms.'

There wasn't a sound now as Chewy talked on. All the parents were hanging on his every word. Jolly just sat there, his mouth open. He hadn't heard anything like it before.

'In Design and Technology there are two main areas which pupils have to cope with, unlike any other subject. The academic side is as demanding as any other area of study but with an additional demand. Children have to *think* for themselves. They aren't used to doing that. They like to have it on a plate, pre-digested, ready to fork the stuff down their little throats without having to chew it.'

A few of the parents were busily swallowing involuntarily at this.

'The Design process is a continuous set of decisions which must be made the whole time and as the work continues if any real progress is to be made. No other subject is like that. And that's quite apart from the pure creativity which needs to be released along the way. There is also the problem of asking children to grapple with materials, tools and processes. No longer is it just one of three simplistic areas, Woodwork, Metalwork or Technical Drawing. Today, Design and Technology is a very complex and sophisticated world of many separate disciplines. But what do we get?'

Jolly covered his eyes with his hands, expecting the worst.

'Parents simply say, 'little Mary or little Johnny are good with their hands, so they should be able to cope with your subject'. Let me tell you now that Jack the Ripper was 'good with his hands' but I doubt whether he could have coped with the National Curriculum or the need to design anything.'

Silence prevailed.

'So, Design and Technology demands one simple process. A child must develop the skill of THINKING. That's what we try to do and so far it seems to be working.'

Chewy stopped talking and the silence thickened. Then the place erupted with a burst of spontaneous applause, hoots and whistles from almost all the parents. Jolly couldn't cope and simply sat there, his mouth hanging open again. This had to be a first for any parents evening. There were no more questions but just a loud buzz from the audience as Chewy walked back to where Rusty was standing.

Rusty just said, 'Hail Caesar!'

'Piss off!' said Chewy.

Tuesday slid by without the trace of any trouble, miraculously. The boarders were now quite settled into the school routine after the first week back. There had only been five smashed windows and four fire alarms which brought out the whole local brigade. One had been caused by the attempt by a twelve year old trying to warm up his bed with a toaster. The fire damage had been contained to the top floor of the boarding house and the rest of the kids had to camp out below for a few days until repairs were made.

The police had only been called out twice so far by the Wide Mouthed Frog. She had seen yet another flasher, she said, which had more to do with her own peculiar sexual fantasies and the high powered binoculars she tended to use through the front room windows of the boarding house. Other personal 'damage' had been slight amongst the kids for there had only been a mere three black eyes and one broken nose from a Sixth Form 'kick in' round the back of the R.E. room. Hardly any cigarette lighters had been confiscated with very few packets of 'Dunhill tipped', the 'cool' thing to be seen smoking. Very disappointing.

Only seven kids had been caught so far climbing back into the boarding house, pissed as rats, all fourteen years old and at two thirty in the morning. Quite quiet really for a normal week. The town of Braumsley girded itself for the rest of the term. Yet Tuesday evening saw the sun set for once on a calm and placid school community. It didn't last. The kids were just getting into their stride which was more than the staff were. One of these was George Partridge, Head of the Sixth Form. His had been a manic first week. He'd already had to close the Sixth Form common room due to an excessive and ritualistic tendency to 'gang banging' with one or two of the Sixth Form girls as prime targets. Quite apart from the fact that they always 'made themselves available', as the Wide Mouthed Frog would always complain about, enviously, he had no choice but to close the place down for a week until they could begin to control themselves.

All this did was to change the venue from there to one of the other more 'relaxed' boarding houses and the rituals continued. After spending years trying to prevent this 'extra mural activity', George was now beginning to be affected by it in the most counter-productive way. He staggered into the staff room one early evening when the full Escape Committee were there enjoying a last drink. Stopping in the middle of the room and shaking with frustration he came out with a line which will live in educational history. It was, "Why isn't there a woman on the staff who can stop an erection!"

"Not now, dear. Later on perhaps." Lill had said calmly.

The daily routine of lessons were relatively peaceful but the evenings could be a particular pain to those on the staff who had been allocated as assistants to House Masters or Mistresses. The idea was to give the staff in charge of a boarding house a night off once a week. Chewy had the misfortune to be assistant to 'Adolf', Henry Short, teacher of Chemistry, who ran his house along remarkably similar lines to that of a P.O.W. camp. The only things missing were barbed wire and machine gun towers. Consequently the house, called 'Coldacre', was known to all as 'Cold-titz'.

All of this was as nothing compared to Adolf's regular lectures to his charges about his experiences in South Africa, were he'd taught for fifteen years before coming back to the UK. His dismissal of the indigenous population of that part of the continent via references to 'kaffir's' and 'the blecks' always featured highly in his tirades of blind racism.

The evening of every Wednesday during the term was Chewy's 'slot'. This should have lasted from 7.00pm until 10.00pm but Adolf would invariably be late, pissed and very argumentative when he returned. Chewy largely ignored him when he did get back but he rarely managed to leave before 11.00pm most of the time, which did not help his overall enthusiasm for having to be there.

On one Wednesday evening Chewy arrived, Adolf left and Chewy settled down with the paper in Adolf's office trying not to look at his watch every few minutes. Forty five minutes later he patrolled the three storeys of the place just to make sure that a relative peace and quiet prevailed. The kids, between the ages of eleven to eighteen, were grouped in batches on each floor in several bedrooms with up to four per room. Beds, desks, shelves, drawers and lockers were squashed into these with various items of personal belongings scattered all over the place. Tidy they were not and, without exception, all were rather malodorous. The two common rooms on the ground floor were far worse as no one age group felt responsible for them. Chewy, after his second tour, decided to do something about it. He walked round again, delivering the same orders into each room.

"O.K. you 'orrible little wazziks! You have twenty minutes to clean this place up and the common rooms downstairs. Anything left lying around after that will go straight into the bin! And I mean *ANYTHING!!* Got it?"

Heads nodded grudgingly without looking at him and he left them to it. Half an hour later he patrolled again and the place had changed dramatically. The pong still hung in the air in most of the rooms and they were indeed tidier but there were still a few things on some floors, stuffed behind doors and on the staircase. Fed up with this he 'nominated' one kid from each year group with strict instructions to clear up the remaining 'rubbish' and stick it all in the large bin outside. Ten minutes later the job was done and even Adolf, when he stumbled in at 10.50pm, was impressed. Chewy waved goodbye and thankfully made his way home. During the midmorning break a couple of days later Adolf strode over to Chewy who was sitting with Rusty.

"I want a word," he almost snarled.

"Do you now," Chewy smiled. "Would you like 'Piss', or 'Off'?"

"*BOOTS!*" Adolf snapped.

"Boots, eh?" Chewy asked calmly. "That's a new one for me. Unlike your good self I don't speak Afrikans."

That only infuriated Adolf even more.

"You know exactly what I mean!" he said, his hands clenching into fists. "Your big tidy up the other night dropped me right in it!"

Less than a minute later Adolf had stomped out of the staff room to the sound of great guffaws of laughter from Chewy and Rusty. During the tidying up that night all the 'rubbish' had been cleared but the following day one kid couldn't find a very, very expensive pair of rugby boots, a present from his proud father, only three days before. Chewy's orders had been carried out dutifully and the stuff collected, dirty socks, shirts, ties, a few half eaten sandwiches, many empty packets of crisps and sweet wrappers *and* the boots were dumped in the outside bin. That had been collected during the following day. That evening, after the owner of the boots found out what had happened, made a phone call to Daddy and Daddy had contacted

Adolf, haranging him for half an hour and threatening legal action! That then forced Adolf into paying £85 for another pair!

8

Now that Braumstate Cathedral School had fully emerged from the two and a half months of the summer hibernation there was not only the ridiculous tide of useless paperwork to wade through but the impending 'post-mortem' of the A Level and GCSE results from earlier in the year which were sitting heavily with all subject staff They awaited the dreadful prospect of a memorandum arriving in their pigeon holes summoning each one of them to Jolly's manic need for a detailed examination of these academic entrails It was always an alphabetic process, subject by subject instead of departments, so, the whole interminable inquisition lasted far, far longer than it should have done. Chewy knew his time was coming when he spotted the Art, Biology and Chemistry staff trudge into the staff room one lunchtime, looking as if suicide was the only thing left to them His results hadn't been too bad but he knew Jolly would find something to agonise about He checked his pigeon hole and there it was, the memo from Jolly 'inviting' him to 'discuss' his results What was worse was that Jolly had 'suggested' Chewy's two free periods that afternoon as a 'convenient' time

'Ahh, shit!' Chewy muttered, screwing up the memo and throwing it into the bin. After lunch he arrived outside Jolly's office and greeted the Mad Hatter.

'Good afternoon, you delectable creature.'

'Up yours!' she replied, not even looking up from her paper strewn desk, 'You can go straight in.'

He didn't bother to knock, he never did. He simply opened the door and walked in. It was a deliberate ploy to throw Jolly's pathetic attempt at authority and it always worked.

'Oh... ahh..., Mr Chambers, Arthur!' Jolly flustered, standing up with a handful of paper, quickly thumbing through the sheets for Chewy's results.

Chewy just stood there, waiting, hands in pockets and quietly grinning. He hadn't bothered to bring his own paperwork as he knew Jolly would have several copies of every child's grades. Jolly continued to flick through the sheets trying to find the relevant ones so Chewy sat down, uninvited, sighed, gave a small yawn and waited for the cross examination to begin.

'Ahh! Here we are,' Jolly said, brandishing the lists. He sat down and scanned through each page before looking up, frowning, and saying, 'There aren't many A grades here, are there, Arthur?'

'One,' Chewy said flatly, 'and that was a minor miracle.'

Jolly was slightly taken aback by his answer.

'But… but…,' he began, 'there was surely the prospect of more, wasn't there?'

'Well,' Chewy replied calmly, crossing his legs and fixing Jolly with a pointed stare. 'Churchill summed things up pretty well for circumstances like this.'

'Churchill?' Jolly asked, completely thrown by Chewy's reply, 'Churchill?'

'Yes, Churchill. You know. Two fingers up, 'Never in the face of human conflict…', and the really important one, 'Give us the tools and we will finish the job.' That Churchill.'

Jolly was totally confused but Chewy kept going.

'Look, my problem is that I don't get the 'right material' coming into the department. All I get are the ones who can't cope with the so-called 'important' subjects, Maths, English, Science and the rest. Design and Technology is not regarded as 'academic'. I thought I'd made that case the other day at the parents evening. So, I tend to get the dross, the kids who don't know what else to do and, although I know they do their best, the results are sometimes disappointing… to some.'

Jolly opened his mouth to speak but Chewy hadn't finished. It was time to deflect Jolly in a completely different direction.

'So you see it's a problem every year. A lot of the characters who choose D&T for GCSE and A Level could be seen as 'wastage' from the whole pupil body. It's not unlike the wastage we suffer from as far as tools and materials are concerned.'

Chewy waited briefly while that sank in.

'Wastage?' Jolly asked, his eyes widening.

'Yes. Wastage,' Chewy began again. 'You wouldn't believe the stuff that goes missing over every year and then there's the way the bins fill up.'

Jolly sat back heavily, his mouth hanging open but Chewy hadn't finished.

'I'll give you an example. Give a kid a piece of wood, metal or plastic and I can guarantee that 50% of it will end up in the bin.'

'50%…?' Jolly repeated.

'Oh, yes. You see, kids don't ever think about being economical. No. They'll hack away at anything to produce what they want. Give any one of them a sheet of plastic, say two feet by three, and they'll always draw what they want, right in the middle of it, and cut the rest away. That usually ends up as useless bits in the bin. And that's the fascinating thing. I have a theory about that. I'm sure they look at anything as a sheet of paper. They draw what they want on it and get rid of the rest. It's as simple as that.'

Jolly was speechless. Chewy sat back, a wide grin on his face.

'Well,' he then said, getting up. 'Thank you Headmaster for such a useful discussion.'

He walked out of the room, closing the door behind him. The Mad Hatter looked up.

'How did it go?' she asked.

'As well as could be expected,' Chewy said, calmly. 'Yes. As well as could be expected.' He sauntered off knowing that Jolly would be in a state of shock for the rest of the day.

Having suffered the blizzard of the beginning of term paper and the mindless need to justify examination results there was another disaster looming which would affect everyone on the teaching body. On Friday morning a single statement from Jolly at the staff meeting took all completely by surprise and largely scared the shit out of most of them. The morning meeting had begun and continued with the usual crap but then, at the end, Jolly dropped the bombshell on them.

He flapped a letter in front of him which he'd received the previous Saturday morning. Since then he'd been fretting about its contents but, at last, he'd screwed up his courage, such as it existed, to tell the staff. The letter was from the Department Of Education and Science, as it was known then, always a peculiar description to non-scientists, which he read out. The gist of which was as follows,

Dear Sir,

In accordance with the wishes of the Secretary of State for Education, we hereby give you notice of the inspection of your school in the second week of November, this year.

Total and numbed silence was the result. A few of the staff sagged and nearly fainted A few others swore to themselves. The rest just looked helpless. Wooden had gone completely rigid. The Wide Mouthed Frog as self styled 'Mother Earth', sat there, the blood draining from her face. Sheamus Gilpin, the Head of Middle School, was as stunned as the rest, his mouth hanging slackly open. November was only just 6 weeks or so away. Through every mind ran the same basic set of thoughts. First there would have to be the evidence of 'lesson plans'! Not one of them had used a lesson plan for years. They got on their legs and taught. Even with the changes which had arrived in education over the last few years, the essential nature of each subject hadn't varied that much. It was still a matter of 'delivery' though a mixture of 'chalk and talk', encouragement and, sometimes, straightforward intimidation. Now they would almost certainly have to produce dozens of lesson plans to justify their educational direction and existence.

Then they had to think about mark books. They had either lost them, thrown them away or in some cases had never used one. That would have to be rectified and quickly. The thought of creating a series of marks for previous work set filled them with pure despair. That would take days to prepare but the inspectors would almost certainly want to see them. Mark books were considered to be the 'tablets of stone' of progress. The notion of them being rather like an M.O.T., only good for the day, never surfaced with these perfectors of Inspectors. There was a lot to be done before these Inspectors arrived! Unlike today where schools are usually inspected every four years, inspections were few and far between. The independent sector had its own inspectors and they were rarely seen.

Jolly tried to put a bold face on it.

'I have to say to all of you,' he began, 'I look forward to this. I am convinced that we will show the Inspection team how well we are achieving the highest possible standards. I have great faith in all of you and your ability to demonstrate our impeccable standards which are the direct result of all your hard work over the years.'

'Lying bastard!' said Chewy, not too quietly. 'He's shit scared!'

There was one other person on the staff who reacted rather badly to this announcement but not for the same reasons. That was Compton Beardsley, Head of Drama in the school. He didn't give a damn about what these 'philistine' Inspectors might think of his performance as a teacher. He was more concerned about the performance of the end of term play. This was a major blow to all his plans. How would he be able to concentrate on that with all this shit to wade through? The end of term play could be in serious jeopardy.

By the time the Inspection team arrived he would be well into the whole thing. Casting was already in progress, the lighting was being organised and the set was in the last stage of finalisation, on paper at least. In another few weeks he would be ready for major rehearsals with all the kids. The last thing he wanted was a bunch of insensitive arseholes trampling all over him in the middle of a major school production. It was all too much, 'darling'!

Later on in the early evening Chewy, Rusty, Lill, Vic and Harry sat quietly round a table in the local pub. They hadn't much to say. A heavy blanket of depression hung over them all. It had nothing to do with being worried about the Inspection and how they would cope with it. No. It was the prospect of the paperwork which would now begin to engulf them, each and every one.

Inspections were a paper merchant's dream. Everything about the school, in the finest of fine detail had to be recorded and prepared for the Inspectors. Every Faculty, Department, Subject and member of staff had to present a encyclopaedic catalogue of information about every single aspect of the teaching process almost down to their inside leg measurement and what size underpants they wore. That then had to be committed to an endless process of checking, counter-checking, rechecking and form filling to wear out the most durable of wrists and writing instruments. Even if they had been fully computerised their wasn't a database known to man which would have been able to cope with, organise and regurgitate the amount of paper fodder which the inspection team required and Jolly would, inevitably, add to.

Only Harry and Vic had been through the hell of this before. For Harry it had been ten years previously in an inner city school. Two members of staff had topped themselves during that one. Vic hadn't had that experience. His had been while he was a probationer at a large comprehensive in the early seventies. He'd never seen as much paper in his life on that occasion and didn't want to see it again. He almost gave up the idea of the profession at the time but here it was again, ready to test him, just like last time.

Willy Broadhurst, the landlord of the pub came over to sit with them.

'What's the matter with you lot?' he asked. 'This is a pub y'know. Drink the bloody stuff or it'll evaporate!'

Chewy grunted and Rusty looked up. The others didn't move except for a nod or a slight wave.

'Hello, Will,' Lill said.' How's things with you?'

'Obviously a damn sight better than it is with you lot,' Willy replied. 'Why are you all so bloody miserable?'

'Sorry, Will,' Vic said. 'We've just been told we have an inspection coming, that's all.'

'Ah. That explains it,' Willy grinned and he turned and waved to one of the staff behind the bar. 'I thought for a moment it was something serious!'

Young Tommy came over and asked Willy what he wanted.

'Give these poor buggers a drink on the house. I think they need it.'

The door flew open and dear old Compton Beardsley breezed in, a part time member of the Escape Committee. He was wearing a long scarf lightly and widely wrapped around his neck with a look of pure torture on his face.

Willy turned and looked at this latest apparition. 'You'd better get him one too!'

This had a distinct and heartening effect on all of them. Draining their glasses they handed them over and Tommy who went off to organise another round, not bothering to ask Compton. He knew what he wanted. A large scotch. Compton came over, off-loading his scarf but not his expression.

'Compo! You old bastard!' Chewy greeted him loudly, getting up, towering above him and planting a kiss on his balding head.

'Don't do that. People might talk!' Compo snapped.

'Let 'em!' Chewy said, pulling over a chair. 'Sit down you old bugger!'

'Not so much of the old,' Compo said, putting on the most camp attitude he could muster.

'How's things, Compo?' Rusty asked.

'Bloody awful!' Compo replied. 'But I think you know that.'

'We do!' Vic said.

Tommy brought the drinks over, passed them round and then left them to it. The conversation continued as they swapped notes about the usual things. Jolly's manic attitudes eventually, and inevitably, began to emerge again as the main source of conversation. In an attempt to break this habit Lill leaned over to Compo.

'How's the play coming on?' she asked.

'Don't ask!' Compo replied. 'If I had any co-operation from the 'Design' Department I might be able to say, 'reasonably well'.'

Chewy didn't rise to that but just sat there, sipped his beer and said, 'Pardon?'

'You are a sod, Chewy.' Compo said. 'I've been waiting for weeks now for the completion of the final set. When the hell are you going to let me have it?'

'Soon,' was all Chewy would say.

'Thanks a lot!' said Compo.

'It's so nice to see the Drama and Design departments getting on so well!' Harry said, diffusing the situation. 'Come on you lot. Have another drink.'

'My shout,' Chewy said and walked over to the bar.

He ordered for all of them and sat at the bar waiting for Tommy to deliver the goods. The rest of them were now feeling a little lighter than they had when they had first arrived. Willy came back from wherever he'd been.

'It's all right Arthur.' he said. 'Park your bum. I'll bring this lot over when it's ready.'

'Thanks, Will,' Chewy said, and ambled back to the group The conversation had reversed to the Inspection again.

'Oh, Christ!' he said. 'Can we talk about something else? Life's too short!'

Willy followed him and had to agree.

'Too bloody right!' he said. 'Get this lot down your necks and make the most of it. The place'll fill up soon with some of the bods who'll be going to the Council dinner.'

'Shit!' Rusty said. 'I'd forgotten....!'

'Forgotten about what?' Lill asked.

'The dinner!' Rusty said. 'What time is it?

Chewy checked his watch. 'You're OK,' he said. 'Calm down. It's just coming up to 5.45. The Dinner doesn't begin until seven.'

'That's not the problem,' Rusty said, getting up and draining his glass.

'So what is?' Lill asked.

'The plan! The revelation! I meant to warn Bernie!'

'What about?' asked Vic.

'That he'll be sitting directly opposite the old Braumsley cow!'

9

Friday, 700pm The Town Hall was busy with the local great and good and not so good It's quite amazing where people come from on these occasions The slightest sniff of free 'nosh' and the woodwork erupts with all kinds of parasites whose only function is to stuff themselves on the pretext of being 'somebody' So it was with this evening The serfs waited for the milling guests to take their seats in the upper chamber, normally used for the occasional dinner dance for the Conservative Association, Rotarians and the like It had been transformed into a banqueting hall Council officials ran over the procedure for later on in the evening and congratulated themselves on their luck in having the old bitch, Lady B, agreeing to their plans for the new road system All was now in place for her final signature and the formal hand over of her land

The place was heaving with sycophants, hangers on and anyone who had been given the 'wink' about this particular 'knees up'. They had all arrived in their parochial party frocks, nodding respectfully to each other but all wondering what 'they', the others, were doing here. Tickets were carefully checked as they shuffled through the main door and then made their way into the building, passed the ushers and on and up to the first floor. They gathered in a large anti chamber next to the banqueting hall to be indulged with sweet sherry and polite 'nibbles' before the main event took place. A large gong had been placed next to the doors of the banqueting hall to be struck by the chief usher when given the signal by the Town Clerk.

Jolly picked up Maggie in the school car from her flat and brought her to the Town Hall. They were joined there by the others, Wooden, the Wide Mouthed Frog, who had somehow managed to screw a ticket for herself, and the Prick with the Fat Controller following behind. Maggie didn't know anyone except this lot. Somehow they still really didn't qualify to her as 'people' so she was feeling just a little vulnerable and alone. Apart from that she had the distinct disadvantage that she had never met Lady Braumsley and really wasn't looking forward to that. But she knew her 'lines', given to her by Chewy and Rusty, and had prepared herself to drop them into the conversation at the first convenient opportunity.

Joining the local worthies, busily engaged in soaking up the sherry, Jolly and the rest of them nodded and had the odd word with a few of the crowd. Minutes later the sound of the gong reverberated through the hall and the doors to the banqueting hall opened slowly. A near cadaverous individual stood there, the catering manager of a local hotel, and with a quavering voice he announced, 'Dinner is served!'

The crowd surged forward and Maggie found herself propelled from behind as they moved as one to indulge themselves on the free food. Then her arm was grabbed from the side and Rusty stepped over, complete with dinner suit and grinning from ear to ear.

'Good round here, isn't it?' he said and led her into the hall, expertly elbowing all aside and clearing a path for them both.

Jolly was not at all amused at seeing him but in the circumstances there was nothing he could do about it. He and the rest were swept along as the locals pushed forward to find their seats, every one of them labelled and waiting to be recognised.

'How did you...?' Maggie tried to ask but Rusty just winked. They reached the top table and he took the seat next to her, his name in front of him on the official place setting. Wooden sat next to him with the Wide Mouthed Frog and then Jolly, almost at the end. He was not at all happy. He was supposed to be sitting next to Lady Braumsley but then he hadn't known about Chewy's covert manipulation of the seating plan with Maisie's help. The Fat Controller found his place on the other side of the hall. He sat down with a pained expression on his face. His personal 'plumbing' was acting up and he began to fret about where the gents might be.

Jolly tried to attract Wooden's attention, waving and motioning to Wooden to move places but Wooden just waved back. Then Jolly was buttonedholed by an ancient old trout of the town and couldn't get another word or signal out. The Prick found himself flanked by two very ugly old crones who proceeded to talk across him and in harrowing detail about their recent medical problems and consequent operations, ignoring him completely.

Under the cover of general conversation Rusty was able to discretely whisper to Maggie of little Bernie's presence across the table. She smiled across at him and was rewarded with a huge grin. He was sitting wearing a borrowed dinner jacket at least four sizes too big. He didn't care. This was the kind of 'do' he'd never experienced and he was wide eyed with wonder.

A hush settled over the place as Lady Braumsley arrived, complaining loudly and wearing a terrible old, diaphanous, flowery layered gown, again dripping with pearls but giving the appearance of a leaky old galleon under full sail, shipping water badly and looking as if she was going to sink at any moment. Quentin staggered along beside her, trying to keep her afloat and almost failing. He managed to get her into her seat right next to Maggie in the centre of the main top table then sat next to her, red faced and panting, but nodding to all around, including the Town Clerk who was sitting next to him.

Bernie was loving all this. He just sat there, still wearing his wide, manic toothless grin and having to pull up the sleeves of the borrowed jacket which kept sliding down over his hands. He had his eyes fastened on Lady Braumsley. Her Ladyship just sat there pushing the cutlery around to make a place for her handbag. Quentin fussed about but was given a steely look by his mother and sat rigid for the rest of the time, hoping not to annoy her again. The doors to the banqueting hall closed with a dull thud and the dinner began.

The following day the news of the previous evenings Council dinner rippled furiously through the town. The morning newspapers had a field day reporting what had happened. The headlines of the local rag said it all.

BATTLING BRAUMSLEY!
TOWN CLERK TROUNCED!
CIVIC GUESTS BOUNCED!
BANQUET SMASHED!
ROAD SYSTEM TRASHED!

Last night's Council dinner, held to finalise plans for the new road system, was the scene of a major row between Lady Braumsley, 89, and the whole of the Town Council.

Our reporter on the scene, Reggie Northgood, saw her Ladyship in full cry as she chased the Town Clerk, Mr George Mossop, 57, round the whole hall, smacking him with her handbag and calling him a, 'Snivelling little..'- we think the word was –'Beasthead!'

He ran out into the square, in some distress, where he took cover in the local branch of the Conservative Club before she could inflict any further damage. He was unfortunately ejected from there five minutes later as he hadn't paid his subscription for the last two years.

Witnesses to this bizarre event at the Town Hall said Lady Braumsley suddenly went berserk and assaulted Mr George Mossop, 57, Town Clerk, at the dining table. No one really knows what caused this but there have been rumours and counter rumours that it had something to do with the history of the Braumsley family. **Continued with pictures on page three.**

Page three was a riot of photography, and was in peculiar contrast to the 'tit and bum' photograph of the outrageously and scantily clad local beauty queen, next to the main story from page one.

This showed three large photographs, in full colour, of the old bat in full battle stance, her handbag being swung round her head. A panic stricken group of people were trying desperately to get out of the way. Mr George Mossop, 57, Town Clerk, was just about to have the bag make contact with his head in the largest of the three. Two other, slightly blurred, photographs showed him in full flight down the Town Hall steps and then lying flat on his face where he'd slipped at the bottom.

The text continued, captions and all.

BATTLING BRAUMSLEY BANGS, BEATS AND BATTERS!
A 'swinging' Lady B cleared all before her last night in the Town Hall but her main target was Mr George Mossop, 57, Town Clerk. Was it something he'd said???!!!

The main photograph had this next to it. ' *Mayhem' amongst the worthieeees!'*

The second caption read, *'Down!'*

The third simply stated, *'And out!'*

In the staff room of the school during the morning break there were at least fifteen copies of the same paper being rapidly passed around, many of the staff shrieking with delight at the news and the event itself. The Escape Committee and Maggie, now an honourable member, sat under the louvered cupboard, a highly practical position most of the time, and watched the performance. Chewy looked over at them all and shook his head.

'Just look at the stupid buggers,' he said. 'You'd think it was their friggin' birthday!'

It might as well have been. Their relief at the cancellation of the road system was almost good enough to taste.

'Never mind about those silly sods,' Vic said leaning over to Maggie and Rusty. 'What actually happened last night?'

'Just about everything!' Rusty said, grinning.

'It wasn't that complicated,' Maggie said. 'And I hardly had to do or say much. Mr Mossop triggered things off all by himself.'

The ploy had been simple. Maggie was meant to feed her Ladyship a few subtle lines which Chewy and Rusty had given her. The difficulty would be carefully leading Lady B into a casual conversation. She did not make small talk, ever. Nevertheless Maggie had tried. As the guests began to settle down after Lady B's arrival, most of them were immediately and totally bemused at the ranks of cutlery which lay before each of them. Desperately polite conversation broke out all over the place in an attempt to cover their ignorance. Lady B just sat there like an outside toilet which hadn't been flushed for a long time. Maggie dipped her conversational 'toe' into the silence exuding from the old bitch.

'I understand your ancestors can be traced back to the time of Baron Bathdere, Lady Braumsley?' she asked gently.

'They can!' came the curt reply.

George Mossop was listening intently to this on the other side of Lady B and so was little Bernie.

'Is it true that the Baron gave your family the estate which you still run?' Maggie asked trying to look enthralled.

George was all ears now, so was little Bernie.

'He did and we do!' spat the old bat.

'That's wonderful!' Maggie said, smiling widely. 'You must be very proud.'

'I am!' Lady B said, so was little Bernie. Then there was a detectable softening in her manner. Just for a moment the old bat thought she had someone who was genuinely interested in quality. She had. It was Bernie. Quentin still hadn't moved, staring straight ahead and now lost in his own little thoughts. Before Maggie could develop this any further a serf, somewhere at the end of the hall, banged the gong again and another hush fell over the company, squashing all conversation. George Mossop, 57, Town Clerk, who had been listening to every word, had his ribs elbowed sharply by a Council member sitting next to him.

He rose to his feet, slightly flustered, cleared his throat and said, with an enforced humility which bordered on making a more than a few people feel quite sick, but with his best Town Clerk's voice, 'It is with great honour that we have with us tonight a revered and respected representative of one of the oldest families in the county. Lady Braumsley has graciously accepted our invitation here tonight to seal an agreement which will be of enormous benefit to the town and for all living in the area. I know we will enjoy the dinner which has been prepared for us in her honour and then will come the formal signing of the agreement. Thank you all for being here with us and I can assure you that this will be an evening to remember. Bon Appetite!'

He was right about it being an evening to remember, that's for sure! A polite ripple of applause was then given, the doors opened at the far end of the room and the serfs wheeled in the first course, fish soup. A few minutes later Maggie tried again. Picking her moment carefully she asked another question.

'It must be quite a task running such a large estate, Lady Braumsley.'

'It can be,' came the smug answer.

George Mossop's ears stiffened like antenna again. Bernie put his spoon down and, elbows on the table and, hands on each side of his head, just sat and listened.

'What of the estate property?' Maggie asked. 'Is that still used by all the staff?'

Lady B stopped slurping her soup at this question, looked up and, for the first time, saw Bernie staring at her with a look of proud rapture on his face. She recognised him immediately and dropped her spoon with a loud clang splashing soup across the table. George tried to stifle a 'guffaw' but failed. She misunderstood the mirth from the Town Clerk and bridled at the presence of Bernie. Taking both of these things as personal insults she turned a bright puce, thinking George was taking the mickey and turned on him like a savage beast.

'What the hell are you laughing at, you bloody stupid, little man!'

Quentin stiffened even more, thinking she was talking to him. George made the great mistake of pointing at Bernie, the actual source of his first chortle. Lady B then pushed her great bulk to her feet, letting out a great, 'Arghhh!' and smacked George across the head as hard as she could with her handbag and kept swinging, yelling at the same time, 'What are you trying to say, you little shit!'

That's when the photographers galvanised themselves into action. Rusty managed to pull Maggie clear of the melee which developed very quickly. George, partially stunned by the first blow of that lead-like handbag just managed to duck from the next swing but it caught Quentin full in the face. He staggered back, knocking over chairs and holding his throbbing, bleeding nose. Then he ran away. George by this time was under the table as the bag came back again, sweeping plates, cutlery and everything else away. Bernie just managed to get out of the way as a water jug flew past the end of his nose.

Lady B was now in full screech, mouthing off horrendous oaths at all the Town Council for daring to suggest any 'hanky panky' in her family. She lurched alongside the table swinging at all of them, knocking chairs aside as they were vacated but catching one or two Council members across the backs of their heads with her bag. The rest of them panicked and scattered like sheep as she bore down on them. George made a brave attempt for the doors but slid on the soup which was all over the floor by this time. She caught up with him, yelling, 'I'll have you, you spineless arsehole!' and gave him a sickening kick in the ribs which propelled him forward, smashing him through the doors and out into the lobby. She charged after him, handbag whipping through the air in a vicious circle around her head.

The assembled worthies looked across the wreckage of the dinner, stunned by the whole thing as she galloped after George, stumbling and struggling to keep well ahead of her. A gaggle of photographers ran after them, flash bulbs going off all the time.

The dinner had come to a spectacular end.

'Oh, hell! I wish I'd been there!' Chewy said. 'That must have been bloody wonderful to see!'

'It certainly was!' chortled Rusty.

'I'm not sure about that,' Maggie replied. 'That handbag almost decapitated a few folk. Quentin was lucky. It only knocked his wig off!'

'Well,' said Vic. 'That's all over. Now we can back to the business.'
'What business?' Rusty asked.
'The inspection!' Vic grinned.

As an independent school Braumstate Cathedral School had not been inspected for almost fifteen years, well before Jolly's time and the present statutory four year event for all schools. As November approached and the Inspection loomed, Jolly became more and more agitated. The morning meetings degenerated even further into pure paranoia. He became obsessed with the slightest thing and wouldn't leave it alone. Once it was dirty windows, then it was open windows, then it was broken windows. After that he worried everyone, or tried to, about not being late for lessons, then they were in the land of the 'orange peel'. There was, apparently, too much of the stuff lying around. After that it was the problem of muddy footprints he'd discovered in the dining room.

One of his particular worries was the horrific incident of the 'dead' apple! Some little toe rag in the school had stuck a few knives into an apple during lunch time and left it right in the middle of a table where only Jolly could have found it. To him this appeared to be some form of satanic ritual. They were told to be on their guard against these disgraceful incidents and must report anything like this directly to him. And so it went on and on and on. All through late September and the whole of October he prattled on and it got to the point where they wished the damned Inspection would arrive. At least that would keep him fully, tremblingly occupied and off their backs for a change!

Half term arrived and they all escaped for a merciful few days holiday. When they all came back Jolly was worse than ever. He had now taken to walking round the school, 'popping in' on the staff, in the middle of lessons. It was almost as though he was trying to check up on them, making sure they were all there. The staff didn't like it at all and the kids even less. This was a double torture for them. During lunch times he would make a point of sitting with them. Watching this from a distance became a spectator sport for the staff.

Jolly would queue up with the kids for his lunch boring them all totally with his mindless chatter and then wander off with it on a tray looking for somewhere to sit. After a few days of this the kids had perfected a method of keeping him away. They all kept an eagle eye on his direction and then, if he seemed to spot a likely place, would quickly spread themselves to fill the table or grab other kids passing to sit down with them. This worked very well and Jolly could be seen walking back and forth as spaces on the tables rapidly filled up. He gave it up after a while and reverted to sitting with the staff, much to their great disappointment.

His general paranoia continued to drive everyone up the pole coupled with his continued inability to make the simplest of decisions. During the countless meetings which he chaired every week, and he had initiated, he would always sit doodling while others ranted, prattled or droned on. Never did he bring any order or conclusion to them. Even the Prick was becoming manic in his need to have Jolly resolve, conclude or make a judgement of any kind.

One meeting in particular always provided the low point for the whole term. This was the committee for 'Curriculum Redevelopment and Academic Planning', more affectionately known by its main initials to some on the staff as, 'CRAP', which summed up the whole nature of the discussions held there, especially for some of the poor unfortunates who had to attend it. As Heads of Department Rusty and Chewy were part of this enforced boredom which happened, mercifully, only once a term. They always tried to take the piss out of it and the rest of them but without the others realising it. It was not a difficult process.

As well as the heads of departments the other members of the committee included Wooden, Sheamus Gilpin and the Wide Mouthed Frog with Jolly taking the chair. Wooden always took the minutes which were usually a completely garbled cock up by the time he'd had them typed up and posted on the staff notice board. On the agenda this time were three items. These were the problems of Sixth Form behaviour in the town, smoking, drinking and that other, rather naughty thing which some had been caught doing with each other. Oh dear. Then there was the matter of fire drills. Not enough of these were taking place. Something must be done to improve matters. To round things off there was the destruction of pot plants in the dining room. The catering staff had been right about that.

On the first item it had come to Jolly's attention that the local pubs were not happy with how they were being treated. It actually boiled down to the fact that the Sixth Form didn't drink enough! They would just sit around, filling the places up and keeping the paying punters away. Those few who were reasonably flush went completely the other way and were regularly pissed out of their brains picking fights with everyone. 'Fairly normal', was the contribution from Rusty and Chewy. This was not appreciated by the rest of them, especially Jolly and he suggested a system of 'chits' which would need to be signed by house staff if any of the Sixth Form wanted to go to the pub. More bloody paper!

'A rubber stamp on the forehead might do the trick!' Chewy offered but it wasn't accepted. Sheamus Gilpin had dozed off by now and it was only the low snoring which gave him away. Jolly asked Sheamus, loudly, what he thought. Sheamus spluttered awake and said automatically, 'I think we have that just about right, Headmaster.' Then he slowly dozed off again.

Fire drills came next. Chewy found himself thinking about the last time this was discussed. On that occasion he'd been saddled with the task of making twenty eight bright yellow signs to be held high above the head of each form teacher, the number of each form emblazoned on it in black. These were to be used as targets for the kids to make for on the central mustering point of the lawn outside the main building. That turned out to be a spectacularly stupid and disastrous idea when they tried it out. Most of the kids just sloped off to have a fag or raid the local sweet shop and left all the staff like lemons holding up a forest of signs. They didn't try it again.

The discussion then became quite mindless as Jolly, Wooden, Sheamus, who had now woken up, and the Wide Mouthed Frog ground on about how this last unsatisfactory situation could be prevented. Chewy and Rusty lost interest in the whole thing and were having their own conversation at one end of the table while the others continued to quack on and on. As Jolly brought the meeting to a close it was perfectly obvious to all that as he gave his summary of each point, weighing up the pros and cons, testing the waters, being prudent and all the other inept excuses available to him from his vast cache of gibberish, he wouldn't be making any decisions until he'd given all the options a great deal of thought, again.

Maggie was another who was almost tearing her hair out. She found herself in the same position as the others trying to get a decision about anything from Jolly. She'd spent weeks preparing all manner of proposals but he couldn't cope with any of it and kept side-stepping her at every point. One early evening well after school the Escape

Committee were up in the staff room again. All of them were feeling more than just pissed off.

'What the hell am I supposed to do?' Maggie said. 'He won't make decisions, discuss anything and I doubt whether he's even listening most of the time. I've reorganised the ground staff and now they know what they're doing which makes a change. The Development programme needs to be looked at now that I have a few firm proposals. Advertising and Marketing the place needs to be discussed and I don't know where to start about computers. There's nowhere to put them for a start and no one to run them, quite apart from introducing them to the 'stone-age' administration we have round here. Every time I try to get any sense out of him he's miles away looking over my shoulder, or his, never really with me at all!'

'Ah,' said Chewy, 'You've noticed that, have you?'

'Don't take the mick!' Maggie snapped at him. 'This is serious!'

'Very serious,' Rusty said. 'But you won't get any sense out of him until after the Inspection, and then with difficulty.'

'Yes,' said Lill. 'He's right. Jolly's not very 'jolly' at the moment.'

'Was he ever?' Chewy said.

'Never,' said Vic.

'You could always talk to the Chairman of Governors,' Harry chirped in. 'You never know. He might just do something.'

'Yes,' Maggie said. 'He could sack me!'

Chewy saw the same old frustration rising up and decided to be helpful, which was slightly out of character for him. Nevertheless he tried.

'You should talk to Howard about computers,' he said. 'If anyone knows anything about computers it's Howard.'

'Who's Howard?' Maggie asked.

'Works with me in D&T,' Chewy said. 'Good man. He'll solve all your problems.'

'Right,' Maggie said 'When can I meet him?'

A small highlight of the term was November the fifth, Guy Fawkes Night. The school always arranged its own fireworks display and dutifully, everyone turned up to see it. This was usually organised by the Science Department, recognised as being the only ones who understood the 'physics of dynamic reactions between certain elements'. Well, that's what they said. In truth, they were the only silly sods stupid enough to have volunteered to handle it in the first place. They'd been stuck with it for years and there wasn't a cat in hell's chance of anyone wanting to take it over from them.

As the sun went down half the Science Department were running around the large field above the school setting out the firing positions for the roman candles, rockets and other main displays which had arrived earlier in the day. Darkness fell and they were still crawling around trying to get the things ready to go. All that could be seen were the faded yellow beams from their torches as they rushed to and fro.

Seven o'clock arrived, the appointed time of the show and Jolly, with his entourage of Wooden, Sheamus, the Prick and the Fat Controller, stood in front of the whole school waiting for the first rocket which would signal the beginning of the spectacle. Nothing happened. Minutes went by and still nothing happened. A growing murmur of discontent began to rumble through the kids and staff alike. It wasn't that warm out there in the dark and hands, toes, and noses, as well as other 'sticky out bits' were beginning to feel the cold.

Around the edge of the field, in amongst the trees, could be seen the faint glow of a hundred or so fag ends as the kids took advantage of the dark night. Most of the staff misread what they saw, thinking the trees were full of funny insects. The few who knew didn't say a word.

Jolly became restless and strode up the field to find out what was taking the time. In the inky blackness of the night he stumbled and fell right into the pond at the bottom of the field. A couple of fourth formers thought they had a trespasser. Their yells were heard by the Prick who sprinted up to where they were sitting on Jolly, who was face down and soaking wet, the two twelve year olds holding him down. He dripped back off to his study with the Prick holding him up.

Then at last the first rocket went off but not in the direction it was supposed to. As Jolly and the Prick mounted the steps to the main building the rocket exploded against the stonework just above their heads, showering them with bits of stone and a pyrotechnic nightmare. Other rockets were launching themselves all over the place except upwards. Kids and staff dived for cover or just hit the ground as these multi-coloured missiles, whistling and screaming, scythed through the air towards them. Then the roman candles ignited throwing their molten blobs left right and occasionally up. Some of these landed on the main stockpile of fireworks and the whole lot went up in an ear-splitting, crackling, kaleidoscopic, four levelled detonation. It was just like a visual Beethoven's Fifth Symphony crescendo! Boom, Boom, Boom, BOOM!

The Science staff staggered out from the smoke and flames like shell shocked zombies. Everyone else got to their feet, or peeped out from the bushes, moving slowly just in case there was more to come. But no, the whole pile of fireworks had been dispatched in a mere four seconds. Light from behind them flickered as they pulled themselves together. The trees on the side of the main building were now fully ablaze and one of wooden sheds next to this was well away.

The reason for the cock up didn't emerge until the following day. Two dogs had wandered onto the field and their doggy thoughts were full of those lovely sticks which were obviously there to be played with. The Science mob had tried to 'shoo' them away but they kept coming back with lighted rockets and fizzing roman candles to be thrown for them to fetch. The result was the 'different' display which almost wrote the school off.

Up in the staff room where the Escape Committee had been watching, Chewy and Rusty raised their glasses.

'Good one!' Chewy said.

'Best yet!' said Rusty.

Before the arrival of the Inspectors themselves, on November the sixth, and as the fire brigade were packing up to leave, the first formal communication thudded onto Jolly's desk, having been dispatched by a recorded and registered special delivery. It was a doorstop sized package which contained the first round of questions for all areas of the school. This was needed prior to the Inspection team itself. It would be the platform of information from which they would spring like wily hunters all over the place.

With no experience of any of this himself, Jolly spent the next few days grilling all the staff who'd been around at the last one. Harry and Vic did not volunteer their own experiences from other schools. There were only three others on the staff who could offer any information about the last inspection of the school but at that distance in time they didn't give him a lot of help. This had more to do with the fact that all of them were now near senile and couldn't really remember what had happened or what the procedure might now be.

Old RobHinton, teacher of Classics was the first to be interviewed. He wittered on about how the Inspectors at the time had ignored him completely. What he didn't tell Jolly was that he had hidden during the whole six weeks they had been there, locking his classroom on every occasion and then feigning the flu for the rest of the time.

Jeffrey Lowther, who taught Politics, was the second. Otherwise known as the 'Gardener', Jeffrey was another pot plant freak and had established himself as the unofficial provider of pot plants in some of the rooms in the school. He could remember little of the Inspection itself save for one incident, which he'd been banging on about ever since.

During that Inspection a rather fine specimen, known as '*Livistona chinensis*' to Jeffrey and to everyone else as, '*that bloody horrible, Chinese, spikey job*', disappeared one morning. It had been in the main reception room, next to the Headmaster's study. A few of the Inspectors at the time had used the room for having coffee and a short conference on progress. When Jeffrey had arrived later to water his plant, the thing had disappeared, pot and all. Only a dirty ring on the floor showed where it had been. Ever since then he had grumbled on about 'light fingered Inspections'.

What he didn't know was that one of the cleaning staff had knocked it over and accidentally run over it with a big vacuum cleaner. It was chewed up, chopped up and consequently chucked out, shredded beyond all recognition. The cleaner kept the pot. It was just what she wanted for under her spare bed. Jeffrey had put the whole school through a major inquisition about the bloody thing and still referred to it all these years later. He had bored Jolly rigid with the story again as his contribution to 'Inspections'.

Finally Milly Cawthorne, an old crone in her mid seventies, who had been persuaded to retire as soon as possible, gave Jolly her account of the business. She couldn't remember much about it save for filling in a few forms and simply quacked on about how 'nice' the gentlemen had been. Jolly was not to know what had actually happened. As a teacher of Biology she had allowed her subject to colour her vision. She'd taken a shine to one of the Inspectors and they had both been discovered by one of the other staff in a highly compromising situation on her Biology storeroom table. That particular Inspector had been checking more than just her paperwork.

Jolly was not a happy man. Neither was Wooden. He was positively terrified, although it was difficult to tell. A much slower delivery of speech and his tendency to say everything three times was the only indication of his consciousness having to work harder as he worried about the arrival of the Inspectors. He hoped they wouldn't. But what could prevent them? Perhaps a sudden flood or an earthquake would cut the off town. But arrive they did, complete with their thirst for paper, tons of the bloody stuff. There was almost the sound of bunker lids being clanged shut from the other staff as the Inspectors walked into Jolly's study. There were six of them altogether. Three women and three men. Jolly felt like a victim at a firing squad as they all trouped into his study and lined up in front of him. Stern faced and tight lipped they just stood there until one stepped forward and stuck out a hand. This was the head man, a tall bull of a man and sporting a full black beard. With the name of Mr Block, he was the Chief Inspector, a Chief Examiner, an HMI and an absolute bastard. He'd closed many a school in his time. Things did not look too good, not good at all. The staff meeting, which took place the following morning, was a rather glum affair, much more than usual. Jolly, looking more than a little haggard, cleared his throat and began, forcing an uneasy smile across his face.

'As you may already be aware,' he began, 'Inspectors are now in the school.'

'And he's in the shit,' mumbled Chewy.

'Mr Block, the Head of the team, has informed me that this will be a 'short' inspection.' Jolly took a careful breath and continued. 'This means that they will only be here for approximately two weeks and be looking at our core areas of Maths, Science and English and not the others.'

The feeling of relief passed like a wave through the rest of them. Some sat up grinning, others patted each other on the arm nodding while others, lucky enough to be sitting, the core subject teachers in particular, sank lower in their chairs. One, Cecil Talbot, teacher of Physics, went ashen, and with eyes wide open they rolled up to expose pure white and he slowly slid down the wall to crumple in a dead faint, completely out for the count. The P.E. oaf went back to sleep in the corner, a slow grin forming on his face.

'I am sure you will give them your full attention and co-operation at all times,' Jolly went on, unaware of the extremes of reaction, 'and make their time here a pleasant one.'

'Pleasant?' Vic said, 'He must be bloody joking!'

Jolly handed over to Wooden who began to speak about the usual mindless rubbish but again he was ignored and whatever else he was saying just dribbled to a stop. He had tried to tell them all about the standard information which the inspectors would want from everyone but no one heard him. They were all too busy with the impact of the impending Inspection and what it would, or wouldn't mean to them. Despite the fact that only the core subjects were to be inspected every staff pigeon hole held a thick wodge of paper. As individuals came to check their own after the morning meeting disintegrated, depression again set in like concrete as they opened these things. The pages revealed an endless list of questions, all of which had to be answered. There would be no exceptions. This was something none of them had expected but it was routine for these inspectors and designed to give them a wider understanding of the whole school.

'Oh, shit!' Chewy groaned, leafing through his paper brick. 'This is going to take bloody days to fill in!'

'You think you have problems?' Rusty said. 'What about me? I'm one of the chief suspects, remember, core subjects? That's me, English!'

'Got to do something about this,' Harry murmured, conspiratorially.

'Oh, yeah.' Lill said. 'Like what? Suicide?'

'I'm thinking,' said Harry. 'I'm thinking.'

10

Maggie held out her hand. 'Hello, I'm Maggie Thornton, Development Officer for this 'organisation'.'

Howard Stokes stood up and shook her hand. Chewy had told him she would be arriving.

'Come on in and sit yourself down,' he said. 'I gather you might just have a slight problem about computerisation?'

That was an understatement. She knew very little about computers and said so but then she outlined her problem.

'So you see,' she concluded, 'if this place is to arrive any where near the twentieth century without terminal trauma setting in, I have to introduce a straightforward and simple system which will actually make sense of, and cope with, all the information we have to process.'

'Fine,' Howard said. 'How much money have you got to spend?'

'That depends,' she said with a wry smile.

An hour later she had all the basic information she needed to talk to the Fat Controller. She also had the great advantage of having Jolly's full backing on any new initiative to the needs of her work. The Fat Controller didn't like the estimate one little bit, even though it included VAT, but there was nothing he could do about it. She left him with orders for a state of the art computer networked system with all the trimmings, CD Roms, laser printers, scanners the lot. Anything less just wouldn't have handled the data which needed organising, especially with the volume the Inspection would generate. Now at least she was on her way. She hoped there would be more computer equipment to come, especially for the various departments of the School although where the money would come from was anyone's guess.

Maisie Hatter, the Prick, the Wicked Witch of the West, who handled the salaries, the Fat controller, as well as herself, would be faced quite soon with a steep 'learning curve'. She worried a bit about that. Computers mystified her as much as they did most folk at that time.

In the meantime the whole school became affected and infected by the impending Inspection. The kids in particular were fascinated and the Sixth Form were already taking bets on how many staff would be fired as a result of it. They had quite a list. A lot of money changed hands over that.

Quentin Braumsley was still largely unaware of the actual importance of it all. He was still locked into the continuation of his vast and highly complicated 'Pot Plant Plan'. On a wall in his bedroom he had his large map pinned to the wall showing the whole School covered in coloured stickers. Each colour represented a particular genus, species or variety with secondary colours next to them. These denoted such things as quantity and watering sequences. It was all very comprehensive. His mother, however, was not impressed.

'QUENNNTINNN!' Her voice screamed up through the house to his room.

Flinching involuntarily he gave a quavering answer.

~ 87 ~

'Coming, M..m..mummy!'

He found her in the drawing room but didn't like the way she was sitting there, waiting and glaring at him.

'I need to talk to you,' she said slowly, a venomous glint in her eye.

'Oh, really Mummy?' Quentin said softly, 'What about?'

'About a certain number of people who 'work' at the School.' She shifted her bulk in the armchair and continued.

'It has come to my notice that there is an element within the teaching staff who are, shall we say, less than loyal to the School and anyone who has any connection with it.'

Quentin didn't have a clue what she was talking about but didn't dare to interrupt her.

'I am reliably informed,' she went on, 'that there may be one or two individuals who may well be responsible for the humiliation I had to endure on the night of the Town Hall dinner.'

Quentin said nothing. Every time she summoned him like this he knew there would be something he would have to do, and she would insist on it in a way that only she could. Whatever it was he knew in his water he wouldn't like it.

'I want you to be my eyes and ears,' she said, leaning forward and pointing her stick within an inch of his nose. 'Now that you have this silly 'job' of yours, I want you to listen, observe, and find out who was responsible for the presence of that…, that, that stupid little man being on the opposite side of the table from me on the evening of the dinner in the Town Hall!'

Quentin blinked and blinked again. What was she talking about? What little man was she referring to? Could it have been that odd little character with the floppy dinner jacket sitting opposite them? All he could really remember about the dinner was the sudden interruption to his private fantasy about his 'Pot Plant' scheme by a very hard smack in the face from his mother's handbag. His wig had flown off and he never did find it. It was just as well he had a spare at home. But what else had been going on that night? He was completely confused but had the good sense to simply nod in agreement. It was the only thing to do.

'Did you hear me!' she barked at him.

'Yes, Mummy,' he whimpered.

'Do you understand?' she barked again.

'Yes, Mummy!'

'Then get on with it!'

'Yes, Mummy,' he said weakly, 'Of course I will.'

He was summarily dismissed by a wave of her stick and he scuttled out of the room before she could change her mind. He ran back up to his room and shut the door, glad to be back in relative safety.

Dear old Harvey Sheasby had been responsible for this 'conversation'. After his humiliation at being discovered trying to listen to the Escape Committee's plans, he had been looking for an opportunity to drop the whole lot of them in it. He had put two and two together, after reading the report of that disastrous dinner and then talking discreetly to a few of the Council members who had been there. It was after that he had written to Lady B making a few 'suggestions', but without being too specific about particular individuals. That had been enough. The old battle-axe was now looking for blood.

The first week of the Inspection ground on relentlessly, generating a growing mountain of paper which was now overflowing from Maisie Hatter's office and out into the hall. Even with the computer processing which was now going quite well there were still stacks of the stuff arriving from each department and subject providing the fine detail the Inspection team would need for every single part of the school.

Maisie was not a happy woman. As well as having to cope with the new computer technology, Jolly was driving her up the wall with his constant interruptions and his fetish for writing pointless memo's to everyone. Her work load had quadrupled as a result of the paper coming through the office, not to mention the time she needed to convert it to 'disc'. Maggie was able to help her load a huge amount of information into the database of the computer but it was still a very difficult time for her.

At the end of one of the morning meetings Jolly explained to the staff that Maisie would be under a great deal of pressure and he would be grateful if they could all reduce their need to use her administrative services to the bare minimum. Chewy summed that request up quite succinctly afterwards.

'Sounds as if Maisie has told Jolly to piss off again!'

She had and not for the first time. That was when Harry began to form a small germ of a thought. He'd been trying to think of something to 'inhibit' the Inspection process. He now thought he might have a line to do exactly that. Computers were wonderful things when you could use them properly. He wondered what would happen if you didn't.

The pressure began to mount on all of them as the first two weeks dragged by and then the third week began with no sign of it ending. The Inspectors were still there. The 'short' Inspection was becoming a little longer and other subjects were now being pulled in. It felt like a 'black hole' developing in their midst, getting bigger and bigger with several departments being dragged into this pernicious, educational autopsy. Inspectors lurked in classrooms observing and noting down everything. It was all very unnerving for most of them.

One exception to this was Alfred Soames, a teacher of Chemistry. He'd been with the school for years and was near retirement. He rarely mixed with any of the staff, content to remain in his classroom for most of the day, sandwiches at lunchtime and then straight home. He was not at all fond of having these young upstarts in his classroom, as he viewed all on the Inspection team, particularly as they all had the irritating habit of scribbling away at the back of his room.

On the third occasion when this had happened he was teaching the Sixth Form, a motley collection of boys who were disinterested and bored with the subject. Old Alf was trying to enliven his lesson and create some kind of spark with the kids but not for the benefit of the Inspector who sat in the far corner of the room writing copious notes as usual. Alf didn't give a damn about what he was writing and he tried once more to raise the kids' general torpor to something approaching enthusiasm. The subject he began to talk about concerned organic acids, esters and ethanol, the latter of which just happened to be a member of the family of *alcohols*. Alf thought that if this didn't get this bunch of Sixth Form piss-heads interested then nothing would. He delivered the last word of a short introductory sentence and then repeated it again but this time much more loudly.

'I said *ALCOHOL!*' Alf almost shouted at them.

Heads looked up, including the Inspectors.

'*ETHANOL* is the *ALCOHOL* in spirits, wine and *BEER!*'

The kids were now on full alert. That last word was very dear to their hearts. The Inspector was scribbling again.

'But what does Ethanol come from... and how is it produced?'

Silence, apart from the wretched scratchings of the Inspector still writing maniacally at the back of the class.

'Well?' Alf asked calmly. 'You should have been reading this up before you arrived, shouldn't you... as I asked you to in your last lesson?'

Silence again, more scratchings from the back. That's when Alf lost his rag.

'Then I want *YOU* to tell them!' He bellowed, throwing a piece of chalk straight across the room at the Inspector's head. It bounced off the middle of his balding dome as Alf strode from the room, shouting back some advice as nothing less than an order.

'You have two minutes! *Now get on with it while I go for a leak!*'

A general feeling of misery had now established itself with everyone else on the teaching staff as more and more lessons were examined and then more and more requests for information from the Inspectors in the form of questionnaires kept on arriving. One of these provoked a situation which gave a little light relief to a few observers at the time. It was centred on a double sided, A4 sheet crammed with questions which had been organised by Wooden on behalf of the Inspection team. This was no mean feat as far as he was concerned. In any case it had to be filled in by everyone and was specifically targeted to the use of television in the School. The questions were endless. Which channels did staff use? Were programmes recorded or viewed 'live'? How many times per week was television a part of the teaching process? Were pre-recorded tapes used or hired and who from? And on and on and on.

Most of the staff busily filled these in, cramming in as much detail as they could to keep the Inspection team happy and show how useful television could be to their teaching methods. One member of staff, Chewy, screwed his up and threw it in the bin

'To hell with that!' he said. 'I'm damned if I'm going to fill that bloody thing in!'

He'd had a bad day. Jolly had been in to see him twice. The second time because he'd forgotten about the first. Both visits were completely silent, Jolly nosed around without saying a word. Highly irritating.

The sheets from other staff eventually filtered back to Wooden who checked them, twice, and then fed them to Maisie to be included in the database for the Inspection. Another waste of a day. It was only then that Wooden realised Chewy was the only one who hadn't returned his sheet. He saw him the following day in the staff room and asked about it.

'What's the point?' Chewy asked.

'It's very important that the Inspectors have this information,' Wooden said in his monotone wooden voice.

'Why?' Chewy asked.

'Because...' Wooden began, trying to think why. 'Because they need it to find out what programmes are...'

Chewy broke into this. He didn't have the time to go through this whole rigmarole.

'I haven't filled it in,' Chewy said flatly. 'It's in the bin!'

'It's in the bin!' Wooden wailed.

'Yes!' Chewy said again, 'It's in the friggin bin!'

'But it's very important...' Wooden began.

Chewy held his hand up to stop Wooden starting all over again from the beginning.

'You are missing something here,' Chewy said, 'which is rather fundamental to this discussion.'

A few of the staff looked up as their voices became louder.

'But the Inspectors...' Wooden tried to say.

'Hang on!' Chewy said. 'Hold on! Just stop there! Three years ago I talked to the Fat Controller about 'equipment' for the Department. That 'equipment' included a television set and a video recorder. He told me then that the money for either of them wasn't in the budget for that year. Because it wasn't in the budget I couldn't have them.'

'But...' Wooden tried again.

'Let me finish!' Chewy snapped at him.

Wooden just stood there looking and feeling very confused. This was not difficult for him. More staff were now watching this performance and loving it.

'Each year since then,' Chewy continued, 'I have had the same reply from the Fat Controller, including this year. That was, 'if it isn't in the budget you can't have it.''

Wooden opened his mouth to speak but Chewy ignored him.

'That's where our discussion falls down,' Chewy said.

Wooden blinked, not understanding a word.

'But what about the sheet?' he asked, 'It's very important that the...'

Chewy held up his hand again.

'Look I'll say this simply,' Chewy said very slowly so that Wooden could follow it, with luck. 'Every Department, every boarding house, every office and practically *every shit house* on this site has a television set, right?'

Wooden nodded, blinking.

'Right!' Chewy said. Then drawing a long breath he said, 'I, we, the Department *DO NOT HAVE a bloody television set*!'

This statement slowly sank into Wooden's head. He blinked again then said, 'Can you fill the sheet in as if you did?'

Chewy had to walk away in case he might hit him.

A day or so later Quentin was still trying to do what his mother had told him to do. Keep his eyes and ears open for any information. The trouble was that he didn't have a clue what he was looking for which did give him more than just a slight problem. He didn't dare ask her to be more precise. No, that would not have been a good idea. Instead he crept round the school listening to any conversation he could. There were a few tricky incidents when he was nearly caught eavesdropping by a number of the staff but the worst one was when he was lurking outside the ground staff's tearoom. It also happened to be the most informative. He was on his hands and knees under the window listening. A general argument was going on inside about something. He couldn't identify the owners of the voices but what he heard was fascinating. It went something like this.

'Don't be bloody stupid! It wasn't his fault!'

'How do you know?'

'Cos he told me, that's how!'

'Bollocks!'

'Well, he was there, wasn't he?'

'Yeh, but you know what he's like.'

'What's that supposed to mean?'

'It's just that he's a few bob short of a quid that's all.'

'If he's that short how did he get an invitation?'

'Dunno, but it's a funny thing that he was sitting opposite that Thornton bint.'

'And Lady B. Let's not forget that!'

Quentin's ears widened at this. Were they talking about that funny little man who had sat on the other side of the table?

'Oh, screw her! Bad tempered old cow!'

Quentin swallowed hard.

'I reckon it was a set up, deliberate like.'

'How?'

'I saw that little shit Sheasby in the office a couple of days ago when I was collecting the post. He'd left his poxy clipboard next to the pile of letters I was about to pick up and was busy talking to the Mad Hatter about something. There was a letter to the old bitch on the top of it. I managed to read a bit as I picked up the letters.'

'What did it say?'

'Something about the ones she wanted needed close 'inspection'. There were six of them and the main culprit, I think it said, was tall and bearded.'

'Anything else?'

'No. That's all I had time to see.'

Quentin couldn't believe his ears. That must be the Inspectors! He didn't even think that it was actually a description of the Escape Committee, the true 'conspirators'. He gave out a small squeak of horror and that was his undoing. Fred McBride, 'Big Mac', and Craig Combe, 'CC', came out to find out what the noise had been and found Quentin in full eavesdropping position, still on his hands and knees, his ear up against the window.

'Well, well, well!' Big Mac said, looking down at the now quivering Quentin. 'It's our little boss himself!'

CC grabbed him and held him up against the wall, Quentin's feet completely off the ground.

'Lost something, have we?' CC asked.

'N,n,n,no!' Quentin squeaked, trying to breath against CC's grip.

'Oh. good,' said Big Mac. 'Then you can run along now, can't you... sir?'

CC dropped him and Quentin ran off, terrified. He didn't stop running until he shot through his bedroom door, two miles away. Mummy was out. He could tell that by the skid marks from the open garage which he could see from his bedroom window. Good. At least he would have a short time to himself. He began to calm down and thought again about what he'd heard before being discovered. In his garbled little head he was still convinced that the Inspectors were responsible for the Town Hall disaster. Mummy would be pleased. When she eventually returned he screwed up his courage and told her. Her face coloured up, her eyes narrowed and her venomous glare almost drilled through his quivering frame. Then, to his relief, she turned sharply and stomped off without a word, but an evil idea began to form in her mind of how she would wreak her own highly poisonous vengeance.

The Inspection inquisition rolled on beyond the third week with still no sign of an end. It was now late November with December only days away. Just over two weeks remained until the end of term. The original team of six Inspectors had been enlarged to nine. Jolly was now in a hell of a state, reeling under the paperwork which he ordinarily loved but even this was too much for him. The invitation which arrived later that day did nothing to lighten his general demeanour. It was from Lady Braumsley and was an open invitation to the Management, Governors and the Inspection team for dinner in the great house at the end of the week, Friday, at seven for eight.

This was something he did not dare miss but it was also an event which he wasn't looking forward to at all. Not one little bit, especially after the disaster of the formal dinner for the road plans. He began to write a standard memo to everyone invited but then, for the first time ever, thought better of it. With very little time left before the evening of the dinner he decided to contact the Governors personally and talk to the Inspectors as soon as he could. He was actually quite peeved at the old baggage for not giving him enough time to organise things. A typical Braumsley attitude. As far as the rest of the management were concerned he could see them all during that morning. Maggie found a hastily written note from Jolly later that day about the dinner. She phoned Maisie immediately.

'What's this about a dinner?' she asked.

Maisie told her, sounding just a little stretched.

'I can't make that,' she answered. 'I have to be in London. A pre-arranged meeting for the school.'

She lied. There was no chance of her going to that dinner, especially with that guest list. She could think of nothing worse than spending a whole evening talking to the worst collection of 'dick heads' ever amassed under one roof. Besides, the last formal one she had attended turned out to be rather less than successful. Jolly wasn't happy about that but she spun him a line about 'marketing contacts' and that seemed to appease him, just.

Jolly was able to contact all the Governors and receive their slightly irritated confirmation for the dinner. A few of them suggested that a little more notice would have been useful but the Dean at least recognised the importance of the gathering and agreed without any argument at all. Jolly was relieved. That only left the Inspectors. He talked to Mr Block who answered for all his team. They would be very happy to come. He then gave Jolly the surprise information that by that Thursday the Inspection would almost certainly be concluded. A dinner on Friday evening would now be more than welcome and particularly opportune. Jolly was now a happier man, but it wouldn't last for long. He remembered to inform all the staff during the following morning meeting of the end of the Inspection and a wave of sheer relief washed over all of them.

'Thank God for that!' said Vic, who was probably the only one fully qualified to say it.

As Friday approached Lady B was busy with her own 'preparations'. With the letter from Harvey and the information Quentin had given her she was now looking forward to the dinner with great relish, cackling quietly to herself about the plan she had in mind for that very important event. She had rattled around amongst her late husband's bric-a-brac in the loft where she eventually found what she was looking for. It was a small, old, leather case full of various 'potions' which he had collected over the years. He'd spent a lot of time in India and South America during the thirties and forties and had acquired, amongst other things, this questionable range of concoctions, all in a fine powder form, some of which had been occasionally and 'carnally useful' to both of them on his return from far flung places. In amongst these powdery and near lethal aphrodisiacs were other, but no less spectacular aids to inducing or relieving physical illnesses and effects. Taking great care to read the fading instructions within the case she found the very one she wanted, closed the case and returned downstairs clutching a small glass phial filled with a dirty, grey coloured substance and made straight for the kitchen. Her instructions to her cook and butler were very specific. She gave them the seating plan for Friday evening and then showed them exactly how the powder should be administered and who should receive it. Then she left them to it, grinning from ear to ear.

On Friday morning during break Harvey Sheasby was feeling quite pleased with himself. He'd agonised long and hard about writing to Lady Braumsley but he knew he'd done the right thing in the end. This was confirmed by the letter which he'd just taken from his pigeonhole. It was a reply from her, the spidery handwriting quite unmistakable. He sat with a freshly poured cup of coffee and read it through, savouring every word. The letter was short but very much to the point.

Dear Mr Sheasby,

Thank you so much for your letter. I was particularly pleased to receive it and to realise that there is, at least, one member on the school staff who can show sensitivity, understanding and demonstrate a quite outstanding set of values.

I have noted with great interest all your written suspicions and I can assure you there are certain steps which have already been initiated to deal fully and properly with those who are obviously responsible.

Thank you again for your very kind words.

Yours sincerely,

Lady Braumsley.

Harvey relaxed with his coffee, a tight grin forming on his face. So much for that lot. They were now going to get their just rewards. He only wondered how it would be done. A formal Governors meeting? A full confrontation with Lady B and the Headmaster? It didn't really matter as long as something *was* done. They had it coming, every one of them.

Chewy sat watching Harvey as he preened himself silently on the other side of the room. It was sickening watching the silly old fart smiling away to himself.

'What's up with the Sheasby shit?' Chewy asked the others, nodding in his direction.

Rusty looked round but dismissed it, waving his hand.

'Probably won again at bunji jumping off the Cathedral tower,' Harry said, grinning.

Then Jolly came bumbling into the room in one of his 'states'. He looked quickly around and then, relieved, saw Harvey and shot over to him. Harvey stood, as Harvey would, and the pair of them chattered away in quiet tones for a few seconds and then they heard Sheasby say, 'Of, course Headmaster! I would be delighted! Thank you so much for asking me!'

Jolly beetled off again leaving the Escape Committee intrigued as to what he'd been asking Sheasby about.

'What the hell's going on now?' Chewy wondered.

'Probably won the south west prize for arse licking,' Vic mumbled.

In a way he was right but it was a prize which Harvey would eventually have preferred not to have won. He didn't think so then but he certainly did the following day.

Later on in the early evening the Escape Committee met in the pub for a quick drink before drifting off home. Compo joined them shortly after that and took the opportunity to have another go at Chewy about the set for the play.

'Oh. leave it alone, Compo!' Chewy said. 'You're getting to sound just like bloody Jolly!'

'Wash your mouth out!' Compo snapped back. 'How can you say that!'

'Easily,' Said Rusty.

'It's just a knack he's got.' Lill said

'Thanks a lot,' Chewy said, but then gave Compo his full attention. 'All right, you old bugger. When do you want this set of yours?'

'Yesterday!' Compo replied, emphatically.

Maggie arrived in the middle of this and sat down amongst them. Vic looked at his watch, a puzzled expression on his face.

'Shouldn't you have your party frock on right now?' he asked. 'I thought you were going to the dinner tonight at Lady B's?'

'Not on your life!' she answered. 'I told Jolly a large 'porky' about having to be in London instead'

'That's what Jolly must have been talking to Harvey about,' Lill said. 'I'll bet he's asked him to go as Senior Master!'

She was right.

As the guests were arriving at the great house the kitchen staff were putting the finishing touches to the preparations for the dinner. The butler, Ralph, and the cook, Mrs Dodkin, were busy with the 'brew' which Lady B had given them. This was now an evil smelling grey liquid in a thick, white, ceramic pot, which would have to be applied to each of nine soup bowls, one for each Inspector, before the first course, mushroom soup, was served. They had already selected the bowls and were about to paint it on with a pastry brush. There then had to be careful co-ordination during the delivery of the soup to ensure the bowls arrived in the right places. That was Ralph's job. In the meantime they waited for the mixture to cool slightly so that when applied there would be no visible trace. They left it sitting on a shelf above and to the side of the large range where most of the cooking for the dinner was taking place and busied themselves elsewhere with other tasks. Unfortunately, this was directly above the open soup tureen which was busily bubbling away.

Then Quentin came through the door next to the range but found nobody there. He liked to nose around the kitchen, especially when they were having special posh dinners. The aroma from the food was wonderful. He pushed the door shut just a little too hard and it slammed, wobbling the shelf and the grey 'cocktail' sitting on it. It rocked back and forth and then fell into the soup with a loud 'sploosh'. Quentin panicked, managed to retrieve it, despite burning his fingers in the hot liquid, gave it a wipe, ran to the tap, put some cold water in it and replaced it on the shelf, all in a flurried blur of action. Then he left in a hurry before anyone came back.

Ralph and Mrs Dodkin returned, checked the pot and were surprised to find how clear the mixture had become. Ralph shrugged it off and carefully painted each designated soup bowl. Then he took them all and placed them at each of the positions he'd been told to. With this done he could now announce to her Ladyship that all was ready.

All the guests were by now assembled in the drawing room politely partaking of the sherry. The Governors and the nine members of the Inspection team were all mixed up together attempting profound conversation with each other about education. The Dean and Mr Block were locked into a deep discussion about the progress of the Inspection and the others had the good sense to leave them to it. Jolly and the rest of the management were trying to make sure that everybody was happy. Some were succeeding more than others. Wooden was being his wooden self, boring to death one of the women about his experiences as an ice cream salesman when he was at college. She was not impressed.

The Prick was quacking on about his forces days and the Fat Controller was explaining, in a grindingly slow fashion, about the differences and excitements between 'capital' and 'revenue'. One of the Inspectors was stuck with the Wide Mouthed Frog who became slightly alarmed at her concern regarding the dangers of allowing Sixth Form pupils, boys and girls, to sit together in classrooms. 'One *never knows* what they're doing with their *hands,*' she said, almost whispering and mouthing her words. Jolly flitted about not really saying anything of any importance but very keen to make sure the evening would go smoothly. Harvey was sliding around doing his bum-licking best to praise the work of all of the Inspection team as well as extol the virtues of the school at the same time. Nobody really believed a word he said. There's a surprise.

Lady B slid from group to group, wearing another 'ship of the line' outfit and dripping heavily with the usual pearls and delivering a few subtle lines of veiled sarcasm. Quentin was largely ignored by everyone although he tried several times to latch on to anyone's conversation. Every time he did so the group would break up and re-form with the others. Eventually he gave up and sat down, sulking.

Ralph waited discreetly in the background but then was able to catch Lady B's eye, gave her a discrete nod which meant everything was ready and then he retired, ready to do his best. She then wacked her stick on a rather ugly and dented suit of armour against the wall, not for the first time, it was her version of a gong, and announced that dinner was served. With her at the head of all her guests, her arm on Jolly's, she made her way regally forward. The rest followed sedately into the dining room. The soup was to be the first course.

They settled, the soup was served and the rest of the dinner proceeded without a hitch. The cuisine was a delight and Jolly stood, after the cheese and biscuits, and on behalf of them all proposed a toast to their generous host. Lady B smiled and nodded graciously to everyone but knew it would only be a matter of time before 'things' began to happen. She was looking forward to that. They retired to the drawing room where coffee, brandy and port were ready and waiting. The conversation welled up again and it was interesting to see that

Wooden, The Wide Mouthed Frog, the Prick and the Fat Controller seemed to be completely outside the main body of Governors and Inspectors. Harvey was the next to join them and they stood around, fiddling with half empty glasses, trying to smile but looking rather lost. Quentin joined them but this didn't help at all.

The first sign of something going not quite right was the odd loud gurgle which came from the Fat Controller's stomach. He never had a great deal of control over this area of his anatomy but tonight was different. It was much more spectacular. The gurgles became louder and a few of the others looked round wondering what was making the noise. Then the Prick's stomach joined in closely followed by Jolly's, Harvey's, Wooden's, the Wide Mouthed Frog's and Quentin's. This was rapidly echoed by others from the Governors and Inspectors alike and soon the drawing room sounded like a plumbing system gone mad.

Then there was an almighty shriek and Lady B, a look of sheer horror on her face, went absolutely rigid for a few seconds. Everyone looked round, still suffering the same internal strife, but she was off like a bullet and gone, holding on to her backside and looking very, very unhappy.

Ralph was good. He was very, very good. Always in control, always completely cool and always completely calm. Working for Lady B had given him a great deal of 'experience' over the years. It was he who phoned for the ambulances, five were needed altogether, he who cleaned up the mess in the drawing room and out to the garden and he who managed to find some old joss sticks and assorted air fresheners to take the smell away. He really was worth his weight in gold. He'd also had the good sense *not* to touch the soup on that particular evening.

Governors, Inspectors, Management and Lady B herself were kept in the local cottage hospital for a couple of days, all in isolation, until the worst of their gastric effects wore off. The doctors were taking no chances. They didn't want this unknown mini epidemic spreading throughout the county. That could have been quite disastrous. By the time they were released, all of them in a rather sorry state, the papers had inevitably caught a 'whiff' of the story and yet again the headlines of the local press told all.

BRAUMSLEY'S BIG BLOWOUT!
BIZARRE BACCHANAL BITES BACK!

The Braumsley mansion was the scene of panic and mayhem, it was revealed today, as guests were found running madly to the cover of bushes in the grounds all around the great house. This, apparently, happened after an important meeting between Governors, an Inspection team and the Management of Braumsgate Cathedral School and immediately after dinner.

An eye witness, Mr Ned Tinkell, 33, and a member of the ground staff there, told our intrepid reporter, Reggie Northgood, that he was just checking the identity of one of the maids in the grounds outside the house when the drawing room glass doors flew open and several people galloped past him in some distress, all holding their nether regions. They disappeared behind several bushes and he could hear the definite sounds of exertion and then relief floating up from all around.

Soon after that a fleet of ambulances arrived and took the unfortunates away who were now in a rather 'distressed' and, said Mr Tinkell, 'a partially undressed state'.

The reasons for this event are not yet clear. There are suggestions that it was the dinner itself which had caused their 'indigestion', but this was hotly denied by Mrs Dodkin, 47, the cook.

'There ain't nothin' wrong w'my grub m'dear!' she said.

The Butler, Mr Ralph Holdworthy, 56, was not available for comment.

It would appear that Lady Braumsley was also 'taken ill' and had to be given a sedative before she could attack any more of the para-medics on the scene.

Once at the hospital, the staff there were guarded as to the cause of the malady but after several male nurses, auxiliary and ancillary staff, including porters and the security guards, were able to hold Lady B and her guests down, emergency enemas were performed on all on a strict rota basis.

'Just look what you missed!' Rusty said to Maggie, holding up the paper. 'You too could have had a sore...'

'Rusty!' Lill chipped in. 'Behave yourself!'

Chewy was helpless in the chair, tears streaming down his face with laughter.

'The...the...the best bit,' he managed to say, 'is the wonderful fact that Sheasby was there! I always knew he was a shit and this proves it!'

The rest of them fell about at this and didn't really regain control for a good few minutes. As they were hooting with laughter up in the staff room the Dean, Mr Block and Jolly were heavy with discussion about the Inspection. Not one of them was feeling too well although it had been a couple of days since that fateful dinner.

'So you see Headmaster,' Mr Block was saying, holding a handkerchief to his mouth, having trouble with a few 'repeats'. 'We're almost complete now. I will be taking the information with me, back to head office, and it should take no longer than two weeks before the final report will be ready.'

Jolly nodded and wiped his brow. He still felt terrible but he was trying to put on a brave face.

'Thank you, Mr Block,' he said, rather more limply than he would have liked, 'That will be something to look forward to.'

The Dean cleared his throat and shifted his weight in the chair. He was still having trouble sitting down.

'I have been impressed by your efficiency,' the Dean began, 'and I too look forward to reading your report on our school. There is, however, just one thing I would like you to clear up for me.'

'Oh, yes,' said Mr Block. 'And what would that be?'

The Dean fixed him with a steely eye and said, 'On the night of the dinner and our, err, rapid evacuation, if that's not to much of a misplaced term, why were you calling for the 'bar stewards'?'

Next door Harry had wandered into Maisie's office. He waited until she lifted her head from the computer screen. Then she looked up, saw him standing there, fiddling about with the photocopier, and asked what he wanted, none to politely.

'I just wondered what you were doing,' he said innocently.

'What the hell do you think I'm doing, you silly man!' she spat at him.

'I don't know,' He said spitting back at her, 'I was just asking, that's all!'

'Oh, I'm sorry, Harry,' She said, 'didn't mean that the way it came out. It's just there's a lot to do at the moment.'

'Yeh, sure,' he said, smiling. 'No problem. Carry on. Didn't mean to upset you.'

'You didn't,' She said, pushing her chair back and rubbing her eyes. 'Fancy a cup of coffee?'

'Lovely!' Harry replied.

Maisie walked out to the coffee machine in the outer office and found a couple of cups. While she was out there he slid behind the machine and quickly scanned the desk. A pile of paper on the right hand side almost covered the whole desk but there were two discs sitting there at the back with 'Inspection 1' and 'Inspection 2' written on them. He pocketed these and then looked at the computer screen. The title at the top said 'Inspection 3' and below this was a mass of statistics, a pure data base. She was obviously having to wade through this all this paper on the desk, loading it onto the computer.

Poking round he found spare discs in one of the drawers in her desk. She was now pouring the milk and about to add sugar to his. He quickly rewrote the titles from the original discs and put the blank discs where the originals had been. Now he could hear Maisie stirring the coffee in the cups and realised she was about to return. In desperation he hit a few of the more curious buttons on the keyboard and then shot out of her seat to resume his original position.

Maisie arrived with the coffee. They sat and chatted for a few minutes and then he made his excuses and left, thanking her for the coffee. Maisie deposited herself in front of the screen again and restarted the logging process again. Jolly, the Dean and Mr Block didn't hear the sudden, *'Oh, shit!'* which boomed from the office as Maisie discovered that something had gone very wrong with her precious database.

Outside in the hall, Henry the handyman was bumbling about looking for the weekly black bags. These were always full of the usual dross and paper junk of the week which Maisie religiously bagged up, earlier in the day, ready for Henry to dispatch into the large rubbish skips next to the dining hall. As Henry fumbled about looking for them, his pebble glasses being his main handicap, the Dean, Mr Block and Jolly came out of the side door from Jolly's study.

'Whoozatt!' Henry said, suddenly alarmed at the noise of the door and three hazy figures walking towards him.

'It's all right, Henry,' Jolly said. 'Carry on.'

Henry recognised his voice, if not his face, and relaxing, he continued with his search. With all the paperwork from the Inspection there was more than just the two standard bags of rubbish on this occasion. Six black bags sat there this time for him to manhandle out the back door to the skip. The other four were made up of the junk and mistakes which had been made over the preceding days by staff and management, as a result of the Inspection.

The important documentation, from the Inspection itself, sat next to the six rubbish bags as neat cardboard boxes, twelve of them in total. Unfortunately they all happened to be a very dark colour and to Henry's eyes were indistinguishable from the plastic bags.

Jolly, Mr Block and the Dean were still muttering about their unfortunate experience at the Braumsley mansion but in a rather low key. Henry looked at the mountain of 'rubbish' and then asked a question, right in the middle of their conversation.

'Which of this lot has to go, then?'

Jolly looked round and simply said, 'The ones at the end.'

Henry made for the 'end' as far as he was concerned which just happened to be the gap between the black rubbish bags and the cardboard boxes. Mr Block spotted this and corrected him, 'No. Not that lot, the other end.'

Mr Block, the Dean and Jolly wandered off, still deep in muted conversation. Henry was now very confused. Which end? He took his cap off and scratched his head. Then he made his choice, put his cap back on, and got on with it. Ten minutes later the hall was emptier except for the six black rubbish bags which Maisie had packed up. All the documentation from the Inspection was now sitting crumpled and squashed inside the big waste skip which stood, completely full, in a small courtyard next to the dining room. Bernie the Bin had then deposited several dustbins of waste food on top of the whole lot and today was the day when the collection and dispatch of the skip was due.

11

A definite air of relief and tranquility had begun to settle over the main body of the teaching staff now that the Inspection was over No longer would they have to endure the probing eyes and insidious questions about their methods, approaches, preparations and delivery of their subject They were, however, still very apprehensive about the contents of the inspector's report which would soon arrive What they didn't know about was what little Henry had unwittingly done for all of them, and particularly for the chief inspector, Mr Block

Everyone was sliding back into their old routines and the staff room was no longer the manic hive of industry it had been. Several of the teaching staff had used the place as an office to prepare various reports, fight with endless lists and ask each other nervously about requests for information from the Inspectors. All was more or less as before, empty, save for a few of the Escape Committee relaxing after the school day. Harry walked in, beaming. Rusty saw the smug expression on his face and knew there was something going on.

'You've been up to something, you old sod, haven't you?'
He said.

'Who?' Harry said. 'Me?'

'Yes, you!' Rusty said. 'I can tell from that self satisfied mush of yours that you've been doing something you shouldn't have! What is it?'

Harry slid his hand into his pocket and produced the discs.

'What the hell have you got there?' Rusty asked, intrigued.

'Only most of the results of the Inspection, that's all!' Harry grinned. 'I just need to know how I can screw up the information on them and then we're free and clear!'

There was only one place to go. The D&T Department. If they were quick Chewy might still be there. It was now well after four thirty, the end of the teaching day. Both of them galloped round to Chewy's place. They were lucky. He was still there. The others had gone. Chewy listened as Harry explained what he had done with growing admiration and then looked at the two discs.

'So what do you think? Harry asked.

'Easee, peasee,' Chewy said, and swung round in his chair to a set of drawers. He pulled the top one open and, rattling around amongst the jumbled contents, he found what he was looking for and pulled it out. It was a large, red, horseshoe shaped magnet.

'Ahh!' he said. 'This should do it.'

Laying the discs down he passed the magnet over them, laid it on each one for a few seconds then handed them back to Harry.

'Job done,' he said with a big grin on his face.

'Really?' said Harry, frowning. 'How?'

'Well.' Chewy began, 'putting it simply, floppy discs use magnetic storage. Pass a powerful magnet over them and…'

'You can screw up…' Harry butted in.

…anything on them!' Rusty completed the sentence.

'Exactly!' Chewy said, handing them back to Harry. 'You'd better get them back to the Mad Hatter before she realises they're missing.'

'Come on!' Rusty said. 'I'll come with you to create a diversion!'

Maisie was still there but in a terrible state. The computer was producing gobble-de-gook. She couldn't get it to make sense at all and the damn thing wouldn't print anything which was intelligible to a Martian never mind herself. Whatever Harry had done it had been as successful as Chewy's magnet. Maisie gave up and closed the whole thing down hoping that in the morning things might have sorted themselves out. That's when Rusty and Harry arrived, slightly out of breath. She looked up briefly, nodded, and then began to tidy up her desk.

'Maisie!' Rusty said, bounding forward. 'Fancy a drink?'

Maisie was immediately suspicious. She knew Rusty. There was always another motive lurking somewhere.

'What for!' she snapped.

'To ease your weary load!' Rusty grinned, leading her gently from the desk.

Harry kept his distance hoping for a chance to get the discs back in place.

'Oh, piss off, Rusty!' she said, 'I want to go home!'

'Don't we all, dear heart!' Rusty replied still hanging on to her.

Harry moved in silently as Rusty drew her further from the desk. He deftly retrieved the discs he'd planted and replaced the original ones. Maisie turned to look at him.

'What the hell are you doing, Harry?' she asked.

'Nothing. Nothing,' he said. 'Just looking at this mound of crap on your desk, that's all.'

'Crap is absolutely right!' Maisie said with feeling. 'I've never seen so bloody much of the bloody stuff in my whole bloody life!'

'Come on,' Rusty said, 'Let's get you a drink in the staff room. I think you need it. What do you say?'

'Oh, all right!' she agreed. Rusty led her out, followed by Harry, waited while she locked the door and then they both took her up to the staff room. Harry shot a large wink in Rusty's direction as they made their way there.

A couple of hours later the whole Inspection team came together in the outer drawing room to Jolly's office. They were there to formally bid their farewells and collect the pile of paperwork which had been packed in the cardboard boxes. Jolly had organised a light, late, high tea and bustled around making sure that all was well. Wooden did his best to keep the atmosphere 'jolly'. He failed, as usual. Then Mr Block buttoned a few of the team to help him load the boxes into the back of his estate car. They ambled out into the hall looking for them but no sign of any box of any sort could be found. He came back to find Jolly.

'Sorry to trouble you, Headmaster.' he said genially. 'I just wondered where you might have placed the boxes.'

'Boxes?' asked Jolly, slightly non-plussed. 'Boxes? What boxes?'

'The documentation from the whole inspection,' Mr Block said slowly. 'That was what was in the boxes. Where are they?'

'I have no idea,' Jolly said, a cold chill beginning to envelope him.

'Then may I suggest,' said Mr Block, coldly, 'that we look for them!'

Mr Block released his team but stayed on to hunt down the missing documentation. Well into that evening he, Jolly and Wooden scoured the building but no sign of the boxes could be found. It was hardly surprising. The waste disposal truck had taken them away hours before. They were now so much pulp in the recycling plant outside the town. Jolly began to panic as Mr Block's attitude became more and more churlish.

'Who came in here today?' Jolly asked Wooden menacingly, holding him by the lapels of his jacket.

'Just about everybody!' Wooden replied, terrified at this attack.

'Think!' Jolly said, letting him go suddenly. 'Just think!'

Wooden thought and stayed that way for a long time. Jolly was pacing up and down. Then Wooden walked out into the hall and was away for a few minutes before he came back, a heavy frown on his face, one hand on the top of his head and the index finger of his other hand on his lips. This was his thinking mode.

'A thought occurs to me,' he said in his wooden monotone. This was a monumentally huge and giant mental leap forward for Wooden.

'Oh. that's good!' Jolly snapped. 'A thought! Well that's really going to help, isn't it?'

Wooden either ignored that or didn't hear it. After all he was thinking his 'thought' and that didn't leave much of his brain left for other things. He walked slowly over to one of the chairs and sat, still with hand on head and finger to mouth. Then he put them down, stood up and spoke again.

'Why are all the rubbish bags still outside in the hall?'

'How on earth I am I supposed to know that!' Jolly almost shouted back. 'They should have been taken......' He didn't finish that sentence but stopped in mid flow, a horrible 'thought' of his own breaking as a dam might burst.

'Henry!' he screeched. 'Find Henry!'

Two hours later they found Henry. He was absolutely ratted. He'd been in the local Legion Club since opening time and now he was beyond all pain and singing a rather bawdy 'ditty' about 'ladies in the city with very large....' He was carried out and brought back to the school. It was only about nine thirty at night but Henry was well and truly pissed. As a professional 'cider head' he could drink himself stupid on the stuff, which wasn't very far to go for him.

Jolly frantically demanded two large jugs of black coffee from the dining room and the few staff still on duty grudgingly brought them to his study. He spent two long and frustrating hours pouring the stuff down Henry's throat, hoping and trying desperately to sober him up. Henry was having a lovely time, he thought, being so well looked after by the Headmaster himself as well as the first Deputy and that nice Inspector Block, but his befuddled brain couldn't figure out why an Inspector of Police should be with them. Jolly didn't bother to correct him. They continued to pour coffee down his throat as midnight struck, asking questions all the time, but the answers they got, before he eventually passed out, were less than helpful. The best they achieved was just before he crumpled in the chair, spark out, gently breaking wind.

'Henry', Jolly had soothed, in his best bedside manner. 'Henry, can you please tell me what you did with the rubbish?'

Henry looked up through his pebble glasses, this time seeing nothing at all.

'Hoozeddat?' he asked.

'It was me, Henry, your Headmaster, remember?' Jolly said, gritting his teeth. Henry wobbled his head in remembrance.

'Now. What did you do with the rubbish?' Jolly asked again.

'In-the-skip-it-is!' Henry managed to say.

'And where did the little skip go to?' Jolly said, trying to keep his voice as light as possible.

'Off-to-the-big-pulp-land-in-the-sky!' Henry blurted out quickly and then grinning he let fly a huge belch. 'Bye-bye-little-rubbish. Hic! Bye-bye!' Then he flopped back into the chair, gone to the world.

'This is a complete waste of time!' Mr Block said. 'That imbecile has destroyed all our work! How could you let him do it!'

Jolly didn't like that.

'If I might remind you, Mr Block,' Jolly said, jumping up furiously, and completely out of character, 'it was you, not I, who ordered Henry to dispose of the 'rubbish'! I suggest you think about that! I have the Dean as a witness to the whole event!'

Mr Block remembered. Jolly was right. He had. That did change things. It was his fault. Nobody else. What could he do? What would head office say? He wasn't feeling too well by now and those familiar gurgles of the other day began to start again. A few seconds later he had to run. Jolly sat down again and rocked backwards and forwards, his head in his hands. If the documents had really gone to the plant they would by now, as Henry had said, be nothing more than pulp. If only there had been another record. He sat up suddenly. There was! The database which Maisie had been working on!

Without saying a word he grabbed Wooden by the arm and dragged him out and along the corridor. Wooden didn't know what was going on but he stumbled on as best he could. Jolly fumbled with his keys, unlocked the door and once inside Maisie's office, he snapped on the lights and slightly out of breath, scanned the interior. Wooden asked a simple question.

'Is there a problem here?'

'No, you silly man!' Jolly yelled at him. 'But there will be if I can't find the discs!'

'Discs?' Wooden asked, blinking slowly.

'Yes!' Jolly snapped back. 'The discs! We must find the database discs of the Inspection!'

He began hunting through the office, turning everything over in his desperation to find the database discs. Wooden looked down at Maisie's desk and saw the two discs sitting there marked 'Inspection 1' and 'Inspection 2'. Because they were square, the three and a half inch floppy variety and not circular, so he ignored them. They were not discs. They were squares, even though they had 'Inspection' written boldly on their surfaces. Then Jolly pushed past him pushing the stuff around on the desk and found the discs.

'Ahh!' he said. 'Here they are!'

Wooden tried to tell him they were squares and not discs but Jolly ignored him. Jolly switched on the computer and waited for the programme to come up on screen. He'd been looking over Maisie's shoulder too often to forget how it was done. But that's all he knew. The programme came up and he fed the first disc into the port. He waited but nothing happened. A few more seconds dragged by and still nothing happened. In frustration he punched a few control buttons and by sheer chance he brought up the file with the information on it. He sat looking at total gibberish.

'Oh. my!' he said to himself.

He pulled out the disc and fed the other one in. The same thing happened.

'Oh, no!' he whimpered very quietly. With his inexperience of computer use he thought he'd really done it now. Not only had the actual Inspection Documents themselves been destroyed but now he'd screwed up the discs. If only he'd known how to operate the damned machine this would never have happened. He was not to know that the things had already been 'got at' by another agency and it was highly unlikely that the agency involved would ever tell him. Wooden offered his all-purpose question again.

'Is there a problem here?'

'Problem? Problem?' Jolly said. 'What do you mean, 'problem'?'

'I just thought...,' Wooden began but was cut short by Jolly.

'Don't think! Don't say! Just... don't!' Jolly snapped at him.

He stood up, pulled the disc out of the machine, left it with the other one and switched of the machine. The he walked out of the office, clicking off the light, leaving Wooden in the dark. Wooden followed, almost tripping over the waste bin by Maisie's chair. Mr Block was just coming along the hall as they walked out. He was holding his stomach and not looking too good.

'In the circumstances,' Mr Block said, 'I think we had better re-think this whole business.'

This sounded to Jolly like code language for, 'I've had enough of this and I'm off!'

'Oh, really?' Jolly said, trying to smile.

Mr Block was not in the mood for a conversation. He was rather fearful of another sudden attack of his personal plumbing to hang around too long.

'I shall be writing to you, Headmaster,' he said, and with a quick nod to Wooden he was out the door and gone, a little faster than he needed to have done. His 'plumbing' was having its own way again. That was the last they heard of the Inspection, the team and Mr Block although Jolly did get a short letter from Head Office a week or so later, on the last day of term. It was short but to the point.

Dear Headmaster,

It is with regret that I have to apologise for the circumstances regarding the recent Inspection at your school. I have discussed this with Head of the Inspection team, before he left us, and he has assured me of your more than adequate standards which the Government demands.

In so far as this has now been accepted, there will now be no need for a further visit in the foreseeable future,

May I apologise again for any inconvenience which this may have caused.

yours sincerely,
Department of Education and Science.

Jolly sagged visibly as sheer relief washed over him. But before that gem of a letter had arrived there was still another final problem in the school to be resolved. This time it had nothing to do with the management. It was the end of term play.

Compo was near total hysteria by now. Nothing was going right. There were only two days before the full dress rehearsal and it was looking disastrous. The basic 'facilities' which he had didn't help either.

The 'theatre' which the school used was an ancient barn, stuck way out on a limb from the main school buildings and yet another ancient and conserved 'monument', untouchable and sacrosanct. It was an eleventh century, buttressed, stone slated, slit windowed, narrow arched doored, open timbered roof variety and almost impossible to use for theatrical performance. Concessions had been made over the years with the installation of a basic electrical supply but this was well below the needs for adequate lighting and power for any school production. Every time they attempted to present any kind of performance they had to rig up a huge generator outside to supply the extra 'juice'. That gave its own problems. As another ex-army 'bargain' it regularly blew up and a couple of the ground staff were always seconded to stand by. They were dab hands at 'repairing' it. The thing had been re-built, patched and taped so many times it was fast becoming a dangerous electrical hazard. Apart from the horrendous noise it produced the cable from it stretched everywhere, up to the makeshift lighting rig above, down to the lighting desk at the back, into sound systems, generally draped through all the timber work above their heads like black spaghetti. There was no other way of doing it. The local fire officer would have gone white with sheer fright if he'd seen it.

The 'stage' was a roughly constructed platform at one end and because they were not allowed to interfere with the structure there were no 'wings' at all. The only way they were able to get round this was to sneak in some large hooks, hammered into the ancient, historic, protected, oak beams above with two large curtains suspended from these on either side. They served to close off a thin corridor on either side where scenery and actors could hover. This narrowed the actual stage area alarmingly but there was no other way to present a play, get the 'players' on and off or change the sets without having to cart them through the audience. That would not have been a good idea. As it was there was hardly any room at either side to hump scenery around especially in the middle of a play and when the place was heaving with kids waiting for their cues.

The other practical problems were manifold. A wooden shack at the rear of the building, yes another one, was being used as a changing room and for make up but this was far too small. It also had to serve as the scene dock which left very little space for costumes and props, never mind the kids. The fact that the roof leaked badly and it was a good sixty yards away with a high stone wall between it and the barn didn't help either. Negotiating kids between there and the barn, round the wall in completely black, unlit darkness, sometimes when it was raining stair-rods or snowing or blowing a gale was not for the faint of heart. All very unsatisfactory.

All this was as nothing as far as Compo was concerned. The kids didn't know their lines, some of them forgot to turn up for rehearsals and the set still wasn't finished. Chewy was working flat out constructing it but it might be another day before it was on site and painted. Compo wasn't having a nice time. This time the play was to be 'Wind in the Willows' and kids of all ages would be involved from the little ones in the Junior School right up to the Sixth Form, and that's where the problems started. With little ones from five years old going up to lurching great six foot plus Sixth Formers, organisation became a nightmare. There were well over eighty kids performing in the play as well as an additional thirty or so who were to be stage crew, callers, runners, dressers, prompter, lighting and sound crews, and ushers. On top of this lot were the musicians. Oh, yes, this was to be a major production. They brought the full complement up to just over a hundred and thirty. In full rehearsal it felt like a thousand. The row from them all was horrific. Even Cecil B. De Mille would have been tearing his hair out.

Compo was sitting up at the back dolefully watching the last scene, with the whole company on stage. Standing a few feet away from him was a diminutive, shrieking, Welsh, harridan. This was Geraldine Candell, teacher of drama for the little ones in the school. She dealt with all ages, adults included, as she did the tots, viciously, if they didn't do as they were told. This was one occasion. She stopped the last song, walked down the hall to the front of the stage and bellowed at all of them.

'WILL YOU ALL PLEASE LISTEN!'

The barn echoed with her voice and a hush settled over all. Compo was full of admiration. How could someone so small project a voice like that? Truly amazing!

'Will the rabbits STOP giggling ALL the time, the weasels and stoats STOP 'Ninja Turtling' all over the stage and will Mr Badger keep his hands OFF the washer woman when he makes his entrance!'

They all nodded as one.

'As for you Mr Mole,' she continued, 'I will NOT have you enter stage right with a 'Gameboy' in your hand AGAIN! It's not in keeping with the play, IS IT!'

Mr Mole shook his head, looked at his feet and shuffled uncomfortably in the strained silence.

'Right!' Geraldine said. 'Let's try this last scene again, and this time I want to *HEAR YOU ALL SINGING!*'

The kids bumbled off to either side of the stage, waited for their cues and then ran through the final song again, the 'walk downs' and the finale, this time to her satisfaction.

'Well done!' she beamed, applauding. 'Now! There are just a few other points which I want you all to listen to!'

Everyone of them sagged visibly as she began to go through each section of the last scene. Compo crept out and walked briskly up to the D&T Department to see how Chewy was getting on with the set. The workshop was heaving with flats and bits of scenery. The Fifth Form had been 'volunteered' to help and they were scattered around the room, working on various finishing treatments, sanding down corners, making sure screws were fully tightened and looking thoroughly miserable and bored stiff. There were tools everywhere and the floor was covered in off cuts from the construction process. Chewy was in the middle of all this, now sitting on a workbench, sweating.

'Compo, you old bugger!' he said, seeing him walk in. 'How's it going?'

'Don't ask!' Compo answered. 'The Jerry-Can's in there now marshalling her troops!'

'Jerry-Can', Geraldine Candell, would not have liked her nickname. She would have liked the one Chewy had given her even less. That was 'Candlewick', or as he actually preferred, 'The Wick', because she got right on his. Other less than savoury references of his to the use of candles would have been equally offensive.

'I don't know how you stand that bloody Welsh witch.' Chewy said. 'She drives me up the bloody wall with all her Celtic theatrical crap.'

'Don't hold back now,' Compo said, forcing an 'understanding' expression, and repeating a familiar line from Escape Committee sources. 'Just tell us how you really feel.'

'Up yours!' Chewy said. 'Come on you old fart. Let's have a cup of coffee.'

By mid evening Chewy had the scenery finished, painted and in the scene dock ready for use. Compo was a little happier now. In the pub afterwards, the full Escape Committee with him, Compo finished his quick chat to Chewy about a couple of slight changes to one of the sets and now joined the conversation with the rest.

'Sorry about that, all.' he said, 'I just needed to check a few points. Now. Seeing as you're all here, I wonder if...?'

'Oh, here we go!' Vic said. 'Time for more 'volunteers' is it?'

'Well, now that you come to mention it, yes!' Compo beamed at them all.

'No!' said Rusty. 'I haven't forgotten the last time!'

'Nor have I!' Lill agreed. 'Fumbling around in the dark from the changing room, trying to find three lost 'pixies' and in the pouring bloody rain, was not my idea of fun!'

'Oh, come on you lot!' Compo said. 'Just because the generator packed up twice and the set fell over at the beginning, well, it could happen to anybody!'

'It fell on me!' Rusty said.

'I know, I know!' Compo tried to save the situation. 'But the damage wasn't that bad. You only had to have three stitches after all!'

'Thanks!' Rusty said, picking up the remnants of his beer. 'It must be your round then.'

Compo took this as a partial agreement to be involved, scooted over to the bar, organised another trayful and came back, ready to plead if necessary.

First night arrived and the barn was full. Governers, parents, staff and kids were all crammed in, shoulder to shoulder on those bloody awful plastic chairs, waiting for the play to begin. The Dean, Jolly and the Wide Mouthed Frog were sitting on the front row. An expectant hum filled the air. The musicians struck up the opening chords of the introductory music and the 'house lights' slowly dimmed. The music faded away as the place became completely and absolutely black. It stayed that way for about four minutes. The generator had packed up again. Outside was a scene of manic activity as spanners, screwdrivers and insulating tape flew in all directions. Then a switch was thrown and the first scene lighting came on with a 'crack!' It scared the hell out of the audience who were feeling less than comfortable in total darkness. The play continued uninterrupted and everyone behind the scenes were crossing everything they had and hoping that nothing else would go wrong. It did.

Rusty and Lill were up at the back supervising the kids on the lighting and audio desks. Chewy was round the back of the stage directing traffic for scene changes and Vic was acting as main 'crowd control operative' for the several kids involved throughout the play. The damned place seemed to be alive with little 'bunnies' and assorted 'furry' animals. They were everywhere. It was a hell of a task to keep them quiet as well as away from the stage. When they were not actually on stage, all they wanted to do was to poke their heads out from behind the curtains and wave at their mums and dads.

'Bring back bloody myxomatosis!' Vic was mumbling under his breath as he kept having to grab several 'bunnies' by the scruff of their necks and pull them back.

There were only two small incidents in the first act. Alfred, the horse, was in the middle of one his speeches when his trousers fell down, revealing a 'cool' pair of 'Lethal Weapon 3' boxer shorts. That went down quite well with some of the audience except Jolly, the Dean and the Wide Mouthed Frog, although she had time to take a photograph of it before Alfred managed to pull them back up. The other one incident happened during the scene with the 'Wild Wooders'. Stoats and assorted Weasels rushed around, chanting and generally being 'beastly' about Mr Toad. Two of the silly little sods didn't watch where they were going and in their excited leaping around collided, head on, front centre stage and dropped like stones where they lay in a crumpled heap. The audience thought this was part of the play and a great series of hoots and whistles came up from the middle of the barn. The rest dragged the pair off as the lights went down and the scene and the act came to an end. A massive round of applause came up as darkness fell again. The two kids were out for a day and a half after that bump and each of them had a lump the size of a chickens egg as a trophy of their performance. But, so far, so good, everyone thought. Wrong. Act Two, Scene One began. Deep in the 'Wild Wood'.

Up at the back Rusty checked the cues as the Fifth Former next to him pushed the sliders forward to bring up the lighting. Then he looked up and just said, 'Oh, shit!' There wasn't a stick of scenery visible, nothing, zippo! There was a completely empty stage where a jungle of contorted, evil trees and branches should have been.

'Chewy'll go bloody mad about this!' Lill said. 'He spent days making them!'

Chewy was in no position to say anything at that moment. He was pinned up against the wall underneath the scenery, with all the other stage crew. Someone had given the Stoats and Weasels too early a cue and they had arrived, flooding in, stampeding over Vic, squashing everyone in their path, including Chewy, massing on the sides, ready to come on.

The whole scene had to be played in partial mime. There was nothing else they could do without the set being there. No one in the audience seemed to mind or notice and afterwards Jolly actually congratulated Compo on such an 'innovative ' idea. The rest of the play went ahead without any other misfortunes but at the end, when everyone arrived on stage for the jolly, 'isn't everything all right, song', Mr Badger was still groping the hell out of the washer woman and she was loving it. The audience went wild with applause, whistles, shouts and stamps and they all had to come back on and go through the last song again, the audience joining in this time, so that was all right. Compo slumped at the back with Rusty and Lill.

'Thank God that's over!' Rusty sighed.

'No it's bloody not!' Compo said.

'No!' Lill agreed. 'There's another three performances yet!'

The last week of any Michaelmas term was usually a total and absolute waste of time for everyone. The kids were completely switched off with the prospect of Christmas only a couple of weeks away and several staff had a pile of videos ready and organised for their daily 'in flight' movie for the journey over the remaining days. Jolly wouldn't have that. He insisted on all the staff and the kids continuing as normal, right up to the last day. Needless to say most of them ignored his instruction but nodded to him at the time to keep him happy.

Some of the more misguided of the staff were putting the finishing touches to an event which was being repeated in many schools all over the country. This was the staff play or pantomime, and an excruciating experience which would make even the most stout-hearted burn with total embarrassment. Why some staff inflict this kind of 'am-dram' crap on their comparatively innocent charges is beyond reason but they do it every year as a means of attempting closer relationships with the kids, failing to realise it has exactly the opposite effect. The Braumstate version, a single performance of a one act pantomine of 'Cinderella', was no exception. To the Escape Committee the word 'pantomime' was an apt, accurate and sardonic description of this thespian nightmare. But then again, every cloud has a silver lining and it was the Wide Mouthed Frog who provided one.

The kids, herded into the old barn once again, were not looking forward to it one little bit and they had good reason to be feeling that way. Previous 'performances' over the years had seen particularly dire theatrical attempts ranging from 'Star Trek', based on the original series, to 'The Fall of the Roman Empire', a comedy! Each one was, thankfully, only an hour long which was just as well. Anything longer than that would have had the kids attempting a mass breakout.

This time the generator, fortunately, held and the house lights dimmed, the curtains opened and the stage lit up for the performance to begin. Twenty minutes later silence had been the only reaction from the kids as several of the staff cavorted around on the tiny stage. It was bloody awful, as usual. But then came the scene where the fairy godmother arrived and in she came, the Wide Mouthed Frog in full costume, long fur coat, wings stuck on her back, silly hat, Dame Edna specs on, feather duster in one hand and a large, furry muff on the other. Not a pretty sight but she was loving every moment.

The appearance of this apparition triggered a huge intake of breath from the audience but then the place erupted with whistles, cat calls and general verbal abuse from all the kids. They had never seen anything like it and she thought, stupid cow, that they were loving it just as much as she was. In the midst of her saying to little Cinders, 'You *shall* go to the ball!' played by the Art mistress, the Poison Dwarf of all people, the kids in the audience were still making a hell of a racket. Giving up the struggle, Wide Mouth took offence, stopped suddenly, strode to the front of the stage and fixed the whole audience with a steely eye. What she said then will go down forever in the school's pantomime history.

She said, *'Watch it you lot! I have a lot of spells up my muff!'*

The place exploded in raucous laughter at that but, somewhat confused, she tried and eventually succeeded in continuing despite the furore from the kids. The following day Chewy congratulated her on her performance. A sickly grin spread over her face but Chewy hadn't finished.

'And that was a cracker of a 'muff' line he said.

Her reply to that was even better than her stage delivery.

She smiled again and said, 'Well, I don't know what they were laughing at. It's not as if I'd said 'Up my pussy!'

As the last few days ground on, the time for the 'House parties' arrived which were a mixed bag, to say the least. The biggest 'mixed bag' was the Wide Mouthed Frog, who organised her 'gells' in rows and then insisted on playing party games which would have driven a three year old to a rapid suicide. The kids hated her end of term 'parties' and one by one sneaked out for more adventurous venues, the boys' Houses. They had the good sense to stay clear of Adolf's place who, as House Master, was usually well pissed very early on every 'party night' and would inevitably harangue the kids, yet again, with his African 'experiences' for hours on end. After a while there were very few kids left in that House as well.

Most of the 'action' tended to focus on two other Houses which sat next to each other. One was a girls' House and the other, and this was planning gone mad, was for boys. The mixed 'knees up' which took place between them was legendary throughout the school. So was the aftermath the following morning. The ground staff usually had a running bet as to how many fag packets, 'tinnies', beer bottles and 'preventative devices' they would find when they were given the job of clearing up the gardens at the back. Thirty five was the highest figure ever reached for one of those categories. It was usually the last one.

After the mid-week House Parties there were only two days left of the term and they tended to grind on forever. Video supplies were getting low all over the school on the penultimate day and a few staff were beginning to become quite panic stricken as they realised they might have to actually communicate with their charges in an attempt to keep them happy.

The afternoon of that day was always given over to 'clearing'. 'Clearing' was the overall description given to tidying up Houses, classrooms and the school itself. The first two areas were usually organised in a quite straightforward fashion by the kids with little supervision by the staff. The last area, clearing up the school, was always given to the 'naughties' who had been placed on detention, usually by the same staff every week who couldn't cope with the more individualistic natures of some of the pupil body.

These 'unworthies' were provided with black plastic bags and ordered off into the school site to pick up rubbish, of any kind, for one full hour. Off they went, grazing through all the buildings picking up all kinds of unsavoury bits and pieces. At the same time another member of staff, Hilda Chaseborn, Home Economics teacher and 'Cheeseburn' to all others, House Mistress and also in charge of lost property, had dispatched four kids to collect any obvious gear which was always lying around. Boots, jumpers, blazers, cases, socks, hockey sticks and all manner of lost bits and pieces were always scattered around the place, no less at the end of term.

The only flaw in this dual system on this particular day was Chewy. His was the unhappy duty of checking up on the team collecting rubbish. A rota system existed for all the staff and his turn happened to fall on this occasion. He wasn't happy. To make things worse it began to rain heavily and he wandered about, complete with large brolly, making sure that the 'naughties' were doing their stuff. He made the basic mistake of assuming that the four kids he found collecting lost property were part of the detention team. They tried to tell him but he shouted them down.

'Do as you're damned well told!' he said, standing in the pouring rain and telling them to pick up all the damp, and by now rather tacky, detritus which was lying about. Shrugging, they did so filling their bags with all manner of evil junk and then, with the bags full up they reported back to Hilda Chaseborn. The four of them stood there, dripping in the rain, holding their sacks of soggy crap, scooped up from all over the place. Hilda brought them into the house and through to her own private lounge, fussing about them getting soaked and what a wonderful job they had done. The kids looked at each other wondering what the hell she was talking about but then stiffened as she asked them to tip it all out in the middle of the floor! Hilda, who was expecting a vast collection of shoes, ties, sweaters and other similar apparel, had to ask again for them to tip it out there and then so she could have a look at it.

'Are you sure?' one of them said quietly.

'Don't be silly!' Hilda said. 'Come on! Let's see what you've got!'

'But...' one of them said.

'Will you do as I ask?' she snapped. 'And right now!'

They did, all four of them, all over the carpet. The look on her face as all that crap folded out in a soggy, stinking mass was unbelievable. The stain which it left on the carpet was beyond cleaning and she never forgave Chewy for that.

The day finally ended, to everyones great relief, all of them now ready for the 'big finish' the following morning, the end of term service in the Cathedral. Vic would be giving the sermon. That was usually well worth listening to. This one would be no exception.

Vic came into the staff room and slumped into a chair. It was still early with half an hour before the end of term service was due to begin in the Cathedral. Vic was not very happy and it showed. Chewy and Rusty arrived with a few other staff and came over to him.

'And how are we today, Chaplain?' Rusty asked brightly.

'Suicidal,' Vic answered.

'What's up, Vic?' Chewy asked him. 'It's the last day, remember? Escape beckons!'

'Don't ask,' Vic answered miserably, waving a limp hand. 'Just don't ask.'

'You've been telling the truth again Vicar, haven't you?' Rusty said. 'I've told you about that before. Not a good idea round here as well you know.'

'It's Jolly, isn't it?' Chewy asked, recognising the signs. 'Come on, spit it out. What's the silly bugger said this time?'

'He doesn't like the sermon,' Vic sighed.

'You haven't given the bloody thing yet!' Rusty said. 'What the hell's the matter with him now?'

'He wanted to 'vet' it,' Vic answered.

'Oh no, not again!' Chewy said. 'He's nuts!'

'Well spotted,' Rusty agreed. 'So what now? There's not a lot of time left before 'curtain up' is there?'

'Exactly,' Vic replied then fell silent, hands clasped together, deep in thought.

Rusty and Chewy looked at each other. Then Vic was on his feet.

'To hell with it!' he said. 'No changes! Not now!' and stomped off.

'This I have to hear,' Rusty said grinning.

'I wish I had that pocket tape recorder with me,' Chewy grinned as they left for the Cathedral.

In only one hour from then the Cathedral would look as if a whirlwind had swept through the inside. Hymn sheets would lie crumpled all over the nave together with the odd comic, hundreds of sweetie papers, chairs dislodged from rows, hymn books on the stone flagged floor and hassocks, which had been used as footballs would be everywhere but hanging on chairbacks. Several gobs of long forgotten chewing gum would be squished on the bases of several of the columns and the vergers would be blowing steam from their ears at the sight. It would need at least two hours to put it straight again. There was nothing new about this. It happened every time the school massed for a service but that would come later. Right now the whole nave was filling up with the school. Other visitors, the general public and one or two tourists were being jostled and buffeted out of the way as the kids made their way in and eventually took their seats, some having to be brow beaten and manhandled by several staff at the same time.

Within a few minutes they were reasonably settled and the organ began to play, vibrating through the building. Then the Dean, followed by Jolly, processed through from the vestry at the side with Vic behind them, complete with surplice and with his 'holy' look on. He climbed to the pulpit as everyone stood and he greeted them all, reminding them that Christmas was almost here, as if they didn't know. Rusty and Chewy were standing at the back, better placed to capture any would-be 'escapees' amongst the kids, of which there were always a few, and then the first notes of the first hymn boomed out from the organ towards them, 'Hark the Herald Angels Sing'.

After that the Head Boy and Head Girl gave a garbled, mumbled reading from the pulpit which few of the kids were listening to or understood. It came over rather vaguely as something to do with two squatters, a baby, an asteroid, three tourists, a King, income tax and a few assorted animals. Another hymn followed this, so up again from the chairs and the whole school launched into it singing lustily, the 'lyrics' of which became oddly changed into, 'While shirkers washed their jocks at night....' Sadly there were one or two in the Sixth Form who used a similar sounding word to 'jocks', but it wasn't 'jocks' at all. As the echoes of the hymn died away Vic appeared in the pulpit again and casually laid his notes in front of him.

'Here we go,' whispered Chewy.

Vic folded his arms and rested on the edge of the pulpit. A few seconds drifted by as he scanned the congregation slowly but he didn't say a word. It was as if he was lazily looking out from a first floor window just watching the world go by, a slight smile on his face. There were a few stifled sniggers from the younger kids and the staff. Jolly in particular moved uncomfortably in his seat. You could have heard the proverbial pin drop. Then Vic stood upright, unfolded his arms, placed his hands on the pulpit and leaned forward delivering his opening line.

'I'm absolutely fed up with stupid, silly stories!'

There wasn't a sound. Every one was fascinated. What was he going on about? And more important, what was he going to say next? If Rusty and Chewy could have seen Jolly's face they would have cracked up completely. He was almost purple with rage. In that single opening sentence it was perfectly obvious to him that Vic had ignored everything he had said about his sermon earlier that same morning. But Vic didn't care anymore. He continued, ignoring the venous look Jolly was giving him.

'They are the kind of stories which always bounce around at this time of year perpetuated by people who should know better. The ones I'm talking about are the 'baby Jesus, cuddly animals in a barn and three peculiar fellas who arrive from nowhere with goodies' variety. Then there's a young teenage girl who suddenly becomes pregnant... and nobody wonders how or why!'

A few of the staff were squirming with annoyance and others were in mild shock at this 'disgraceful' statement but the kids were following his every word. Vic soldiered on and with every sentence he uttered there was a startling re-appraisal of the whole Christmas story. It was pure delight for Rusty, Chewy and the bulk of the congregation, mostly the kids, listened as they'd never listened before. Chewy looked to his left at one point and saw Compo shaking with laughter, a hankie stuffed in his mouth to stifle the noise. Lill sat next to him in the same state, her hand held tightly across her own mouth. Harry was next to her but he had a dictaphone in his hand, held up discreetly in front of him, hoping to catch every word as it was spoken. A good ten minutes later Vic wound up his thesis. It had been a stunner, but the final summary really did it.

'So. There we are. I hope you can all see what I've really been driving at. Jesus isn't just a pink, plastic doll surrounded by cuddly animals with a funny light bulb stuck on top of his head. He's a man, a real man who doesn't want to know about all these sugary stories and I suspect he'd be very annoyed at finding a fat old man getting in the way of everything, dressed in a silly red dressing gown, dishing out presents and surrounded by reindeers. That's a bit like taking advantage of what Jesus was trying to do and did for all of us. Neither would he be too happy hearing someone with a guitar in here singing about little donkeys all the time. I don't like guitars in church either, or plastic, pink babies or silly furry animals getting in the way of the real message. Jesus Christ gave up his life for us. The least we can do for him is to celebrate his birthday properly. Just try to remember that, if you can. Now, let us pray.'

Every head bowed in silence, except Jolly's. He was beside himself with fury. After the prayer the Dean stepped forward, gave the blessing and the organ rose up to play them all out. On the way back to the school the Escape Committee were swapping hilarious notes about Vic's sermon as all the kids swarmed past them to find their parents in the log jam of cars which surrounded the place. Well ahead of them were Jolly, Vic and the Dean, all three of them locked in heavy conversation as they walked briskly on.

'Looks like Vic's getting a good bollicking from both of them,' Chewy remarked.

'Again,' Lill sighed. 'He really doesn't deserve that, not this time.'

She needn't have worried.

Half an hour later, back in the staff room for the traditional last drink of the term, the Escape Committee sat round with Vic. Chewy asked the question again.

'Please?'

'Why?' said Vic.

'I just want to have a transcript of that sermon,' Chewy answered. 'It was bloody marvellous!'

'Ah, well, someone else didn't think so,' Vic grimaced.

'I wonder who he's talking about?' Rusty said.

The rest of them shrugged altogether in mock ignorance.

'It might have had something to do with that reference to Mary being pregnant,' Compo said, breaking up again into giggles.

'Oh,' Vic said grinning. 'You mean the bit about how would you feel if your young girl of a wife said she had a bun in the oven and you weren't the baker?'

Compo could only nod. He was shaking with mirth again.

'I wish I'd heard it,' Maggie confessed. 'I was trying to get rid of the last bits of paperwork up here.'

'You missed an absolute treat,' Lill told her, 'and the kids were hanging on Vic's every word all the way through it.'

'And that's just what the Dean said,' Vic told them all, a huge smile breaking over his face. 'I couldn't believe my ears when he said that walking back from the Cathedral! He said that it was the most honest sermon he's heard for years!'

'So it wasn't a discussion about your P45 at all!' Harry grinned.

'Nope!' Vic laughed. 'That's why Jolly isn't that 'jolly' right now. When we arrived back at school he took it out on Wooden instead!'

'So nothing changes, eh!' Chewy gaffawed. 'Here's to the end of term!

As evening approached, the 'End of Term Christmas Dinner' for the staff was now almost ready. The catering staff had surpassed themselves and a veritable banquet was waiting to be served. A bar had been set up at one end of the dining room and after the dinner a disco had been organised for anyone who wanted to join in and have a 'bop'. Staff and spouses began to arrive and were offered 'The Sherry'. This was, again, one of those occasions where unrecognisable people mysteriously turned up from everywhere to partake of a free meal. Almost twenty per cent of the full compliment there had never been seen by any of the staff and they probably wouldn't be seen again until the next one. Such is the way of main celebratory events.

'What the hell am I doing here?' Chewy said.

'Getting pissed by the look of it!' Rusty offered.

They and the rest of the Escape Committee, together with the newest honorary member, Compo, were up in the staff room, getting a 'lining' on for the rest of the evening.

'Thanks a lot,' Chewy said. 'It's just that every year I swear to myself I'll never come to this dinner again, but here I am! I must be bloody mad!'

'I'll drink to that!' Harry said, draining his glass.

'So will I!' Maggie said, holding her glass high.

'Well,' said Vic. 'It's been an interesting term, that's for sure! I wonder what the next one will bring? Truth? Trust? Professionalism? Better still, I predict there could be an 'outbreak' of common sense!'

'Listen to old Nostradamus!' Lill said. 'Fat chance any of that'll happen!'

'Now, now, girls and boys!' Compo interrupted. 'No more negative thoughts! We're here to enjoy ourselves! It's nearly party time! Come along now! Large and lively! Large and lively!'

'Shut your face!' Chewy said. 'This will be the usual and painful, 'Isn't our Headmaster wonderful' routine. All the toadies will run around licking everything as close to his nether regions as possible and expecting the rest of us to join in. Fuck that!'

'Glad to see you're getting in to the party spirit!' Rusty said.

'Come on,' Maggie said. 'We'd better get down there. All ready for a 'fun' evening?'

'NO!' came the collective reply.

'Niceness' flowed over all of them as soon as they arrived in the dining room. Simply because of the time of the year an awful 'understanding of one's fellow man' seemed to seep from everyone. It was quite nauseating. Chewy made a mental note of this. The same technique might come in useful at a later stage. He wasn't sure how or when but it might just be a powerful tool for next term.

Jolly could be seen through the crush, flitting through the assembled company, making light and polite conversation and deliberately trying to establish a general feeling of calm and serenity for all at this last meeting of the year for the staff and the Governors. Then he came across Lady Braumsley. She was standing there, balancing on her stick in yet another 'all weather' frock and with the cascading pearls. Quentin was, as usual, in fawning attendance but fully aware of his secondary position next to her. She greeted Jolly, looking him up and down, and deigned to swap a few words with him before 'sailing on' to someone else. That was the Dean. Another short and vaguely polite few words and she moved on again. Chewy noticed all of this and had the distinct feeling she was almost 'notching' her stick. It was like watching a checklist being gone through. Odd, he thought. She eventually sat at the top table next to the Dean with Jolly on her other side but with a wicked grin spreading across her face.

Wooden began to float amongst the crowd, suggesting the time had come to take up their seats. A few people actually took notice of what he was saying and made their way around the tables looking for their names. A seating plan had been organised in advance and staff had been invited, two weeks before, to nominate their chosen positions on a large sheet in the staff common room. Chewy and Rusty had made a few minor amendments to this to ensue a more lively evening. Ten minutes later many of the staff found themselves sitting opposite or next to someone they loathed. As a diversion from this mild irritation some of them began to pull the crackers placed on the table with their spouses and a few of the staff actually donned the dreadful paper hats which fell out. The jokes which came with them were the standard kind. *'My dog has no nose'. 'How does he smell'. 'Awful!'* and *'My wife's gone to the West Indies'. 'Jamaica?' 'No. She went of her own accord'.* It was truly rib tickling stuff.

The Escape Committee sat glumly watching all the other guests responding to the contents of the crackers with large smiles but were revived by the catering staff, some of whom had been given the role of dispensing the supply of wine. They arrived bearing red and white, 'drinking for the use of'. It was good stuff but only because Chewy and Rusty had suggested to the catering Manageress, a lady of exceptional girth and stature, that there might be a few more palatable labels available locally than the ones which usually appeared and which might go down particularly well that evening. She was grateful for the advice. Her own experience of wine was either the filthy, sweet, French stuff or the even more bloody awful German hock which the frogs and the krauts wouldn't drink even if they were pissed out of the heads.

Kathy Bains, an assistant cook, had taken a shine to Rusty a while ago and kept him, and them, supplied as often as she could. By the time the main course came round the Escape Committee had acquired a total of twelve bottles, red and white, by the careful manipulation of Kathy and the other wine staff who regularly came round checking on the tables.

The dinner, which was in fact very good, a beef base with an exotic selection of vegetables, continued with all of the guests really appreciating the fare before them. Eventually, the worst part of the evening arrived. It was time for the speeches. The Escape Committee were all well away by this time. Jolly then stood and tapped his glass for attention. The room became quiet.

'Lady Braumsley, Mr Dean, Governors, Ladies and Gentlemen. It has been a very busy term. A great deal has happened and I am very proud of all of you.'

A loud gurgle came up from somewhere. Lady Braumsley grinned widely. Jolly carried on, ignoring the noise.

'Next term will be just as hectic....'

Gurgle...Gurgle!

'...and I am confident....'

Gurgle...Gurgle...Gurgle!

'...that we will all be able to continue....'

Gurgle...Gurgle...Gurgle...Gurgle......!

The whole dining room was now awash with the noise of protesting stomachs. A few of the guests had to get up quickly and leave hurriedly, all of them holding on to themselves in fairly obvious places. Lady Braumsley was now smacking her stick on the table and laughing raucously. The assembly broke up completely. People were fighting each other to get out, in any way they could to somehow relieve themselves.

The Escape Committee, somehow saved by the antidote of a substantial alcoholic intake which they had consumed throughout the evening, gaped at the sight, all of the guests falling over each other to get out. One large group galloped over the tables towards them and they had to jump out of the way, flattening themselves against the wall as another mob rushed out past them. Lady B was now helpless, totally hysterical with laughter by this time. The old bitch, after that disastrous dinner of her own, had somehow doctored this one and was now revelling in the spectacle before her, everyone gripped in the effect her own gastronomic revenge.

'What the hell's going on!' Chewy said, nonplussed by the whole thing.

'God knows,' Vic said.

'Well, He would, wouldn't He!' Harry said.

'Not sure about that', Rusty said.

'I am,' Lill said.

'What's that?' asked Compo.

'Simple,' Maggie said, nodding at Lill and raising her glass. 'It's the end of term!'

THE ESCAPE COMMITTEE

The Mad Hatter
(Maisie)

Compo

Harry

Lil

Chewy

Rusty

Vic

Maggie

'For every person wishing to teach
there are thirty not wanting to be taught'

W.C.Sellar 1898-1951

LENT

TERM

1

The four week Christmas break of 'playing with grown-ups' was over They were back in the nut house and really, *really* looking forward to another term It was a cold, late morning and a couple of the staff were up in the staff room looking out of the window as their precious pupils were arriving back 'bursting' with enthusiasm for the new term ahead Fat chance of that They surveyed the growing traffic jam as parents arrived with their offspring in huge '4 by 4's', 'Jags' and assorted 'turbo' models, all adding to the grid lock which always happened in and around the School at the beginning of every term As vehicle doors opened and mums, dads, kids, trunks and bags filled up the gaps between the cars the comments from above followed the usual pattern

'Look at that one!'

'Which one?'

'The one with the thighs, teeth and....'

'Oh, that one!'

'New?'

'Think so. Too 'smiley'. Doesn't have that guarded look, somehow.'

'Who's that?'

'Which one?'

'The one climbing out of that red, Japanese 'bullet' thing.'

'Oh, him?'

'Yeh.'

'Gun-runner.'

'Gun-runner?'

'That's what they say. Someone had a contract out on him last year.'

'Contract?'

'Yeah. He used to arrive in an old Cortina until the 'heat' came off.'

'Really?'

'Yeah.'

'Why?'

'Something about a 'duff' delivery of rocket launchers, or was it anti-personnel mines. Can't remember now. Either way they didn't work, so he had to stay 'low' for a while.'

'Oh.'

'I see she's back.'

'Which one?'

'The red head. Been 'on the game' for years.'

'Has she?'

'Yeah. Only way she can afford to get her kids through this place. You can tell by the way she walks.'

'Oh, yes!'

'I see he's back.'

'Who?'

'That one!'

'Oh, him!'

'I thought he'd been expelled?'

'No. Just suspended.'

'Oh. I suppose that means the 'management' bottled out again?'

'Well, it was only a medium sized fire.'

'True.'

'He'll have to try harder next time.'

'He will. Give him time.'

And so the Lent term began.

The beginning of term morning meeting was its usual vibrant self. Staff filed slowly in and took up their cramped positions. This was the day before lessons began and was another complete and utter waste of everyone's time, but nobody had the guts to say so except for the Escape Committee. Everyone was feeling depressed. The only concession to the event was the time. It was eleven thirty in the morning. Jolly, Wooden, the Prick and the Fat Controller arrived, all in mufti, which was a partial lift for some of the staff.

'What the hell is he wearing?' Lill whispered looking at Jolly.

'God knows', Harry said, 'but he's certainly got a sense of humour if he can walk around looking like that!'

'No he hasn't,' Rusty said.

Jolly was wearing a bright pink jumper, livid blue and white checked trousers and a floppy yellow scarf round his neck. This was his 'relaxed' image.

'He looks like Rupert the bloody Bear's Granddad!' Chewy said, stifling a laugh.

'What about Wooden!' Rusty hissed. 'Just look at him!'

Wooden had a tasteful, green, all in one job with thick straps coming up and over a pale blue, crew-necked jumper. He had a definite 'Wooden Top' look to him which had several of the staff creased up, but quietly. The Prick and the Fat Controller sat side by side, each of them in modest, tasteful, servile, dark blue blazers, white shirts and both of them wearing cravats, one pale blue the other dark.

'Hello sailors!' Lill giggled.

And so the meeting started. Jolly took a deep breath and came out with his standard opening. 'Good morning everyone!' The buzz faded slowly, everyone resigned to receive his beginning of term tedium.

'As we all know,' Jolly began, 'This is the busiest term for all of us in the build up towards the examinations.'

'Well spotted!' whispered Vic.

'There are many tasks ahead of us,' Jolly continued, 'and we must maintain our resolution to ensure that all our endeavours will provide the highest possible standards for the testing time ahead of us.'

'Here we bloody go again!' Rusty thought.

'Wasn't this one of Churchill's speeches in 1940?' Harry wondered.

'I really should have stayed in bed!' Vic grumbled.

'What the hell is the silly old bugger talking about?' Chewy hissed.

'How the hell should I know?' Lill hissed back.

'Only eleven weeks to go to the holidays,' Compo thought.

'I think I'm going to be sick!' Rusty said.

Unaware of any of this, Jolly burbled on for another few minutes about how they should all make sure they arrived to lessons on time, did not allow certain pupils to shirk and their need to maintain educational stands of excellence. These were, in fact, basically insulting remarks to their intelligence, which any headmaster with any commonsense would never have thought of saying. Lulled into near sleep through all of this, they were quite unprepared for his next two announcements.

'In view of the many new considerations and the consequent moves towards additional educational legislation, which have appeared in the last year, with regard to the pupils in our care, I have appointed Mrs Hilda Broadstead to be Second Deputy.'

The proverbial pin, if it had been dropped at that point, could have been heard as a deafening metallic crash as they struggled to absorb this hugely depressing piece of information. Hilda Broadstead was the Wide Mouthed Frog! She had been boring everyone rigid with her incessant droning about the 'Children's Act' for months. She almost waved it as a stick and was the most unsuitable personality Jolly could have chosen, but for someone like him, without any real brains at all, this came as no real surprise to a number of the staff.

'Christ!' Chewy said. 'He's done it again!', summing up how Jolly always made the wrong decision, on the rare occasions when he ever did.

'How can that silly sod appoint the most evil bitch on the staff,' Rusty said. 'She has no idea of the truth and wouldn't recognise fair play if it came up and bit her on the bum. She doesn't possess an understanding molecule in her whole bloated body!'

Vic sat forward, his head in his hands. His pastoral role would now be completely knackered by this. She would be hell bent on muscling in on all matters to do with the kids' problems. Lill just closed her eyes, lowered her head and shook it slowly. Harry was speechless and Compo sat with his mouth open in disbelief. The Wide Mouthed Frog sat with a smug, self satisfied grin extending almost round to her ears. Then she took out her hankie and performed one of her little rituals. She blew her nose. It sounded like a tug's foghorn stuffed with unmentionable, immovable, unidentifiable crap, but it had the effect of releasing the silence. Everyone started talking at once. Jolly had a difficult time getting their attention again.

'Ladi..., Ladies and... , *Ladies and Gentlemen*!' He shouted above the buzz. 'As I was saying…!'

Grudgingly, the noise died down and he was able to speak.

'Mrs Broadstead will share responsibility with the first Deputy on all matters regarding discipline, planning and the organisation of the administrative side of the school day.'

'That'll leave Jolly with sod all to do!' Chewy hissed.

'Don't be daft!' Rusty hissed back. 'He does sod all as it is!'

Jolly had now turned to another matter.

'As you all know, the increasing pressure of the National Curriculum, coupled with new innovations to many subjects, makes for a difficult time tabling process quite apart from the need to have a clear overview of all subjects with regard to our pupils needs.'

'What the hell does that mean?' Rusty whispered.

'That he can't bloody cope and doesn't understand!' answered Chewy.

'Because of all this,' Jolly continued, 'I have appointed a well qualified professional teacher to handle all curriculum matters. A Mr Neville Condon will be joining us tomorrow.'

'Oh, shit!' Rusty said. 'Another bloody dead-head appointment from Jolly. I wonder what this silly bugger's going to be like?'

'He did say 'Condon', didn't he?' Lill said, smirking

Maggie was spared all of this. As Development Officer she didn't have to join the infamous morning meetings, although Jolly always invited her to do so, at any time. Not a chance. She could always find something else to do that was much more productive, like going to the loo.

With a new term ahead of her she was determined to somehow corner Jolly into agreeing about something. It didn't matter what it was as long as he did it, and within a week of her asking, whatever it was. That was her goal and she was going to bust a gut to do it although she knew it was going to be very, very difficult. Looking out of the window she could see that the parental traffic jam was easing but the weather wasn't. It was cold and miserable. No snow had yet fallen but the forecast wasn't very hopeful and the sky looked terrible. She gave an involuntary shiver. Her coffee was now stone cold so she ambled through to see the Mad Hatter and make another. Maisie was up to her elbows in the beginning of term 'explosion' of paperwork. Updates and dozens of copies of the school rules, staff lists, every form list, house list and the whole school list were lying around all over the place.

'Keeping busy?' she said to Maisie.

Maisie just gave her a long, lugubrious look without saying a word.

'Sorry,' Maggie said and beat a retreat to the kettle.

With a fresh coffee on her desk Maggie looked again at the latest piece of rubbish from Quentin Braumsley, her Clerk of the Works. This one was a scribbled note describing his latest thoughts about 'improvements'. Maggie didn't really want to know how the 'ambience' of the school could be raised by this new but equally pathetic offering. Window boxes on all of the buildings did not 'grab' her as a meaningful contribution. Holes in several roofs, rotting window and doorframes as well as preventing lumps dropping off the stonework seemed to be more important somehow. She crumpled the note up, threw it into the bin to join all his other hair-brained ideas and looked out of the window at the solid grey sky. It did not look good but she wasn't to know that this was just the beginning of a period of freak weather.

In the staff room, the meeting was over and most of them had sloped off leaving the Escape Committee sitting around helping each other to come to terms with being back in the arms of 'academe'. The contents of the cupboard on the wall were doing its best to calm the situation. They were trying to ease their depression about the Wide Mouthed Frog's appointment for they knew that anything she would do would help no one, especially the kids. As for the appointment of this Neville Condon, they would just have to wait for the series of disasters which they knew would follow. It was as sure as night follows day. If Jolly thought he was good that was a certain indication of how useless he would be.

'We need a bloody good shake up at the top of this place!' Compo moaned. 'Why can't these silly sods see we need change, and change for the better?'

'*Sed semper hoc facimus in hoc modo*,' Vic said.

'What the hell does that mean?' Compo asked.

'Well,' Vic answered. 'You asked why things don't change round here, didn't you?'

'Yes.' Compo said. 'So?'

'So, '*Sed semper hoc facimus in hoc modo*' means, 'but we've always done it this way'.'

'We should have that as the school motto!' Lill said.

Maggie came in.

'Hi, team!' she said.

'Get yourself a drink,' Rusty said pointing to the wall cupboard. 'You might find a few drops of something still there.'

She did and sat down with them.

'Good to be back, eh?' she winked.

'NO!' came the collective reply.

'That's what I thought,' she said, grinning.

'What the hell are you so happy about then?' Harry asked.

'Hardly 'happy' exactly,' she said. 'Optimistic perhaps.'

'For what?'

'Getting a few things done,' she said. 'It's about time things changed round here.'

'*Sed semper hoc facimus in hoc modo*,' Vic grinned.

'What?' Maggie asked, nonplussed.

Vic explained.

'We've been working against that for years now,' Chewy said. 'and still nothing happens.'

'There is a fixed routine in this place which would take an atomic bomb to shift,' Rusty said.

'Two or three,' Lill chipped in.

'It's like being back in time in this place,' Vic said. 'Most of them haven't a clue about the real world and I doubt whether they know it exists.'

'So why are you all here?' Maggie asked mischievously.

Vic answered for all of them.

'Let me tell you a story,' he began, taking a deep breath. 'Back in the 80's a time of change was brewing, bubbling a definite whiff in the air of, 'what are those buggers doing'. That was the Government looking at all of us and deciding something had to be done. Just imagine. It's around '86 and you, a recognised professional in a state secondary school, discover that a few highly ambitious, manipulatory Government persons of questionable birth are nosing around education mumbling about 'improving' things.'

The rest of the Escape Committee just sat back listening. When Vic got going it was always entertaining. Maggie was all ears. Vic continued.

'Disconcerting? Certainly. But then 'things' were suddenly changed without any real consultation and rushed into place. They called it 'GCSE', the new examination. It would solve everything. Then a couple of years later, they do it again! This time it's called the 'National Curriculum' and the world had been saved. The only problem is that we knew, in our water, that it felt like a time warp back to the 50's. It didn't work then and it sure as hell wouldn't work thirty years later. Not only that but we all began to suffocate in the paperwork necessary to service all this bright new world crap. Now, how would you feel?'

Vic carried on, not waiting for a reply.

'To make matters even worse, we then found out that the other mob, the Independent sector, on higher salaries anyway, which is even more galling, didn't have to follow these new changes. It was just the rest of us who had to grudgingly comply. Now, what would you do?'

Maggie tried to say something but Vic kept going.

'Would you have accepted it? Hardly. Strike? Painful. Look for another job in the Independent sector? Damned right! I saw this job advertised, applied, got it and joined 'Independence'. I left State education with all the union propaganda, teacher abuse, working to rule, graffiti, muggings from the kids and their parents and took up position in a 'Public School'. Almost a thousand years of history and with a bar in the staff room. And that's where the real time warp began. As I said earlier, *Sed semper hoc facimus in hoc modo!*' And here we all are.'

The Escape Committee gave him a round of applause.

'Well,' Maggie said. 'I'm glad to see how you all appreciate the place!'

Since they'd been sitting there a few snow flakes had wafted down. The sky was now an angry dark grey and a few hours later snow began to fall steadily. By midnight it hadn't stopped. All through the night it became heavier and then increased to a raging and full-blown blizzard. It eased slightly during the following morning but by lunchtime a good three or four inches had fallen. This provided a few problems for the day kids arriving in the morning but most folk were taking their time driving in and no real problems occurred. There were a few tricky moments when they were going to and coming from the beginning of term service in the Cathedral, but apart from two twisted ankles and a painful elbow, after sudden contact with the slippery path, everyone arrived back safely.

Later, as the kids began to congregate outside the dining room for lunch, the air was full of snowballs and screaming. Miraculously, not a single window was smashed. That didn't last. During the rest of the day the snow continued to fall more heavily without a break and by the time school was over a thick, six-inch layer covered everything.

This was the first time in living memory that as much snow as this had fallen in this part of the world. No one was prepared for it or knew how to deal with it, particularly the driving public. As the afternoon wore on the road surfaces began to ice up and with slush everywhere, roads and footpaths began to freeze solid. Mayhem does not describe the situation which developed. Parents, arriving to take their day pupil offspring home, found themselves in a nightmare of spinning wheels, uncontrolled skids, dented body work and smashed head and tail lamps as they attempted to negotiate a way passed each other. In amongst all of this the kids were now charging around like wild animals, sliding across roads, pathways, inside and outside the school, throwing clumps of ice and freezing snow at each other, stuffing it down necks, fronts and rolling each other in the stuff, barely missing the wheels of cars on their way in to pick other kids up. A total of twenty six windows were smashed in the space of a mere fifteen minutes as snowball 'warfare' broke out throughout the school site.

The snow didn't stop for the rest of that day but most of the collecting parents did, sooner or later. Jolly and Wooden were now gripped in one of Jolly's self-induced crisis panics. Something had to be done. If this weather kept up, the following morning would be less than easy for the day pupils arriving back, if they did or could. The weather forecast that night scared them even more with the prospect of more snow arriving and pushed them into a ridiculous 'contingency' plan.

As dawn broke over a universal white landscape, Jolly was still fretting. He had talked round and round in circles with Wooden the previous evening and continued that by phone later on. Then he hadn't been able to sleep at all with worries about the day ahead. Wooden hadn't had much of a night either but he trudged into school the following morning and waited dutifully and silently, outside Jolly's study for his arrival and the instructions for the day. When Jolly arrived they began the whole process again but by the time of the morning meeting they had worked out an 'idea' for the 'problem'.

Most of the staff lived within walking distance of the school and they managed to slip and slide their way in for another fun packed day. They didn't realise that almost half the kids would be missing, their parents unable to bring them in due to the road conditions. The half that remained, the boarders, now with a few of the day kids, were lying in wait for several of their 'favourite' staff to appear. They were not going to miss the golden opportunity of bombardment with hard packed, white, missiles. Some of those 'missiles' had more than snow as their ingredients.

Boots, galoshes, wellies and even a pair of snow shoes littered the area at the bottom of the stairs to the staff room. The floor of this was covered in gobs and crunched up blobs of melting snow, much to Jolly's disapproval as he picked his way over them. Wooden followed him, lost in the several pages of written gibberish he always committed to this, his infamous note book, the thing which he used instead of a brain, and which was stuffed full of the notes he'd had to feverishly scribble down at his previous meeting with Jolly. The staff were sitting moaning about the weather but some of them were nursing lumps on the head and tending other places on their bodies where contact had been made from shoals of snowballs from behind walls, corners and anywhere which gave shelter to dozens of adolescent marauders in full target practise. Harvey Sheasby had a wonderful black eye, the Poisoned Dwarf was dabbing at a very red nose and the Wide Mouthed Frog was holding a throbbing right ear. Each one had been the victim of a hail of snow 'bullets' as they walked through the School site. Not one of them had caught a single child, either in the act or as they ran away, such was the extent of the fusillade which suddenly engulfed every one of them. The Escape Committee sat watching these casualties without a scrap of sympathy.

'Couldn't have happened to a 'nicer' bunch!' Chewy said quietly to the rest.

That's when Jolly and Wooden walked in and depression settled over each and every one of them instantaneously. Wooden had his little, red, woolly scarf on so everyone knew it was winter and it must be cold. The scarf would now stay in place for another month before he took it off. It was always the same every year. Jolly was fidgeting around with his bits of paper and by the body language it was perfectly clear that he was in one of his 'states'.

'Good morning everyone!'

'Is it?' Chewy said.

'I am pleased to say Mr Condon will be with us soon,' Jolly said. 'Due to the weather conditions he has been delayed, but I received a phone call just a few minutes ago letting me know he should be with us by this morning's break.'

'Oh, good!' mumbled Vic.

'Which brings me to my next point,' Jolly continued. 'As you are all aware the weather is not good.'

'He's noticed then!' Rusty grinned.

'We have been giving great thought to this', Jolly went on, 'and it is important for all of us to be ready for the worst.'

'Worse than this?' Lill mumbled.

'Should the weather deteriorate a plan of action must be ready,' Jolly said and eyebrows lifted in astonishment throughout the staff room.

'Did I hear that right!' Harry said sitting up. 'Did I hear that a 'plan' is about to arrive!'

Jolly ignored the mutterings and continued.

'We have decided to set up a 'Snow Desk' in the school so that parents or pupils can call in or call out to ensure their safe arrival or departure during this difficult time. A telephone will be set up in the outer office and will be available within the next hour.'

He handed over to Wooden who began to give the detail of how it would be used. He missed the point that everyone actually knew how to use a telephone and ground on about the need to tell everyone that the kids should be informed about the 'snow desk' hotline. In any case the staff were all too busy talking to each other to listen to him. He gave up, again.

With only half the kids in school the great debate was now about how to organise the school day. The hub-bub grew louder and Jolly knew he'd lost them. He made a vain attempt to get them going to assembly but then realised that there wasn't a great deal of point in that with half the school missing. The more 'urgent' members of the staff were busily discussing how they could group kids here and there so that they could continue with the important task of teaching but one, a member of the Escape Committee, was trying to work out something else. Chewy murmured about a idea to get out of teaching that day if he could get away with it.

'You can't do that!' Lill said.

'Want to bet?' Chewy said. 'Watch me.'

He got up and walked over to the other side of the room where the Wide Mouthed Frog was sitting.

'What's he up to?' Rusty asked.

'Search me,' Vic answered

'He's going to try and con the Frog into something I think!' Lill said to both of them, shaking her head.

'He's what?' Rusty asked.

They all looked over and Chewy was leaning down to the Frog, smiling and chatting. She was listening intently, a puzzled look on her face. A few more words from Chewy and she smiled and started fluttering her eyelids. It was not a pretty sight.

'What the hell is he saying to her?' Rusty wondered.

'I don't think I want to know judging by the look on her face now!' Vic said, a worried look on his own.

Chewy stood up, had a final word with the Frog and then walked back over, a very wide grin on his face. He sat down, still grinning.

'Well?' Lill asked. 'What's up?'

'It's amazing what you can achieve,' Chewy said, 'when you're 'nice' to people.'

'What's he on about?' Rusty asked.

'I'm 'on about' being 'nice',' Chewy said, tantalisingly. 'Last term, just before the end of the term dinner actually, I thought what would be the effect of being 'nice'. It would have either one effect or the other.'

'He's gone.' said Compo. 'It's been too long a term.'

'Looks like it,' Harry said.

'I think I've just proved that it works,' Chewy said.

'Will you please just tell us what you have done!' Rusty said.

'O.K.,' Chewy said. 'It's like this. I just told Wide Mouth how well she was looking, that was a tricky moment, congratulated her on her new role and asked for her advice. She absolutely bloody loves it when you do that.'

'Better you than me!' Vic said.

'Too right!' Rusty agreed, pulling a face.

'Go on then,' Lill said, ignoring the others. 'What did you say?'

'I asked her if she could advise on some of the kids,' Chewy said grinning again.

'What about!' Lill asked again.

'I said we all seemed to have a few of the older kids with too many 'hormone' problems and she immediately volunteered to talk to them about it, you know what she's like. She loves getting into all that.'

'You sod!' Compo said. 'How could you inflict that on the kids!'

'Don't underestimate them,' Chewy said. 'She's a source of great entertainment for them. They all think she's crackers anyway, so it won't do them any harm. Besides I have just released you all from having them until this afternoon. She's going to give them the 'special'. The 'pop - up' book!'

'Oh, God!' Lill said. 'Don't let it be true!'

'He will,' Vic said. 'He will!'

'There's only one snag in all that,' Harry said.

Everyone turned to him with the unsaid question hanging in the air.

'All of us,' he said, 'have free periods for most of the morning, so we wouldn't have had the kids anyway!'

'Ah well,' Chewy said, crestfallen. 'It was a bloody good idea at the time!'

He had, in fact, proved his theory. Being 'nice' could reap rewards. The other side to this 'nice' technique was exactly the reverse of this when he and Rusty tried it out on a couple of the other staff. That didn't happen until a couple of weeks later.

The morning rolled on and then it was time for the first break of the day. The Escape Committee made a point of arriving to view this new 'white hope' for the curriculum, Neville Condon. He turned out to be another faceless, safe, cretin who walked, talked and even moved more slowly than Wooden. He also seemed to be on his guard the whole time. They were not impressed and as the academic year ground on they had their first reactions totally confirmed.

The man was useless and didn't have the first idea of weighing the importance of subjects and how they could react together. All he eventually demonstrated was a profound skill in misunderstanding the nature of education, attempting to translate it into a convenient mathematical arrangement. But all that was to come. For the moment they had the weather to deal with.

A thaw had settled in and already the evidence was falling past the window as the snow began to melt in an erratic drip, drip, dripping from the blanket of snow above. But there was still the 'Snow Desk'. Just about everyone took advantage of this and a long line of kids and staff queued to make phone calls. Hardly any of these were anything to do with the weather. The odd bet to the local bookies was quite popular as was the 'party line' call. By lunchtime the whole place was slopping with messy slush. As the school day ended there was water everywhere with only a few blobs of snow left. Then it began to rain. So much for more snow. None came, just lots and lots or rain.

During the afternoon hardly any teaching was going on apart from the 'dedicated' few like Harvey Sheasby and the Wide Mouthed Frog who, between them, had only seven kids. Very productive. Quite a number of the staff, again mostly the Escape Committee, were driving Maisie up the wall by calling her under 'Snow Desk' conditions from different phones on the site with silly voices. Chewy was the worst offender.

'Hello, Hello!' he would say. 'This is Drift Number One calling 'Snow Desk'! Drift Number One calling 'Snow Desk'! Come in 'Snow Desk!'

After four or five calls like these Maisie was not a happy woman and told Chewy to do something. It wasn't very 'nice'. Relative normality broke out the following day but the weather didn't really improve. The rain eventually died away but after a brief calm a cold breeze developed which quickly grew into a gusting, buffeting gale.

'Bloody weather!' Chewy grunted as he came into the staff room. 'Bloody snow storms one minute and bloody hurricanes the next.'

He didn't know it then but the last part of that remark was a very accurate description of what was heading their way. Later that same day an embarrassed Meteorological Office issued storm warnings for the whole of the south for the next forty-eight hours and that's where the fun began. Throughout the night the wind gained speed and strength and by the following morning it had already caused a massive amount of damage over hundreds of square miles. Braumston lay on the edges of the worst of it but that still had the strength to blow more than cobwebs away. The School took a bit of structural damage but the most hazardous factor of all was loose roof slates which were flying around like frisbees. The whole school was back after the farce of the snow but this gave another problem for Jolly to solve. He came in for the morning meeting, distinctly windswept and red in the face from simply trying to walk over to the staff room.

Slightly out of breath he said, 'As you are no doubt aware we seem to have another weather problem,' he said.

'He's quick, isn't he?' Chewy muttered.

Wooden just stood next to him, staring his wooden look straight ahead, unblinking, but with his little woolly scarf tied tightly round his neck.

'Until the day parents can collect their children I think it would be unwise to allow them to move around the school,' Jolly said, still slightly out of breath.

A groan came up from everyone. This meant they would be stuck in their classrooms all day with the little cherubs. What a prospect.

'Any normal movement around the site,' Jolly went on, 'would be rather dangerous, putting yourselves and them at the unnecessary risk from so much flying debris.'

The muttering continued but Jolly kept going.

'During assembly I will tell the whole school to stay in the first classroom which they would normally attend.'

More mutterings. None of the staff liked the sound of that. There would be no point having them all day. Vic was getting restless and then spoke up.

'Wouldn't it be better for them to go to the boarding houses?' he asked. 'In that way we can keep them together more easily, surely?'

This took both Jolly and Wooden by surprise. Neither of them had thought of that. Well, they wouldn't have, would they?

'That would place a great burden on all of the house staff,' Jolly managed to say after a few seconds, pondering and twitching.

'I thought the buggers were paid for that,' mumbled Chewy.

'Not if we all help,' Lill piped up.

The mutterings grew louder with a few heads nodding. The wind outside was now a tearing fury, rattling the windows and buffeting the whole building. Jolly reacted to every windy noise but had to agree that it would a much better idea to bring the kids together into the boarding houses.

'Vic,' Chewy said. 'You're a bloody marvel. You've just managed to eliminate teaching for the whole day!'

The rest of the Escape Committee grinned to each other but the rest hadn't got that far yet. There were several staff who thought it outrageous that they should not teach. A little bit of wind was not going to stop them. Coincidentally, these were the same staff who did not have their own rooms or a base from which they worked. They usually moved from room to room during the day. Most of them did not have enough brain cells to realise that wandering around in the face of such horrific weather was not a good idea. They insisted that they should take the children to an available classroom and try to perform as normally as possible.

Jolly sagged under the loud arguments which were now breaking out. He managed to restore some order and agreed to allow them to do just that. The Escape Committee just sat shaking their heads The habits of a 'peripatetic' lifetime would now be put to the test but there was one small point which Jolly and the others had missed. This was that all the classrooms were still locked from the previous day and, because of the weather, no one had thought to unlock them. Before the meeting eventually broke up Jolly made a final statement.

'If it is necessary to go outside, will you please ensure that the children are always accompanied.'

'D'y know, I would never have thought of that!' Chewy said slowly and none too quietly.

Jolly shot a poisonous look at him but didn't say anything.

2

By the time they had managed to get the kids from assembly to the boarding houses the wind had reached official hurricane strength. Debris was flying everywhere. Bits of trees, street signs and all manner of rubbish was scattered through the site, filling the streets around them and the air itself. It was really quite scary and positively dangerous. Inside the boarding houses there wasn't a great deal of room to spare anywhere. The kids were sitting around all over the place, on staircases, along corridors with the staff occasionally patrolling around to make sure that no 'unseemly' behaviour was taking place. Chewy wandered round inside one of the boy's houses but ignored the card games and the odd fag being lit up. The morning dragged on while the wind howled outside. He happened to be standing by one of the front windows when he saw a line of kids staggering past, hanging on to each other against the force of the wind, headed by one of the same idiot staff who had argued for normal teaching.

The wind was still at full hurricane strength and there they were being blown around, all over the place, with 'dozy', Dora Hapgood, nicknamed 'Happy', which she never was, leading them all up through the school. She taught French and was looking for an unlocked classroom. Five minutes later and she was back again, still looking for any classroom she could get into. Vic joined him at the window.

'Look at that stupid bitch!' Chewy said to Vic. 'What the hell is she doing?'

'Oh, she came by about half an hour ago,' Vic said.

'Has she been wandering about in this for all that time?' Chewy asked.

'Probably,' Vic said. 'You know what she's like. Head up her arse most of the time.'

'She's going to have more than her head up there if she doesn't get those kids inside!' Chewy said. 'She'll probably end up with a few decapitations before long with all the crap that's flying around out there!'

As if to confirm his last statement the sound of breaking glass could be heard coming from yet another window close by. Wooden came in a few minutes later looking very worried. He found Vic and Chewy still standing by the front window.

'Could you help out with patrolling the grounds?' he asked in his monotone way.

'What for?' Chewy asked 'A few buildings blown away?'

Wooden didn't flicker.

'No nothing like that,' he said. 'It's just that we need a few staff to make sure there are no pupils wandering about by themselves.'

'If any kids have tried,' Vic answered, 'they would have been whisked away by now with this wind.'

'Do you think so?' Wooden asked him wide eyed.

'Without doubt,' Chewy said, winking to Vic.

'I'd better tell the Head that,' Wooden said and padded off out into the wind where he almost lost his little woolly scarf.

They watched him skittering off to see 'sir' and then pulled their coats on to see if any kids were out there. Keeping their eyes peeled for wind blown pieces of the school, they made their way round the site, sometimes having to hang on to each other in the face of the main fury of the wind. They did find a few stupid little sods who had ventured out for a dare and had to rope them together with their own scarves to make sure they didn't actually blow away, dragging them into the nearest boarding house.

Dora Hapgood came round a corner at one point followed by a line of kids hanging onto each other. The silly cow was still trying to find somewhere to teach. They had to manhandle her, almost protesting rape at the top of her voice, all the way with the kids into one of the other houses. The kids were immensely relieved to get under cover but they almost lost one as the wind caught him and rolled him off over the lawn, arms and legs flailing the blustery air, across and in front of the main building. Chewy just managed to catch him by jumping onto his flapping coat before he fell into the pond. Once he was safely inside the building with the rest of them they continued to patrol around but after a few minutes had to take shelter. How that silly woman had kept it up for the better part of an hour was beyond them. They were near the ground staff buildings so they dived behind the hedge and round into the first one. The lads were all in there, in the middle of an important meeting. It was five card brag again. As they opened the door the gale blew in scattering cards and notes all over the place.

'*Shut the fuckin' door*!' yelled Big Mac as he tried to pin the money and the cards down. The ground staff cat, who was lying under the table at the time, was not too happy about it either. It shot off when the first gust blasted in through the door. With some difficulty they managed to shut the door and the air became still again. The lads picked up their cards and spent more than a few minutes and a lot more choice language sorting out the money.

'Nice to see you all keeping busy,' Vic said.

'If you think we're goin' out there,' CC said, 'you must be bloody mad!'

Chewy was looking out the window, across the playing pitches and up to the fields beyond. There were a dozen or so big black and white lumps lying on the grass but they were moving.

'What the hell are they?' he asked. He couldn't make out what they were.

Big Mac ambled over and looked out over his shoulder.

'What?' he asked.

'Those things,' Chewy said pointing at the black and white things.

'Oh, them?' Big Mac said. 'They're cows.'

'Cows?' Chewy asked.

'Yeah. Cows. You know, 'moo'?!'

'Well, if they're cows,' Chewy said, 'What the hell are they doing?'

'Grazing,' came the answer.

'How does a cow graze lying down, you silly bugger!' Chewy answered back.

'Watch!' was the only reply.

Vic came over to have a look. Big Mac lost interest and wandered back over to the card game which had been reorganised. They both looked across to the fields and waited. Sure enough a few of the black and white things scrambled up to their feet and, yes, they were cows. They began grazing immediately but then a gust of wind would hit them and wallop! Over they went, bouncing horrifically, legs thrashing around but with their stupid cow expressions of slight surprise and still chewing. This repeated itself over and over again.

'You were right,' Chewy said over his shoulder.

'Yeah,' Big Mac said. 'That's been goin' on all bleedin' mornin'.'

Vic spotted something else.

'What's that!' he said with some urgency, pointing upwards.

Chewy tried to find what he was looking at but had difficulty tracking down whatever it was. Vic's head was dodging around following the thing he'd seen.

'Where?' Chewy asked.

'There!' Vic said, pointing, but his finger was moving quickly all over the place.

Then Chewy spotted it, a black, furry ball swinging around in the air.

'It's the cat!' he said, bursting out laughing.

When they had arrived the cat had scooted off and then shot out of the door before they closed it. As soon as it hit the wind it was scooped up and thrown around willy-nilly, incapable of grabbing anything with its claws. Big Mac came over and just said, 'Oh, shit!' He flung the door open, blasting the cards and money all over the room again. Vic and Chewy heaved the door shut again and watched him running around in the gale trying to catch the cat. It was wailing and mewing the whole time, swiping the air with claws fully extended. Big Mac made a few dives for it then caught it by the tail. It pulled round and dug its claws into his arm, the pair of them screeching against the wind. Chewy and Vic almost collapsed with laughter at the sight.

The wind began to ease towards lunch time but it was still a tricky business getting the kids organised and over to the dining room. They managed to get everyone through and back to the houses unscathed and then they just had to sit it out, waiting for the day parents to arrive.

Chewy was getting a bit edgy by this time.

'What's the matter?' Vic asked.

'My roof,' Chewy said. 'I'm a bit concerned that my eighteenth century pile of rubble might end up as just that in this wind.'

'You'd better go and see to it then,' Vic said. 'Go now. There's nothing to do here. I'll be all right. There are other staff here after all. Go on.'

Chewy did. He drove off, weaving his way through pieces of stone, branches which had been ripped off and the occasional dustbin which rolled past. He had to drive around the outskirts of the town, reversing out from two roads blocked by fallen trees. The hairiest moment was his confrontation with a damaged power line. The road ahead was blocked by half of someone's roof so he had to make a detour through a few streets to get back to the main road. As he pulled round a corner a thick, black cable was whipping around in front of him across the road. Flashes and sparks were cascading down over the pole which should have held it high in the air. It was lying over at a steep angle across the road, the cable dipping and slapping onto the road surface. He had no time to brake but had to accelerate in the blind hope that the thing wouldn't make contact with the car as he came towards it, sparking and fizzing on the tarmac. Then it then suddenly flicked up in the wind, just clearing the car and he passed under it.

A few minutes later he pulled up in front of his own place on the other side of the town, a little tense but safe. He checked the roof, front and back as well as all the windows and the interior and the outside area at the back of the house and then, satisfied, drove back to the school, but this time he had to use a completely different route. His attempt to go back the same way had been cut off by a large tree across the road.

Driving along one of the few main streets which was still open he barely had time to perform an emergency stop as the complete roof of the house ahead deposited itself with a frightening 'crunch' on the road in front of him. A huge cloud of dust and minor debris showered the car, which was then whipped away by the wind, but with no damage to the car. He breathed a huge sigh of relief and moved forward slowly. He was just able to squeeze past the pile of destruction and on to the school.

Maisie had spent the whole morning on the phone, desperately trying to contact parents to ask them to collect their offspring. With many of the lines down she had to ask the ones she was able to contact to 'spread the word'. There was nothing else she could do. At one point she deliberately went up to the staff room to gain some 'fortification' from the louvered cupboard on the wall. Thus fortified, by a quadruple scotch, she came back to the office and the phone and continued through the day school list.

Trees, power lines, chunks of masonry, slates, tiles and all kinds of rubbish littered the streets and many of them were now blocked. It was a nightmare for anyone driving through the town which only delayed the parental arrival by another hour. Eventually all the day kids had been collected and as darkness began to fall the wind eased further. By the middle of the evening it had fallen to just a medium breeze.

Maggie walked through the school the following morning. The wind had died completely but the grounds, just like the town, were covered in detritus and an enormous amount of broken glass. Many of the older trees around the whole site had given up under the strain and now lay flat having been wrenched out of the ground by the force of the wind. Others were shredded and broken, their branches lying around amongst all the other devastation. Two of the 'temporary' buildings which the Science Department used had their roofs damaged but good old 'Shanty Town' was completely intact. Nothing had been damaged there at all. There was no justice.

Quentin padded along beside her uttering the odd comment. 'Oh my!' 'Look at that!' 'What a shame!' She couldn't think why she had bothered to bring him along. His most animated reaction centred on the state of some the plants in one of the gardens of the houses. 'Oh dear, and I'd only just planted them a few days ago!'

But over the whole site they'd been lucky. Apart from the roofs of the Science buildings the damage was largely superficial yet there was still a hell of a lot to do. The ground staff worked well over the next few days and by the weekend had repaired most of it. With that done Maggie now sat in Jolly's office and talked him through what the ground staff had done and how much it had cost.

'Oh dear,' he said. 'As much as that?'

'Well,' Maggie replied. 'That's just to keep us going and put us back where we were before the hurricane. It really doesn't do anything at all to improve things or give us any more than we had before.'

Quentin sat beside her, an obligatory presence as Clerk of Works, but even Jolly was beginning to regret giving this buffoon the job in the first place. Quentin wasn't really listening to what they were talking about. All he was doing was looking at the two plants in the room. One was a 'busy lizzie' and the other a small cactus which, as far as he was concerned, needed a bit of love and attention.

Relieved at the low level of damage to the School Jolly now felt he could bring Maggie into his confidence. The only reason why he did so was the frightening prospect of all the building work which the school would need for further improvement over the next few years and the problem of funding it. That's when he told her about a substantial property which had just come up for sale. Unknown to Maggie, he'd been looking into this for a while but hadn't said a word to anyone. Less than ten miles away an extensive complex of buildings had been vacated some months before. It had been built during the last century but was now coming to the end of its life for the primary function for which it was built. It was too large and was proving difficult and costly to maintain the required level of security for its inmates. It was, in short, altogether out of date for the modern methods which were now required. It was up for sale and, for its size and scale, at a very cheap price.

'I telephoned the agent only yesterday,' he said, 'and here are the details. I think we should look into this as soon as possible.'

He pushed the paperwork over to her and she flipped through it quickly. It was big enough and, on the face of it, would allow much more space than they had at present.

'I see,' she said, somewhat surprised by this amazing demonstration of lateral thinking.

'But this place would still need tidying up even if we did or could move.'

'True,' Jolly agreed, 'But it would be less costly to simply 'tidy up' than to commit ourselves to a major building programme, wouldn't it?'

There were times when Jolly could come up sheer and brilliant flashes of ordinary thought. For him it almost bordered on commonsense.

'Well, yes,' Maggie said. 'I suppose it would be, but only provided that this place you're talking about wouldn't require a lot of work doing to it before we could move in.'

'Quite,' Jolly said, 'Quite. I just thought that this might be a way out of all our difficulties. Just think. Buildings and grounds we could be proud of and would solve all of our problems.'

Quentin drifted back at this point. He'd been lost in his little world of watering, planting and pruning again. He only heard the last bit of Jolly's statement and thought that it sounded rather interesting. 'A building we could be proud of.' That sounded rather nice. He went off again into his own private reverie.

'Well,' Maggie was saying, 'perhaps it would be useful to see this place quite soon before we decide either way.'

'I so agree,' Jolly said. 'I think we should organise a visit in the next few days if we can.'

'Before the end of the week then?' Maggie asked.

'Indeed, indeed,' Jolly nodded.

'Anyway, the science building will still need some work,' she said. 'but that shouldn't take too long or cost a great deal more. It's just guttering and a few other minor things. A more permanent structure wouldn't have given us this problem.'

Quentin returned again from the land of pot plants and 'ambience' as Maggie said this. 'A more permanent structure'. Now he really had something to work on. First there was, 'A building we could be proud of,' and now, 'A more permanent structure.' He was off again into his own little world.

'Quentin.'

Maggie and Jolly were waiting for him to come back. This happened all the time.

'Quentin!'

'Oh, sorry,' he said. 'I was just thinking...'

'Yes,' Maggie said. 'Of course you were.'

Quentin cleared his work table up in his bedroom in preparation for his new project. This was his chance to really show them all what the Clerk of Works of Braumstate Cathedral School could really do. But where to start? He had to produce something which would astound all of them. He scuttled downstairs into the library. There should be something in amongst all those books which could inspire him. He was halfway up the library ladder when his mother, Lady Braumsley came in.

'Quentin!' she barked at him.

He almost fell off the ladder with shock at her sudden shout.

'Oh, Mummy,' he quavered. 'It's you!'

'Of course it's me, you stupid boy!' she snapped. 'Who do you think it was, Supergirl?'

'Well, no Mummy...' Quentin answered.

'What are you doing?' she said, cutting him short. She was always watching him. She knew how inept he could be and since he'd been working at the School he was more than his normal irritating self. She hated the School. She was convinced that they were somehow behind the disaster of the road proposals last year and even though she'd had a certain revenge at the end of term dinner, she was still looking for any opportunity she could find to make life uncomfortable for them. If only her idiot late husband hadn't rented them the land for a fixed pittance she would have jacked the rent up years ago. As for now, anything that her buffoon of a son was doing down there she wanted to know about, just in case she could sabotage it.

'Well!' she snapped at him again. 'I asked you what are you doing!'

'Just a bit of research,' he said meekly.

'Research? Research?' she asked. 'What kind of research?'

'Building, history, architecture,' he answered, still hanging on to the top of the ladders.

'Which one?' she asked, tapping her stick on the floor. 'Which one!'

'Well,' he said. 'All of them.'

'Why?' She was beginning to lose patience and Quentin knew he would have to be very careful about what he said from now on. He stepped down to the floor, straightened himself up and took a deep breath.

'As Clerk of the Works,' he said, slightly warily, 'I thought it would be nice to be able to help the School...'

'Nice to help the School!' she snapped. 'What's the matter with you!'

'It's my job, Mummy!' he dared to squeak. 'The School suffered a great deal of damage because of the storm and we really will have to do something about that. I just thought it would be rather nice to design something on a grander scale, and more in keeping with the history of the place. Something which they really deserve!'

This was one of the very few occasions when Quentin managed to get more than just a few words out in the face of his tyrannical mother. She was slightly taken aback at his comparative outburst and a short silence hung between them. Then, to his horror, she began to grin. Her shoulders slowly came back and she straightened, still grinning. An evil thought had been triggered in the wizened old bat's head. It was the final part of what Quentin had said that gave her the germ of an idea. That was now growing rapidly. Those last few words of his had planted it. 'Something they really deserve'. That was quite a thought.

Jolly's announcement at the morning staff meeting met total and absolutely stunned silence. The few comments that were then made by the staff revealed a very mixed response.

'Did I really hear that?'

'That's different!'

'Where?'

'He's off his bloody trolley!'

'Very interesting!'

'What the hell is he talking about?'

Feeling slightly disconcerted at the initial and totally silent reaction he had received, Jolly developed his original statement but this time hoping for a more sympathetic attitude.

'So,' he said, 'I am sure that the prospect of looking at this vacant building complex will be a beneficial exercise for all of us and maybe for the future of the school.'

The response he had hoped for still didn't materialise. He took it, hesitantly, a little further. Wooden stood by, unblinking.

'I...err...do believe that...err...it will be of great benefit to...err.' Jolly dried up in the face of a staff room full of eyes, staring at him, unmoved.

Wooden seemed to wake up and mumbled something to him.

'Ah, yes!' Jolly then said, in a much more assured fashion, as if he'd forgotten something. 'I have arranged to have the school minibus available to you for three separate visits to the site during the week. If you would like to see the complex at first hand please sign up on the sheet which will be on the 'urgent' board later today.'

He then swept out, forgetting even to tell everyone to hurry along to assembly.

'He must be off his head!' Vic said.

'Bearing in mind the 'complex' he's been talking about,' Harry said, 'That's about right!'

'What's about right?' Lill asked.

'Don't you realise why?' Chewy asked, grinning.

'Not really,' she said. 'But then nothing Jolly says or does has any basic common sense attached to it. Why should this be any different?'

'He's surpassed himself this time,' Rusty said, grinning as widely as Chewy.

'Come on then, you lot,' Lill said. 'What is it I don't know about?'

'Do you really want to know?' Vic asked.

'Yes,' she said.

'Are you sure?' Rusty asked.

'Yes!' Lill said, exasperated.

'Positive?' grinned Chewy.

'Will you please just tell me!' Lill growled.

'There's only one place around here which justifies the words 'vacant building complex' which Jolly was talking about,' Vic started.

'It is a centre of great renown,' Chewy continued.

'Known far and wide throughout the region,' Rusty chipped in.

'Oh, for God's sake!' Lill said, 'Just tell me!'

Harry had just been sitting the whole time watching this deliberate wind up. He cut in to put her out of her misery.

'What this lot were eventually going to say it that our esteemed Headmaster has pulled one of his truly wondrous stunts, without realising it. The 'complex' he's been going on about was once the property of the National Health Service. It used to be a centre which specialised in one thing and one thing only.'

'What was that?' Lill asked.

'High security for the criminally insane!'

The 'complex' was originally built at the turn of the century. The main building was on three floors, built in a large square enclosing an open quadrangle. The front was quite imposing. There was a hint of St Pancras Station about the place but without the architectural fuss. A central and impressive arched entrance, set into a projecting square tower with a squat spire on the top, led to the open and extensive courtyard beyond. On either side of this the building ran on to two other slightly smaller corner towers. From these the rest of the structure continued to two other identical corners and then back to the middle and a smaller open gateway.

On either side of this main structure were other no less imposing but smaller buildings and then behind them were other more straightforward, two storeyed structures. They were all linked by red tiled, covered walkways, the roofs of these supported by lines of columns set a few feet apart. The impression, which anyone might have gained driving up the wide, tree lined approach, was prestigious to say the least. It could easily have been a college and certainly had the atmosphere of erudition and scholastic endeavour.

On a bright clear morning the Braumstate Cathedral School minibus drove down through the trees towards this mature and substantial edifice. It had been on its way for the better part of twenty minutes. The bus was full with staff who were peering out of the windows over each other, busily appreciating their surroundings and the impact of the facade. A few ripe comments floated up as they approached it.

'Christ! Look at the bloody place!'

'It looks like a bloody mausoleum!'

'Trust Jolly to find another nut house to move to. Isn't he happy with the one we've got?'

Harvey Sheasby, the Wide Mouthed Frog and a few other of the more narrow minded and poisonous 'prissys' amongst the staff bridled physically at this disgraceful behaviour, their faces looking as if they were in the middle of chewing at least two lemons but said nothing. They simply sat stiffly, their elbows jammed to their sides, trying not to come into distasteful, physical contact with their so-called 'colleagues' who were, by coincidence, the full compliment of the Escape Committee. Maggie had the good sense to say nothing and, more importantly, be seen to say nothing in front of the other lot although she couldn't help a few smirks sliding across her face.

Wooden was driving but it was impossible to detect whether he had heard. As he pulled up they all piled out at the main entrance and were met by a small insignificant 'hunch' of a character who was not particularly happy about showing them round. He stood there, fag in mouth and wearing a very grubby, dirt smeared, brown workshop coat, his hands stuffed into the pockets. This was not the first time he'd had to do it. For the last four months he'd had to stay on in the place. He was still employed as caretaker. He was well pissed off with the whole thing and it showed.

The School party were only one of several previous groups who had visited the site with a view to buy it. None of the previous prospective purchasers had bothered to follow it up. It was becoming a substantial 'white elephant' and that was the reason why the price had gradually dropped to well under the current market value. The brown 'Hunch' turned and walked off, not seeming to care whether they followed him or not. Wooden panicked slightly at this and quickly followed, leaving the others to amble along behind, taking in the facade, the view all around and chattering amongst themselves.

The Hunch had entered the arched entrance and disappeared through a door to the left, Wooden chasing after him. The others, quite unaware of this, continued to walk through into the large open courtyard beyond, wondering where to go next. The Escape Committee stayed together and had the sense to stop, noticing that Wooden had vanished.

'Where's the silly bugger gone?' Chewy wondered.

'Does it really matter?' Rusty said.

Maggie walked back and found the door.

'I think he may have gone through here after the caretaker,' she called to the rest of them.

They followed her through to a reception area where Wooden was talking to the Hunch but it didn't look as if he was making any headway at all.

'So you see,' Wooden was saying, 'We're really quite interested in this 'complex' and what it could mean for the School.'

'Oh, yeah,' said the Hunch, and walked off again, leaving Wooden standing there. He continued to walk away but then stopped at a main doorway on the other side of the reception area. He looked round, hands still stuffed into the pockets of the brown coat and still with the fag hanging out of his mouth.

'This way!' he grunted, pushing the door open with his backside and plodding off through it. The door began to close and Wooden, again, ran after him. The others followed, highly amused by the performance.

'He's really pissed off!' Chewy said.

'Who?' Maggie asked.

'Old brown coat,' Chewy answered.

'He's not the only one,' Vic said.

They pushed open the door and followed down the wide corridor. On either side there were several rooms which, at one time in the near past, must have been the administrative offices for the asylum. There was a rather tired look to everything and the decor was ghastly. Floral patterned wallpaper seemed to be the norm contrasted with swirling multi coloured spirals in the carpets of the offices. A strong stomach was needed to view this place. Although all of the offices were empty there were a few vestigial remains of previous occupation. The odd postcard from Majorca, Clacton or Afganistan were still to be seen pinned to some of the walls and a few sheets of paper, in various colours covered in rules, regulations and obscure information were scattered around on all the floors.

The Hunch and Wooden pushed open another door at the end of the corridor. By the time the Escape Committee passed through Wooden and the Hunch had disappeared. A large empty lobby with a staircase which wound up through the building to the top floor was all they found. There were no sounds of footsteps above them.

'That's it then,' Rusty said. 'Looks as if we're on our own.'

'Wonderful!' Harry said and launched himself through another door off to the right and into another dreary corridor leaving them feeling totally unimpressed. The rooms were small, just as the ones they had already seen and without the help of a bulldozer, none of them could see how they could possibly be used as classrooms.

'Come on,' Lill said. 'We're being very pessimistic here. We haven't seen the rest of the place yet.'

'Oh, joy!' Chewy said, grimacing.

'Look!' Harry said, pointing out of a side window.

Harvey Sheasby, the Wide Mouthed Frog, the Fourth Reich and the Poisoned Dwarf were running across the courtyard outside, pursued by two very large black dogs. They were barking, the dogs that is, at the four of them who were wide eyed and terrified at this sudden attack.

'Just look at them go!' Vic chuckled. 'Who do you think will win?'

'The dogs will,' Rusty said, 'with a bit of luck!'

They ran out of sight and as the Escape Committee walked on they heard the crashing of doors further ahead.

'Must have made it inside,' Maggie said.

'Pity,' Chewy said.

A couple of minutes later, out through the door at the end of the corridor and into another lobby, they found Wooden, the Hunch and the others, all breathless from the headlong race from the dogs.

'Security,' the Hunch was saying. 'Dogs are on the site to stop vandals. Lot of them about round here.'

'Does he mean vandals or dogs?' asked the Wide Mouthed Frog, still panting from the race and, as far as she was concerned, canine death.

The Hunch walked on again, uninterested, not waiting for anyone. They all followed into a third corridor but this time the rooms were larger and much lighter than before and only on the outer side of the building. Here at least was the opportunity to think of them as teaching areas. That didn't last. As they passed through another main doorway and then round the next corner of the square they were back again to small rooms and a central corridor. There was something different about this section. Chewy noticed the important difference first.

'Look at that,' he said quietly to the rest of the Escape Committee. He was pointing to each door and particularly at the area around the door handles as they walked along. Each one had a large hasp bolted on to the outside. Just the thing to hold a padlock. These must have been the high security cells. They walked on, passing the others who were looking out of one of the windows, oblivious of the previous use of these rooms. As the Escape Committee passed them Rusty saw that one of the rooms was open, the door standing wide as they came up to it. He looked inside, caught a 'whiff' of the interior and wrinkled his nose.

'God,' he thought to himself. 'What the hell have they been doing in there?' He had a fair idea but didn't like to expand on that. Then he realised what he'd seen and stuck his head in again. He bounced back with a look of sheer joy on his face.

'Take a look, quick!' he said.

Chewy stuck his head in and burst out laughing just as the Wide Mouthed Frog and Harvey Sheasby came up behind them.

'This must be the management's wing!' he said still laughing.

'What are you on about?' Vic asked.

Chewy was leaning against the door frame still laughing.

'I think I've found what might just become the Headmasters room!' he managed to say.

Harvey and the Frog looked inside. It was a padded cell. They were not amused and stomped off in disgust at Chewy's behaviour. The Escape Committee just managed to contain their mirth and with the others now at a deliberate distance from them, continued the circuit of the ground floor of the main building, arriving back at the main entrance. The other two floors above were mostly a series of open areas which were marginally better suited to educational use. After this they were on their way to the other buildings on the site, still following the uncommunicative Hunch. Altogether it was an impressive arrangement.

Compo was wide eyed and speechless as they walked into the first one. It was a very large space and an ideal size for a theatre, concert hall or assembly area for the whole School. 'This is great!' Compo said. 'I'll bet there's room next to this for dressing rooms…'

'Compo,' Rusty said, his voice echoing around the hall. 'Calm down! You'll just upset yourself!'

Beyond this they found another large room which could have been a central focus for the School for displays of work and parents evenings. The school didn't have anything like it. After this came the revelation of finding a large, self-contained laundry which, not surprisingly, the present school didn't have. Then, behind the laundry were the workshops and maintenance buildings. The School had nothing to compare with any of it.

'Just think what Quentin could do with this lot,' Chewy said wryly.

'Yes,' Maggie said. 'He'd probably bury it in pot plants if he didn't wreck it!'

'Where's Vic?' Harry asked.

Vic had disappeared.

'He was here just a minute ago,' Rusty said

The Hunch was walking on so they had to follow him, still wondering where Vic might have gone. They needn't have worried. Vic was busy checking out another aspect of the site. As they walked along behind the Hunch to the next building, a large Victorian Chapel came into view. Vic was already inside this checking the potential of the place. He'd been crawling around inside this for some time. When he eventually caught up with them he was covered in dust and cobwebs.

'Been at the 'Dracula rites' again?' Chewy said as he reappeared.

Two fingers were given in reply. Although these last areas were admired and clucked over, the Escape Committee realised that the whole idea of the school moving here was a complete waste of time. The cost of opening up most of the many smaller rooms to make sensible teaching space for the whole school would be enormous, far greater than repairing and refurbishing what they already had, such as it was. The 'management' wouldn't see that and there was the prospect of this dragging on for months before that could be admitted. The Hunch brought them back to where they had started and simply turned and left them there without a word.

'Chatty little tyke isn't he?' Rusty said.

Wooden was looking a little uneasy, which wasn't difficult to detect. Having had plenty of practice, the Escape Committee knew the signs. He was definitely very unhappy.

'Something wrong?' Chewy asked.

Wooden just pointed ahead. The minibus had gone!

It took three taxis to get them all back to the school but, after phoning the police to inform them of the theft of the minibus, they had to wait for another hour until the taxis actually arrived. It was well after lunchtime before they were back in school. The rest of the staff were less than happy as they had been knobbled by a particularly twitchy Jolly who was fretting rather badly, wondering where on earth the others in the minibus might be. Several members of staff had to look after all the groups of kids in their absence so all the free periods they thought they had were lost as they trudged off to quell the noise coming from the staffless classrooms.

When they did arrive back the Wide Mouthed Frog and Harvey Sheasby were more than embarrassed and immediately scuttled off to Jolly's office to make their excuses and blame everyone else while they had the chance. Back in the staff room later that day the Escape Committee were mulling over the visit to the nut house. The 'snags' to this whole prospective move were obvious. Chewy summed it up reasonably well.

'Jolly must be bloody mad!' he began.

'And I thought you'd never notice,' Rusty said.

'Well,' Chewy went on, 'the whole idea is crackers! The purchase price is one thing, but what these silly buggers don't realise is that it would take at least three times that to refit the place for the school. The internal walls, quite apart from the external structure, are well over a foot thick so opening the place up will cost, not a small fortune but a bloody great vast one!'

'Wouldn't that be worth it for the padded cells alone?' Rusty said. 'After all, that's just what this management need!'

'You're right there,' Chewy said, 'but the time factor alone would mean at least two years of reorganisation before we could even begin to think about taking up 'residence' in the place.'

'Nice Chapel,' Vic said.

'Nice theatre,' Compo said.

'Nice padded cells,' Rusty said.

None of them bothered to pass on their thoughts on to the management. Even if the school had been able to buy it, which it couldn't, it was light years beyond their financial reach and it was, in fact, far too big. In another twenty years time it might perhaps be suitable, and that would depend upon the school growing in size, but not now. Nevertheless, on the face of it this appeared to be a wonderful opportunity to Jolly, Wooden and the rest of the naive idiots who couldn't understand the difference between a structure and a truss. The Escape Committee were content to sit back and wait for that particular, large penny to drop. Another few weeks were to drag by until a final decision was reached about new buildings, of any kind, but that came from a rather unexpected direction.

3

One Saturday morning, after the fiasco of viewing the former high security complex and the theft of the minibus, Chewy was in the D&T office leafing through a set of plans he'd drawn up, prior to the disaster Rick O'Shea had inflicted on the department. He was thinking that this might be a time to talk to the management about improving the whole building. The ground staff had done their best to repair the place and the heating system made a big difference, now that it was working properly, but it was still a bloody awful place to teach in.

The singular problem Chewy had was 'the management'. Was it possible to get these numbsculls to recognise that the two storeyed, 14th century barn he had could be improved? Depression settled over him as he wondered how on earth he could persuade Jolly Jack to spend any money on the place and that's when Rusty arrived.

'How's it hanging?' he said, grinning widely, plopping down into the chair opposite.

Chewy didn't look up but simply said, 'As limp as ever.'

'What's up with you, you miserable old sod. It's Saturday, remember? No more teaching until Monday.'

'It's not the teaching I'm pissed off about. It's this bloody place,' waving an arm in the direction of the door and beyond. 'I'm fed up trying to teach in a place which has hardly any natural daylight, floors which undulate, furniture which is almost falling apart, hardly any storage space for the kids' work or raw materials, lighting which hardly penetrates the gloom…'

He tailed off and slumped back in his chair.

'You're not a very happy pixie today, then?' Rusty said.

'Let me show you something,' Chewy said, standing. 'This way,' and led Rusty across into the workshop. The ceiling was rather low, only seven feet from the ground with substantial oak beams stretching across it. The three windows, on the right as they looked into the room, were all on one side, very small and of the leaded variety. At the far end a step raised the floor level and ten feet beyond that led to an ancient arched door barely five feet high. The room was filled with work benches without a great deal of room to manoeuvre between them and an assortment of hand tools were hanging on racks on either wall.

'D'you see that door?' Chewy asked.

Rusty nodded.

'Well, there's no key to that and there's no chance of opening it as it was sealed up when Adam was a lad. To open it would mean 'major surgery'. So, we have a fire risk already. If anything happened down here there's only one way out and that's the way we came in. But that's not all. There's more. Come upstairs.'

Rusty had to admit it wasn't the most exciting of teaching venues he's seen but he wondered what upstairs would reveal. He'd only been into the office before and this was becoming as depressing for him as it obviously was for Chewy. Climbing a very narrow staircase to a tight half landing they continued up to the first floor and through a rickety door to the 'design studio'. This was no better. Only two windows, on the right again and similar to those below, illuminated the area, albeit gloomily. Behind the desk Chewy used, a roller blackboard was fixed to the wall and beyond his desk a haphazard arrangement of bog standard desks filled the room with a couple of tables on either side where pens, pencils, paper, a pile of small drawing boards and other drafting equipment were stacked. Thick oak beams stretched across them, as below, but above these the underside of the roof sported a substantial arrangement of beams with a single, vertical, oak support connecting to the centre of each horizontal beam from the apex.

'Note the wondrous light level,' Chewy said, nodding into the gloom, 'and the lack of any other way down. Another fire hazard, quite apart from the crap furniture.'

Rusty could only nod. This really was bloody awful. Back in the office Chewy folded up the drawings he been looking at and sighed.

'Why don't you stick those drawings under Jolly's nose?' Rusty asked. 'I'm no architect but I can see there would be no alteration to the structure of the place, apart from another staircase at the other end. The rest is pretty straightforward.'

Chewy nodded. 'With a little help from the ground staff the staircase would be an easy matter to install. I could do the rest myself.'

'Then go for it,' Rusty grinned. 'What the hell have you go to lose. Don't forget the 'parent factor'.

Chewy grinned. That was something that usually worked.

On the following Monday, after school, Chewy went round to see Jolly. 'Has he anyone with him?' He asked Maisie. She shook her head so he just walked into Jolly's office without knocking, as usual. Jolly looked up, flustered at his sudden appearance but before he could speak Chewy was leaning over his desk and opening the plans to his department.

'We need to do something about my place before the parents complain,' Chewy began.

Jolly was quite startled by this. Anything that the parental body were unhappy about always had his immediate attention. Parents were to be revered, honoured and most of all kept happy. Without their 'fiscal input' the school would be up shit creek and Jolly knew it.

Chewy continued not allowing Jolly to speak. 'The department is a death trap and has been for some time.'

Jolly's face stiffened, the blood draining from it at those last words.

'If a child made a mistake with a soldering iron, as they often do, or a few sparks from a grinding wheel ignited the dust in the place we could be in trouble. The building might go up in minutes and on both floors we have a major problem in getting them out, 'if', and I emphasize 'if', we could. The cost of this would be minimal and I'm prepared to do a lot of it myself. We're talking about no more than a couple of thousand to make the place safe and keep the parents happy.'

Jolly was reeling from the prospect of even slightly singed pupils but he fastened onto the potential lifeline that it might not cost too much.

'I… err… yes,' He stammered. 'The cost would be important so I think you should see the Bursar about this.'

Chewy groaned inside. A classic side step from Jolly. He always passed anything which needed a decision on to someone else.

'Fine,' Chewy replied through gritted teeth, folding up the drawings. 'I'll see him as soon as I can. Thank you.'

Two days passed before he could see the Prick who was just as 'useful' as Jolly had been. Another 'pass the parcel' statement came from him.

'In view of the cost I think it would be wise to have a word with our Financial Controller, don't you?'

Chewy's hands formed into fists at this but he kept his cool and made for the FC's office. The same 'passing of the buck' took place as the FC said, 'I would need official permission from the Headmaster to allow this. It isn't in the budget, you know.'

A week later and Chewy was no further forward. He gone round the same carousel from Jolly to the Prick to the FC, twice more, and not one of them, and they probably never would, made any kind of decision. He was even more pissed off than before. He had to do something to focus their attention. The threat of parental unhappiness hadn't worked as he'd hoped it would so another 'tack' was needed, but what?

A couple of days later, and in total frustration, he phoned Jolly, the Prick and the FC, one after the other, asking them to come over to the department after school was over so that they could see the full extent of the plans he had and what he wanted to happen in the department. They were all more than reluctant to come but the 'parental' and 'safety' factors which Chewy emphasized, yet again, were the trump cards he used to ensure they would come. None of them could ignore either.

What they didn't know was that he'd given each one the same time for the 'appointment' so when they all arrived they were somewhat nonplussed to see each other. Jolly was furious at being duped into such a meeting. The Prick viewed Chewy as someone he would have put on a charge for insubordination, if he'd been able to, while the FC was more concerned about his personal plumbing having been upset by this sudden request to appear outside his closeted domain.

'Gentlemen,' Chewy said benignly, before any verbal complaints could be made. 'Thank for coming. I apologise for bringing you together in this way but on the last three occasions I have talked to all of you it seemed that we were going nowhere. I now want to explain to you, on site, as it were, the real problems which exist in this building and you will see for yourselves I have not exaggerated anything. Now, if you will please follow me.'

They did without a word. Chewy took them all on the same route he had taken Rusty, excluding all the expletives he used then, and at the end of that, upstairs, he showed them all of the plans he had drawn up and went over them in detail.

'Much of this can be done with the ground staff helping and I will be willing to work, for as long as it takes, to complete the job. So,' he said, winding up his lecture, 'as you are all aware we have an open day coming up soon. I have a feeling that prospective parents will be unable to ignore the shortfalls of the building. If they ask me about that I feel duty bound to tell the truth, as I have just done with you. However, there is still time to rectify the situation before then.'

Not one of them said a word as Chewy finished his speech but he could see the confusion in all of them and the realisation that the 'parental factor' was something which could not be ignored. Jolly was the first to speak.

'Yes.... well.... errr... I think that this should be looked at by the Bursar and the Financial controller very carefully. A full and detailed costing of this will, of course, be necessary and the Clerk of the Works will need to be informed. We will all discuss this when the details of that expenditure has been assessed.'

They trouped out and left Chewy in a more depressed state than ever. Any decision from them now seemed more remote than ever and if that twat Quentin was going to be involved then that was probably that.

Another Saturday rolled around and, after the morning lessons, Chewy was up in the staff room with the Escape Committee moaning on about what, or rather had not, happened. The others were sympathetic but there was nothing they could suggest. One by one they drifted off until there was only Chewy and Rusty sitting despondantly but partaking of the contents of the louvred cupboard. By almost five in the afternoon they were both quite pissed.

'Ahh,' Chewy said. 'Why should I fucking bother? Let's just wait and see. But if something does happen, God forbid, like a fire in the place, Jolly only needs to apologise to parents for having their offspring roasted, so that's all right, isn't it?'

'Yup,' Rusty said. 'He's good at that. I mean being servile to parents. Best ever. What an arsehole!'

Chewy nodded, mouthing 'arse... hole' slowly. Then he sat up, blinked a couple of times and said, 'Arse... hole. Hole! That's it! That's it!'

'What's it?' Rusty asked, bemused.

Chewy stood, draining his glass. 'Drink up! We've got work to do!'

Minutes later they had staggered over to the D&T Department and were standing upstairs at the far end of the design studio with Chewy looking at the floor.

'What the hell are you looking for?' Rusty asked, peering at the same patch.

'Evidence,' Chewy replied. 'Evidence.'

'Evidence of what?' asked Rusty, who was completely confused.

'Woodworm,' came the reply.

'Woodworm?'

'Yup, woodworm. The answer to my problem.'

Rusty didn't have a clue what the hell Chewy was talking about. 'Have you lost the plot?' He asked.

'By no means,' Chewy replied, a huge grin on his face. 'Come on, we have things to do!'

'We?' Rusty asked but was then pulled along and down into the workshop below.

Two hours later, and almost sober again, they had completed their task using two cordless drills from the workshop, fitted with 2mm diameter drill bits, and a circular saw. At the far end of the design studio Chewy had pulled up a few of the floorboards, assessed the direction of the supporting beams, marked a rectangle and with the circular power saw cut a hole in the floor big enough to fit a sensible sized staircase to the workshop below. Some of the timber from the hole was dispatched to two of the large waste bins outside while other suitable lengths were used to line the hole they'd made. So far so good. Then they drilled thousands of holes into the ancient wooden floor around the hole. They were as close as anything to the effect woodworm has on woodwork.

The tiny holes around the new hole were just right. Who would be able to say that woodworm had not been found? Certainly not Jolly. All they needed now was a staircase to complete the job. That would be the tricky part in that he would have to talk to Jolly again. That wouldn't be easy given what he'd done to a Grade one listed building! They found a wooden ladder at the back of the ground staff's place and brought it back to serve as a temporary access, up and down. Then they made a makeshift barrier with a few pieces of plywood around it so any kids wouldn't be at risk. Satisfied with that Chewy swept up the detritus from their efforts and sat down.

'Jolly will go bloody crackers when he finds out, or you tell him, what's happened,' Rusty said.

'Fear not,' Chewy said. 'In the first place I won't tell him you had anything to do with it. This is going to be my problem and mine alone. I can't think of anything else I could have done. Those silly buggers will never come to any kind of a conclusion so I have, as they say, taken an 'executive decision' on my own. One Jolly will almost certainly call a 'cavalier action' which is, in fact, a pretty good description!'

At the same time Chewy was slightly apprehensive that Monday might be a bit tricky when he told, and showed, Jolly what they had done but the 'safety' and 'parental' factors would, he hoped, work.

With lessons over on Monday Chewy, as usual, strolled into Jolly's office without knocking. Taken by complete surprise yet again Jolly flinched as Chewy walked in.

'Headmaster,' Chewy began without waiting for Jolly to say anything. 'We have a serious problem in the D&T department. Or rather, we did have.'

Jolly was speechless not knowing what Chewy was talking about but then he found his voice and asked, weakly, 'Problem?'

'Yes,' Chewy said very calmly. 'Infestation. To be precise, woodworm. A rather bad case of it I'm afraid but fortunately it has given us a surprise advantage to the conditions I outlined to you recently. Have you the time to come and have a look?'

Jolly was completely dumbfounded but he nodded his head and meekly followed Chewy back to the D&T department.

'So you see, Headmaster,' Chewy said, looking down into the hole in the floor, 'I think we can install a staircase here and do something about the rest of this floor,' waving a hand at the rest of the area. 'The evidence of woodworm, which you can see for yourself around the hole, can be dealt with quite easily. If we don't, we certainly have a potentially dangerous teaching area, something the parents will not be happy about. No, not happy at all.'

'But this is a Grade one listed building!' Jolly squeaked. 'We need to have planning permission before anything like this....'

'And how long would that take?' Chewy asked. 'Are you prepared to risk pupils lives in these conditions. It won't take long to install a staircase and, as I've already said, I can do the rest. The cost would be in the region of two and a half thousand pounds, at most'.

Jolly was beside himself with worry but he realised that he had to do something immediately, not a situation he enjoyed or had ever had to do before. He skittered back to his office without saying another word and immediately phoned the Prick and then the FC. A day later Chewy had a phone call in the D&T office from Maisie Hatter.

'Himself has just told me to inform you that you've just been allowed to spend two and a half grand,' she said and hung up.

Chewy couldn't believe his ears! He talked to the ground staff, organised the materials and prepared himself for a lot of work in the evenings, the only time he would be able to work unhindered. In two weeks they had finished and the transformation was amazing. He now had a new sensible staircase at one end, purpose made desks in the studio and adequate lighting. All he needed now was to have that arched door in the workshop opened up and maybe, just maybe, begin a campaign for a networked computer installation. Wouldn't that be good?

'Don't push your luck' was not a term he believed in!

The days rolled on and then came one of the annual events which some of the staff hated, at least those with any brains did but there were few who qualified in that respect. These were a series of 'outings' for the non-examination groups intended to allow the victims of GCSE and A Level some space for reviewing their subjects and concentrating on the impending examinations which were not that far away. The fact that the 'lower orders' would be away for the day, always on a Friday, had never made a scrap of difference in the past to those about to embark on their examinations. Most of them were as indolent as ever as the day progressed and none of the staff who had them during that day bothered to mention that to the management as, together with many other things they could have said, it would not have made a blind bit of difference. The reference which Vic had made at the beginning of term rang as true as ever. 'Sed semper hoc facimus in hoc modo.' We've always done it this way.

Four venues had been organised, all quite different and, as the management hoped, they would be a truly rewarding experience for all. Well, they got that one wrong again. It did turn out to be an experience for each group but not exactly 'rewarding'. Three of these outings were to be in Bristol. The Bristol Zoo, SS Great Britain, Brunel's famous ship, and the third would be the Bristol Museum. The remaining one was organised for Wookey Hole, twenty miles or so south of Bristol which was famous for an underground extravaganza of stalagmites and stalagtites and the famous, apocryphal, Witch of Wookey.

Four private coaches were waiting for the kids to transport them, and, a mere forty five minutes after their arrival, the kids, accompanied by four staff to each coach, were all on board and on their way. Chewy and most of the Escape Committee were not, thankfully, included in this collective jaunt but Compo, poor sod, had drawn the short straw and he was now on his way to Wookey Hole.

The following day, Saturday, a few staff sat around the staff room including several members of the previous day's 'outings'. They languished there enjoying the fact that they didn't have to rush off to morning assembly. Monday to Friday yes, but not on a Saturday. Compo sat there looking particularly drained. Some of the Escape Committee who were there tried to sooth him, all except Chewy.

'Serves you bloody right for volunteering,'he said.

'I didn't!' Compo spat back. 'I was knobbled by Wooden because some arsehole in the Science department had a bloody cold! A likely bloody story!'

'So it was not an invigorating experience?' Rusty asked.

'Oh, for fucks sake! You have to be bloody joking!' Compo replied. 'Who would want to go down into the bowels of the earth with a gaggle of little shits whose only interest is stealing whatever they can get their sticky little hands on, eh? It was worse coming back out. Going through the old paper mill, that was interesting I have to admit, and then this penny arcade they have there and the souvenir shop. It was a bloody nightmare! I had to frisk the buggers before we left, to replace what they'd 'lifted', otherwise we'd have had the local plods wacking them into the back of the local Black Maria!'

'Black Maria?' Lill asked.

'Police wagon,' Chewy explained. 'Compo's showing his age and historical terminology!'

'So, it was not an invigorating experience?' Rusty repeated, grinning.

'NO!' Compo answered loudly.

The other groups hadn't had much of an 'invigorating experience' either. The group destined for the Bristol Zoo had been thrown out due to several of the kids who had somehow managed to climb into the monkey cage to steal a few bananas. Not only were the monkeys pissed off but so were the staff of the zoo. At SS Great Britain, in mid restoration stage, several of the kids thought it was the Titanic and totally freaked out, shrieking that the thing was going to sink at any moment. Bristol Museum quickly placed a ban on anyone from the school ever entering the place again. Some of the kids had climbed up through the dinosaur skeletons and began shrieking manically from the top of a particularly valuable specimen, 'Jurrasic Park lives!'

And so, yet another wondrous 'experience' for the pre-examination groups had foundered, the management, primarily Jolly, being totally unaware of this until the formal complaints began to arrive.

Chewy walked back to his department, chuckling about poor old Compo's day. When he arrived he was not amused. Parked in front of the door of the building was a Land Rover, the nose of which was almost touching the door. This was not the first time it had happened. Chewy managed to squeeze past and unlocked his door. He went straight to the store, found what he wanted and squeezed back out through the door to apply his own brand of warning to this vehicle. A liberal amount of sprayed glue was applied to the windscreen and then a large, A3 page of felt tipped, non too subtle written 'advice' was carefully rubbed onto that. No bad language was used but the essence of the message was, 'Don't park here ever again, you silly person!'

A day later he had Seedpod, Mr Runner, the Junior School Headmaster on the phone and he was not a happy man.

'I have had a complaint from one of my parents about the 'sticker' you applied to his windscreen yesterday!'

'Oh, really,' was Chewy's simple response.

'Yes, really!' Seedpod spat back. 'It took him almost an hour to scrape the thing off!'

'Good' replied Chewy. 'That may make him think twice about not only parking and blocking the entrance to my department as well as screwing up a vital fire exit, don't you think?'

There was silence at the other end of the phone.

'So you'll be having a word with whoever the dick-head was who parked here, will you,' Chewy said. Silence. 'Well, I think that covers that problem, don't you think?' and he put the phone down. Seedpod didn't phone back.

Of all the three terms of the academic year, in those days, and I suspect today, the Lent term for the school, post Christmas to the end of March, give or take a week or so, was always the most stressful not only for the kids but for all the staff. During this time the important coursework for every subject had to be completed, refined and, if necessary, reviewed for the later assessments which would be necessary prior to the final examination process. As the days rolled on more and more pressure was being applied, not to the kids who were near to completing their work but to those who hadn't. As always, the latter category was larger than the former and that was further aggravated by the fact that the ones who were well behind didn't seem to realise that time was slipping quickly away. 'Twas, as they say, ever thus.

Jolly didn't help any of this. His morning 'bulletins' were riddled with, 'We must be assured that all that can be done will be done,' and 'All students must be made aware of their need to do their best,' and, 'I am sure you will do your utmost to maintain an atmosphere for the most positive of endeavours.' It was all too depressing for everyone, even the creeps on the staff, and almost insulting to have to listen to the crap he insisted on coming out with.

Chewy was one who was particularly depressed by the way his kids were performing, both at GCSE and A Level.

He found himself 'remonstrating' with many of them, on a daily basis, and that, after a parent had complained, brought another 'interview' with Jolly.

Chewy arrived to see Jolly after finding a memo in his pigeon hole requesting his presence. As usual he simply walked into Jolly's office and deliberately sat on the sofa rather than be intimidated by the low chair in front of Jolly's desk. Jolly didn't like that but as he saw Chewy wasn't to be moved he came over to a chair opposite and opened a file.

'There seems to a problem with this particular child,' Jolly began, not looking at Chewy at all.

'Problem?' Chewy asked. 'What problem? What child?'

'Harvey Warburton Smith,' Jolly replied. 'His father is less than happy with your attitude to his son. He telephoned me yesterday.'

'Did he now,' Chewy replied, sounding totally unimpressed.

'Yes, he did,' Jolly said, still without looking up.

'So,' Chewy said, getting more comfortable, 'what's the problem?'

'Well,' Jolly began, 'the problem is the way you have been talking to young Harvey. It hasn't been exactly encouraging.'

'Oh, I don't know about that,' Chewy replied. 'I thought what I said to him recently made a very big difference to the way he's performing now.'

This threw Jolly slightly in that he'd expected Chewy to apologise for his words to the said Harvey Warburton Smith.

'So you don't disagree about what you actually said to this child, do you?' Jolly asked and for the first time looked directly at Chewy.

'Child?' Chewy said, 'Child? This 'child' is almost eighteen years old, is a complete piss-head, smokes all kinds of grass, fornicates whenever he gets the chance and is the top candidate for the laziest little bugger in the school. Ask any other member of staff and they'll confirm that!'

Jolly was completely taken aback by this but managed to ask, 'So you don't deny what you said to him?'

Chewy sat forward, glaring at Jolly and said, 'No! I told him, and I will now quote, '*Stop farting around, get your head out of your arse and complete your coursework as soon as possible or I'll eviscerate your bloody manhood, you little, idle sod!*'

Jolly looked down at the file he held and saw that the exact words Chewy had just thrown at him were there as given by the 'child's' father.

'Wasn't that a touch too strong? Jolly said quietly, without looking up.

'Not at all,' Chewy said, settling back. 'Since then he's actually caught up and might well be in line for a grade A, with luck, or at least a grade B. He has the talent to do that with the right 'stimulation'. Between now and the examination itself it's up to him, but he knows that I won't ease up on the pressure for him to perform. Does his father realise any of this? Or for that matter, does he know that his 'child' is in the same boat in all his other subjects?'

That was the killer blow to the 'interview'. Jolly closed the file he was holding, stood up and said, rather stiffly, to Chewy, 'Thank you. I will keep you informed of any further developments.'

-4-

One of the biggest problems the School had was the organisation of space for public examinations. Apart from the sports hall there wasn't a single building which was adequate for the numbers of pupils who would be taking their finals later in the year. Well before that the problem of the mock exams was just as difficult to solve.

A partial system had evolved by itself over the years, rather than through a rational piece of logic, which used classrooms and other buildings all of which were scattered at extreme ends of the site. If they had actually planned it they couldn't have made a bigger cock up of the whole thing. One of the buildings in Shanty Town was mainly used for the GCSE brigade, with some A Level places included here while the rest of the A Levellers were herded into another shed at the other end of the school. This was normally Compo's base and he wasn't very happy about it. Added to this were other 'overflow' rooms, in various other places which produced the effect of staff and kids having to charge around like startled pigs, all over the site between lessons during the examination period. Nobody had given a thought about using the cavern of the sports hall until one member of staff, who was totally pissed off at having his working area taken over for almost ten weeks in every year, changed the locks on his room and refused to let them in. This was Compo. He used the place for Theatre

Studies and was fed up with being turfed out twice a year. He even squatted in the place for more than a week just in case the ground staff were ordered to break in. Jolly wasn't 'jolly' about this at all. The Mocks had to be delayed until they resolved the problem. That few days of management agony was a classic of bone-headed nonsense.

Jolly, Wooden, Wide Mouth, Neville Condon, and the Prick sat at the large table in Jolly's office worrying the problem around from one to the other. Condon, known to the kids as 'the Rubber', due to his name having a similarity to a certain 'protective' product, slowed everything down to a near stop in the way he 'communicated'. To the Escape Committee he became known as 'Deep Throat', again due to his unbelievably slow and deliberate speech pattern. It would send a lot of folk off to sleep in the months ahead. He always seemed to open his mouth before he spoke as if he was about to take in a complete banana, or maybe something else. Either way he was now Deep Throat to all.

'We must do something soon!' Jolly said. 'We can't delay the mocks any longer. What will the parents say?'

Wooden just sat, a fixed stare on his face.

'What would you suggest, Headmaster?' said Wide Mouth, not having a thought of her own.

'My feeling is this,' he began. 'We must find an alternative venue for the examinations and quickly. Have any of you got any suggestions?'

He had an extraordinary knack of stating the obvious and then wanting other people to solve it for him.

'This... is... a... very... important... problem... to... solve,' Deep Throat said, very slowly, which he always did. 'As... I... see... it..., we... need... somewhere... big... enough... to... take... all... the... examination... groups... at... any... one... time.'

This was a remarkable breakthrough in the application of pure, blinding, intelligent reasoning. As he had spoken they had all begun to lean instinctively forward, following his every slow word, waiting for the answer which they were sure was about the fall at any moment onto the table. But that was all he said. The disappointed silence was broken by the Prick.

'What about the Town Hall, Headmaster?' he said beaming. 'That's big enough!'

'That's a point!' Jolly grinned. 'Well done!'

'There is of course the cinema,' Wide Mouth smiled. 'They only use the place for bingo these days and I'm sure we could come to some arrangement with them.'

'Now we're getting somewhere!' Jolly said, rubbing his hands together. 'I had thought of the Cathedral myself, but I doubt whether the Dean would go for that.'

And so they sat weighing up the Town Hall against the Cinema when the Mad Hatter came in with a tray of coffee. She couldn't believe what they were saying as she poured and then distributed the cups to all of them. She didn't care what she said at the best of times but this was an opportunity she wasn't going to miss.

'Headmaster?' she asked.

'Yes, Maisie?' he said, slightly surprised at her interruption.

'I'm sorry to butt in,' she smiled, 'but wouldn't it be better to use the sports hall?'

'Sports hall?' Jolly blinked at this. 'Sports hall?'

'Yes,' she continued. 'Most other schools do.'

'Do they?' he blinked again. 'Do they?'

'They do,' she said and walked out of his room with the tray, her eyes rolling to the ceiling.

Over the next forty eight hours the five of them spent a great deal of time creeping round the sports hall during the day. It was very strange to watch them and a few staff thought they'd all gone even barmier than they already were. Then, one by one they dropped out. Wide Mouth gave it up first as she was concerned her 'gals' might not understand why she insisted on checking the boys changing rooms so often. The Prick cried off saying he had too much administration building up and Wooden just floated away without saying a word.

Deep Throat was the next to go. He moved so slowly he couldn't keep up with Jolly's frantic scuttling from one end of the building to the other, stopping suddenly, cocking an ear in some undetermined direction, listening. He kept turning up throughout the following day at different times, walking in and listening in different parts of the large interior. No one could work out what the hell he was listening for. That didn't come to light until he made an announcement at the morning meeting the following day that on his last visit to the inside of the hall he had the distinct impression the kids were taking the mickey out of him but he didn't have the 'bottle' to do anything about it.

There were about fifteen kids inside the hall when Jolly came in, yet again. One of them had an enormous pair of ears. They stuck out like sails from his head, large and red. It was sad really but the kids had nicknamed him 'wing nut'. They were all playing short tennis at the time but, as the member of staff had gone off for a quick pee, they had given up playing and were all jigging about, holding the plastic rackets up to their heads to mimic poor old 'wing nut'. That's when Jolly walked in. He misunderstood this completely and was mortified at seeing them cavorting about with huge black, perforated ears. It was a tricky moment for him. Jolly scuttled out, not knowing what to do. He didn't come back.

At the next morning meeting he revealed to all of them what he'd been doing for the last few days. The Escape Committee were particularly interested. They had hoped he'd gone nuts but that was too much to hope for. They knew he was already.

'The problem of finding the right kind of building for public examinations has been with us for some time,' he said, a serious expression on his face, 'and after a great deal of thought and consideration we have been looking at several options, one of which is the sports hall.'

'About bloody time too!' grumbled Compo.

'My main concern has been noise levels. As you will no doubt agree we need peace and quiet for all examination candidates and after a great deal of research into other venues the sports hall became the main centre of interest. I have been able to ascertain that even with the noise of the fans in there, which circulate the air, the sports hall seems to be the most likely building which will give us the space and flexibility to house all examinees. Several others of the management team, after checking noise levels with me, have agreed that this should now be the centre for the final examinations of both GCSE and A Level pupils.'

This was an absolute piece of total bullshit. He hadn't consulted any one of them but they didn't have the guts to say so.

'So that's what the silly bugger's been doing!' Chewy said. 'I had hoped he'd gone completely nuts. What a shame!'

Two people sat up straight at Jolly's last remark. One was Compo who couldn't miss the reference to only the finals being held in the hall.

'What about now?' he almost shouted. 'The mocks should take place in there as well!'

Jolly stepped back as if he'd been slapped in the face. He wasn't used to this kind of verbal attack from a member of staff he had thought to be docile and easy to control. That was his big mistake. The worms may well have begun to turn.

'Well... I suppose... we might think of... ' he stuttered.

Wooden of all people, came to his rescue, nearly.

'I think we should keep calm about all of this...' he said without blinking but Compo had his dander up and cut in to what he was saying.

'I'm very calm,' he said forcefully, 'but I would like the luxury of being able to teach GCSE and A Level pupils, just like the rest of you, instead of being thrown out to find a room which is always a very difficult thing to do when every one of them is in use!'

Jolly was now being forced into an instant decision, something which was totally alien to his whole being and he couldn't help noticing the ripples of agreement which were flowing through a number of the other members of staff. He looked helplessly at his deputies. They looked away.

'You're on your own, Jolly!' hissed Chewy.

The rest of the Escape Committee were right behind Compo and levelled stern expressions in Jolly's direction, nodding their heads. The only other member of staff, who was now sitting bolt upright at what Jolly had just said, and had eventually realised something was going on which he hadn't been informed about, was the P.E. oaf, Duane Hedley or 'Dick Head'. It had percolated slowly into his small kernel of a brain that his precious sports hall was going to be taken away from him. He didn't like that.

'What am I going to do?' he suddenly asked, just like a little boy who'd lost his lollipop.

Jolly ignored him completely. He was more concerned about the full frontal assault he'd just had from Compo.

'Well, err... perhaps you and I need to talk, Compton,' he said, looking distinctly ill at ease. Half an hour later all had been settled. The sports hall would be used for the mocks as well as the finals.

Rusty, as Compo's Head of Faculty, had gone with him to Jolly's study and they both sat there simply saying 'NO!' until Jolly agreed. And so the mocks began. Dick Head, dejected and defeated, had to move out to play outside in the cold for a while. He wasn't happy but everyone else was.

As the weeks dragged by the old frustrations of trying to teach and work in a total madhouse were right back on full throttle. The Escape Committee were no less affected by this. Chewy was one in particular.

'You know what that stupid bastard has just told me!' he said to Rusty, as they walked down through the school.

'Which one?' Rusty simply asked. 'There's quite a few of them as well you know.'

'That little shite, the Fat Controller, Hunt,' Chewy almost spat the name out, 'has just informed me that I haven't answered his last bloody stupid memo about how many paper bloody towels we used in the Department last year! Plus a request for chits for this and bloody chits for that. He's paper bloody mad, just like Jolly!'

Michael Farnsworth Hunt, the Financial Controller for the school really was, as Chewy often eloquently described, 'a nasty, incompetent little shite'. When his appointment had been first announced by Jolly everyone knew they had another dead-head amongst them. He went on to prove their worst fears. Jolly had expressed his delight in being able to find a replacement for the previous accountant who had resigned three months previously. He couldn't cope any longer with such a bunch of nutters and had gone on to a successful consultancy. The consequent announcement from Jolly, of the appointment of a new Financial Controller some weeks after this, raised quite a few eyebrows.

Jolly told them all, 'Of course Mr Hunt was the Financial Controller of Marstons so we're very lucky to have him with us now.'

Harry couldn't believe his ears.

'Bloody hell!' he had mumbled to the others. 'Marstons went bloody bankrupt three months ago! Before that he was working for another business. That went down the friggin plug hole as well. Now he's here! Lucky old us!'

'Jolly rides again,' moaned Chewy.

'How does he do it?' Rusty asked, referring to the unerring list of Jolly's disastrous appointments

'Just lucky,' Vic grunted.

Either way Michael Farnsworth Hunt was still a nastly, incompetent little shite and he was probably the only one who didn't know it.

'Oh, not you too!' Rusty said in reply to Chewy's complaint. 'He sent me a similar memo to that a few days ago. I think I've still got it.'

He dug around inside his jacket and pulled out a crumpled sheet.

'Here it is,' he said. 'Listen to this!'

It said, 'Will you please inform your Department members that they should return their green forms, the monthly requisition for photocopying, to you by the end of this month. This needs to be countersigned by the Head of Department, yourself, and entered onto the blue form for this office and to be entered on to the yellow form, the central record, as a means of cross checking all photocopying work throughout the school.'

'How the hell,' Rusty said, 'can I tell what my lot are going to need in the next month? I haven't got a crystal bloody ball! And does he really think I'm going to piss about filling bloody stupid multi-coloured forms in just to keep him happy? No chance! The man's not just paper bloody mad! He's coloured bloody paper mad!'

By the time they had reached the staff room they'd both calmed down again. A cup of coffee later and they were feeling much better, but there was still a need to take the pressure off these stupid situations which the so-called management constantly applied, at all times, to very simple situations. Chewy remembered his 'niceness' routine of some weeks ago. He wondered if this would have an effect and maybe, if practised generally, would help to take the irritation out of the mindless memo's and statements made by the management and even the more witless members of the staff. Both Rusty and he decided to try being 'nice' to everyone. It might actually prove to be an antidote, a stepping back from being sucked into the quicksand of trivia which surrounded them. Either way it would make a change from complaining about the silly buggers all the time. A positive approach, that was the thing. They agreed that they should be 'nice' whatever happened. The actual test run of this new technique proved to be extremely interesting.

When Chewy and Rusty had arrived in the staff room the place was empty. After a couple of minutes young Ray Butcombe, a teacher of Biology came in, poured himself a coffee and sat down opening a copy of the 'Times Ed'. Chewy and Rusty launched into their 'nice' mode.

'Ray!' Chewy said. 'How *nice* to see you again after all this time! It's been *ages*. How are you? Everything running smoothly?'

Ray looked up from the paper wondering what was going on. He'd seen Chewy not half an hour before.

'Oh,' Rusty said. 'Don't be so pushy, Chewy. Can't you see he's busy trying to find another job?'

'Now, now,' Chewy said, wagging a finger in Rusty's direction. 'I just thought I'd like to spend a little time with a *very nice man* and say 'hello' to a fellow professional!'

Ray folded the paper and looked at both of them.

'What the hell are you two up to?' he asked, a worried expression on his face.

'Up to?' Chewy grinned. 'What could we *possibly* be up to?'

'That wasn't very nice, was it?' Rusty said, looking at Chewy.

'Well, no it wasn't,' Chewy answered, 'but I don't *really* mind. Ray is such a *nice* man. I can forgive him.'

Ray was looking decidedly anxious by now. This was totally out of character for both of them. Harvey Sheasby came in, deliberately ignored them, and clattered around the crockery making himself a cup of coffee.

'Harvey!' Rusty said, turning in his chair. 'How *are* you? It's so *nice* to see you.'

'Yes!' Chewy followed. 'It's so *good* to see such an upright member of the common room.'

Harvey turned his head slowly, a puzzled look on his face.

'Doesn't he look *well*!' Chewy said to Rusty.

'I was thinking that!' Rusty agreed. 'I haven't seen him looking so fit for a long time. How *do* you do it, Harvey?'

Harvey had stopped what he was doing and now faced them with a confused expression on his face.

'What are you two doing?' he demanded.

'*Doing*?' Chewy asked.

'*Doing*?' Rusty echoed.

'I won't stand for this!' Harvey squeaked, clenching his hands into frustrated fists. 'It's not fair!'

'But *Harvey*,' Chewy soothed. 'We so *admire* your presence. Where would we be without your example to follow?'

'How true!' Rusty said. 'How *very* true!'

Ray sat watching this performance, completely nonplussed. He knew they couldn't stand Harvey so they had to be setting something up. They were never like this normally. Harvey stood there, his face becoming quite red as he struggled to keep his temper. Rusty and Chewy sat looking directly at him, huge wide grins across their faces. Harvey couldn't take any more and stormed out, slamming the door behind him.

'Oh, *dear*,' Rusty said, a look of sadness coming across his face. 'I *do* hope he's all right. There are times when I *worry* about dear old 'Harve'.

'I know *just* what you mean,' Chewy said. 'Do you think I should follow him, just in case he does something *silly*?'

'Oh, I don't think so,' Rusty said, a huge grin spreading across his face. 'I don't...chuckle, think... chuckle, chuckle...that would be... ' He collapsed back into the chair as did Chewy.

Ray stood up and threw down the paper as the pair of them hooted with laughter.

'You two are bloody mad!' he said and walked out.

This only fuelled their mood and it was another few minutes before they could begin to think about speaking without creasing up again. One thing was certain. Being 'nice' had its advantages.

At the beginning of every academic year a fresh crop of cannon fodder, better recognised as children, were fed into this ancient, educational sausage machine from the tender ages of five in the junior part of the school and then from eleven, twelve and thirteen in the senior part. There were usually a sprinkling of older ones as well but all of them had undergone the entrance test farce. Some managed to squeeze in well after this, having sat the same tests under supervised conditions in their former school. Either way most of the new arrivals had already been to see the school, with their parents in tow, on one of several Saturday morning visits which happened regularly throughout the academic year. Both of these events, the entrance tests and particularly the visits, were a sore point with most of the staff and were treated with less than enthusiasm.

Parents would usually be taken round in ones or twos by various pupils of the school but it seemed that the management had a knack of choosing the most stupid of all of them to do this. The consequences of this produced some terrible explanations of what was going on from the kids to the parents of potential newcomers. Many a time something as fatuous as, 'This is where we do experiments,' or 'This is where we add up,' or 'This is where we learn about old things,' would be heard. These kinds of 'explanations', quite apart from the disruption of people barging in during lessons, were the greatest source of irritation to all of the staff. Chewy had his own reaction to it. During one Saturday lunchtime he was banging on again about his latest visitation.

'If I find,' he said, 'another one of those little sods say, as they walk into my building, 'This is the woodwork room,' I'll fucking kill!'

It was an ongoing campaign of his to instill something approaching the correct terminology for his subject but he knew in his water he would never really win. Nonetheless he continued to try but a memorable example of the way he dealt with these invasions happened a few weeks later and moved straight into the mini-folk lore of the School.

Wooden, in his little head, and all by himself, had thought up a new wheeze for parents visiting the School. There was to be an open day. Everyone groaned inwardly at this. The very thought of having the place heaving with hundreds of punters did not fill them with joy. As a means of calming some of the more 'difficult' on the staff he did have the sense, which was a first for him, of pinning up a sheet on the staff notice board for anyone who did not wish to have large groups coming round on that day. Chewy's name was on the top of it almost before he'd finished pinning it up.

'I'm buggered if I'm having any of them in my place,' he grunted, grumpily.

'Come, on," Rusty said, 'You love it really!'

'Bollocks!' was the reply.

The day arrived and several groups of twenty or so parents and kids were being trailed round the whole site. Unfortunately someone had not informed the leaders, the kids again, of the staff who *didn't* want to see anyone or have their teaching areas swamped by rubber-necking cretins. Chewy was in full flood with the Sixth Form when the door opened and the room filled with people, pushing each other to get in. A small terrified fourteen year old had brought them in and had immediately spotted Chewy's face which was quickly turning purple with silent rage. Chewy had great difficulty in preventing himself giving vent to his feelings and with some effort tried to ignore them. That was difficult with some of them looking over his shoulder and one snotty nosed brat began fiddling with his paperwork. It was a tricky few minutes. The Sixth Form were waiting for the explosion but it fortunately didn't come. As they traipsed back out Chewy began to calm down and as things began to return to normal another mob came stumbling in. That was too much for Chewy. He drew himself up to his full furry height and gave forth, loudly, stunning each visitor into complete silence.

'Ladies and gentlemen!' he boomed. 'Would you mind leaving. We're a little busy at the moment and cannot have you here. Now, if you would just turn and go, thank you!'

They did. The Sixth Form relaxed visibly. They knew what Chewy was like when he snapped. It could be quite dangerous being within reach when he did. Then as they all calmed and settled again the worst of possible noises could be heard coming from the stairs. Many feet were coming up and a small voice could be heard 'explaining things'.

'And this is where...'

Chewy was across the room like a rocket, slamming the door and flicking the lock shut. He walked sedately back to the Sixth Form and picked up where he had suddenly left them. On the other side of the door there was a muffled conversation going on and then a knocking began. Chewy ignored this completely and carried on talking. The knocking became louder and Chewy stopped. He sighed deeply and scratched his head, looking up at the ceiling. Then he walked off down to the other end and disappeared down the other new staircase. The Sixth Form were fascinated about what he was going to do.

The knocking stopped and then the shuffling of feet could just be heard going back down the stairs. By this time Chewy had walked back along through the workshop below and locked that door from the inside. He was damned if they were going to get in there. That left the entrance. He listened as the last visitor bundled out of the building then emerged from the workshop to lock the door to the staff office as well as the front door to the building. Now the place was secure. What he didn't know was that a particularly nosy couple with their brat of a child had walked into the office, and were happily turning over papers and sifting through the shelves, looking at everything.

He climbed back up the stairs to the Sixth Form and continued the lesson with them. As he did so the father of the little trio in the office tried the door but found it locked. Upstairs Chewy ignored the sound of knocking and then the hammering on the inside of the office door, dismissing it as another group of punters trying to come through the front door. The mother of the family became quite hysterical thinking they would be there until their bodies were found. Her husband began to push and heave at the door but it wouldn't budge. He waved frantically at people passing by but they couldn't see through the window because of the security plastic over the glass. The brat began to cry and then wet itself, sinking down in one corner and blubbering.

An hour later Chewy came down after the lesson, unlocked the outer door to allow the Sixth Form to leave, and opened the office door. By this time the trapped couple were in a hell of a state. Their small brat was still hunched in the same, rather damp corner, tears streaming down its face and the row which then took place, between Chewy and its parents, was quite educational, from a language point of view at least.

At this point in the term an event which had many staff moaning about were the entrance tests for the next academic year. This was yet another total farce and hated by most of the staff. The exceptions to this were the management and particularly the Wide Mouthed Frog and Harvey Sheasby. They viewed the whole affair as a stimulating event in which they could pick and choose the cream of those applying, so ensuring the highest possible standard for the school and the league tables, a very important consideration. It had, of course, nothing to do with the fact that they, the parents, had forked out fifty pounds a head for the privilege of subjecting their kids to the ordeal. This was literally one of the most profitable days for the School, although no one ever found out where the money, all five thousand pounds or more, ended up.

The business of the tests began with a briefing which Wooden always gave. He began weedling on in his monotone, twerpy voice but most ignored him as usual. They'd been through the routine so many times before. Still he kept going like a clockwork monkey who eventually winds down. Some of the staff were to handle the written tests of Maths, English and an essay. The rest were plugged into the interviewing process, including most of the Escape Committee. Not one of them was looking forward to it.

'Last year was bloody awful!' Chewy complained. 'The lot I had could only talk about bloody 'Barbie dolls' or 'Rambo'!'

'You should have seen one of the little smart arses I had,' Rusty said. 'Eleven years old and she was telling me that this wasn't so nice as her last school and the test papers in the morning were very boring. She'd already done them at home twice before!'

The main irritation for the staff wasn't just the tedious business of the tests or awful chore of interviewing gormless, precocious or just plain stupid little kids. It was the fact that they were expected to give up the better part of a Saturday to do it when they would rather have been anywhere but at the School.

The written tests were relatively straightforward. Staff would read through questions and then the kids were expected to write their answers down through a series of timed sections. The interviews were quite different but were completely flawed in their fundamental organisation and approach. With normal grown ups they may have stood a chance at getting some sense out of the kids but with a staff like this they didn't stand a chance. The interviews took place after lunch, which had been provided for the kids who, by now, were mostly drained and bog-eyed from the written tests.

Staff were paired, male and female, and given groups of around ten each. These forlorn little groups were then marched off to a classroom where they were interviewed one by one. This was supposed to give a 'valuable' indication of personality, interests, enthusiasm and God knows what else. Jolly emphasised to all the staff how useful he found their written comments of each interview when he came to deciding which of the little darlings would be allowed in and permission given for their parents to shell out thousands of pounds a year for the privilege.

In any staff room there is a wide range of types and characters and this was certainly true of the School. Given that the most bizarre collection of headcases inhabited the place, a reasoned interview from any of them was, in fact, a total and absolute impossibility. A standard sheet had to be filled in for every child from notes and comments made during the interview. This always took place in the common room afterwards. Some of the comments which floated around in there later on were choice. The Poisoned Dwarf, Art, and Action, the

Outdoor Activities nutcase, were agonising over all of the kids they had interviewed. A more diverse couple could not be imagined.

'Well, I don't know,' she was saying. 'I asked all of them what they thought about the 'T'ang' period of Chinese art and how that might have influenced European art forms, but not one of them could give me an answer!'

Action came out with an equally mindless statement.

'I know exactly what you mean,' he said. 'None of them knew what a crampon was!'

The average age of the group they had been interviewing was just less than eleven years old. Interview comments and the results of the tests were duly assessed by Jolly and a final list of new entrants was drawn up. It bore no relation whatsoever to the brighter or more enthusiastic ones. It seemed totally random in choice. The Escape Committee looked down the list which appeared on one of the notice boards in the staff room a week later.

'That one sat and picked his nose during the whole time I was talking to him!' Lill said.

Chewy clapped his hand to his face.

'I don't believe it!' he said. 'That one couldn't stop farting!'

There were other equally unsavoury individuals who had squeezed through the net.

The worst was the one Harry had seen.

'See that one,' he said.

The rest nodded.

'He didn't listen to a word I was saying, didn't give me a single answer to any question and when I managed to catch his attention he told me to piss off!'

'Could have been worse,' Vic said.

'God only knows what we have ahead of us for next year!' said Chewy.

'Something to look forward to then!' Rusty said.

So much for entrance test day but the crop of kids who had arrived at the beginning of this academic year had been testing all of them in a way they hadn't experienced before. Most normal eleven year old kids, when they arrive in a new, large, school are usually open eyed, open mouthed and as busy as hell to find out as much as they can. Enthusiasm at this age is absolute. They quickly realise that they not only have a larger measure of freedom but are also dealing with 'bigger' people and 'bigger' subjects and usually in much 'bigger' environment which they haven't experienced before.

That was true of most of them but some in this new mob were quite different. Within three weeks the staff found that out. They were dishonest, lazy, foul mouthed and evil in a way which extraordinary for such a young age. 'Laid back' is an expression which fitted most of them but there were other, more pertinent, single word descriptions. Most of them didn't extend beyond four letters.

'Have you come across that little shit, Hampton?' Harry asked one morning.

'Hampton, Farson, Brooke, Panford, Brotherton as well as Lomas-Teasden!' Rusty said, having just had a belly-full of all of them.

'Full marks for the memory man!' Compo said.

'Harry's right,' Lil said. 'Hampton is pure poison and so are the others you've just mentioned.'

Vic had to agree. He'd had more contact than most with these little buggers and as priest, chaplain and counsellor he'd been unable to make a dent in their emotional make up. Chewy had. His had been a much more basic relationship. Only the previous day he had all six of them, amongst a group of normal kids. The first few minutes of that session had shown him he was dealing with a dangerous bunch of spiteful, evil little bastards. One of them had openly stuck a compass into one of the other kids and drawn blood, and when Chewy had 'extracted' him, with one hand, by the scruff of the neck, he'd attempted to do this same thing to him. Chewy had been too quick and grabbed his hand turning it deftly into his attackers own hand. The scream which he gave out was much appreciated by the rest of them.

Chewy held this creature above the floor, gently squeezing his neck until he stopped wriggling. Then he was dropped, before the blood supply to his neck became critical, with one word being spoken. That was, *Sit!'* He did and, with the other five, was no further trouble for the rest of the session.

All of the six had been recruited as choristers, always a difficult slot to fill, and it became very obvious that this lot were the scrapings of the uttermost bottom level of the proverbial barrel. During services fights would break out in the ranks and even after that had been quelled, under pain of expulsion from the choir, not the school, they cottoned on to being able to use the system to get out of many lessons.

The multi-purpose story routine was used regularly, one version to the choir master, another to the house master, yet another to various subject staff and by the time all those had been eventually checked they had missed the bulk of their lessons for just over a month.

All of this was reported back to Jolly but, in the true tradition of a man terrified to upset the parents, he did nothing about it. The problem became worse not better. They were a constant source of irritation to all staff for some time but a few simply ejected them, one by one, from their lessons. Every one of the Escape Committee were included in this and on one occasion Chewy frog marched two of them, holding on to them by the back of their collars, round to Jolly's study and unceremoniously dumped them with him.

'You allowed them in,' he said, 'You deal with them!' and he walked off leaving Jolly to do just that.

Eventually after months of chaos caused by the six of them, two of the worst were 'asked to leave', a euphemism for expulsion. This was just another one of Jolly's little ways of not influencing the infamous league tables. If he had only realised that most of the parents would have applauded him for having the guts to kick these little bastards out. With the two most obnoxious and poisonous of the six now gone things began to settle again, but it took a while.

5

As the term progressed they still had a few problem kids and this was not made easier by the inept attitude of one particular member of the 'management'. That was the Wide Mouthed Frog. It took a hell of a lot longer than it should have done to establish a sensible policy in the school for difficult or screwed up kids. Her interference, via her new 'responsible' role as second Deputy, together with 'help' from Rollerball, another nutter on the staff, simply perpetuated the difficulties.

Rollerball was a very interesting character. He taught Geography. Harvey Sheasby was his Head of Department and as part of Harvey's 'empire', he presented a weather forecast once a week. Harvey was very proud of this seeing it as an invaluable asset to the School and a useful 'service' for the many outdoor extra mural activities or game matches which the School participated in, either at home or away. Wherever they'd acquired their 'Mickey Mouse' equipment to do this was a mystery, probably from 'Toys R Us', but Rollerball continued to deliver his ponderous weekly pronouncements, all of which were invariably wrong, much to the chagrin of all.

He also thought he had a certain 'pastoral' skill and became an unofficial second in command to the Wide Mouthed Frog in the hope of gaining more kudos with Jolly. Unknown to him his nickname of Rollerball had been given by the Escape Committee, inspired by the way he walked, hands in pockets, striding along, but appearing to have something unspeakable going inside his trousers.

The Escape Committee eventually noticed how he and Wide Mouth had become more conspiratorial. They were always walking round the place deep in conversation or huddled in one corner of the staff room mumbling in hushed whispers.

'What are those two silly sods up to?' Lill said during one afternoon break.

'They make a lovely couple,' Harry grinned.

'Probably organising a dirty weekend,' Rusty said, not bothering to look.

'What a horrible bloody thought!' Chewy said. 'Can you imagine...'

'No!' Lill said. 'Don't even think about it!'

Vic became quite depressed at what he saw.

'I have a terrible sinking feeling,' he said, 'that they might well be organising some half arsed 'care' scheme.'

He had hit the mark exactly. They were.

'Well,' Wide Mouth was saying. 'I do think we need to be on full alert. There are some very funny things going on in this school and I think we need to be doing something about it. Some of them get up to the most, well, undesirable things! There is a definite need for explaining certain 'things' to them before we have a 'problem' with some of the ones who might 'experiment'. I don't think I'd like to see 'that' happening at all!'

Rollerball nodded, sagely. He was a greasy sod. His whole manner, movement and speech was one of self satisfaction, a smug attitude always being projected. He was, as Chewy had already commented, 'someone who had a face worth punching'. Both Wide Mouth and Rollerball missed the fundamental point that any normal kid would 'experiment' whether it was fags, booze or sex. They wouldn't be normal if they didn't. The knack of helping them over these 'spasms' of experimentation was in guiding them to better things and not jumping all over them for reacting normally. As neither of them had ever been normal it wasn't surprising they were both frustrated, spiteful shits.

'I so agree with you,' Rollerball oozed. 'And I have often thought that some of the Fifth Form need a place to go. Some of them spend far too much time getting up to mischief in various parts of the school where we don't see them. If we had a common room for them somewhere, just as the Sixth Form have, we could at least pin them down much more easily.'

They both had an approach to kids which had more to do with 'correction' than understanding. Their whole attitude was one of a prison system rather than trust, although neither of them would ever have realised it. If staff like these two had been in control of all the kids it would have been certain that a full scale rebellion might have taken place. It was only later and careful sabotage to their plans which prevented anything like this happening.

With an idea worked out between them the pair of them waddled off, sickly, self satisfied grins on their faces, to see Jolly.

'Now,' Jolly beamed at them. 'I understand you both have a recommendation for me.'

'Yes, Headmaster,' Wide Mouth said, as sweetly as she could. 'We have.'

'Oh, good!' Jolly settling himself expectantly in his chair. 'Fire away then!'

They outlined their suggestions but had to do it all over again as Jolly wasn't always able to understand straightforward propositions. He needed time to have any new suggestion rephrased, repeated, restated and then explained again and in the simplest of language before he could grasp anything. It was a slow process but he eventually understood, before he himself usually cocked things up later on. This time someone else did that for him.

'So, what you're suggesting is this.' Jolly said. 'We should extend the P.S.E. programme, the Personal Social Education programme, for the younger ones and provide somewhere for the Fifth Form to use as a common room or centre of some sort. Is that right?'

'Yes, Headmaster!' they both said.

As they left Jolly's study their faces were wreathed in smiles. Rusty walked past them as they emerged from the main building. What he saw he didn't like. Something was up and he had to find out about it. The only person who was likely to know was the Mad Hatter.

'All I know,' Maisie said, 'is that they both had their plans agreed by himself.'

'So what were they?' Rusty asked.

'She's going to give the kids more sex education for a start.' Maisie answered, pulling a face. 'And they're looking for somewhere to use as a Fifth Form common room.'

It seemed harmless enough, but Rusty knew that with Wide Mouth and Rollerball involved there was a very good chance of disaster following quickly behind. He decided he needed to consult with the others on the Escape Committee. They would have to keep an eye on this.

After a couple of days the effect of part of their plan began to show itself. A number of the eleven and twelve year olds were taken with a strange malady. Their symptoms were the same. They all appeared to be in shock but the resident nurse couldn't figure out why. She managed to track down their last few hours by using the main timetable in the office. Then she talked to all the staff who had been teaching the kids. All of them were happy to explain what they had been doing.

English, French, Art and several other subjects had been identified but nothing horrific had been demonstrated or talked about. Even the three Science subjects hadn't covered anything to explain why the kids had been reduced to such a state. Not until she came to the Wide Mouthed Frog, and what she had been doing with them, did the reason emerge. As the nurse walked into Wide Mouth's room she saw immediately what the cause of the problem might be. Along the whole length of one wall were a number of huge wall posters. They were all highly detailed and produced to an enormous scale and in full colour, of the male and female reproductive organs in various stages of 'activity'. Wide Mouth was in there at the time, preparing for her next lesson. She looked up at the nurse entered.

'Oh, hello,' she said. 'What can I do for you?'

The nurse couldn't speak for a few seconds. She was still transfixed by the posters and what they were showing.

'Ah, yes,' she said, pulling herself together. 'Can you tell me what you were doing this morning with the children? We seem to have a few who aren't feeling too well.'

'Really?' Wide Mouth said. 'What seems to be the trouble?'

'Well,' the nurse began. 'It seems that whatever they were doing during this morning has upset them. I'm just trying to find out what it might have been. I've been round all the other staff but they couldn't shed any light on the problem at all. I wondered if you could help?'

Wide Mouth shifted in her chair, a puzzled look on her face. She was totally unaware of the effect the posters had on the nurse or the children earlier

'Well,' she said, pensively. 'I took them through the reproductive process with the help of these posters.' She waved a hand at the heavy 'porn' on the wall. 'After that I showed them a couple of video's on birth, you know, close up stuff so they'd get the idea, but apart from that I can't think what might have upset them.'

She stood up and pulled down a video from a shelf.

'I'll show you what they were looking at if that would help.'

The nurse couldn't believe her eyes. What she was looking at would scare the hell out of anyone let alone eleven and twelve year old kids. Wide Mouth just sat looking at the graphic close up scenes on the TV set, licking her lips at every scene.

'I know some people get squeamish about this sort of thing,' she said, loving every detailed image. 'But it's just life, after all.'

It took the kids three days to come out of their trauma. The Escape Committee had a few ideas about what to do about this and they implemented their best one. A couple of anonymous phone calls were made to the local Vice Squad and they sat back to watch. An hour later Wide Mouth's classroom had been surrounded by police and she was escorted from the place by two policewomen and taken to the local station. The posters were taken as evidence and it took Jolly four hours to have her returned, red in the face and very indignant about having been grilled as a suspect of white slaving. That aspect of P.S.E. didn't surface again.

Meanwhile Rollerball had found what he thought would be the perfect venue for his Fifth Form common room. It was a single storey extension from the back of one of the boarding houses which he thought was empty and unused. He was wrong, but before he found out who actually used it he'd seen Jolly who agreed with him that it would be ideal for what he wanted, a Fifth Form common room. There was only one problem. He didn't have a key to the place. There were two doors on either side of the building but the Bursar, the usual custodian for all keys on the site, had neither.

By chance he saw Compo going into it one lunchtime. Poor old Compo was about to suffer from another act of the withdrawal of his teaching space. Rollerball didn't have the common sense or plain guts to talk to Compo about the place but, instead, went to Wooden to let him 'do the dirty'. Wooden in his usual wooden manner stopped Compo after one of the morning meetings.

'Sorry to delay you Compton but there seems to be a slight problem,' Wooden said in his little monotone fashion.

'Problem?' Compo asked. 'What problem?'

'It's that room at the back of the boarding house,' Wooden said. 'We think it might be useful as a Fifth Form common room.'

'Common room!' Compo said. 'What the hell for?'

'For the Fifth Form,' Wooden said. Always on the ball was Wooden.

'But why there of all places?' Compo asked.

'Well,' Wooden said. 'It's empty.'

'No it isn't!' Compo answered indignantly. 'It's full of costumes and sets for Theatre Arts. Where else am I going to put them?'

Wooden didn't expect that. He didn't know Compo used it for that. He stood staring directly ahead. He was thinking, as much as you could ever detect it.

'Somewhere else,' he eventually said.

'Where?' Compo said, his anger steadily growing at this ridiculous conversation.

'Somewhere else,' Wooden said again, caught in his own mind loop.

Compo threw his hands up and just stomped off.

'Is there a problem with that?' Wooden asked the space where Compo had stood. He waited for an answer but, not surprisingly, he didn't get one.

Another few days were to go by until the situation was resolved and Compo was forced into a compromise which he didn't like. He would take the building over when he was in full 'play' mode. Before and after that it would be used as a common room. Even Rusty's intervention had no effect. The total contents of the place would be dispatched to one of the ground staff's storage sheds which, true to form, was at the other end of the site from the old barn where the plays were performed. Before the Fifth Form took the place over Compo warned the management that it would probably be wrecked in no time by the kids but he was ignored. If they had taken it over they would have done, but as things turned out not one of them ever crossed the threshold. In the staff room Compo grumbled on to the other members of the Escape Committee.

'Come on Compo,' Rusty said. 'Don't let the buggers grind you down!'

'It's not that easy!' Compo snapped back.

Then Rollerball came in and sheepishly asked Compo for the key to the building. Compo glared at him, then fished around in a pocket and thrust it out to him. Rollerball nodded his thanks and crept out.

'He makes my bloody flesh creep!' Compo said. 'It's his whole manner, the whole way he moves.'

The rest of them agreed.

'There has to be some way of screwing his plans up,' Rusty said. 'It shouldn't be too difficult. He's as stupid as the rest of them.'

Rusty had pinpointed the very factor which would play into their hands and give Compo the building back without Rollerball or the management realising how. Rollerball walked down to the room pushed the key into the lock and tried to turn it. It didn't engage. He tried again but couldn't open it. After fiddling about wiggling the key in the lock he gave up. He didn't have any more time before he had to take a lesson.

The following day he approached Compo again and, handing the key back, explained the problem. Compo couldn't understand it. The key worked for him every time. He offered to walk over there and try the key again. With Rollerball in tow off they went. Compo was back in the staff room ten minutes later with a huge grin on his face.

'What's up?' asked Rusty, seeing the glee on Compo's face.

'You know that key I gave to Rollerball?' Compo grinned.

They all nodded.

'It was the wrong one!' He cracked up at this and they had to wait a few seconds before he could tell them the rest of it.

'Oh, sorry about that. It's just so funny!' he giggled.

'Come on then,' Chewy said. 'Share it!'

'Well,' Compo started, composing himself. 'There are two keys, one for each door. The doors are on either side of the building. Both keys look exactly the same. I originally gave him the key to the door on the other side, that's why he couldn't make it open the door on this side! When we went over a few minutes ago I opened the door with the right key but after locking it I switched it with the other key so he won't be able to get in through that door at all!'

'But all he has to do,' Lill said, 'is go round to the other side.'

'Yes, I know,' Compo said. 'But I wonder how long it will take before he works that one out for himself!'

He collapsed into giggles again at the thought. As it turned out Rollerball didn't think of that but brought in a locksmith to check the lock. The following day he sidled up to Compo and told him what the locksmith had said. The advice was that the lock mechanism had 'dropped' and it would need a new lock.

'Oh that can't be right!' Compo said, desperately trying not to laugh. 'Lets go and try it again, shall we?'

He took the key and off they went. Compo opened the door easily and then switched the key again.

'No problem there,' he said. 'Just needs a bit of wiggling.'

He left Rollerball fiddling with the key in the lock.

Meanwhile Chewy had dreamt up an additional wheeze.

'What if I buy a couple of blanks, cut them to look like the real keys, you give them to Rollerball and keep the genuine ones? The he'll never get into the place!'

Compo was delighted and nodded his full agreement.

For the whole of the Escape Committee it was now a spectator sport which continued for weeks. Every other day Rollerball would have a word with Compo about a key and Compo gave him one of the bogus ones Chewy had cut. The whole notion of the Fifth Form common room died slowly. The last touch to this, which the Escape Committee had great trouble trying not to laugh out loud, was seeing Rollerball sitting in the staff room with a key in his hand just staring at it, not understanding why he couldn't get it to work.

As the term rolled on there were other small highlights which kept up the amusement level and one in particular which involved Rollerball again. The first two came from the Music department of the School. Music played a great part in the daily life of the place. Quite a number of the kids were there for just that with a few other subjects 'tacked on' for good measure. The only problem about this was that it made for complicated time tabling and with the buildings the musicians used at the other end of the site an enforced separation between themselves and the rest existed.

Music staff and the rest of them rarely came into contact with each other which didn't help. Kids would come and go to music lessons in the middle of other subjects and this didn't help either. It became a mild irritation for most of the staff, both musicians and academic but there would be no real solution to this without a comprehensive plan for reorganising the whole school with a rolling programme of phased building. This would take years but sooner or later it would have to happen.

In the meantime they bumbled along as best they could with some of the music staff taking advantage of their relative remote position. This was certainly true of the Director of Music, Aaron Crispian. A flamboyant character, Aaron didn't really want to know about anything but making music and developing the skill of musicianship in kids. He certainly had no time for Jolly and his attendant gang of buffoons and would deliberately miss, avoid or forget to attend the endless, mindless meetings which Jolly insisted on inflicting on all of them. He took the same stance to the endless stream of memo's which flew around the place like a paper blizzard.

'Oh, dear,' he would say, looking through his pigeon hole. 'Just look at all this silly paper. It really is too much. Can't people talk to each other any more?'

He made a point of never replying to memorandums of any kind. His philosophy was quite straightforward. If people wanted to communicate with him they could talk to him. It was a simple as that. Two things happened because of this. More memo's would arrive asking for replies to the others and then eventually whoever had sent them, which was invariably one of the management team, would eventually find him and ask why he had ignored them. He would always give the same simple answer.

'Did you want to talk to me?'

The answer was usually 'yes'.

'Then why don't we do just that, old thing, instead of wasting paper, eh?'

After a while they did exactly that, however uncomfortable it was for them, especially Jolly with his chronic paper mania.

Aaron's office was tucked away, together with the necessary administrative staff, in an old building which had originally been a small coach house. It had a pleasant enclosed courtyard and he thought that this should really be used to the full. After all it was a very nice building and needed something to give it that certain edge. Without giving it another thought he ordered hundreds of pounds worth of white, cast iron garden furniture. The weather was improving quickly and he, with others from the music staff, could now spend a few happy hours, whenever possible, enjoying the sunshine while they dealt with the day to day matters of the pupils.

To his surprise this did not go down too well with the other staff in the main school and Jolly was particularly upset. On one of Aaron's rare appearances at the morning meetings Jolly took him to one side and had a word with him.

'Aaron,' he twitched, 'the furniture outside your office is not really what your Departmental budget is for!'

Aaron dismissed that with a casual wave of his hand.

'Oh, come now, Headmaster!' he said smiling broadly. 'What's a few pounds when the whole feeling and ambience of the courtyard and the building has been uplifted by a few pieces of furniture?'

'Yes, but...' Jolly tried to say. Aaron didn't give him a chance to finish that but cut through with a devastating comment which Jolly couldn't cope with.

'Besides,' he said, with same cheery grin on his face, 'when I've had various parents in to see me, they so enjoy it! It makes such a difference being able to sit and converse in such pleasant surroundings and in such a civilised fashion.'

Jolly treated the parents as if they had the power of life and death over him. With that single reference to them Aaron had won his case and no more was said about it. The Fat Controller, Michael Farnsworth Hunt, tried to make a few waves but Jolly was not of a mind to pursue it. At the same time there was another furniture problem which had been developing, or rather shrinking, for some time. That was the next little problem which Jolly had to face.

The Music Department organised a regular series of concerts throughout the year. These ranged through solo performances and small ensembles to full symphony orchestral events. Lunchtimes and after school in the evening were the times designated for these performances and although they used the Cathedral for the large orchestral pieces, most of them took place in the small concert hall of the Music Department itself. At the end of one week, almost halfway through the term, they were getting ready one evening for a concert involving a number of soloists when they hit a major problem. The conversation which then took place between two of the music staff went something like this.

'Hang on. There's something wrong here.'

'What?'

'They're missing!'

'Missing?'

'Look!'

'But they were there yesterday!'

'But where are they now?'

'I don't know. But they were definitely there yesterday!'

'But they're not there now!'

'I can see that!'

'But who would take them?'

'How the hell should I know!'

'Well, we'll have to do something!'

'What?'

'God knows!'

They were talking about the rather annoying fact that fifty, fully upholstered, brand new chairs, delivered only a few days before, had disappeared from the concert room. This was a mystery which took another few days to sort out. The chairs were never found but the individual who had moved them was. After a few sneaks had dropped the odd word here and there to members of staff, it came to light that a Fifth Form pupil, and by this action a highly enterprising member of the symphony orchestra, had taken every one of the chairs out and, with the help of the driver, had loaded them onto the back of a truck the day before. No one had thought to ask what he was doing or had stopped him.

He was paid two quid per chair which he then blew completely on an elicit 'piss up' with the rest of the hooligan fringe of the Fifth and Sixth Form in a quiet, shrub covered corner of one of the boarding house gardens. The management found the pile of 'tinnies' and the carpet of fag ends a day later. Again Jolly was not jolly.

The whole affair was heavily suppressed. That didn't help the story from flashing round the school well before the culprit was found. Everyone, staff and pupils alike, waited for the 'judgement' from on high. They were not surprised by the decision. Instead of immediate expulsion he was sent home until the beginning of the following week. That statement was made on a Thursday, so the lad had the awful prospect of being denied his education for a whole two days plus the terror of a letter home! Jolly really knew how to hand out punishment.

Another event was equally enterprising. One particular Sixth Former, who had a tendency of being an 'individualist', performed a feat which on one hand gave him a certain cache in the eyes of the Sixth Form and at the same time drew abject horror from many of the staff. The Escape Committee felt themselves to be caught between both camps. After one of the Sixth Form parties, which the school organised about twice a term, there were a few who managed to get themselves, as usual, totally pissed. One of them, a rather bolshie character with a slight chip on his shoulder for a few of the staff, particularly the management, decided to raid the staff common room. His approach was direct and, in the circumstances, surprisingly daring. He didn't break the door down. No. He climbed up the drainpipe and came in through one of the unlocked windows.

Once there he emptied the booze cupboard on the wall and then proceeded to help himself to the contents of the fridge. He had a tricky time clambering back down with a very heavy, black plastic sack which tended to 'clank' a bit, but with great drunken determination he made it safely into the arms of the few who were waiting for him below and the rest of that night was a liquid delight for all of them. The morning was less delightful. Several of the Sixth Form were given odd looks by several staff but, if they'd had any brains, they would have recognised the obvious hangovers which were not being handled very well.

The 'burglary' wasn't discovered until early that evening and then the witch hunt began. Jolly, Wide Mouth and even that shit Rollerball intimidated every Sixth Former who they knew could be manipulated to their will. They were questioned endlessly and eventually a name came forward as the likely suspect. He, naturally, denied it but the staff who had a more easy relationship with the Sixth Form knew it was him. Even so Jolly decided to take punitive action. No, he didn't expel him. What would the parents say? He sent him home for a week!

The name of this character was Hoddinott and from then on every time the Escape Committee, or anyone else who used the cupboard on the wall, an 'Hoddy' would be offered from the optics in recognition of both the offence and the leniency of the sentence passed down by the terrified management. Quite a few 'Hoddy's' were consumed over the following weeks to the health of that adventurous young man. More than just the Escape Committee were glad to see that some straightforward 'guts' were still around in the pupil population.

The pathetic statement Jolly made after both of these incidents was one which left the Escape Committee in despair. Could he have really said that? The statement he made went something like this.

'As you all know this has been a rather disturbing affair. Although the police have not been involved there may be some interest shown from the national press. If you are approached by a reporter will you please say nothing at all and refer them to me and me alone. I do not want the parents upset any more than they need to be.'

He wasn't referring to the parents of the kids involved but to the whole parental body. As far as the national press being involved, well, that was hardly likely, but no one bothered to tell him. They were happy to let him fret about that all by himself.

The other Rollerball incident was one which had the Escape Committee rolling around with great mirth for quite a while. One of the Sixth Form who had witnessed the whole thing took great delight in telling Lill, although Jolly thought he had successfully covered it up. Rollerball had, apparently, been applying his sickening avuncular mode, trying to perform as an understanding and pastorally, squeaky clean, good egg. One of the Sixth Form, a girl, had been looking a little upset about something during his lesson and as the rest of them trouped out afterwards, he took her to one side closed the door and slimily coaxed out of her what the trouble was.

He didn't have the sense to realise that anyone with any brains at all would never, never place themselves, in private, with an emotionally stressed young girl, especially one who was known to be on the 'rampant' side. She had just broken up with her boyfriend, a simple enough situation, but instead of treating it lightly he went into full sympathetic mode. This had a reaction which had him running from the room, his hair disarranged, his tie skewed from his neck and holding on to the top of his trousers, which had somehow come undone.

A few of the Sixth Form had been peering through the window and had seen all. After patting her hand she began to cheer up and then, as her general demeanour had improved so had the urge for which she was notorious. Suddenly, she was all over him, pulling her shirt out and dragging his hand into, for him, highly personal territory. Then she had yanked at his trousers and that's when he managed to pull away from her and leg it out of the room, looking terrified at the near rape which had almost occurred. He didn't provide comfort like that again.

As half term appeared on the educational horizon most of the staff were looking forward to disappearing to recharge their leaking batteries and massage their ailing enthusiasm. The only person on the staff who was anywhere near being positive and excited about the near future was Quentin Braumsley, bless him. His project was now beginning to take shape. His room had proved to be too small for the work he'd already started and weeks before he had taken over the main floor area of the library. He'd done this with the blessing of his mother, Lady B, who had been more than willing to help in any way she could. Anyone else would, and should, have been extremely suspicious if not downright nervous about her enthusiastic support for this project. She had never been one to show such outright and emphatic understanding for any single idea her brainless son had ever had.

She had suggested the move to the library in the first place. After all how could he be expected to run backwards and forwards from the shelves with all the reference material which he would need for this highly important scheme? Quentin saw this as an undertaking which the School would be delighted with and would treasure. The effect upon the overall image of the School would be so much more forthright. They would be forever in his debt. Well, that's what Quentin thought. Her thoughts were of a darker and much more evil nature.

'Oh, Mummy!' he squeaked. 'This is coming on so well! It's such fun!'

'Yes dear,' she said, a terrible grimace sliding across her face which was as close as she could get to a smile.

He was bobbing up and down, patting his little hands together, a look of sheer delight on his face, in front of a large, long table which had been temporarily and specially rigged up for the project. At one end of this a confused mass of paper was strewn around mixed with rolled up plans of the whole school site. The rest of it had the beginnings of a large scale model of a building. Before he began he had spent weeks researching the project from the enormous collection of books in the family library which had been scrupulously organised and brought together by his father over many years. Centuries of Braumsley's had been careful to add the great works of their day to this, now vast, cornucopia of information.

All the great works of architecture and architects had been consulted. Lady B had followed his progress at all times giving encouragement and support as he struggled with the more complicated mathematics of structure and the subtleties of aesthetics. When he actually began the design process his mother had offered suggestions and pointed out various kinds of reference material from the extensive collection of publications from art to architecture all of which, she said, would be of particular use and importance in this prestigious proposal.

With the design complete, and to her immense satisfaction, he then began the next stage. This was to be a highly detailed model of the building which would show everyone exactly what it would look like. He didn't want to rely on drawings alone. No, this was something which could be used to show prospective parents. It was to be a show piece in its own right. He had even thought of adding a simple electrical circuit and tiny bulbs to illuminate the interior. He wanted everything to be as perfect as possible.

Once it was finished there would be only one place, the ideal place, to exhibit this architectural masterpiece. That was in the reception area immediately outside the Headmaster's office. It was the only place it could go, the only place it should go, and wouldn't he be pleased? Of course he would.

'It's coming on very well, dear,' Lady B said, patting Quentin on the head.

'Oh,' Quentin beamed. 'Do you really think so?'

'Of course,' she said. 'Of course.'

'I'm so pleased you do,' he said. 'I know it's taking a long time but I'm trying to make it as perfect as I can.'

'I know you are dear, I think it's wonderful how much you've been able to achieve already. You mustn't rush these things you know. We wouldn't want any silly mistakes now, would we?'

Quentin shook his head and smiled a sickening smile. Lady B hadn't been this good to him since he was tiny. He didn't want anything to get in the way of that and he was very careful to be as adoring as possible during the whole project. He needn't have worried. She was oblivious of his sycophantic quackings and fawning prancing. All she wanted to ensure was the full delivery, in three dimensions and in perpetuity, of the statement which he had first come home with. That was, 'Something which the school really deserves'. By the way the project was going it would be exactly that and worth every penny. She patted him on the head again and left him to it, clacking out from the library with her stick, her huge bulk plodding forward with great purpose into her private boudoir where she made a long and detailed phone call.

6

They were half way through the second hymn in the Cathedral when Chewy noticed one of the staff sidling over to him.

'Oh, shit!' he thought to himself. 'Not again!'

There was no possible way he could escape. The self righteous pompous bastard would be handing it over any minute, a smug grin on his stupid bloody face. The person in question was Nigel St John Burroughs, ex public school, graduate from Cambridge, teacher of Economics and Statistics, one of the members of the school choir and a total snob. He was also the Chairman of the staff common room and loved his position immensely. His role was a simple one. He made himself available, as he described it, as a 'conduit' for information to Jolly. The fact that no one ever bothered to tell him anything, except what he could do with his 'conduit', didn't give him the clue to what they all thought of him.

Known to all as the 'Head Boy', he lived in another world, rarely coming into the real one. And here he was again, with one of his 'funny' alternatives to the words of this hymn. They were, in fact, singularly unfunny but this silly bugger thought they were 'rather splendid' and 'rather racy, what?' Insisting on sharing them with whoever was unfortunate enough to be standing next to him. Luckily the service came to an end and, by some deft footwork, Chewy was able to get away from him in the throng of kids who had stood and were now walking back to School. Nigel had been on the point of dredging out all the other 'alternative' lyrics he had written for hymns so that Chewy and he could have a 'chuckle' on the way back. All of them were dreadful bits of doggerel. Chewy made sure he increased the distance between him and Nigel as much as he could.

Back in the staff room the usual scrum for coffee took place but then Jolly walked in. This was unusual. He normally didn't appear there at all after the service. It had to be a special. It was. Taking up his normal position he waited for the clatter of cups to die down, fiddling with his file of paper, and then as the staff settled he began.

'Good morning, everyone.'

A grudging hush fell over them all.

'I know that I don't usually see you at this time,' he said. 'But I have some news which I'd like to share with you all.'

'He's leaving!' Lill whispered.

'He's staying!' Haffy mumbled.

'He's useless!' Rusty said.

'He's a twat!' Chewy added.

'I received a telephone call yesterday,' Jolly said, beaming a wide smile, 'which gave me a wonderful surprise!'

'He IS leaving!' Lill hissed again.

'He's lying!' Vic mumbled.

'He's barmy!' Haffy whispered.

'He's still a twat!' Chewy rumbled.

Jolly continued.

'It came from a source which I would prefer not to reveal at the moment, but it concerned the offer of a major new building for the school!'

'He's joking!' Vic mumbled.

'He's isn't!' hissed Lill.

'He must be!' Haffy whispered.

'He'll always be a twat!' Chewy mumbled.

The buzz of muted, but intense conversation whipped round the room but Jolly made a final statement above it all.

'I shall keep you informed as soon as I have any more news.'

With that said he closed the file he was holding and strode out with Wooden scuttling along behind him.

'Bloody typical!' Chewy said. 'When does he ever give us enough information? It always has to be dished out in bloody silly little bits. I wish he would just save it up and tell us all in one go instead of these bloody 'magisterial bulletins' he insists on delivering!'

The rest of them nodded. Chewy was right. Jolly was always doing that.

'I'd like to bet that he keeps this going for weeks,' Rusty said. 'We'll be having up-dates right up till the end of friggin term.'

He was right. They did.

The telephone conversation which Jolly had told them about had been with Lady Braumsley and it was mostly one way, her way. When the Mad Hatter had first transferred the call to Jolly he'd picked it up and then immediately stood to attention. It was his funny little way of giving his own form of mindless respect for the one member of the aristocracy who literally had him by the 'buildings and land'. He hardly had a chance to speak on this occasion and spent most of the time nodding and adding the odd 'umm' or 'ahh' or 'yes' with an occasional 'of course' to all she said.

'And that brings me to my penultimate point,' Lady B was now saying. 'I will be not be able to show you the final project until nearer the end of this term. As you will appreciate there has been a great deal of preparation behind it and the architect is very concerned that it should only be 'unveiled', as it were, to those individuals who are directly involved. We must be sure that there will be no chance of any news of this leaking out.'

Jolly's thoughts were running wild. This was obviously a huge project for her to be devoting so much time, effort and what must surely be a very, very large amount of money. He didn't give a thought about why she was doing it. He was completely thrown by the fact that she was. Lady B continued to drone on.

'Finally, all the necessary paperwork will be handled by the estate solicitors. This will also include all the applications for planning permission and building regulation approval. I am most concerned that everything should fall into place without any hold ups or unnecessary delays.'

This was just another way of saying she didn't want him involved at all. She had seen the way he usually cocked up everything he touched. She was still going strong.

'So I need your written agreement, which will also be drawn up by my legal team, that you will fully accept the building which is even now being finalised. Do you understand?'

Jolly nodded. Lady B couldn't hear that and pulled the classic of looking down into the mouthpiece of the phone and bellowing the same question again.

'*DO YOU UNDERSTAND!*'

'I... I understand!' he squeaked.

'Good,' she said. 'Then the final signature, from you on behalf of the whole Governing body, for the full acceptance of the design and consequent construction, will take place in your office on the last day of term, immediately before the unveiling of the model.'

'Y..yes,' he whispered, 'Th...th...thank you very much', as she put the phone down on him.

Not a lot happened over the next few days. Things moved on towards half term but a minor event, a conversation overheard by Maggie between Wide Mouth and Harvey, gave her a real test of controlling her laughter. She reported this to the Escape Committee and as they smirked at her tale Lill succinctly summed up their collective thoughts.

'Only that stupid old bag could have said something like that.'

Maggie had walked up to the staff room to borrow a few spoonfuls of coffee as Maisie's stock was running a little low. When she arrived, Wide Mouth and the School nurse, Grace Sawyer, the same one who had discovered the graphic posters on Wide Mouth's wall, were sitting at the same table. Grace wasn't too happy at being alone with the old trout and was on the point of leaving when Harvey Sheasby came in. He went straight for the notice board, as he usually did, scanning it for 'important' notices. He always found something insignificant to fret about and, sure enough, he began reading something which qualified. Grace was on her way out when Harvey turned and spoke to her.

'Oh, Grace. Glad you're here. It's just that I'm having a bit of trouble with this.'

He pointed at the notice he'd been reading, written by her about one of the girls in the Lower Sixth.

'You say,' he said, 'that this young lady has a problem in that she is... I can't read that next word.'

Grace flapped her hands and apologised. 'Oh, I am sorry, my handwriting! The girl's just been doing too much and needs rest. The word you're probably having a problem with is '*exhausted*'. Do you know, I can never spell that word properly.'

Before either of them could say anything more Wide Mouth made one of her classic responses. Sitting back in her chair, legs wide apart – yukk! – she said, '*Eeehh, j'know I have the same problem with 'diarrhoea'.*'

Totally misunderstanding this Harvey's reply was, 'Oh, I am sorry!'

Half term arrived and the whole School drifted through the last day to 4.30pm when they could all vanish to distant lands and a welcome ten days of peace and relaxation. The Escape Committee, all with free periods, began their countdown in the staff room making a final check on the contents of the wall cupboard. There was no point in thinking about going yet as the place would be completely hemmed in by parents' cars arriving and departing with day and boarding pupils. That always took at least an hour to clear.

Two hours later Lill had gone home followed by Compo, Vic and then Harry. Maggie had made a brief appearance but now only Rusty and Chewy remained. They were well on their way to being less than co-ordinated. After another 'educational libation', then, 'one for the road', and a final, 'here's to god'ole Jolly!', they staggered out of the staff room and down the stairs. Once outside they found the place was deserted. Not a single child in sight. It was a wonderful experience. It was also quite dark.

'Juss think what y'could really do with this place,' Rusty said, whimsically

'Yeah,' Chewy replied. 'Me first on the bull-dozer!'

On their way through the site they came across a greenhouse. This was an ancient structure which had been around, as they say, 'since Adam was a lad'. They peered in through the streaked and dusty panes of glass. Along one side they could just make out a short row of seed packets, all bunched up together, with a label sitting on top of them.

'Wazatsay?' Chewy muttered.

'Dunno,'; Answered Rusty. 'Lezfineout!'

They set off along the greenhouse side, bumping off each other and round to the door which was unlocked. Once inside it was quite a cosy atmosphere, a good ten degrees higher than the air outside. Chewy unsteadily picked up the label from the seed packets and handed it, in a rather formal and ceremonious fashion, to Rusty.

'You're the Head of English,' he said pompously, 'you read it.'

Rusty took it from him and blinked several times, trying to focus. Then he straightened up and read it out loud, as if he was delivering a heavy Shakespearean text. It was a brief message, which stated, 'Seeds for all School gardens. Planting must take place during the half term break. See drawing on reverse'

'Couldn't agree more,' Chewy said, with a hic-cup.

Rusty turned the label over and found a sketch of the site with different dots indicating where all the packets should be planted.

They both then had the same idea at the same time. After another few minutes they had 'adjusted' the sketch, replaced it and teetered out into the night. What ever came up in the gardens over the next few weeks would be an interesting spectacle. It certainly wouldn't be the plan that Quentin Braumsley had orgainsed.

After the half term break two further examples of brief and barmy skirmishes with stupidity took place. One was 'foreign' and the other was 'fire power' and both provided a few smiles for the Escape Committee. The first was to keep them entertained through the remaining part of the term but the other one, in the second part of the term, was quite extraordinary.

The first event concerned an exchange of staff from abroad. Staff exchanges had been going on for a number of years and the one Braumstate had managed to organise was no exception if only a little more exotic than most. At the beginning of the academic year Jolly had seen an ad in Times Ed. and written off to reply. A couple of weeks later a letter from a school in Pusan, a coastal city in the south of Korea, dropped onto his desk. A long process of correspondence then took place over three months. The Mad Hatter took that over. She knew that Jolly would screw it up completely if she left it to him.

She handled all the arrangements and an exchange of staff between the two schools proceeded without a hitch. Maisie might have appeared to be an old battle axe sometimes but she was extremely efficient, which was probably just as well with someone like Jolly around. Two of the science staff agreed to go to Pusan and they were looking forward to the experience but not the language. With little fuss off they went.

Just before half term the two Korean, Pusan staff arrived. Jolly had arranged for them to stay with him during the break. The idea was to allow them to settle in over the week of the short holiday and then they would move to rented accommodation, paid for by the School. Once that was done they would join the rest of the staff to begin the remaining half of the term. The Escape Committee wondered how they would be able to remain sane even during that short time with Jolly. The slightest contact with him usually had a devastating effect on any normal person's mental state. It would be interesting to see how they would actually cope.

On the first day back after the holiday two diminutive figures walked into the staff room for the morning meeting and were introduced by Jolly to all. Both male, one was a chemistry specialist and the other a former Olympic pentathlon champion. He would be helping out with P.E. The school they came from didn't have another Science teacher so the Science Department of Braumstate would just have to cope. They were not happy.

Rusty was not impressed. When the Mad Hatter had told him that two Korean teachers were due to arrive he had hoped that one of them would be female. He had a 'yen' for Orientals. So did Lil. She perked up considerably when she found out they were both male. No one on the staff could understand the coincidental fact that a small crop of six Korean kids arrived at the School at the same time.

'Jolly must have a deal going,' Rusty said. 'Let six in and you get two free!'

The plus side to this was that the Korean staff could at least speak English, albeit broken and halting. The negative side was that the kids couldn't speak a word. That eventually resolved itself, for by the time they left the school the following year, they could communicate easily in the most horrific expletives known to western society. The indigenous population of the School had seen to that. Such is the power of 'passive' education.

The beginning of the remaining half term proved to be a traumatic period for Duane Hedley, the P.E. oaf. It was the first time in years that he'd worked up a sweat. The Korean rang rings around his flabby body and old Duane, 'The Pain', as he was now known, began complaining of pulled muscles, cramp and a wide catalogue of bodily ailments as he tried to compete with this 'sideways job', as he called this Korean fitness freak.

The one teaching chemistry was no less effective and he kept the whole of the Science Department on their toes for the rest of the term. The only area where both of the Koreans were less than sure about were the niceties of English social language and how best they could communicate the every day things of life. They had worked long and hard to improve on this but there were still areas of doubt in this new language which still mystified them but they continued to grapple with it.

This lack of a full working knowledge of the language had been their salvation while staying with Jolly. Not fully understanding what he meant most of the time had acted as an antidote to all his little ways. Ignorance can be bliss some times. The Escape Committee were slightly disappointed by this but there was at least a small bonus coming for all of them. A session in the staff room, one lunch time, saw the Koreans asking yet another set of basic questions in their quest to come to terms with the English language. This time they were concerned with being polite and being sure of saying the right thing at the right time. Wide Mouth and Harvey Sheasby were sitting with them. The Escape Committee sat around in the background listening.

'Iss velly difcult some time to be collect!' One was saying. They were both very keen on being 'collect'.

'How tlue!' said the other. 'Fo inst, when should say 'goo bawning'?'

'No, no. That's 'good morning'', Harvey said, smiling knowingly, and explained when that would be an appropriate greeting.

'Ah!' said the first. 'I see. Good. Good. But what bout 'Hell how yoo!' That tlicky one!'

Wide Mouth took that and explained it to them.

'The 'correct' greeting,' she said, smiling smarmily, 'is 'Hello, how are you?'. That should give you a better reaction.'

'Ah, so. Good Good,' came the reply. Then they both yabbered away quickly to each other before yet another question popped out.

'This one very impolt,' one of them said, leaning forward to Wide Mouth. She sat back casually waiting for the question.

The Korean thought for a moment, his lips moving slightly to make sure that his pronunciation would be right. Then he nodded to himself and came straight out with it.

'When should say 'Fuck Off?''

The Escape Committee almost exploded with laughter, not just at the words but mostly at the reaction from Harvey and Wide Mouth. They were both stunned and speechless. The Korean said it again, 'Fuck Off!', echoed by the other one, 'Fuck Off!', and Harvey with

Wide Mouth left the room quickly, leaving the Korean's with puzzled expressions on their faces but still muttering 'Fuck Off. Fuck Off? Fuck Off!' to each other.

Jolly made another two non-announcements about the new building. The first of which was typically vague. 'Things', he said, were proceeding very well but he didn't say what the 'things' were. Speculation was high amongst the staff about what kind of building it would be and which subject was going to benefit. Frustration was also beginning to build.

'If he does that once more,' Chewy said, 'I'm going to ask him, point blank, what's going on!'

'It won't make any difference,' Lill said. 'He won't know, and won't be able to shed any further light on it. Don't waste your time.'

Chewy wasn't happy with that. The next time Jolly came out with another non-statement he was going to push the point, just to see what would happen. He didn't have long to wait. Jolly came out with the second of his non 'bulletins' the following week.

'I would just like to bring you up to date with how things are proceeding with regard to the new development,' he said.

Chewy didn't wait for any more.

'Can you tell us,' he asked loudly, 'when we will be able to see this new development?'

Jolly was taken aback at this sudden 'attack'.

'I... I'm not sure,' he said.

'Will it be this week?' Chewy asked.

'Well.. I...,' Jolly tried to say.

'Will it be next week?' Chewy pressed him.

'I... I...' Jolly said.

'Or next month?' Chewy fired another question.

'Well... err.' Jolly was floundering now.

'This term?' Chewy kept going.

'It might.. err...,' Jolly was now on the verbal run, stepping back with each salvo from Chewy.

'Or next term?' Chewy continued.

The whole of the staff room were following this with great interest. It was just like watching the crowd during the finals at Wimbledon. Jolly was now up against the wall, literally. Finding nowhere else to go he had to say something. With an effort he pulled himself together and answered, slightly flustered and red in the face.

'We should see a presentation before the end of this term,' he answered feebly.

'Thank you very much,' Chewy said, and sat back in his chair.

The buzz which followed this exchange continued for some time, but they still hadn't been given any more information. Jolly was in a bit of a state and left the staff room in a hurry followed again by Wooden. Two of the staff were shocked at how Chewy had pursued their Headmaster. Harvey Sheasby and the Wide Mouthed Frog. Both of them sat there as if they were sucking on another lemon.

'I thought that was just *so* common!' Wide Mouth said.

'I so agree,' said Harvey. 'But what can you expect from people like that?'

'I told you,' Lil said. 'I knew he wouldn't be able to give anything useful.'

'Had him going for a while though!' Chewy grinned.

The second incredible event, the 'fire power' incident, happened the following week. Sheamus Gilpin 'organised', in his own cack-handed fashion, the small unit of 'would-be' military headcases amongst the kids in the school. Many independent schools provide the opportunity for pupils of all ages to play soldiers or pilots or matelots, after school, in a half arsed attempt to interest these silly little buggers in joining the armed forces. It's something which has been going on for a long time in the independent sector. Quite sad really. Anyway, as far as Braumstate was concerned the kids involved, or conned into this, would spend a short time once a week running around the place dressed in their 'can't see me' clothes, khaki squaddie gear, or strutting up and down in the blue uniforms of the R.A.F. Now and again they were given small calibre rifles to play with. Fortunately, all of these weapons were loaded with blanks and that was just as well. If they'd been allowed live ammunition the School population would have dropped rapidly.

The weapons were the property of the Ministry of Defence and, being a responsible organisation, they insisted on checking and overhauling the things on a regular basis. While they had them for checking another batch would be made available to the school. The time for that 'swap' had now arrived and Sheamus booked one of the mini-buses, gathered the guns together and set off for the M.O.D. camp which serviced them. It was out in the wilds, about thirty miles from the town and was, in fact, one of the main arsenals in the country.

Sheamus arrived and drew up outside the large heavy wooden gates. These were swathed in chains and padlocks but no guards were visible anywhere. The camp buildings beyond showed no signs of life whatsoever. Nonplussed by this Sheamus honked the horn and a few minutes later a squaddie dressed in civvies ambled over from one of the nearest buildings.

'Yes, mate,' he said, his hands in his pockets. 'What can I do you for?'

Sheamus, still puzzled by this casual approach, wondered if he'd come to the right place.

'I said,' the squaddie said again, 'What can I do you for?'

Sheamus rolled the window down.

'This is the M.O.D., isn't it?'

'Yup!' came the reply.

'Ah, right!' Sheamus said, relieved. 'Got some guns here. Need to swap for checking. O.K.?'

'O.K.,' said the squaddie.

Sheamus started the engine of the bus and waited while the other began unlocking and undoing the padlocks and chains. Then he was in through the gates and waiting while the gates were closed and secured as before.

'Just pull in over there,' the squaddie said, pointing ahead to a low brick, windowless structure beyond the first few buildings.

Sheamus still hadn't seen anyone else. The squaddie ambled up to the one steel door which gave access to this brick box and fumbled about in his pockets.

'Where is everyone?' Sheamus asked.

'Cut backs,' came the answer. 'Reorganisation.'

That was the only explanation Sheamus was given. After a couple of seconds of fumbling the squaddie pulled out a large key and opened the door. This led to an inner door with a combination dial in the middle of it. Before he tried to select the correct numbers for entry Sheamus tapped him on the shoulder.

'What?' the other said, turning his head.

'Don't you want any identification from me?' he asked.

~ 215 ~

Sheamus couldn't believe he had been able to get this far without showing something to prove who he was.

'Oh, bugger. Yes.' said the squaddie. 'All right. Got anything?'

As it happened Sheamus had nothing at all with him to prove his identity. He went through his pockets again but still couldn't find anything except a receipt from Woolworths. Embarrassed by this, all he could do was to shrug with a silly grin on his face.

'I'm sorry about this,' he said. 'I don't have anything.'

'Where did you say you were from?' came the question.

'Braumstate Cathedral School,' Sheamus answered.

'Ah, that's all right then,' said the squaddie, grinning, and he turned back to the combination lock.

He was about to turn the dial but then stopped and clicked his fingers.

'Damn!' he said. 'Forgotten the bloody number again!'

He began fumbling around in his pockets again but without any luck. Sheamus picked up a piece of crumpled paper from the ground between them.

'Is this what you're looking for?' he asked.

The squaddie took it and then grinned.

'Great!' he said. 'I'd be for it if I'd left that lying around!'

If they had been under attack he would have been right.

The squaddie read the combination numbers from the piece of paper, fiddled with the dial in the centre of the door, it clicked and he pulled the thing open. This revealed a metal framed lift. The brick box was just the top of a large subterranean construction and as the squaddie pushed a button on the side wall of the lift they slid down to fifth underground level. A short walk from the lift and they were standing in front of an enormous rifle section and extracting the number of rifles Sheamus had asked for. These were then loaded onto a special rack, fitted with thick, wide rubber rollers, which they pushed to the side of the lift. The rack clicked into specially machined connectors on the side of the lift and back up they went.

'New system this,' the squaddie said. 'Just finished putting it in. First time it's been used.'

Sheamus was impressed and almost honoured to find himself on the maiden voyage of this mechanical marvel. He was easily impressed. He was also amazed to see, through the open front of the lift, how much raw weaponry was held in this place. It was stuffed with it. Each floor was packed with rows and rows of death delivering devices. The lower floor held the rifles and machine guns and as they slid back up to the surface he glimpsed pistols, rocket launchers and all manner of mechanical 'delivery'. As well as this there were thousands of cases of ammunition and a wide range of explosives.

As they reached the top the squaddie pressed a button and the rack loaded with the guns swung round from the side of the lift to engage with the specially prepared framework on the back of the security door.

'See that!' he said. 'Don't have any humping to do with that. That rack detaches and you can roll it to wherever you want to go! It's great!'

Sheamus was again impressed. They really had thought this one through very cleverly. He stood back to allow the squaddie to open the door. It opened outwards, or should have done. There was only one problem. The guns were sticking out on either side of it. It didn't occur to either of them to detach the frame from the door as they should have done. No. Instead of this simple act they laboriously unclipped every rifle from the rack and stacked them against the wall. A few minutes later Sheamus had off loaded the guns he'd brought with him and was on his way with replacement rifles, a moving clanking heap in the back of the bus.

The incredible thing about all of this was that an unidentified male, without identification of any kind and with a heavy Irish accent, had entered a top security M.O.D. arsenal and then had been helped to load a score of rifles into an unmarked minibus and allowed to drive off with them. It could only have happened to Sheamus Gilpin, 'begorra'!

Chewy was now totally pissed off with Jolly. Another non-announcement had been made but that had only given them the knowledge that an application for planning permission had been accepted by the local authority and was being looked at favourably. Chewy hadn't bothered to push him with questions this time. There didn't seem any point. Jolly breathed a sigh of relief when he left the staff room. After giving them the latest news about the new building he had stiffened, waiting for another 'attack' interrogation, but it didn't come. Maggie had been sitting with the Escape Committee this time, hoping for some news herself.

'Who the hell is the architect for this bloody building?' Rusty grumbled.

Nobody knew.

'No idea, Maggie?' Chewy asked.

'None,' she answered. 'Jolly hasn't said a single word to me about it.'

'Bloody hell!' Vic said. 'The very person who should know, our Development Officer, and she hasn't been informed at all!'

Maggie shrugged.

'What can I do?' she asked. 'I've asked Jolly several times but I've had nothing but waffle back from him every time. It's almost as if he's hiding something.'

It seemed they were fighting a losing battle but a chance remark, later that day, opened up the secret of the new building which the Escape Committee took advantage of immediately. Just after six in the evening, Maggie was clearing up her desk, on the point of leaving, when Quentin came bustling in.

'What's this?' she asked him. 'Are you the night shift?'

'Oh, Mag!' he said cheerily. 'You are so funny! No. I just popped back to see if we had one of those little plastic document covers.'

Maggie opened a drawer and handed him one. It was blue. The School colour.

'Oh, no,' he said. 'Not that kind. I was hoping you might have one of the see through jobs, the transparent kind.'

'Nope!' she said. 'Don't use them. Why do you want one of those?'

'Windows,' he said dreamily. 'I need it for the win...,' then clapped a hand over his mouth.

'Oohh! I shouldn't have said that!' he hissed.

Maggie was now intrigued by his 'windows' statement and his odd reaction.

'What's this about 'windows', Quentin?' she asked. 'What are you up to now?'

'Ooohh! I shouldn't have said that!' he said again. 'You won't tell Mummy, will you? Will you? She told me to keep it a secret! She'll be furious if she finds out you know. Please don't tell her! Please, please, pleeeease...'

Maggie held up both of her hands to quieten him down.

'Quentin, Quentin,' she soothed. 'Calm down. Calm down. Just calm down and tell me what you're talking about.'

A few minutes later and she had the whole story. Quentin was holding himself and in quite a state. He was terrified at the prospect of his mother finding out that he had told someone else about the new building. Maggie managed to calm him down but then had to persuade him to let her see this 'wonder' of architecture.

'Quentin,' she said gently. 'I have to see it.'

He shot a look of pure terror at her and physically stiffened in the chair.

'Must you!' he squeaked.

'I must,' she said, leaning over him. 'And now!'

Fifteen minutes later and they were rolling slowly up the drive to the house, the car lights switched off so that they wouldn't be seen in the darkness. The moon broke through the clouds as they stopped. Once out of the car they closed the doors carefully and crept up the steps to the front door, opened it and entered, tip-toeing along the hall to the library. Quentin was trembling with fright for fear of his mother arriving and finding him there with Maggie. He closed the doors behind them without making a sound and then took her over to the model.

The moonlight gave the library a ghastly atmosphere. Maggie came closer to the table. What she saw there was unbelievable. Lady Braumsley had done an efficient job of conning her son and if this monstrosity was ever built it would frighten the life out of anyone.

The Escape Committee arrived one by one and sat in a circle around one of the tables in a side room of the pub. Maggie had phoned all of them. This was an important meeting. Quentin had told her everything. Now she told them.

'So if I have this right,' Lill said. 'The old Braumsley bag is going to foist onto us a large pile of crap, this so-called new building, the major development Jolly's been wittering on about, just to take the piss out of the school?'

'Got it in one!' Maggie said.

'Bloody hell!' Chewy said. 'That old crone's crackers!'

'That 'rich' old crone,' Rusty said.

'If she's prepared to spend that much money,' Vic said, 'she must hate us!'

'If she has got that kind of money to throw away,' Harry said, 'couldn't we do something about it?'

'Yes,' Chewy said. 'We could.'

They all turned to him.

'If we pool our ideas,' he said, 'this is what I think we could, and should do.'

The plan was sound. It would need a fair amount of work, but there was just enough time before the end of term to organise and implement the idea. The only thing they needed to do was to see the thing which Quentin had been working on for all this time. That was an important and basic factor. Chewy needed to know how big it was before they could finalise their own operation.

'Well then,' Chewy said. 'There's no time like the present!'

'What, now?' said Lill.

'Why not?' Chewy replied. 'I can't see why we shouldn't. What do you think Maggie?'

Maggie wasn't too keen. Quentin wouldn't be a problem. She could deal with him even if he did become a bit hysterical. It was the old bat herself they'd have to bypass somehow and it was getting late. If they did go there now it would be well after eleven by the time they arrived.

'Let me make a phone call,' she said.

She was back a few minutes later, grinning.

'We're in luck,' she said. 'The old bag's in London and won't be back until tomorrow. Quentin's all by himself. He's expecting us.'

'How did you manage to persuade him?' Lill asked.

'Oh,' Maggie said. 'That was easy. I told him that if he didn't let us see it I'd tell his 'Mummy'!'

'Brilliant!' Rusty said.

'Right!' said Chewy. 'Let's go!'

They parked the cars at the back of the house and came in through the large glazed doors of the sitting room. That had been Quentin's idea. He didn't want anyone to see them but as the house was set all by itself in acres of estate land there really wasn't a chance of that happening anyway. Now they were in the large hallway and walking over to the library where Quentin was waiting for them. Very few lights were on and, mixed with the moonlight, the house was an extremely creepy place to be in.

'This place feels like a bloody morgue,' Compo muttered.

'Yeah,' Rusty said. 'Cosy isn't it?'

Harry closed the library door quietly once they were all inside and followed the others over to the large table. Quentin stood in front of it with a look of abject misery on his face. He was wringing his hands and wiping his sweating face with an enormous handkerchief.

'This won't take long will it?' he whined to Maggie. 'I really shouldn't be letting any of you see this. Mummy will be so cross if she finds out!'

'There, there,' Maggie soothed, patting his hands. 'Don't worry. We'll only be a few minutes.'

The others surrounded the table and surveyed the model. It was one hell of a sight. A large Christmas cake nightmare of a building sat there complete with little trees and people. The single lamp above it and the moonlight coming through the library window helped to accentuate its awful outline.

It looked like a mixture of neo-classical, Victorian gothic with dollops of fascist megalomania and hysterical, twisted versions of baroque and rococo thrown in for luck. It was something straight from a horror movie or maybe the manic imagination of a total lunatic. Gormanghast would have paled to the status of a holiday camp atmosphere compared to this. Every one of them was speechless. They'd never seen anything quite like it before, even in their worst nightmares. Quentin broke the spell.

'How much longer will you all be?' he quavered.

'Hang on,' Chewy said. 'I need some measurements.'

He whipped out a steel tape measure and a small notebook. In a few seconds had taken all he needed.

'O.K.,' he said, 'That should do it. I think we've seen enough.'

'That's an understatement!' Harry said.

'Then would you mind...' Quentin began but didn't finish.

The noise of a car engine pulling up at the front of the house had stopped him.

'Oohhh!' Quentin squeaked. 'That might be Mummy!'

It was. She'd decided to come back that evening instead of the following day. Ralph the butler had picked her up at the station and now he was helping her out of the car. They all made a bolt for the door but they were too late. As they piled into the hall the front door began to open. Turning on their heels they shot back into the library and closed the door quickly but quietly.

The 'clack, clack, clack' of Lady B's stick echoed down the hall, getting louder as she approached the library door. Chewy grabbed Quentin and slapped a hand over his mouth just as he was about to screech something hysterical. He squirmed and struggled as the noise of the stick grew louder and stopped on the other side of the door. The handle began to turn and the door opened slowly.

'I'll just have a quick word with my son,' Lady B said to Ralph as she stood in the open doorway.

The rest of them were flattened against the wall behind the door, Chewy still holding on to a trembling Quentin.

'I think you'll find he's in bed m'Lady,' Ralph replied. 'He was on his way there when I drove off to collect you.'

'I see,' she said, tapping her stick on the wooden floor. 'In that case I'll see him in the morning. Switch the light off in there, will you? That silly boy is always leaving it on!'

She clacked off across the hall and made her way slowly up the stairs. Ralph walked over to the door, leaned forward to reach the handle and flicked off the light with his other hand. As the door closed they all breathed a sigh of relief. That had been close, very close.

'Give it a few minutes,' Rusty whispered, 'and then we all leg it!'

Nods came from all of them in the darkness of the room. Chewy whispered in Quentin's ear.

'Don't make a sound or I'll break your bloody neck!'

Quentin nodded. Chewy still held him and then slowly relaxed his grip. Quentin didn't move or blink an eye. He was too terrified to do so.

'Come on then,' Maggie said. 'Let's go!'

Once in the cars they drove slowly away without lights. It had been just as well that they had left them round at the back. If the old bat had seen them in front there would have been hell to pay. Quentin crept into his bedroom and worried all night. He daren't say anything to his mother and hoped that she would never find out they had been in the house and seen his 'masterpiece'. He didn't dare think about what she might do if she ever found out. She never did find out but she did have a surprise coming. It would take another few weeks and on the very last day of the term for that to happen.

7

With only a few weeks left of the term, Jolly was well through his social calendar. This involved a carefully planned series of events to 'keep people happy'. A regular number of dinner parties every other week were held at his place involving Governors, the more well heeled amongst the parental body and various members of the staff.

He was, however, very particular about never, ever, mixing the staff with any of the Governors or some of the more influential parents. They might, he thought, say something 'untoward' about him or the so-called management he surrounded himself with. That would never do.

The theory behind these 'do's' of his was simple. A relaxed atmosphere around a dinner table would help him to get to know all of them a little better as well as shroud the fact that he was bloody useless. Anyway, that was his theory. The only flaws in that theory were the fact the most of the staff who were invited didn't want to go in the first place and then there were the frequent, and often disastrous, 'mis-matches' of personalities which Jolly always managed to organise. This time Maggie had received an invitation. She mentioned it to the Escape Committee.

'Ah,' Rusty said. 'One of the honoured few!'

'Absolutely!' Harry grinned. 'If you behave yourself you might even get invited again!'

'What do you mean,' Maggie asked them, 'by 'honoured few'?'

'Jolly always invites new staff to dinner,' Vic told her. 'If you keep your nose clean and follow his every wish, you get invited back. Simple as that.'

'How many times have you been?' she asked all of them.

'Once!' they all said.

'Oh, I see,' she grinned. 'By the way. Where's Chewy?'

'He's rather busy at the moment,' Lill said, winking. 'An important project. He's been at it for days. He mumbled something about getting it ready as soon as he could.'

Lil was concerned about other ears listening, flicking her eyes in the direction of Harvey Sheasby and the Wide Mouthed Frog who were sitting too close for that part of the conversation to develop further. Maggie nodded, understanding exactly what Lil meant.

'That sounds a bit mysterious,' Harvey whispered out of the corner of his mouth.

'They're like that sometimes,' Wide Mouth whispered back. 'We'll find out soon enough. They never could keep something to themselves.'

The evening of the dinner came round and Maggie arrived at Jolly's house. She was ushered in by an effusive Jolly in his best 'party' suit, accepted a glass of dry white wine and after the introductions to the others she settled amongst a few of them on a large settee. She already knew most of them but they were still a very mixed bunch. Wide Mouth and Harvey sat together nattering away to each other, 'Aimit', short for 'Actually, I Mean, I Think', a line he always used in his conversations, had brought his little, mousey wife, Greta, who hardly said a word the whole evening. Rollerball had brought his big, blowsy tart of a wife, Sharon, who said far too much and that left Maggie paired with Deep Throat, of all people. This was going to be some evening.

They all sat around in the drawing room making painfully polite conversation as Jolly busied himself by flitting about making sure everyone had their glass full. His wife, Portia, a large woman with a huge chest, kept popping out to make sure all her preparations were bubbling along nicely. Having eventually dispensed with an endless discussion about the weather, the behaviour and dress of some children and the disgraceful amount of litter in the streets, as a means of keeping the conversation going, they were now quickly running out of things to say to each other.

Then, thankfully, Portia announced that dinner was served. They all trouped into the dining room and took their places, every one marked by a tasteful little card. Maggie wondered who she would be sitting next to, not that there was much to choose from. Her heart sank when she saw the names. Harvey was on one side and Deep Throat slid into the chair next to hers. He immediately began an extremely tortuous conversation about education. Just what she wanted to talk about.

'So... as... you... can...see...,' he droned on, a long bony finger waving slowly in tune with each slow word. 'It's... something... you... have... to... be... very... careful... about.'

She nodded and smiled but she didn't have a clue what he was talking about, nor did she particularly care. She was praying for the first course to arrive so that his mouth would have something else to do. On her other side, Harvey was listening in rapt attention to Wide Mouth prattling on. It was something to do with a portrait of herself.

'Oh, it must be twenty years ago now,' she was saying. 'It's hanging on the living room wall. A lovely piece of work.'

Harvey nodded as she continued to explain.

'The artist was a friend of the family,' she said. '*So* talented. He could turn his hands to anything. Of course now he's *very* well known. Exhibits in the Royal Academy regularly. As a special present for last Christmas, my hubby commissioned a head and shoulders sculpture from him.'

'Really?' Harvey said, completely taken by this startling and new piece of information.

'Yes, he did,' she said, and then came out with a cracker of a line.

She leaned closer to him and simply said, 'You *must* come over and see my bust!'

Maggie almost choked trying not to laugh and was saved by everyone's attention being taken by the soup arriving. The dinner ground on with Jolly performing as waiter for most of the time. Portia was the kind of lady who didn't like to see him lounging around when she'd been slaving away all day preparing for the evening, and said so on more than one occasion.

'Come along dear!' she would say or, 'Don't just stand there!' and 'Will you listen to me?' Maggie was having a difficult time keeping a straight face. Jolly's wife kept him running around during the whole meal and he wasn't able to relax after that either. When they all retired from the table he was virtually ordered to see that everyone's glass was kept fully charged. No wonder he was so twitchy at school. Deep Throat was still grinding on about education. Maggie couldn't seem to get away from him.

'It's... a... very... difficult... time... for... all... teachers... departments... and... schools,' he said at one point, after what had seemed like a full hour of crass, educational gibberish. 'The... Government... are... very... keen... to... ensure... the... best... for... all... the... children.'

The same bony finger continued to emphasise every word. On the other side of the room Rollerball's tarty wife was quite pissed by now and becoming louder and louder as the evening dragged on. He was looking decidedly worried as he tried to deflect what she was saying but failed completely.

'The trouble with things today,' she said at one lull in the general conversation, 'is that there's not enough being done about sex!'

Wide Mouth pricked her ears up at this. Was this a kindred spirit?

'There's far too much of it!' Sharon continued after swigging down the contents of her glass. 'I sometimes have to send the videos, which my husband insists on buying, back to that funny little company in Soho. Do you know the one I mean?'

She looked directly at Harvey as she said this and he immediately shook his head frantically, going bright red at the same time. Then Aimit spoke up and launched into some garbled statement, hoping that Jolly would recognise that he was trying to deflect the conversation elsewhere.

'I do think that we have it about right in the school,' he said. 'Actually, I mean, I think that we do our best to make sure that the pupils are fully aware of all aspects of social responsibility.'

Sharon knew a bullshitter when she heard one. She'd also had far too much to drink.

'What the hell is that supposed to mean!' she snapped over the table.

Aimit just opened and shut his mouth. Nothing came out.

'You bloody teachers are all the same!' she said testily. 'Patronising little sod!'

A silence fell over the table like a wet, soggy blanket. Maggie wondered where this was going to lead. Rollerball tried to calm things down.

'Come on Sharon,' he said in his oiliest fashion. 'Let's just relax.'

'Relax!' she snapped at him. 'Relax! I am relaxed! Tell that little shit over there to 'relax' and start talking some sense instead of through his arse!'

Portia, Jolly, Harvey and Wide Mouth were stunned by this. Then Aimit's little mouse of a wife Greta suddenly added something which acted like a safety valve.

'I do like your wallpaper!' she said quietly.

Sharon burst into loud, raucous laughter. The others shifted uncomfortably but the danger had passed. Maggie just sat back watching all of this. The Escape Committee wouldn't believe it, but then again they probably would. They'd been around these nutters for much longer than she had. In any case it would make a very good story for tomorrow. The gathering broke up shortly after that and

Maggie was glad to get away from it, hoping that she wouldn't be invited again.

Chewy stood back and looked at it.

'Yes,' he thought to himself. 'That's about right!'

He was in the storeroom of the workshop and it was quite late. Having worked out the basic size, length, width and height, he now had a better idea of how long it would take to complete. The baseboard was well over six feet long. There wasn't a lot of time left until the end of term so he'd have to get a move on. The time consuming part would be the construction itself. The design was not going to be a problem. That was almost finished. It was something he'd been working on for years, well before this opportunity arrived to demonstrate his ideas. The rest of the Escape Committee had thrashed out a few more details and then left him with the final overall arrangement. Now that he'd organised the base, he switched off the lights, locked up and went home. He had a long night ahead of him before he could start the actual piece itself. There were still a few things to do but it was almost complete. His drawing board awaited for the final details.

Report time had arrived at Braumstate Cathedral School. Once a term all the staff delivered their considered, caring, understanding and particular educational comments about the performance, attainment and potential of the pupils under their charge. All was positive. None were negative. At least that's what Jolly always wanted. The truth was somewhat different. The process began three weeks before the end of term and continued until the beginning of the last week.

This time the suggestion had been made to get them out of the way a week earlier. Everyone seemed to think that was a good idea. It would take away the pressure of the last week. The actual reason behind this was that Jolly wanted to be away to his holiday retreat as soon as School closed down and this would ensure he could do just that without having to spend days of the holiday endorsing the whole lot.

Depending upon how many groups each individual member of staff actually taught it would mean anything between eighty or up to a hundred and twenty separate, hand-written statements about each child. R.E. had the worst of it with every single pupil in the school needing to be covered. Not that it posed a problem for Vic. Although he was the school chaplain he didn't teach R.E. That was handled by Rob Hinton, code name 'Tripod', a rather tasteless religious reference to the Trinity. His reports were a wonderland of economy. Without exception every report he issued ran thus, *'He/She has attended well to the issues raised during the term.'* He got away with it every time which said a lot about Jolly's role. He was supposed to read every one of them.

For most of the staff, regardless of the number of reports to be written, it was a period of total, mindless boredom. Formula statements, similar to Rob Hinton's, were standard. Slight rewording of these covered the near identical statements from most of the staff. Only the high flyers and the dross were ever given a little more attention. The bulk of the pupil body which lay between these two extremes were virtually rubber stamped. A few days into this process and the Escape Committee were moaning to each other in the staff room. None of them had finished their reports and there were only two days before the final deadline.

'I'm running out of things to say,' Harry said.

'I've run out,' Rusty said

'How many times can you say the same thing?' Lill complained.

'As many as it takes,' said Compo.

'How do you say to loving parents,' Chewy said, 'who have shown their complete faith and trust in our professional ability to deliver the best in education, that their darling child, the apple of their eye, is an absolute, top rank, diamond studded little bastard?'

'Tricky!' said Vic.

Other staff had the same kinds of problems but there were some who were daft enough to create even more work than was ever necessary. One of these was the Fourth Reich. Being German she had the good old Teutonic tendency of insisting on absolute perfection. A distinct struggle in this place but she kept trying. She looked after one of the middle school forms and was meticulous about making sure all the reports arrived in good time, particularly the games reports.

'Vare are my games reports!' was a familiar cry to many.

Rusty happened to be on the receiving end this time.

'Soon, soon!' he said, waving her away in the vain hope she might forget. She didn't. She never did. Every day she hounded him. Rusty was not of the opinion that games had any lasting value. He didn't object to them, he just didn't see the point in filling in reports about something he knew nothing about. It was a pointless exercise but the Fourth Reich didn't want to know about that. She had to have her reports one way or another.

For the umpteenth time she asked him again, 'Vare are zey?' Short of telling her where to look he gave up and scribbled one there and then. She wouldn't be happy until he did so.

'There!' he said shoving it under her nose.

All it had on was the child's name, form and one other word. That was '*Football!*' Still she wasn't happy.

'For God's sake woman!' he said. Taking it back he scribbled an addition and handed it back again.

This time it read '*He has played Football!*' She was happy with that.

'Und ze rest please, zoon!' she ordered and marched out.

A few of the staff had taken computer technology by the horns, still a rare event in those days, and committed everything to 'disc'. This was in fact a good wheeze as it could save a great deal of time. Once the reports had been logged, via a computer onto a disc, it was a simple matter to adjust them if necessary, and then simply print them out like baked beans. That worked well but one member of staff found a fault. Well, he would wouldn't he. That was the Head Boy. Nigel bloody St John Burroughs.

One afternoon a female member of staff, young, blonde and, everyone had thought, very demure and attractive teacher in the Science Department, was sitting by herself in the staff room when the Head Boy walked round from the pigeon holes with some of her reports in his hand.

'I say, Hilary, old thing,' he said. 'You haven't signed these.'

He handed them over and she blushed slightly.

'Sorry,' she said. 'After I printed them out I must have forgotten to do it.'

She signed them and handed them back. The Head Boy condescendingly took them and walked off. Then he was in front of her again with another batch.

'I know,' he said, in a very smarmy, pompous manner, 'that computers are wonderful, time saving devices but yours doesn't seem to be able to keep them intact.'

He was referring to the fact that they were in triplicate and had come apart during the printing process. Not a big problem in itself and not really worth mentioning, but he did. He shouldn't have, as she'd had a long day and he was being particularly patronising. She looked him straight in the eye and just said two words. They were, *'Tough shit!'*

Activity increased as the deadline for the completion of the reports approached. Staff were frantically scribbling anything just to get them out of the way. The usual latecomers were shouted at for holding the system up but at last they were done, finished for another term.

Now they were into the last week and it was all downhill from now on. An atmosphere of slight detachment crept into the staff room in those last few days. No longer were the staff wound up and tetchy. Most of them were looking forward to the prospect of escape for a whole four weeks. That was just enough time to realise that they, or rather some of them, really were adults before the misery of the Summer term began and the last minute panics of the final public examination which always threw them back into teaching twitches.

The conversation was relaxed yet varied. At one end of the room the scientists were discussing at great length the latest syllabus which would be upon them in the new academic year and several others were scattered round reading the quality newspapers. It had the atmosphere of a gentlemen's club. Erudite comments floated over from one group to another, the height of academe still lived. At the other end of the room other comments, which were far less intellectual, were being made. Two or three tabloids were being flicked through. The contrast in comments was fascinating to listen to.

'I'm not sure that modules will really work in my subject, you know.'

'Oh, no! The bloody price of a pint's going up again!'

'Wonderful review in the Times here, for the latest economics of administrative cost effectiveness in staff training.'

'Just look at the size of them! How does she keep them up!'

'I'm afraid the acidity level would prove too high for any relevant factors in that experiment.'

'Struth! He did it eight times before he got off! I bet that made it sore!'

And so on, and so on. The Escape Committee were swapping ideas about what they would be doing during the break when Wooden came in looking slightly lost but then made straight for Chewy. Wooden looked after staff cover if any of them were away and Chewy had drawn the short straw for a 'special' which had just developed.

'There seems to be a slight problem,' he said in his standard monotone, 'which you might be able to help us with.'

'Oh, yes,' Chewy said suspiciously. 'And what might that be?'

'One of the P.E. staff has a slight problem. Can you cover for this next lesson?' came the monotone answer.

'What kind of a problem?' asked Chewy.

'Well,' Wooden said. 'It seems that he had some part of his body caught in the door when the kids tried to come in. It's only a sprain so he should be all right tomorrow.'

That had to be either Action or the P.E. oaf. Only those two could have something like that happen to them.

'Catch his head in the door did he?' Chewy asked.

Some of the Escape Committee snorted.

'No, not exactly,' Wooden said. 'It was something lower down.'

More snorts and chuckles.

'So it's nothing serious then?' asked Chewy.

'No,' Wooden replied. 'He'll be fine tomorrow.'

'Pity,' Chewy mumbled.

The cover period was for the sports hall. By the time Chewy turned up the place was in absolute turmoil, thick with eleven and twelve year old kids, all rushing around like maniacs. Whoever had been looking after them was nowhere to be seen.

'Typical!' Chewy grunted. 'Why do some bloody staff just disappear when they judge their time is up?'

There must have been at least thirty of the little sods in the hall creating total bedlam. He bellowed at the top of his voice and there was a sudden halt from all of them. They turned to look and he beckoned them over. The noise level increased as they ran, walked, trudged, or sauntered over to him. Some of them were dishing out the odd clip round each others' heads as they came. Others were trying hard to trip each other up. Chewy was not looking forward to this at all. He had all the head bangers from both year groups and there was always trouble of one sort or another when they came together.

The situation was made worse by the fact that it was almost the end of term and their adrenaline levels were on full output. It was always the same at the end of any term. The kids would gradually go potty in the last few days, gearing up for their own escape from the place.

As they eventually gathered round him he noticed a crumpled heap lying in the far corner of the hall. He couldn't make out what it was at first and then it moved. It was 'Splinter', Richard O'Leary, language teacher and a younger version of Wooden. The same comatose personality and dead eyes. He wobbled to his feet rubbing the back of his head as Chewy wandered over to him. Behind his back mayhem broke out again as more than half the kids started kicking and thumping each other. Chewy ignored this. He couldn't be bothered to sort it out and continued walking. Whatever was happening behind him might help to slow them down a bit. Splinter was shaking his head when Chewy reached him.

'What's up?' Chewy asked. 'You all right?'

'What? Oh, yes,' Splinter said. 'Think so.'

'Get a bang on the head or something?' asked Chewy.

'Something like that,' Splinter said, 'I think. I was supposed to be helping one of the P.E. Staff but he had to go after being smacked when the door suddenly opened and this lot came in.'

Splinter had tried to control them by himself but what had happened then was just another example of the effect this little lot of potential terrorists could have on the staff. They'd been playing something similar to football when the ball shot straight for Splinter. The kids all charged forward after it, smacked right into him and sent him flying into the wall, backwards. They didn't hear the 'crack' as his head connected with the brickwork but just stampeded over him as the ball bounced away. He'd been lying there, out cold, for twenty minutes before Chewy arrived. During that time the 'game' had degenerated into absolute warfare, the ball ignored completely. Splinter walked off unsteadily, a huge egg bump sticking out from his hair. Chewy turned to the enemy.

'Come here you lot!' he yelled.

They gathered round him again, this time sporting a few black eyes and a couple of cracking bruises.

'Right!' he said. 'There's only another half hour to go. What do you want to do?'

'Go home!' one little smart arse said.

'Yeah! Yeah!' they all shouted and began jigging around again, kicking and smacking each other.

'Pack it in!' Chewy yelled, 'Now!'

Gradually order was restored.

'You!' he shouted at a tiny eleven year old.

The kid almost left the ground in shock.

'Me!' it squeaked.

'Yes, you!' Chewy snarled. 'Get the ball!'

It ran off, terrified, and brought it back.

'Thank you,' said Chewy as he took it. Then he took a deep breath.

'Now, I want you in two teams, so sort yourselves out.'

That took up another few minutes of chaos before Chewy gave up waiting and charged through all of them, squashing a few feet in the process, but splitting them roughly into two groups. A few choice remarks floated up but he ignored them.

'O.K.' he yelled, flinging his arms around. 'You lot defend that end. You lot the other!'

They charged off to either end of the hall and Chewy was left all by himself in the middle, holding the ball.

'The ball's over here, you dipsticks!' he yelled at them and bounced it as hard as he could, walking back quickly. By the time the thing came back down they were all waiting for it and the warfare began all over again. Chewy leaned against the wall and left them to it but then he was careful to keep moving and not to come anywhere near the marauding gang who, as well as chasing the ball, were knocking seven bells of hell out of each other. It was a dangerous place to be.

Chewy looked at his watch. Depression set in immediately. There was another twenty minutes of this to go before he could think about releasing them. He kept moving as the swarm ricocheted round the hall, still chasing the ball, still fighting. Then the door flew open and another thirty, damp and bedraggled kids spewed in. Behind them Compo appeared, puffing and panting.

'What the hell are you doing here?' they both said together.

'I was knobbled just after you were!' Compo yelled above the noise. 'Aimit should have been looking after this lot but he had to go home with a headache, poor thing!'

'Why the hell did you bring them here?' Chewy shouted above the row.

'Because it's pissing down outside!' Compo yelled back.

With sixty kids in the hall the warfare had now escalated into third world war proportions and both Chewy and Compo spent the rest of the time pulling wriggling, kicking, biting and screaming kids apart. By the time the session was over, and only in the space of ten minutes, all manner of damage had taken place.

'I just hope the nurse has plenty of field dressings,' Compo said as he herded the survivors outside.

'Too bloody right!' Chewy said and looked around at the carnage. Ten little, twitching figures lay around all over the hall in various states of collapse and injury. It had been quite a session. Isn't sport wonderful?

Later that evening Chewy was putting the finishing touches to the structure he had started a few days ago. The overall size was about right and once in place nobody would know until the moment of 'exposure'. He was looking forward to that. Oh, yes! All that needed to be worked out now was a 'modus operandi' for the final day of term. That's where the others came in. The rest of the Escape Committee were gathered round his creation.

'Chewy, that's terrific!' Maggie said.

'I agree with you completely!' Chewy answered, grinning.

'All right, smart arse,' Rusty said. 'Now that we have that what do we do with it?'

'That's not going to be easy,' Harry said. 'It's a hell of a size.'

'No bigger than the other,' said Lill.

'That's true,' Vic added. 'But the other one's arriving soon, isn't it?'

'When?' Rusty asked.

'Tomorrow morning,' Maggie said.

'Well,' Harry said, 'it's just a matter of how we get that one out and ours in.'

'That shouldn't present a problem,' Compo said. 'We have all the things we need right here on the site. It's just a matter of 'arrangements'.'

'How?' the others said.

'Well,' Compo said. 'It could be done quite simply.'

They all listened as he outlined his thoughts to them. After a couple of minutes they had their plan of action totally organised.

There were only three days before the end of term and that left a few of the Escape Committee with their last formal act. The once a week House Duty. It was another mindless task but at least it was the last one of the term. The only problem with this, as with the cover periods both Compo and Chewy had been given, was that the kids were that much nearer to the end of term and they were likely to react in a much more demonstrative fashion, particularly the older ones.

Rusty, Harry and Lill were due to take over their various positions in three different houses that night, from early evening until around ten. Then they usually met in the pub with the rest of the Escape Committee. By the time they arrived on this occasion they had plenty to talk about. Maggie, Chewy, Compo and Vic were sitting in the lounge bar of their local, nattering away to each other, going over some of the more hilarious moments of the term, generally unwinding from the last few weeks. The time ticked by and still the others hadn't arrived. Five minutes to eleven arrived and then Lill came through the door, closely followed by Harry and then Rusty. The others looked up as they walked over and sat down, all of them grinning widely.

'What's up?' Chewy asked.

'You wouldn't believe it!' Lil giggled.

'Try us!' Maggie said.

'This bloody school!' Rusty said.

'What's happened now?' Compo asked.

'Mayhem!' Harry said.

'Tell us!' pleaded Vic.

They were just in time for a drink before time was called. Then they told their collective story, some of which had been given to them by the kids themselves. The three of them had been involved in a bit of boarding house to boarding house, extra mural activity. Jolly, Wide Mouth, Rollerball and good old Harvey Sheasby had been involved as well which hadn't made life any easier. Things had been going fairly well for the first part of the evening. The Houses were quiet, the kids were getting on with various bits of prep and then, at nine, the time came when they could leave their work and relax. Quite a few of them didn't. They had something else in mind altogether. Unknown to the staff on duty the kids, Sixth and Fifth Formers, had organised an end of term party, but not in any of the houses. Just a short distance from the school a public garden known as the 'Paddock' was to be the venue. It had at one time belonged to a large private house but was bought by the local authority and became public property.

It was a rough oval in shape surrounded by a thick, mature belt of trees which thinned out to a central expanse of rich grass. A wide path ran all the way around it with a few well trodden ones in place which weaved their way through to the centre. This was at a lower level, the ground gently falling to a flat irregular shape with the odd clump of bushes here and there.

Just after nine o'clock a gradual, covert drift from the houses began to take place. In ones and twos they meandered in that general direction and as soon as they were out of sight of the boarding houses they galloped off. Most of them had 'supplies' with them, disguised carefully under jumpers, stuffed down in pockets and inside coats, which had been purchased by the older ones over the last few days from town. Ten o'clock came round and none of them had returned as they should have done. Lill wondered what was going on and, having a suspicious mind, phoned Harry to see if the same thing was going on there.

'Same as you,' he said. 'Most of the little sods are still missing. I wonder what's happening with Rusty?'

Lill tried to phone but didn't get an answer. Rusty was busy elsewhere. He had wandered up through the house, checking on the kids, and found one of them halfway out of the window.

'Come here you daft little sod!' he said, pulling him back inside. 'It's three floors down from here! What do you think you're doing!'

After a couple of minutes grilling followed by a quick 'frisk' he had the answer. That's when he heard the phone ringing downstairs.

'You stay put or I'll have your guts for garters!' he said and left the Fifth Former there, sulking. Lill was on the phone when he picked it up. She told him about Harry and her own situation and he told her what he'd gleaned and what he'd found on the Fifth Former upstairs, four cans of lager.

'Yeah,' he said. 'If that little bugger had tinnies you can bet the others have. He was on his way to the Paddock. That's where they'll be.'

'Oh, shit!' Lill said.

'Come on,' Rusty soothed, 'It's not that bad.'

'Yes it bloody is!' she hissed down the phone. 'Wide Mouth has just arrived!'

The Wide Mouthed Frog was the House Mistress. Lill would have to tell her the kids were still out. She told her and Wide Mouth panicked immediately.

'I must tell the Headmaster!' she squeaked and ran for the phone.

Lill just sighed.

'When will this silly bitch ever react normally?' she thought to herself. 'Never!' came her unspoken reply.

Jolly was on the scene a few minutes later, panting for breath and carrying a torch.

'I've been in touch with the other house staff and they are making their way to the Paddock as I speak!' he said, a manic tick developing in one eye.

Lill gave him a limp smile and looked at Wide Mouth, as if to say, 'Over to you.' Wide Mouth took the point and rose to the challenge.

'I'm right behind you Headmaster!' she said.

'Your lucky day, sunshine!' Lill thought.

Both of them scampered off in the direction of the Paddock. The two other house staff who had already arrived were Rollerball and Harvey Sheasby. Neither of them had noticed the lookouts which had been posted by the kids and as they both were carrying torches, switched on, it would have been impossible for the kids to have missed them coming. The two Fifth Formers who had been standing guard had plenty of time to warn the others. Oh, how we underestimate kids! The word flashed through the assembled mob in the Paddock that staff were on their way and the whole lot disappeared in seconds into the trees. Harvey and Rollerball were making their way to the open ground in the middle and just missed all of that, switching off their torches as they left the trees.

'Don't want to forewarn them!' hissed Harvey.

'Good thinking' Rollerball whispered behind him.

They found not one single pupil but they did find a hell of a lot of empty tinnies and a thick carpet of fag ends where they'd been. With their torches still switched off they poked about amongst the debris. That's when Jolly and Wide Mouth arrived, skulking on the edge of the trees, their torches ready to use. Both of them skirted the edge of the tree line looking for anyone who shouldn't have been there. Then they saw two shadowy figures in the middle of the Paddock acting very suspiciously.

While all this had been going on, the folk who were living in the large house on the edge of the Paddock had phoned the Police. They were more than concerned about what was happening. Not only had they heard the laughter and squealing of young people, they had just seen flashing lights and then strange ominous figures walking around in the middle of the whole area. Three squad cars were dispatched immediately. Jolly and Wide Mouth crept closer, picking their way carefully across the grass to the two dark shapes they could see moving ahead of them. They inched closer, determined to catch all these naughty pupils in the act of whatever they were doing. As they snapped on their torches another barrage of light flooded over them from behind. Rollerball and Harvey froze in the illumination. Jolly and Wide Mouth turned, holding their hands against the light, wondering who had lit the place up.

'Stay where you are!' came a disembodied voice. 'This is the Police! Stand perfectly still! Do not move!'

A uniformed Police Sergeant stepped forward followed by six officers, all carrying large, powerful lamps.

'Well, now,' he said, playing his lamp over the four of them. 'What do we have here?'

Jolly pulled himself up to his full height, trembling slightly, and faced them. Wide Mouth and the other two cowered behind him.

'I'm the Headmaster of... ' Jolly began.

'Yes, yes,' the Sergeant said with a bored expression on his face. 'And I'm Dame Edna Everage. Come on. What are you lot doing here at this time of night?'

'Tracking down children!' Jolly said pompously.

'Oh, yeah,' the Sergeant said. 'One of 'them' are you? That'll get you ten years, you dirty old man!'

Jolly was taken aback at this. So were the others, particularly Wide Mouth.

'How dare you!' she shrieked. 'I'll have you know I'm a very respectable person as we all are!'

'I'm sure you are, madam.' said the Sergeant dryly. 'And that's why you're here in the middle of the night, crawling around in the dark with three men!'

'I reckon it's a gang-bang, Sarge!' one of the other Policemen muttered.

Wide Mouth spluttered with rage.

'I beg you pardon!' she gasped. 'I've never heard...'

'That's enough!' said the Sergeant. 'Come on. This way. You can do all your explaining down at the station!'

'Now just a minute my good man!' Jolly said. 'You have no right...'

'Shut up!' the Sergeant cut in. 'Come along, there's a good gentleman. Just do as you're told.'

The six Policemen surrounded the four of them, still protesting, and led them back through the trees. Some of the kids were still there, watching the whole thing and desperately trying not to give themselves away. As the group came out into the street and under a lamp, Wooden was there walking towards them.

'Is there some kind of problem here?' he said. He was quick, old Wooden.

A few minutes later they had the whole thing sorted out but there had been a few moments when Jolly and the others thought they might be spending the night in the cells. It couldn't have happened to a nicer bunch.

The end of term was at last upon them. The service in the Cathedral had been the usual forty five minutes of drafty, piousness from Jolly this time. Vic sat listening to the stream of twisted, quasi religious drivel, as did the whole School, but there was no way of leaving. The Escape Committee tried to close their ears to it but kept their frustration to a minimum by flicking the ears of a few kids who wouldn't sit still.

'If we have to listen,' Chewy murmured to one particularly stroppy Fifth Former, '*so do you!*'

As before, most of the staff were careful to stay well out of the way of the Head Boy. He was at it again, rewriting the words to the hymns. This time Aimit was getting the treatment and he was obviously not enjoying it. Eventually the Dean gave the final blessing and they were released. The rest of the day was filled in with videos to keep the kids happy, they were not in the mood for anything else, and then later in the afternoon the big clear up began. All over the School the junk of the term was dumped into the nearest bin. So were a few of the kids. They had a funny sense of humour sometimes. The afternoon dragged on and on but then the magic moment arrived which they'd all been waiting for, the end of term. Kids streaked out in all directions, closely followed by most of the staff. Up in the staff room the Escape

Committee were celebrating and talking about the evening ahead. Seven o'clock was the time scheduled for the 'presentation'. The Mad Hatter had told them that.

'So it's in there now, is it?' Rusty asked.

'Yep!' Maggie answered. 'Quentin had it brought in during this morning. It's sitting on Jolly's big table ready for later on.'

She was talking about the model of the monstrosity they'd seen at the Braumsley house. It was now in position waiting for Lady B to perform what she thought would be her act of vengeance on the school. All the paperwork was ready and she was looking forward to the handing over 'ceremony'.

'In that case,' Chewy said grinning. 'I think we'll have to put plan A into operation right now!'

At six thirty everyone had assembled. Wide Mouth, Wooden, the Prick, the Fat Controller and Jolly waited nervously for Lady Braumsley to arrive. They were in Jolly's office. The big table sat there with Quentin's model on it, shrouded in an expansive blue cloth. They had all been tempted to peep under it but Jolly would have none of it.

'I gave my word,' he said, 'that no one will see it until we formerly accept it from her Ladyship.'

He was quivering with excitement. This was going to be such a boost for the school. A purpose built, brand new building and right in the heart of the school where everyone would see it and admire it. He would be bound to get the credit for having had such foresight and vision. The parents would love it. The sound of a car engine interrupted his daydream as Lady B's limousine pulled up outside followed by another carrying her legal advisers. They jumped from their car; all dressed identically in dark, pin-striped suits and almost formed a guard of honour as they opened her door. Quentin popped out first to help the bulk of Lady B emerge. Taking Quentin's arm she thumped up the few steps and left him, plodding on through the open door of the building and down the hall to Jolly's office. He stood at the door waiting for her, hands clasped together and grinning inanely as she approached.

'My dear Lady Braumsley,' he said, giving a slight bow. 'How very good to see you. Do come this way.'

She clacked past him, accidently jabbing his foot quite hard with her stick as she did so. He didn't flicker, his grin fixed. Only his eyes, which widened slightly, gave away the pain. The entourage fussed around the old bat trying to help her into the arm chair at the head of the table. She swept them away with her free hand and dropped like a beached whale onto the deep upholstery. They arranged themselves behind her while Jolly and the others dithered about, not knowing where to stand. Quentin floated between the two groups, fretting about which side he should go to. Then he simply gave up and sagged where he stood. The old bag ignored him completely and an evil grin slowly spread over her face.

'Jenkins,' she said, and one of the smaller, dark suited flunkies behind her skittered round with a large, leather bound wallet. He opened it and placed it before her, holding out a fountain pen, uncapped and ready to use. She took it without looking at him and leaned forward, pen poised but staring hard at Jolly. This was her moment of triumph!

She had lied, bribed, intimidated, blackmailed and applied every underhanded, manipulative kind of pressure on many members of the local authority to achieve her goal. They had all, under her awful influence, rubber stamped every stage of the project so that nothing would stand in the way of it being built. Many of the standard procedures had been bypassed. Now she was on the point of having the satisfaction of seeing Jolly's face when he saw the model but would also have a cast iron, legal contract which gave no release to either of them from the actual construction of the building.

'Two signatures,' she said. 'Yours and mine, will seal this agreement and make available all the necessary funds from my private account. I understand this will be in the region of one point six million pounds.'

There was an audible intake of breath from all of them as she said that.

'Nonetheless,' she continued, 'the building will be yours to be built exactly as you will see it when the blue cloth is removed.'

The tension in the room was excruciating. Nobody moved. Nobody breathed. Everyone's eyes were now fixed on her hand and the pen. She signed with a flourish and handed the pen to Jolly. His palms were sweating as he took it and with a trembling hand, added his own name below hers. Everyone breathed again. The tension began to relax but there was still the 'unveiling' of Quentin's 'masterpiece'.

Her grin became even wider and her bloodshot eyes widened as she revelled privately in her victory. This building would make the school a laughing stock nationally, quite apart from the pleasure it would give every time she herself saw it. Then, again, she called for her tame, pin-striped solicitor.

'Jenkins!'

The little man sprang forward again and took hold of one corner of the blue cloth. He turned to wait for her nod. She settled her great bulk further into the chair and looked straight at Jolly. He had his eyes fastened on the hand holding the cloth. The others were holding their breath. Her head came forward and the hand began to pull back the cloth.

Then the tension and the silence were shattered by the ear-splitting, groaning whine of an old style klaxon warning horn suddenly blaring up in volume. Someone shouted 'FIRE!' and black smoke billowed across and outside the windows. The shout, 'FIRE!' came again and that's when panic took over. Startled and ashen faced, Lady B was dragged out of her chair by her pin-striped squad and bundled out of the room, closely followed by Jolly and the others. Quentin fought his way with the rest of them as they galloped along the hall, burst out through the door and ran away from the building on to the lawn. Great clouds of smoke gushed from the base of the building, rolling towards them and engulfing them all. Coughing and spluttering they could now hear the 'hee-haw' of a fire engine in the distance. They all had to stumble further away up the lawn to clear the smoke.

Jolly wiped his eyes, now streaming with tears from the smoke, and looked back through the thick billowing clouds which still spewed up. The main building could hardly be seen and Jolly immediately began to worry about his precious, gibberish paperwork stuffed in the groaning filing cabinets in his office, where would he be without them? Under the cover of the smoke and the noise of the ancient fire horn, six figures had negotiated their way into the building through another entrance and were frantically at work moving something through to Jolly's office and then back out again, unseen by anyone.

Then the fire engine arrived screaming to a halt, men jumping from the cab, pulling on breathing apparatus as they walked into the heart of the smoke. Minutes later they had dealt with the problem, the smoke had cleared and the firemen climbed back into the vehicle.

Their chief was not a happy man. Jolly had been standing as close as he dared but now came closer, timidly walking up to the chief.

'You the Headmaster?' the chief grunted.

Jolly nodded.

'You should look after your gear more carefully,' he said, glaring at Jolly's puzzled face.

'Gear?' Jolly asked.

'These!' the chief snapped and handed Jolly three, still warm, metal, cylindrical pot-like things. 'Smoke canisters!' he said. 'You have a cadet unit here, haven't you?'

Jolly nodded again holding the canisters which still gave off slight wisps of smoke. He'd seen the cadets using them when they'd been playing soldiers. 'Simulating battle conditions', was the reason given by the staff in control.

'Then one of your little cherubs has been playing games with you *and us*,' the chief growled. 'We haven't the time for silly games, sir. I'll have to file a complaint about this!'

With that he climbed up into the cab and the engine drove off leaving Jolly standing, still holding the canisters. The rest of them had been slowly walking back during this and now stood dolefully in front of him, except Lady B, her face a fury and being held up by her pin-striped following. Jolly threw the canisters down in disgust and clasped his hands together. With a bowed head he began to whine to the old bat.

'Your Ladyship!' he began. 'How can I begin to apologise for this awful business?'

'By shutting up and getting me back inside!' she snapped. 'Now!'

Back on the chair with a cup of tea Lady B was now composed and ready for the unveiling. Nobody had noticed the slightly different shape under the blue cloth. She nodded her head again. Jenkins pulled the cloth away and a collective intake of breath was the instant reaction to what they saw before them.

Instead of the nightmare of Quentin's model a completely different structure now met their eyes. Quentin fainted. Nobody noticed. It was a superb, modern piece of architecture with just enough sympathy with the ancient surroundings reflected in its lines and materials. Large glazed sections could be seen, three levels for a wide use of subjects and activities, two tree lined courtyards and gardens with open space woven through the whole complex. It would blend perfectly with the rest of the school.

Lady B's face drained of all colour and she dropped the teacup. Nobody noticed the tinkle of broken crockery. They were all enthralled with the arrangement of the building. As the others moved forward to look closer she stood and shuffled towards it, her mouth hanging slackly open.

'Magnificent!' Jolly cried, clapping his hands together.

A resounding crash made them all turn at once to see Lady B flat on her back, out for the count, arms wide, pudgy legs sticking straight up in the air and displaying a terrible pair of voluminous bloomers.

At the back of his building, Chewy smacked the lid down on the large waste unit. The others applauded. The truck would be there tomorrow to take that nightmare away. His model was the one the others had seen, the one he'd been busy with for days. A short while later, in the pub, they all raised their glasses to the end of term.

'And here's to Lady B, the old bitch!' Chewy said.

'Hang on, why her?' Maggie asked.

'Why not?' Chewy grinned.

'That old bat,' Vic said, 'has just tried to pull one of the most evil schemes on us, and you want to toast her?'

'Sure do!' Chewy kept grinning.

'What the hell for?' Harry asked.

'Why her?' Compo said.

'You must be barmy!' Rusty snorted.

'Probably!' Chewy said, 'But just think. That bloody thing Quentin 'designed' was an act of pure revenge on her part and would have cost her quite a bit. That was the measure of her hatred. She was prepared to pay that much.'

'So?' the rest of them said.

'Well,' he said. 'The one she's now committed to build won't be any less.'

They all nodded waiting for his reason.

'So I think she's going to need all the 'toasts' she can get,' he said, still grinning.

'Why?' Maggie asked.

'Because,' he said, 'the new one, ours, will cost her at least twice the amount of Quentin's. That should be just over three million quid.

She'll have to realise every asset she has to comply with that contract which she had drawn up and insisted on both she and Jolly being bound by. That will keep her busy for years and off our back completely! So, cheers!'

A whoop of delight went up from all of them. Glasses came together again, clinked, and they drained every drop to good old Lady B! This was one hell of a way to end the term!

THE FAMILY

Bernie 'The Bin'

Lady Braumsley

Quentin

**'With what measure ye mete,
it shall be measured to you'**

The Bible St Mark 4-24

SUMMER
TERM

1

Well, at least the weather had improved. Morale was another matter. Only a few days ago they'd been feeling relatively normal. Well, some of them had.

'Six weeks to go,' Rusty said.

'The end of term?' Chewy asked, looking puzzled.

'No, chance would be a fine thing. That's only until half term. The end of term timing's a bit more depressing,' Rusty said. 'It is exactly eleven weeks, two days, one hour, four minutes and...,' checking his watch, 'thirty five seconds and counting.'

Enthusiasm hardly overflowed. The Escape Committee sat around in Chewy's office, silently and listlessly stirring and staring into their coffee cups.

'Well, come on,' Vic then sighed. 'Up and at 'em!'

'Time already?' Harry almost wailed.

'Come on then,' Lill muttered. 'Let's get it over with.'

'Here we go,' Compo said. 'All along the yellow brick road to 'Worry Land' again.'

'See you all later,' Maggie grinned.

They trudged off, preparing themselves in their own way for the 'Jolly' hour. The four week break since the previous term was never quite enough and this was only the day before teaching actually began. What a prospect. What a happy school. What next? Jolly swept in with his entourage in hot pursuit. Wooden looked just the same, as wooden as ever. The Prick and the Fat Controller began to whisper to each other as they sat down and the Wide Mouthed Frog started blowing her bloody nose again. Harvey Sheasby sidled down next to her and sat back waiting for 'his master's voice.'

'Good morning everyone!' Jolly began. 'I hope you all had a restful break?'

This was a standard cue for all the sycophants to nod their heads.

'Good, good. All ready for the term ahead?' he said, a sickly grin spreading across his face.

More nodding dogs.

'Well, we now have a few weeks ahead of us to ensure our pupils are ready for the final public examinations,' he said. 'I know you will all concentrate on this so they will have the best possible chance of the highest possible grades.'

'He should come and see some of mine,' Chewy muttered. 'No chance!'

'Snap!' Rusty whispered back.

Jolly went through all of his standard warnings, worrisome recommendations and cautions but after the first few minutes he'd lost most of them as they applied their own mental 'fail safe mechanisms' to the crap he always shovelled out to them. The P.E. Oaf had dropped off almost immediately, his snoring only just audible at the back of the room. A rich and varied range of activities had started up as a means of keeping sane and were going on quite unnoticed by Jolly. As well as the crossword puzzles and books, fiction still unfinished from the break, there were quite a few drawings, doodles and mindless scribblings going on, side by side with knitting patterns, various attempts at origami, and one rather cack-handed attempt at macramé which looked more like a hangman's noose than anything else. In the circumstances it was fairly appropriate.

Anything was better than listening to the inconsequential rubbish which Jolly insisted on churning out. He continued to witter on and on and on as he always did. They'd heard it all before. The only thing which had changed was the date. Chewy looked at his watch, grimaced to himself and sighed. The others knew exactly the meaning of that look of sheer despair. There was at least another half an hour of this drivel before any of them could escape.

Maggie and the Mad Hatter were griping a bit about how much holiday the teaching staff were given as opposed to their paltry amount.

'It's not that I really mind that,' the Mad Hatter said. 'It's just that every time 'you know who' comes back, he brings with him a bloody mountain of meaningless crap for me to process. Memos by the bloody hundred, all kinds of futile letters and usually the latest rewritten rules, regulations, do's and don'ts for the staff and the kids. Just look at that lot.'

Maggie turned to where she was pointing. On the end of Maisie's desk a tray was stacked high with paper.

'If only there was less holiday,' the Mad Hatter said, 'then he wouldn't be able to produce so much bloody rubbish. He wouldn't have the time!'

'Do you mean to tell me,' Maggie asked, 'that he dumped all that with you when he came back?'

'That's it,' The Mad Hatter said. 'That's all he seems to do during every holiday.'

'Oh, Maisie,' Maggie said. 'I'd stick it in the bin!'

'What do you think I do?' she grinned. 'I take the first twenty pages off the top and the rest I chuck away. By the time I feed him that first batch he's usually forgotten about the rest of it!'

The Mad Hatter was not that mad. She had Jolly summed up and knew exactly how to handle him. More often than not it was with straightforward contempt. There had been one glorious occasion when Rusty had overheard a pathetic plea from Jolly to Maisie when she was not feeling too enthusiastic about organising his diary a mere five years in advance.

He'd been in Maisie's office checking on some simple task when Jolly had arrived asking for help. Maisie was feeling particularly pissed off with him and didn't want to know.

'Too busy!' she snapped.

Jolly had slunk off but then had reappeared a few minutes later, sticking his head round the door, not realising Rusty was still there. As Rusty was leafing through a file behind the door he heard Jolly plead with Maisie.

'But it's important,' he whined. 'I must get my diary organised.'

'Tough!' Maisie spat at him, not even bothering to look up.

Jolly stood in the doorway, sagged and then tried again, saying one single word to her, a desperate note in his voice this time. 'Please?' he said quietly.

That story had flashed round the staff room as soon as Rusty had been able to pass it on to the Escape Committee.

Almost an hour had grated by and a few of them were beginning to get restless. Jolly was still beating his little gums and it was a minor miracle to witness just how long he could talk and talk and talk about so little and say nothing of any real value. Now he was going on about the second half of the term.

'So there will still be the opportunity,' he said, 'for educational visits during this time, but we must be on our guard about the number of them. At the present time parental concern is very high about additional expenses. I will be issuing you all with a special form to fill in so that the co-ordination committee can review all intended excursions.'

'More bloody paper!' Chewy grunted. 'They'll want to fill forms in about farting next!'

'Well,' Jolly beamed. 'I think that's all I have to say for the moment. Is there anything anyone else would like to say?'

Some of the Creeps tried to, but just happened to be sitting next to staff who didn't want that. Most of them were the Escape Committee. Their hands went down very quickly under glaring eyes and the vicious silent gestures which could not be misunderstood. As the meeting broke up The Escape committee were more than a little surprised Jolly hadn't mentioned the 'New Building'.

'What's his game?' Rusty said. I would have thought he would be busting to tell all about it.'

Chewy shrugged. 'He's waiting for the 'right' moment so he can take all the credit, stupid sod.'

'And when will that be?' Lill wondered.

'That's anybody's guess,' Chewy replied.

It was a little busier than usual in the pub just before lunchtime but the Escape Committee managed to find a corner where they could all squeeze in together and settle to give each other solace after the beginning of term meeting.

'He's getting worse,' Rusty said.

'Was he ever better?' asked Chewy.

'Never!' they all said.

'Come on you lot,' Compo said. 'He's never going to change.'

'I've a feeling,' Lill said, 'that he's never going to go either.'

That tended to halt the conversation for a while. The prospect of years and years of Jolly Jack ahead of them wasn't a good one. The image of the Times Educational Supplement filled every head. There had to be a job somewhere without the 'Jolly's' of the world in control.

'Well, there is one thing we do need to do,' Rusty said.

Everyone looked at him.

'That's the need to organise our various visits well in advance,' he said.

'We already do!' Harry reminded him.

'Yes, I know that,' Rusty replied. 'But now that he's going to feed all 'requests' through that bloody silly committee, it'll take weeks for an agreement to come back.'

A few glum drinks later and they had departed to their various homes. Such was the Jolly effect.

The following morning began with the whole school assembling at the Cathedral. The Head boy stood all by himself. He couldn't understand why no one wanted to share his latest 'lyrics' on the present hymn. He looked about but all the other staff were careful to sit as far away as possible from this mindless bore. He continued to scribble away anyway. It would be another little 'gem' for the next dinner party. On their way back from the Cathedral the Escape Committee were feeling less than vibrant about the first day of teaching but before that could begin there would be another morning meeting.

'What on earth will the silly sod talk about this time?' Harry wondered.

'Sod all, as usual,' Chewy said.

He was right. Jolly wittered on again but no one except the creeps had listened. He handed over to Wooden and that was of even less value to anyone. After the meeting there were quite a few staff who asked the same questions and received the same answers from their colleagues.

'What did he say?'

'Who?'

'The Head.'

'Dunno.'

'What about the deputy?'

'What about him?'

'What did he say?'

'Dunno.'

'What did anyone else say?'

'Dunno.'

And so another day of another term started.

Those on the staff who were about to see their examination groups during that first day were not looking forward to it at all. They knew by bitter experience what they would find. After a four week break anyone might have expected some work to have been done. What did they find? Nothing. None of their charges had lifted a book, checked through any notes or given the slightest thought to the examinations which would be upon them within weeks. What a surprise. Others, who didn't have that joy ahead of them, had the younger ones to cope with instead. It was a toss up between which camp would have the more difficult and stressful time. The staff room at break that afternoon saw a forlorn mixture of staff who were already looking distinctly battle weary. It was going to be a long half term.

'Never mind,' Rusty said. 'It's only eleven weeks, one day, thirty five minutes and... ten seconds until the end of term!'

'You say the nicest things,' Compo said. 'Any more little gems like that?'

'Yes!' Rusty said. 'And that involves you and you!'

He pointed directly at Chewy and Compo. Both of them sat up. What was this about?

'I think we need to organise some cross curricular activity!' he said.

'That sounds rather smutty!' Lill grinned.

'Chance would be a fine thing!' Harry offered.

'Come on then,' Chewy said. 'What's the plan?'

The plan was a joint trip to London, taking in 'Theatre Studies', 'English' as well as 'Design and Technology'. Not only would it be a natural bridging of subjects, pulling all of them together for one main event, but it would save a hell of a lot of money if they all went off in one bus. The added bonus was that it might end up as a great day out. Anything to get away from the place if only for a day.

'There's a production coming on later in the term,' Rusty said, 'Which is ideal for all three of us. It covers a set text for us, gives a wider understanding of theatrical technique as well as a pretty good example of how a designer can create an illusion of complete reality in a totally false environment.'

'Cor!' Lil said. 'I love it when he talks 'erudite'! I bet he does the same, or better, when he talks dirty!'

'Try me!' Rusty grinned.

'Sounds all right to me,' Compo said.

'Well,' said Chewy. 'Let's get the details so we can plug it into this half arsed committee.'

The trouble that trip was to cause later in the term was, as far as the 'management' were concerned, an 'infringement of protocol' and the important need for the correct 'paper procedure'. Things were getting steadily worse.

'Examination coursework' were two words which all teaching staff hated. It always happened at this time of year. All attempts which were made to finalise, complete or at least gather in something from the kids which could be assessed in good time were usually met with blank stares or a mixture of apathy and inertia from them. It's extraordinary how kids of fifteen plus can appear to be so dense and unmotivated. A few of them were on top of the work but too many of them were still messing about without any sign of urgency. It was probably the worst part of the academic year for all of them and there were still five weeks of this to go. On the second Saturday of the term, after morning lessons, two of the Escape Committee were in the staff room, moaning.

'My lot are driving me up the bloody wall!' Rusty complained.

'You think you have problems,' Chewy said. 'I'd swap my bloody lot any day!'

A few other members of staff wandered in to the staff room as they were talking. Two of them were Lill and Harry.

'Happy coursework time?' Lill asked as she sat down with them.

'No!' they both answered.

'Well,' Harry said. 'This should cheer you up.'

He was standing over by the notice board, checking over a few things, a big grin on his face.

'What,' Chewy asked, 'could possibly cheer me up?'

'This might,' Harry said. 'According to this 'ere list, posted by our esteemed Head of Sport, the King of P.E. and all round intuitive selector of the most qualified members of staff for sporting activities...,'

'Get on with it!' Chewy said. 'What does it say?'

'You are down, you lucky person, for an away match this afternoon with the 'Colts'!' Harry said. 'Not only that. The venue for this momentous contest is in, wait for it..., Sherton Abbot!'

'Oh, shit!' was all Chewy could say.

There was one sport which Chewy really couldn't stand. Most of the others he tolerated but this one, with the 'Colts', for the under fifteen year old kids, he loathed. It was tennis. Chief in charge of running the teams was the Parrot, Derek Matthews, teacher of History and a total head case. He'd been given the 'joy' of organising tennis in the school by Jolly, not the P.E. Oaf, when old, and now doddery, Jeff Lowther, teacher of politics, couldn't cope any longer. Old Jeffrey had been glad to get rid of it and now bumbled about the place, still boring everyone rigid about pot plants. Even Quentin, bless him, steered clear of old Jeff when he saw him coming.

With not a shred of enthusiasm Chewy was now resigned to a complete and total waste of a day. It was bad enough having to be with the kids while they played this silly 'ping pong' game, but Sherton Abbot was miles away. It would be a two hour drive just to get there, then probably four hours of boredom while they ran around the courts. He wouldn't even get the chance to read, and then there would be another two hours on the road after that. They'd be lucky to be back for eight that evening. Joy of joys! He made his way down to the dining room with the rest of them hoping that he might be missed. No such luck. The Parrot joined them for lunch.

'Don't say a bloody word!' Chewy said as the Parrot sat down. 'I know already!'

'Know what?' Parrot asked, with a mock smile on his face. He knew damned well but didn't want to show it. This was a good chance to wind Chewy up. It didn't happen that often.

'Ping bloody pong!' Chewy said.

'Is this some new code language I'm supposed to know about?' Parrot asked, still smiling benignly.

'What time are we leaving?' asked Chewy, ignoring that.

'Leaving?' Parrot asked. 'Leaving?'

'Put him out of his misery, Parrot!' Lill said. 'He'll go on about it for days if you don't!'

'Oh, you mean the tennis!' Parrot beamed. 'Well, I reckon in about... twenty minutes.'

'Five!' Chewy muttered.

'Ten!' Parrot countered.

'Done!' Chewy agreed.

Almost an hour later they were still waiting for all the kids to turn up. They were still two short. Parrot had put the word out for them to arrive on time but few of them had done so for the appointed time. He'd been round the school twice, gathering up some of them but they still couldn't find the other two. Chewy was sitting in the front of the bus, seething. Then he suddenly got out shouting at the kids.

'Right you lot!' he bellowed. 'You have two minutes to find the missing two or you'll all be on detention with me for the rest of the week! Now go!'

Every one of them shot off in different directions and before the two minutes were up they had found the missing pair. Neither were in their tennis gear but one of the others had bundled it up in a bag and stuffed it into their hands. They knew what detention with Chewy could be like. He took a joy in handing out half inch brushes to sweep the studio and workshop. That always took hours. They didn't want that experience or cleaning out that awful sink of his either. That was the worst task of all. But now they were thankfully clear of that and they could at last go. Parrot and Chewy frisked them all before they left. This was standard procedure. Three assorted tinnies, two lighters and four packets of fags later and they were ready, the names of the malefactors registered in Chewy's mental filing system. He'd be dealing with them personally when they returned. The minibus they were using was a hired one, complete with driver. The one that had been stolen when they viewed the old nuthouse never did turn up. The two other school buses were in use by other staff and the driver of this one was not a happy man. He didn't like kids using 'his' bus and made that fairly obvious all the way there and all the way back. Before he started the engine he laid down the ground rules for the journey.

'I have just cleaned my bus,' he said to Parrot and Chewy. 'Would you mind if I had a few words with this lot.'

'Feel free,' Parrot said.

Chewy waved a hand in compliance. The kids were jumping around all over the place, not taking a blind bit of notice as he began to speak.

'If I can...,' he began. 'I just want to say...' he started again.

Chewy closed his eyes in partial despair but then turned in his seat and bellowed down the bus.

'SHUT IT!'

The kids sat down immediately and silence took over.

'Thank you,' Chewy said. 'This gentleman would like to say something to you.'

He held up a hand in introduction and the driver began again.

'Well, err, yes, thank you,' he said, collecting himself together. 'I just wanted to say that I don't want any chewing gum stuck up anywhere, feet on the seats, rubbish on the floor, damage to the upholstery or anybody eating anything at all. Don't fool about when we're moving. You must put your seat belts on and leave them on until we stop. Thank you very much.'

He turned back to the controls and started the engine. The kids had switched off long before he had finished. Three of them were picking their noses and a few others were scratching themselves in strange places. Most of them were gazing out of the windows, lost in their own private thoughts.

'Belt up!' Parrot yelled, which brought them back to the world. As the bus moved off they struggled into their seat belts and the two hour journey had begun. Chewy closed his eyes and dozed off. He slept, all the way. He came too with a start. Parrot was shaking him gently.

'We're here,' he said.

Sherton Abbot is a tiny village, deep in the heart of Devon. Its only claim to fame was the private school which had been there almost as long as Braumstate had. There was a rumour that it had been founded by another 'bent' member of the aristocracy, one Maximillian Sherton, way back in the fourteenth century. He had blackmailed the local clergy about the misappropriation of church funds and the shady 'doings' of the Abbot of the local Monastery. To keep him quiet the Abbot had built him a large country house and then, against all expectation, moved in with Sherton, leaving his order forevermore. The Abbot turned out to be just as 'bent' and just as insatiable as Sherton in his 'tendencies'. To serve both their peculiar 'needs' they had, with the same misappropriated funds, extended the house to take in the male offspring of the local gentry to train and educate them, and not just academically. And so the school had begun and continued to maintain itself on the high fees which were demanded from anyone who wanted to send their male issue to them.

After fifty years the initial reputation for their deviant activity had gradually faded and over the centuries it became an establishment for clean, healthy living and hard work. It was still a boy's school and still drew its population from the well to do. Consequently most of the pupils were hateful little shits who despised anyone with less than one 'Roller' in front of the country mansion and a weekly income to match buying one. This was not going to be an easy tennis match. On the outskirts of the village the stone flanked gates to the school came into view. Leaning against one side of the gate was a long tall streak, dressed in immaculate school tennis gear, who had been posted there to meet them. They were usually met at other schools by some scruffy wretch but this one was squeaky clean and very haughty with it. The bus pulled up at the entrance and the tall streak ambled over to them.

'I take it you are Braumstate?' he said, nose slightly in the air.

'That's right, wack!' Chewy said deliberately. 'Take us to the man with the plan!'

The tall streak was slightly taken aback at this but he climbed up behind Chewy and amongst the kids, sniffing the air.

'Oh, I say,' he said. 'Bit rich in here!'

A few choice remarks floated up from the kids in reply to that but both Parrot and Chewy deliberately ignored them, much to the discomfort of the tall streak who, having to sit amongst the 'commoners,' was less than happy. They drove on through the gates and down to the School itself. They were met outside the main building by a tall, greying character in a pin-striped suit with a dark blue anorak pulled over it.

'Oh shit!' Parrot mumbled. 'It's him!'

Chewy wondered what he meant by this but it didn't take long to find out. They piled out of the bus and while the kids were organising their gear, Chewy and Parrot shook hands with Blue Anorak.

'Super to see you!' Blue Anorak said, grinning from ear to ear. 'Good day for it, what?"

'Good day for what, what?' Chewy asked.

'Tennis old boy, tennis!' Blue Anorak said, horribly enthusiastically.

Parrot applied a polite smile, Chewy forced a limp grin.

'We have a real 'urgent' one here!' Chewy mumbled sideways.

'It'll get worse,' Parrot said quietly, without moving his lips.

'Courts are through here,' Blue Anorak was saying, just as enthusiastically. 'Let me show you. This way!'

They followed him through a wide Tudor archway, which passed through and under the main building. Beyond this was a wide lawn, a line of mature trees and then the tennis courts.

'Just look at that lot,' Parrot said, miserably.

He was referring to the twelve tennis courts, all laid out on a specially prepared synthetic surface. Not like the crap they had at Braumstate, a surface which was fine grit and breaking down. This was the 'state of the art' for tennis court surfaces, good for playing on throughout the year, whatever the weather. Neither of them noticed the rectangular sections set into the surface at either end of each court or wondered what they were for.

'Must have cost thousands and thousands to install this lot,' Parrot said.

'Hardly surprising,' Chewy said, 'when you consider the fees this place charges.'

Blue Anorak was standing rubbing his hands together.

'Shall we get started then?' he said brightly.

He launched into a rapid delivery of tennis gibberish which left Chewy well behind, and Parrot with a fixed grin on his face. Chewy gave up after five minutes of it and left Parrot to cope. After all, this was his 'bag' and not Chewy's. Chewy didn't give a stuff about the silly bloody game and didn't want his ears worn out listening to the Blue Anorak quacking on about it. He wandered around for a while looking for something to sit on. He wasn't looking forward to the next few hours and was intent on staying away from Blue Anorak as much as possible.

'I don't believe you!' Lill said.

'It's true!' Chewy said. 'That's exactly as it happened.'

'Wish I'd seen it,' Harry said, grinning.

This was the following Monday after the Saturday 'match'. The Escape Committee had loved the story Chewy had given them.

Chewy had found somewhere to sit while Parrot and Blue Anorak were discussing the order of play. Just outside the open wire enclosure and placed centrally to the twelve courts was a low, grey, metal box with a wooden, shed-like canopy over it. It was just over seat height but it would do as far as he was concerned. He hitched himself up onto it and settled himself. The thing gave slightly under his weight, gave off a couple of complaining, straining clanks but it held and he thought no more about it.

All the kids had warmed up by now and the match was underway, The twelve courts were full of kids, all rushing around the place, defending the honour of their own school. Blue Anorak was rushing from court to court, analysing every stroke, scribbling notes and bobbing and weaving, echoing the motion of the players. He became extremely animated with Parrot a couple of times as he was discussing the action but Chewy could see, even on the other side of the court, that Parrot was just as pissed off as he was. After half an hour Chewy was as bored rigid as he'd expected to be but then an argument about a point broke out in the middle of the whole area. Their side were disputing the last delivery. This became very interesting; much more so than the silly game itself.

'No, no!' one of the Sherton Abbot twerps was saying. 'That was definitely out!'

'Bollocks!' came the Braumstate reply.

'I say!' replied the opposition. 'Hardly language for the courts, old man!'

'To hell with that!' said one of the kids, 'The bloody ball was in!'

'Would you mind being a little more civilised?' was the snotty answer.

By this time they were up to the net and Chewy was helpless, too far away to prevent the smack in the mouth which zapped over from the Braumstate kid. Everyone stopped playing as the other crunched over backwards, lip bleeding. Then he was up again, leaping over the net and swinging his racket. The other side-stepped and kicked him up the backside as he flew past. That's when the rest joined in and the real contest of the day began.

Chewy shot up from the metal box he was sitting on but a horrible clank from behind made him stop. The top of the box fell off, exposing a row of levers. He tried to fit it back in place but accidentally pushed some of the levers as he did so. All over the courts the rectangular sections at the back of each court opened and a machine slid up from each of them delivering a fusillade of tennis balls at a great rate of knots. The air was now full of yellow missiles.

Chewy fought with the levers but had to give up. Within seconds the courts were covered with balls and they were still coming from the machines. Blue Anorak, Parrot and the kids were rolling around trying to walk but with so many balls on the ground this was impossible. Still the missiles came. They didn't stop until Blue Anorak fought his way round to where Chewy had been sitting and closed the control unit down. Surprisingly, the match was abandoned.

Jolly Jack was fretting again. This time it was about the need to make potential parents more aware of the school and what it had to offer their offspring. This was Maggie Thornton's domain and as Development Officer she was putting forward a few suggestions.

'As I see it, Headmaster,' she said, 'there are several ways this can be done, some more costly than others, but all of them will be effective.'

Jolly sat back like an expectant little boy and allowed her to continue.

'Temporary exhibition units could be used for two purposes,' Maggie began. 'First in the school itself to show parents and visitors a wider aspect of what we are doing. Then this could be taken around the region or even further afield. The I.S.I.S. venues are a good example.'

'Oh, yes,' Jolly said. 'I.S.I.S. is a very good idea. We have used them in the past, and I do believe that the next exhibition is being planned for quite soon.'

I.S.I.S., or the 'Independent Schools Information Service' was a Nationally organised body which promoted the Independent sector. The School, as Jolly had said, had used it before to display its 'wares' to possible punters.

'Yes,' Maggie said. 'That's right. It's next week in fact and I've already booked our place there. I've found the school's exhibition unit, and that's in the process of being reorganised.'

'Oh, good' Jolly intervened. 'You will talk to the Financial Controller about that won't you? We must be careful about additional expenditure during these difficult times.'

'Yes,' Maggie said slowly. 'I will.'

It was difficult talking to Jolly most of the time. She wished he would just listen instead of picking up everything she said and worrying about it.

'As well as that,' Maggie continued, 'wouldn't it be a good idea to move the model of the new, proposed building from your office and have set up in the main reception area?'

She didn't bother suggesting that it was also about time he told all the staff about it; at least those who didn't know it existed. Just moving the model would be enough. Then he would have to say something.

'There are two other areas of general advertising which need to be looked at,' she continued. 'One of these revolves round the printed word, publications and straightforward advertising and the other is a more recent trend. This is the use of videos of the School either for sale or as free 'samples' of what we are, where we are and what we do. This last one will take more time to organise.'

'I say!' Jolly said. 'Videos! That sounds very interesting. Are we thinking about a lot of money there?'

'That's something I'm looking into,' Maggie said. 'Although I have to say that whatever the cost it should be covered by the fees of new pupils to the school. If we were able to take on only three or four more pupils by using this method then they would more than cover that cost.'

'Yes, yes,' Jolly said. 'But do keep the Financial Controller well informed.'

'Yes, Headmaster.' she said, again very slowly and with great control.

Maggie had already started the ball rolling before she talked to Jolly. She'd been with the ground staff earlier in the day and they had recovered the 'exhibition unit' from the store. It was a battered, scruffy thing which really needed junking. A heavy wooden framed arrangement. It was in three parts which hinged together. A soft board panel on each part provided the exhibition surface. With the I.S.I.S. exhibition only a few days away there would be no time to find a suitable replacement.

'Leave it to us,' Big Mac told her. 'We'll get the thing tarted up well before then.'

'Thanks,' she said. 'Couple of days from now?'

'Easy!' he said grinning from ear to ear.

That left her with another problem. Finding something suitable to exhibit. She spent a day in the library with Betty 'Flash' Gordon, the Librarian, but didn't find much to use. There were a few old photographs of the place but nothing up to date. Quentin faffed about trying to help but just managed to get in the way. She gave this up and tried the other members of the Escape Committee. They might be able to help.

'I've got a few shots of past productions,' Compo said. 'You can have those. They're a fair size, not just silly prints.'

'Great!' Maggie said. 'That's a start.'

'There's a number of projects the kids have done over the years,' Chewy offered. 'Plenty on negative if you want to look through them.'

'Yes please,' she said. 'It all helps.'

The others didn't have anything but were willing to help take a few shots around the school. After seeing Jolly and another day later she had all she needed and had the negatives and new film processed. From the prints she chose a selection which gave a flavour of the place, had these blown up to sensible sizes and after another day she now had something to show. Big Mac and the lads had the unit tidied up and freshly painted and the day before the I.S.I.S. exhibition was due to be mounted she was ready. It wasn't perfect by any means but it would do for now until she could have something more purpose made. A minibus was ready and the unit stood waiting to be loaded. Quentin was still fussing around but hadn't added anything to the process. She was due to leave in the next few minutes when the Mad Hatter came running up.

'Phone call!' she said. 'It's that Video Company you were talking to the other day.'

The Company were very keen to help with the promotion of the school and would be in that part of the world later that day. That gave her another problem. Who would take the bus and the unit to the venue? As she looked out of the window she saw Quentin fiddling about with the unit, waiting for her to come back.

'Me!' Quentin said. 'But I...,'

'It'll be all right,' Maggie said. 'I must see these video people, which means you have to take the exhibit to the exhibition. There's no one else who can.'

'But...,' Quentin tried to say.

'Quentin,' Maggie said firmly. 'Mr Gilpin will be with you. You won't be by yourself. Now come on!'

'Oh, All right,' he said slightly sulkily. 'If I have to.'

'You have to!' Maggie said.

Sheamus Gilpin turned up, all bright eyed and bushy tailed.

'Are we all ready?' he asked in his lilting Irish accent, rubbing his hands together.

'The units over there,' Maggie said. 'Quentin's taking my place. I have to see some folk about some other school business.'

'Fine, fine!' Sheamus said. 'Let's get on with it then!'

Maggie left them to it. She did have a slight worry about these two. Of all the staff they were the most likely to cock things up, but, on the other hand what could go wrong? All they had to do was put it in the minibus take it to the venue, stand it up and then bring it back. She dismissed her concern and concentrated on the job in hand.

She had a good long chat with the Video company representative. They had quite a lot of experience for this kind of work and he was very helpful. Everything he said was straightforward and she couldn't see any problems at all. They would require some kind of shooting script, the voice over could be handled by one of many professional actors which they had on their books, and as soon as they had organised the actual script he reckoned they could have the whole thing sewn up in a couple of weeks.

'That sounds great!' Maggie enthused. 'I'll get on to that right now. If you can let me have a reasonable idea of cost, I can take that to the Headmaster and we can get going!'

It didn't quite work out that way. She spent the rest of the day preparing a basic script and then worked on some advertising material for local and national press. By the end of the day she had both more or less complete but still had a few things she needed to check through with Jolly. That would have to wait until tomorrow. Time had been ticking away and it was almost seven when she emerged from the building. As she walked up through the School, she saw the minibus parked awkwardly in the forecourt. Sheamus was leaning over a distraught Quentin at the back of it. The back doors of the minibus were open and Quentin was sitting on the step, crying his eyes out.

'Quentin?' she asked. 'Quentin? What on earth is the matter?'

Sheamus stood up and rubbed his forehead. Quentin continued to weep, holding his head in his hands without looking up.

'It's a long story,' Sheamus sighed.

2

The story Sheamus Gilpin told Maggie was an absolute cracker. When Maggie had left both Sheamus and Quentin earlier that day, they had picked up the exhibition stand from the ground staff and brought it round to the back of the bus, both doors wide open and ready to receive it. It was a fair old width and try as they might they couldn't get it inside. They turned it round and tried again. It just wouldn't fit. If it had only been a few inches less than there would have been no problem. Horizontally or vertically it just wouldn't go in to the back of the minibus. Neither of them had actually thought about pushing it in *diagonally*. No, that would have been far too simple and they may have been accused and then found guilty of using common sense.

'If we take the two sides off,' Quentin said brightly, 'we could get them inside without any problems. They're much narrower. Then the other big piece can go up on the roof rack!'

Sheamus had to agree with him. As far as he could see it was going to be the only way to get the whole thing transported to the exhibition site. Having scrounged a screwdriver from the ground staff they took the sides off. Sheamus had asked Chewy first but he'd told them to go and do something unpleasant. He'd lost too many screwdrivers like that in the past. With the two sidepieces inside the minibus, they carefully heaved the main part onto the top with all the new photographic panels mounted on it.

Sheamus left Quentin to secure the whole thing on the top and wandered off to see whether Jolly and Wooden had gone on ahead to the exhibition venue. They were to be there for the first part of the day. Harvey Sheasby and Wide Mouth were then due to take over in the afternoon. The Mad Hatter confirmed they had already left so Sheamus came back to the minibus to find Quentin already in the driver's seat. He climbed in to the passenger seat and off they went.

Forty five minutes later they arrived in the middle of a large market town and found the community hall which had been booked for the event. Sheamus jumped out of the bus and went on ahead to find the actual position for the unit and to see if Jolly and Wooden had arrived. There they were on the small area designated for the school, waiting patiently, having checked through all the school propaganda which they'd brought with them. They had organised a table and a couple of chairs and all that remained to do was to erect the display unit itself. The hall was a hive of activity. Some of the stands were finished, their owners standing back admiring their own amateur handiwork. Others were still in 'blu tac' and 'sellotape' modes, sticking hundreds of photographs, school rules, and general 'tat' all over the place. Some of the stands had gone 'high tech' and were bristling with video monitors, slide shows and garish lighting. It was enough to put any prospective parent off completely. Collectively it was a nightmare of the most naff display work ever seen.

Jolly wasn't looking very happy. Sheamus wondered why. They had arrived in good time so what had upset him? Wooden gave him a quick resume, as far as he ever could, of what had happened not fifteen minutes before. Jolly had stomped off to the gents while he explained, the shoe of one foot slipping off on every step as he walked.

The stand next to them had been screwed, bolted and nailed together by the staff of that school, a minor prep school somewhere in the wilds of Wiltshire. When they had finished their labours one of the organisers of the whole exhibition had walked by, checking all exhibitors. When he saw this one he'd gone slightly 'apeshit', much to the distress of Jolly and the stunned silence of Wooden. Both of them thought they might be blamed for it. What this official had said was 'pithy' if nothing else.

'Too bloody tall!' he barked at them. 'Cut it down! You should know by now that no one is allowed a stand over seven feet tall! Every stand must be the same height. Cut it down to the correct height or leave the building, NOW!'

Jolly was taken aback as the official shouted this last word directly at him. He made a weak attempt at an explanation but one of the staff who had just erected this nightmare of a stand stepped forward and, hands up, said simply, 'O.K., O.K! We'll sort it. Just give us a minute or so, that's all.'

'I said now and I mean now!' the official repeated, standing there, arms folded, insistent on an instant 'adjustment'.

The other staff member shrugged and walked back to one of the toolboxes he'd been using. He pulled out a saw and walked over to the stand, beckoning to his colleague. The other one hoisted the stand up off the floor while he attempted to saw a foot off one of the uprights. The thing was wobbling about all over the place and almost fell over a couple of times while he was sawing away. He stopped sawing and called over to both Jolly and Wooden who were just standing there staring.

'I say,' he asked. 'Could you both give us a hand?'

Jolly looked as if he'd been slapped across the face, his hand coming up to his chest in surprise. Wooden just blinked.

'Just for a minute or so?' the other asked again.

Feeling distinctly ill at ease Jolly came forward and held the stand just above the point where the other had been sawing. Wooden blinked as an automaton seeing his lord and master complying to the request and positioned himself behind Jolly, hanging on at the back while the sawing started again. Twelve inches of substantial timber flopped onto the floor.

'Three more to go!' said the one with the saw and the process was thus repeated three more times. Unfortunately on the last 'cut' Jolly almost had his foot taken off by the exuberance of the character in charge of the saw, his shoe being badly chewed up as the saw passed through the remaining wood and down to the floor. What had been a perfectly good pair of black, shiny shoes now had the right one with a terrible gash across it, the laces shredded. Jolly was not happy. That wasn't helped by Wooden trotting out his standard line, 'Is there a problem here?'

Sheamus scuttled back to the minibus before Jolly reappeared from the gents. He found Quentin in a state of great distress. He was standing up against the minibus with his hands to his mouth, his eyes like saucers. The two panels from inside the bus were standing against the bus, but there was no sign of the main, central part.

'Where's the middle bit?' Sheamus asked.

'I...I...don't...know!' Quentin squeaked.

'Whajamean, you don't know?' Sheamus asked.

Quentin could only shake his head. A horrible thought managed to surface in Sheamus's brain.

'Didn't you tie the bloody thing down?' he demanded.

'I thought it was quite safe!' Quentin whined. 'It must have come off on the way here!'

It had. About half way there the speed of the bus and a sudden gust of wind had lifted the whole thing off the top and it simply floated away like a large, wooden leaf, unseen by the pair of them as they sped down the road. There had been no other traffic on the road in front or behind them so no one else had seen the thing sail away. Sheamus smacked his forehead and wondered what the hell he was going to say to Jolly Jack.

'Get in the bus and go and look for it!' he snapped, 'Quick!'

'W, w, where?' whined Quentin.

'The same way we came, you idiot!' Sheamus growled at him.

Quentin climbed back into the bus, and with a grinding of gears, shot off the way they had come. Sheamus watched him go and then turned back to the hall. He would have to tell Jolly but for the life of him he didn't know how too. He walked slowly inside, wringing his hands. Jolly spotted the worried look on Sheamus's face and this just set him off into one of his own 'worry' modes.

'Sheamus!' he said, his whole face a complex wreath of furrows. 'What's the matter?'

'Well...I...there's...' Sheamus tried to say.

'Is there a problem here?' Wooden chipped in chirpily.

By sheer chance, twenty miles down the road, Quentin found the missing section which was lying in a field. It had sailed up into the air as they had whipped round a bend in the road and then floated down amongst a few grazing cows. Miraculously it had missed every one of them, or the school might have had a rather large, bovine legal problem on their hands. It was only slight scuffed and with some effort Quentin struggled with it and managed to hump it over the hedge and heave it back on top of the bus. He drove back to the hall at high speed. Screeching to a halt outside the hall he ran inside to find the others. Panting and out of breath he pushed through the other staff from other schools, all still busily putting their exhibits together, and found them. Jolly wasn't any happier. He only had half an exhibit for the day and that didn't even have the name of the school on it. Having only one serviceable shoe didn't help either.

'I've got it!' Quentin wheezed. 'It's on the minibus!'

'Right!' Sheamus said. 'Let's get the thing up here, fast!'

They both ran back to the bus but when they arrived there was nothing on the top. It had disappeared again! Quentin's knees buckled under him and Sheamus smacked his forehead again, his eyes closed, a grimace of total frustration on his face. Jolly stood waiting inside the hall. Sheamus bundled Quentin back into the bus and they shot off again. Three hours later they had travelled backwards and forwards along the same stretch of road a dozen times looking for it, Sheamus hanging out of the window looking over hedges and fences as they passed them. But the unit had disappeared forever into a stream, where it had slowly sank and then drifted along the bottom until it became stuck in an outcrop of weeds and silt, never to be seen again.

Back at the hall Jolly and Wooden had to cobble the two remaining pieces together and produced a badly hand-written sign on a piece of paper from a wide roll used for drying hands they had found in the gent's loo. It wasn't quite the same as the original which was now lying in a soggy, disintegrating state in the stream, together with photographs, statistics and several other bits of relatively vital information about the school. That was the morning session.

The afternoon session was no better. It was far worse. Wide Mouth and Harvey Sheasby arrived to relieve Jolly and Wooden and were taken aback by the state of the stand but didn't dare say anything. Jolly stomped off followed by Wooden, leaving them to it without saying a word. Jolly was glad to get away but Wooden wasn't looking forward to the journey back to the school with him. Wide Mouth just sat there in the hall feeling totally embarrassed at having to sit under a loo roll banner with the school's name on it. Harvey pretended not to belong at all. The parents who did approach them walked on quickly when they saw the stand, such as it was.

Later in the afternoon, during a lull in parental activity, Harvey noticed the paper name of the school had sagged a bit and tried to adjust the position of the two sides. All he did was to nudge one of them back too far and it clonked into the stand immediately behind them. Two seconds later a terrible 'crunch' hit the air. Harvey made the great mistake of wanting to find out what had happened and stuck his nose round the stand, still holding the part of the School stand which had connected with its neighbour. Lying on the floor, in front of the stand he'd bumped, and in a thousand pieces, were the remains of a six foot wing span biplane. This had been the pride and joy of the other school. It had been carefully constructed, over a period of six months by staff and pupils, especially for this exhibition, and had formed the whole focus for their stand. Now it was so much matchwood. Harvey, in nudging the Braumstate School 'stand' had knocked this thing off on the other side and now looked at it in abject horror. The staff from the other school were almost in tears at what had happened.

'Oh, dear. Anything I can do?' he said uselessly.

The slow look he received from the others was pure unadulterated venom. Harvey beat a hasty retreat on the excuse of finding himself and Wide Mouth a cup of tea. The I.S.I.S. exhibition for the school had not been a resounding success.

Quentin was in a hell of a state for a couple of days, desperately trying to think of something he could do to make amends. Then he did find something which seemed to be a very good idea, at the time. The idea he developed came from a conversation he overheard between Maggie and the Fat Controller. Maggie had asked him to come over to discuss the idea of the video for the school. Quentin was lurking in the fbackground tending one of his ghastly pot plants. She outlined her thoughts to the F.C. as Quentin listened, much as she had to Jolly, and then asked him about the financial side.

'How much are we thinking about?' he asked.

'Probably around three thousand,' she said.

'Is it in the budget?' was his first question. That was always his first question no matter what the conversation was about.

Maggie realised quite quickly that she was dealing with a complete automaton, someone without a shred of thought other than a balance book. His eyes gave him away even before he opened his sly little mouth. They were dead, lifeless, enlarged orbs, due to the thick lenses he wore, but nonetheless still quite dead. A typical accountant. He didn't even qualify for that classic definition given by Oscar Wilde, 'A man who knows the price of everything and the value of nothing.' He failed that one miserably on both counts.

'What budget?' Maggie asked.

'Ah,' he said, leaning back in the chair. 'There we are then. If it isn't in the budget we can't do it, can we?'

Maggie nearly delivered her first thought which was, 'You patronising bastard!' Instead she smiled sweetly and said something which changed his mind instantly.

'The Headmaster is very keen that we should go ahead on this.'

He sat up immediately. That had made quite a difference. It even changed the way he talked. He began to lisp, in a rather effected and distinctly slimy manner.

'In that case,' he said, 'I'll see what I can do. How much do you think may be involved for this new venture?'

Maggie had a difficult time trying not to throw up at the way this creep was behaving.

'As I said before, around three thousand,' she said. 'But I expect to be given a more accurate figure in the next day or so.'

'I see,' said the Fat Controller, relaxing again. 'Then as soon as you have a more positive quotation you'll no doubt let me know.'

'Of course,' Maggie said.

'Normally we would need three competitive prices,' he said.

'That won't be possible,' Maggie said. 'There are few companies who can do this in the time available. Besides, as I said, the Headmaster is very keen to move on this quite soon.'

'Ah, yes,' the Fat Controller said. 'You'll be in touch then?'

'I will,' she answered, but didn't like the thought of being 'in touch' at all. Not with him.

The Fat Controller slithered out with a smug expression on his face and Maggie just sat there. "How can anyone take that greasy sod seriously?" she thought.

Quentin had absorbed all of it. He'd been fiddling about with the same pot plant during the whole conversation. He thought that this might be the chance to redeem himself after the disaster of the I.S.I.S. exhibition. If he could get himself organised quickly before this other company were brought in he might just pull it off. By producing a video for the school and thereby saving it a great deal of money he would be back in everyone's favour. It didn't seem to be much of a problem. A few scenes here and there should do it. After all he'd had quite a lot of Amateur Dramatic experience. Not everyone had staged the epic 'Ben Hur' on an eight foot wide stage! He thought he knew enough about presentation and timing and, oh, it would be so much fun! All he needed was a camcorder.

With the first week well over the management now turned their full attention to one of the most important events of the year. This was nothing to do with the public examinations, the worried planning for Sports Day or the agonised, endless discussions which continued to ensure a smooth and perfect series of events for Open Day. No. Their minds, such as they could ever be defined, were now concentrated on the day for the 'School photograph'.

It was always a nerve racking experience for all of them. Even though the School did not have a large number in the pupil body it could not have been organised under cover. When the kids, teaching staff, ancillary and administrative staff were brought together the overall number was close to eight hundred bodies. It was a strictly outdoor event. For obvious reasons the weather tended to play a rather important, if not vital, role in this.

There was, however, a new secret weapon in the school, recently acquired and at great expense, which was now at their disposal. This was the system of all systems, the latest in computerised, electronic, satellite sensitive, state of the art, high tech wonderland. This was F.O.G., 'Future Observation Guidance'. A weather forecasting system. Harvey Sheasby had installed it, after conning the management that this was an absolutely vital piece of equipment and fundamental to his subject, Geography. To the great irritation of Rollerball, it had replaced his 'dinky' set up but he couldn't do anything about that as Harvey was his departmental head. Other staff had other opinions about this latest 'innovation'. Chewy had a better explanation of the initial letters of this device. 'Fucking Obscure Guff!' He had a chat about this 'state of the art' addition to the School with Howard Stokes, his second in command in the department, just after Harvey had the thing up and running. Howard had been around a bit and knew more than most about the electronic world.

'What do you reckon then, Howie?" he asked.

'It's a piece of crap,' Howard said. 'That silly sod Sheasby has blown a few thousand quid on something which a piece of bloody seaweed can do more accurately than that ever will.'

Chewy wasn't really surprised but pushed for more background.

'What's it like?' he asked.

'Crap, as I said,' Howard replied. 'I saw the test run and that was embarrassing to watch. He's got the thing linked to some half arsed satellite, and God only knows how much we're paying for that. The resolution on the monitor is as good as watching domino's linking up or, at best, a chess board with huge squares. The U.K. looks like bloody 'Legoland'. There's no detail at all! It's really is crap!'

Harvey, on the other hand, was beside himself with pride. As far as he was concerned it was an incredible and wonderful device, far in excess of anything he'd seen before, which said a great deal about him and his experience of life as a whole. Yet, notwithstanding that, he now had the heady task of providing the school, on a daily basis, with the weather forecast. He'd been supplied, as part of the F.O.G. installation, with a special plastic wall hanging, 'F.O.G. STAT', which he could adjust for every day. It was just like the kind of thing some folk stick outside their door to let the milkman know how many bottles of milk they wanted, only slightly bigger.

A number of little dials and windows would reveal whether it would be, 'bright', 'sunny', 'overcast', 'rain', 'cloudy' and then wind direction which was indicated by a dial and pointer with a simple, 'N', 'S', 'E', 'W' on it and, gosh!, a pretend thermometer which had to be set every morning. It was appalling!

On the very first day the kids thought this was hilarious and one bright spark managed to screw the whole thing up with superglue, after setting the thing to 'snow' and minus thirty degrees celsius. Harvey quickly ordered a replacement and set it up again in a lockable glass case. He was not amused.

As the day for the school photograph drew nearer, Harvey was consulted twice a day to ensure the weather would be fine. He had a slight problem with this. Every reading which came from the satellite he was using predicted heavy rain for the duration and there was nothing he could do or say which would pacify Jolly. Needless to say it remained bright and dry. The whole of the management were now infected with this new worry. Would there be rain? Would there not be rain? Nobody knew and Harvey's little system began to shrink in their esteem.

Then the day before the photograph was due to be taken, dear old Harvey got it 'right' and the Met. Office got it 'wrong'. At least that's the way it looked at the time. He'd predicted sunshine and the National forecasting organisation, with all their vast resources had informed the nation that there would be heavy showers which would last for twenty four hours. At that morning meeting he had the nerve to say something which most of the staff thought was a slight overstatement of confidence.

'I have been in touch by telephone with the Met Office,' he said, in a smarmy, self satisfied fashion, 'to let them know we can always help them out with any future predictions.'

'Can you imagine,' Rusty said after this, 'What you would say if you'd received a phone call like that?'

'That's easy,' Chewy said. Everyone else nodded. Chewy didn't have to say anything.

The following day was the day of the photograph. At seven thirty in the morning Harvey tuned in the system and waited for the monitor to show him what the day had in store. He grinned and then scuttled off to set his little plastic display board. 'Sunny', 'Light breeze', '22ºC'. He stood back to look at it and then ran off pulling his anorak tighter.

Most people were looking out of their early morning window at the same time. It was pissing down, blowing a gale and bloody freezing! Time would tell. By morning break nothing had changed and Harvey was not feeling very well. Jolly arrived and stood in his 'delivery' position waiting for them all to quieten down before he began. Staff sighed and settled, waiting for the cancellation announcement for the photograph. It didn't come.

'Good morning everyone.' he said. 'I thought I'd just have a quick word with you about the School photograph. As you can see the weather isn't exactly conducive to our needs and so my feeling is this. We shall review the weather in one hour before making a final decision.'

A general buzz came up from all of them.

'The company organising the event are already constructing the stand, I believe?' He looked at Wooden for confirmation. Wooden nodded, woodenly.

'The company organising the event are already constructing the stand,' Wooden said, right on the ball again.

'I wonder if we're going to have a 'Rain Desk'?' Chewy muttered.

The next hour dragged by but just before the sixtieth minute the rain stopped. The clouds began to break up and within half an hour sunshine played down everywhere.

'It's a bloody miracle!' Rusty said in disbelief.

The photograph would go ahead. If the three characters putting the stand together had been told it was off they would not have been happy. They'd been working away in the pouring rain, at the top of the main lawn, constructing a massive, aluminium, stepped structure, ready to take the whole school. As the sun came through they finished tightening up the last few bolts and then sat on it to take a fag break before the chore of setting up the kids began.

'I bloody hate doing this,' one of them said. 'It always takes bloody ages.'

This was no reference to the construction. It was particular to organising the kids.

'I know,' said the other. 'It's like chasing bloody chickens. You get one and lose another. Get one kid in place and the rest of the little sods have moved.'

'Yeah.'

'Still,' the other said, 'there is one thing.'

'What's that?'

'Think of the money!'

'Oh, yeah!'

Fifteen quid a head multiplied by more than eight hundred wasn't bad for a few hours work. Everything had a good side. And so the process began. The kids were marshalled into a long 'crocodile' which stretched right round the School. Year group by year group they were 'loaded' on and packed together. Staff not shepherding the waiting multitude ambled about chatting and Harvey strutted around waiting for the congratulations to flood over him for his forecast. Nobody bothered.

Compo was having a bit of bother with his group until he hit on a wheeze which kept them, and the rest, as happy as sand boys. Seeing a 'Mexican wave' running around a snaking line of hundreds of kids did pass the time, although Jolly wasn't happy. For him it was 'unbecoming', and he despatched Wooden to put a stop to it. He failed.

Eventually, with all the kids in place the staff then began to take up their positions at the front and below the body of kids. That was where the sweepstake which was running amongst the staff, organised by Vic, came into its own. The School photograph was an accurate barometer of status. Nearer the centre was an indication of high favour. The outer edges underlined the opposite but there was no opportunity to choose. No. Wide Mouth was organising that according to Jolly's decision. With loud hailer in hand she walked back and forth with a clipboard, cueing the staff for their turn to sit.

'With a mouth like that to begin with,' Chewy said watching her perform, 'a loud hailer's just overkill.'

One by one they walked over to their designated seat much to the amusement of the kids. Roars, whistles and various cracks were made, depending on their status with them. Some of it was not quite 'nice'. Jolly wasn't happy again but there was nothing he could do to control it. All he could do was just sit on the front row, glowering. High stakes and quite a lot of money was riding on where Rollerball would be placed. He'd been trying so hard to ingratiate himself with Jolly. It would be interesting to see where he eventually sat. Dozens of eyes followed him as his name was called. He walked along the front, getting closer and closer to the centre. Then he kept going and, with Wide Mouth pointing and to his great humiliation, was almost at the other end before he sat down.

'There's hope yet' Rusty said grinning.

The rest of the Escape Committee agreed. They'd just won the sweepstake.

'No there's not,' Lill said as she and the rest of them took up their positions on the other extreme end of the group.

'Nothing changes then!' Chewy said.

Cameras had moved on since the days of kids being able to be on both ends of the photograph. The wide angle lens of this camera prevented that. A few kids tried rushing back and forth but were then pinned down by the staff and several photographs were taken. As the shutter clicked for the last time everyone relaxed but then the heavens suddenly opened, soaking all of them to the skin in seconds. Jolly didn't talk to Harvey for a few days after that.

That same evening Quentin was playing with his latest toy. It was a compact editing desk. As part of his idea for a video for the school he'd bought this machine with his own money as well as a camcorder. He'd now be able to handle the preparation of the final tape. All he had to do, he thought, was shoot the scenes and put it all together. The next few weeks would see him wandering around, camcorder on his shoulder, squinting through the eyepiece, following various staff and pupils around the school and quite often walking smack into walls and falling over kerb stones and plant pots.

'Just look at that daft sod,' Chewy said, looking out of the staff room window. 'What the hell does he think he's doing?'

'With Quentin,' Rusty said, 'there's no knowing. He's in his own silly little world most of the time.'

'Let's hope he bloody stays there,' Compo muttered, browsing through the Times Ed.

'You any further with this visit idea?' Chewy asked.

'Oh, yeah,' Rusty answered. 'Just had the details in the post today. The production I was talking about is 'The Arrival'. It's on at the National in four weeks time. Just right for after half term and the end of the examinations. Great set and effects. Should be good.'

'What about 'them'?' Compo asked.

'Our esteemed management?' Rusty said.

'No,' said Chewy. 'He means the dick heads who run this place.'

'All in hand,' said Rusty. 'I gave all the information to Wooden after the morning meeting. Numbers of kids, time of the play, departure times, arrival back here and the cost. It's a matinee so it'll be cheaper.'

'When will 'sir' let us know?' Compo asked.

'That's anybody's guess,' Rusty said, 'but they should let us know by next week.'

'Optimist!' Chewy grunted.

'What time will we leave?' asked Compo.

'No rush, really,' Rusty said. 'We don't have to be there until about two in the afternoon.'

That gave Chewy an idea.

'If we left earlier,' he said, 'we could do something in the morning and then take in the play after lunch. After all, if we're going all that way we could take advantage of the place. There's a lot to see.'

That wasn't a bad idea. London did have a lot to offer. It was worth thinking about.

The grind of coursework was still with them. It was coming together but very slowly. Some subjects were better off than others. Chewy's was one of the others. Although the kids had mostly finished their paperwork the projects were far from complete. Designing was one thing. Making was quite another. Most of the kids were running around like startled pigs, busily destroying Chewy's stock of raw materials in their desperation to complete their work. They only had a week left to do it.

'The bins are going to full this year,' Chewy moaned one day. 'I've haven't seen so much bloody crap for years!'

This was a standard statement he came out with every year. He was usually right. Compo, with his Theatre Arts group, was having better luck and was now waiting anxiously for his external moderator. Staff usually marked the kids work and then had another qualified teacher, from another school, arrive to mark it again. This was the 'moderation' process. Not a bad system, depending on the moderator.

They all had horror stories about unsympathetic moderators marking the kids down heavily, but this time, for Compo's lot, it was going to be slightly different. Compo checked his watch again and began to fret. The moderator was half an hour late. The shed they were using was ready, fully blacked out and a few lamps from an overhead rail shone down on the small makeshift stage area. The kids were ready, mumbling through their lines for their short performances and the audience had been sitting for a while. Compo had established the need for an audience to give the kids a real 'feel' for their work. It was slightly scary for them but experience had showed him that it did help to raise their 'delivery' for the moderator.

The audience was a combination of friends and few parents so a 'sympathetic' body was always a plus. But, as the minutes dragged by, they too were beginning to fidget. Then, like the kiss of death, Jolly arrived, fussing and smiling to the parents he could see sitting there. Compo found him a seat just off to one side and hoped his group wouldn't notice him when they performed their pieces.

Then the door flew open and in walked Ainsley Whitcombe, an old actor turned teacher and flamboyant, very flamboyant. He was wearing a wide brimmed velvet hat, a long scarf and a cloak which he whirled over his shoulder as he strode over to Compo holding out his hand.

'Compton, old dear!' he boomed. 'How wonderful to see you again!'

Everyone turned round to witness this apparition. Compo shook his hand and brought him over to a slightly raised seat at the back of the audience. He had been an old style actor manager but as the business had contracted he'd seen the writing on the wall and looked for pastures new. In teaching he could flaunt all his exhibitionist ways without worrying about the box office. As a moderator he was in his element even more so. Compo ran through the candidates list with him and then they were ready.

'On with the motley, dear boy!' Ainsley boomed, and the lights dimmed.

There were seven short performances and, with only a couple of prompts, everything went well. They took a short break in the middle and Ainsley and Compo talked to those who had performed. Then the others went through their pieces and after another interview with them it was all over. Jolly was very impressed and hung back while the audience and performers drifted away.

Compo spent a few more minutes with Ainsley while they agreed the final grades for each of the candidates and then they were finished. The kids had done quite well, Compo was more than happy. Jolly was still hovering. Compo sighed. He thought Jolly might have gone but was then faced with having to introduce Ainsley to him. Ainsley solved that problem for him.

'Headmaster, I take it?' he boomed in Jolly's direction.

Jolly stared at the large hand which shot out in his direction. He took it, nervously and Ainsley pumped it up and down vigorously, shaking Jolly all over at the same time.

'Well, now,' Ainsley boomed again. 'What did *you* think of our little thespian band, eh?'

Jolly didn't know what to say or how to say it in front of such a huge personality.

'Very nice,' he said wetly.

'Nice! NICE!' Ainsley almost shouted. 'They were *wonderful*! Quite *wonderful*! A great credit to young Compton here, don't you think so?'

'Oh, yes,' Jolly said meekly.

'Quite right, old thing! Quite right!' Ainsley grinned at him. 'Especially that little thing with the ... err... you know!'

He held his hands up in front of him, wobbling them up and down just as if he had two melons in his hands. Jolly went bright red. Compo was struggling to keep his face straight.

'And as for that other one,' Ainsley said, lasciviously, with a huge wink and a dig in Jolly's ribs, 'You know, the one with the..err...'

This time his hands hovered round his rear which he wiggled. Jolly spluttered and tried to say something but Ainsley cut him off.

'Which reminds me,' he said. 'I picked up a little something recently which I know you'll just love. Let me show you.'

He looked around and then said, 'perhaps we should be discreet about this and move over there, eh?'

He hooked his arms into theirs and took them over to a corner of the room and, looking sneakily over his shoulder to make sure there was no one else around, he slid a hand into an inside pocket and brought out a brown envelope. Jolly flinched and really didn't like what he thought was coming and tried to pull away but Ainsley held him firmly by the shoulder with his other hand.

'Now, now! Come along, dear boy,' he whispered in Jolly's ear. 'Don't be shy!'

Jolly froze, his hands clasped tightly against his chest. He was terrified about what he was going to see. Compo just shook with suppressed laughter. Jolly thought he was as terrified as himself and gave him one of his pathetic looks. Ainsley flourished the brown envelope high in the air and then brought it down in front of all of them, opening it very slowly and teased from it a postcard sized piece of card.

'What,' he said loudly, 'do you think of...THAT!' and he turned the thing, sticking it right in front of Jolly's face. It was a pensioner's bus pass!

Ainsley fell about laughing. Jolly sagged with relief. Compo was still trying not to laugh and didn't dare look at Jolly's face.

'Oh,' Ainsley cackled. 'Since I reached the age to qualify for this I've pulled that stunt so many times! They all fall for it! Every time! Every time!" His hat fell off and he had to sit down as he was laughing so much. Jolly wiped his face and tried to regain his tattered dignity.

'Well,' he said, straightening his tie. 'I'd...err... better be going now. Things to do you know. Things to do.'

He managed to shake Ainsley's hand, who was still roaring with laughter, and then he scuttled out the door. Compo collapsed next to Ainsley and they were still laughing fifteen minutes later. Wiping the tears from their eyes they left the shed and walked up to the school. Compo had been prepared for the joke. He'd seen it before. It was still just as funny.

'Your Headmaster,' Ainsley grinned. 'Not very 'jolly' is he?'

A couple of days later word came down from 'on high' that the joint trip to London had been agreed. The co-ordination committee had weighed up all the options and given due recognition to the combination of Theatre Arts, English and Design and Technology Departments on one venue.

'This is a true miracle!' Chewy said. 'A decision in less than a week! Never been known before!'

'Don't knock it!' Rusty said. 'Just play 'shtum'! We don't want them changing their minds!'

'This is true,' Chewy said. 'I just wish there wasn't so much bloody paper every time!'

All of them had been given photocopies of Jolly's memo giving them permission. They'd also received a copy of Rusty's original statement about the trip, including Rusty. This was Jolly being efficient again. He didn't realise that all he had to do was use the English language and communicate verbally. After all, he saw them every morning. But, no, it always had to be done on paper so that he and the world at large would have a record. That's why he had so many filing cabinets. They were stuffed full of meaningless, unimportant memos, messages and missives, homage to the God 'Paper'.

The paper didn't stop there. They all had to fill in a form for each kid they were taking which would then go back to the parents, so that they were fully aware of the overall cost of the trip, then that would come back to the school, complete with their signature of approval and everyone was happy. Well, that was the theory. Kids are not known for efficiency where paperwork is concerned, and weeks were to go by before all the forms arrived back.

'Is all this really necessary?' Compo complained.

'No,' Rusty and Chewy said at the same time. 'But it keeps Jolly happy!'

'How many are actually going?' Compo asked.

'With all the kids, some of whom are involved with one or more subjects,' Rusty replied, 'we have around fifty three altogether, plus staff; one full bus.'

Compo whipped out a pocket calculator, tapping out the number of kids and staff against the cost of the bus, £250, and the price of the theatre ticket, £7 esach. As the answer came up he sat back and blew out a breath.

'That works out at £11.71 per head,' he said. 'I'd like to know anyone who can take you into London, from here, in privately arranged transport, plug you into a theatre, pick you up again and bring you back for that!'

There was no answer to that, but Jolly now insisted that all the parents should be informed well before the event. After all it was an 'extra'. In truth he was probably right but it was not exactly an exorbitant amount for what the kids would gain from it.

'You remember that thought I had about doing something else while we're there?' Chewy asked.

They all nodded.

'Well, if we could leave a little earlier I could take my lot to look at the Transport and maybe the Science Museums. You two could plug into something else at the same time which could be just as relevant to your subjects, couldn't you?'

That was quite a thought. They were going to London. It had a lot to offer! That's when they laid their plans which, after the event, were to repeat on them, over and over again, like a bad kebab.

The third week of the term was almost over. Deadlines for coursework were now nudging everyone, staff and kids alike. As the staff battled on to get the work in, there were two of them who were responsible for collecting and despatching the initial marks for all subjects to the examining boards. One was dear old Ray Butcombe, a 'nice' man. The other was Penelope Grisby, a total twitch of a female who always needed to have everything 'right'. Ray had the good sense to let her get on with it. It made less work for him. She was far worse than the Fourth Reich. The Germanic nutcase could always be told, 'we won the bloody war!' which tended to keep her at bay. Penelope, bless her, could not be parried. She bore down on anyone who hadn't given her the necessary paperwork.

'I need your C.A.M.'s,' she would ask.

'I wish you wouldn't talk dirty in public,' Chewy answered.

'You now exactly what I mean!' she countered, not at all amused.

The 'C.A.M.s', she referred to were 'Computer Assisted Marksheets'. All subject staff had to fill these in carefully for their candidates, taking immense care to block in tiny little boxes denoting each mark with an HB pencil, it was all very prescribed. These things were in triplicate. One for the board, the top copy, one for the moderator, the second copy, and one for the subject teacher as a file copy. More bloody paper. A single mistake on one of these things would be a nightmare. They were pressure sensitive so that any mark made on the top copy would transfer itself all the way through. Advice was given about using an 'eraser' but there were more than a few cack-handed cretins on the staff who couldn't cope at all with that. Penelope Grisby did not have a 'nice' time for the next two weeks. Computer controlled mark sheets needed careful handling. So did she, as the slightest remark about them would send her off into a gyrating, twitching spasm.

Maggie Thornton was feeling the same kind of frustration. She'd had the quotation from the video company and passed that on to the Fat Controller. He'd sat on it for a few days then passed it to the Prick. Another few days had gone by and then he'd sent it to Wooden who didn't know what to do with it so he'd given it to Jolly.

Maggie sat waiting while this was going on, unable to do anything at all. Jolly finally found it amongst all his rubbish and went back to the Fat Controller to discuss it. And so it went on and on. With no decision likely Maggie turned her attention to other things. As well as looking after the ground staff and fabric of the school, the advertising and promotion of this 'Centre of Educational Excellence', she was still saddled with the problem of introducing 'Information Technology' to the whole School. It was not the easiest of situations.

The basic problem was not organising the equipment itself, but who was to be the poor sod who would have to take it on, maintain it and then make it available to the kids. Difficult. At least Jolly Jack was aware of the amount of money which would have to be spent, or so he had said. She was still pondering this one morning on her way to the staff room for coffee, as she met Chewy who was deep in thought about something else.

'Hello,' she said, walking alongside him. 'Is there anybody there?'

Chewy turned and stopped.

'Sorry Maggie,' he said. 'didn't hear you.'

Maggie looked at him. There was something going on.

'What's up?' she asked. 'What's happened?'

'Rusty's leaving,' he said. 'He's got another job.'

3

Upstairs, in the large Braumsley House, Quentin was in his bedroom sitting cross-legged on the floor scribbling notes. There were half a dozen videotape cassettes stacked on his desk which were the product of hours and hours of wandering around the school with the camcorder taking everything that didn't move and anything that did. There was no pattern or pre-arranged format to any of it. It was a random selection of shots. All he thought he had to do now was write a script and splice all the best bits together. Simple soul. He should have been on the school site working but Maggie was glad not to have him around.

Apart from Ralph, the butler, he was all by himself in the rambling old place. Lady Braumsley had taken an extended holiday abroad to calm herself down and get away from the recent disaster of her commitment to the new building. She was still smarting from that as a substantial part of her estate had been stuffed into hock to raise the money for it. With her gone from the place the atmosphere was much more relaxed and Quentin was free to get on with his own little life without the fear of her bearing down on him every second of the day.

He continued to scribble away for the rest of the morning and eventually organised a rather cliché-ridden script which he could begin to use with bits edited from the tapes. Unlike the last 'surprise' he had been responsible for, the ghastly model, he was going to keep this one an absolute and total secret. Not even Maggie would know until he was ready to show it to the Headmaster and the Governors. Wouldn't they be pleased!

'Well,' Chewy said. 'Congratulations! A successful escape!'

'Thanks, you old bugger!' Rusty said.

'Hey!' Chewy growled. 'Not so much of the 'old'. The rest I can cope with.'

The Escape Committee had gathered in the pub at lunchtime to drink Rusty's health.

'When did you find out?' Maggie asked.

'Last night,' he answered. 'Had a phone call offering me the job, providing I could take it up at the beginning of next term. It's another Head of Department but it's not here, that's the main thing!'

'That might give you a few problems,' Compo said. 'You need a full terms notice, don't you?'

'He's got a point there,' Vic said. 'Jolly Jack can be a pain in the nethers about 'protocol'.'

'Not this time,' Rusty said. 'I told him this morning and he seemed quite pleased, although he tried not to show it. I mentioned the business of a term's notice but he wasn't too bothered about that either. 'I'm sure we can wave that in the circumstances' was all he said.'

'I wonder why?' Harry said, a smile on his face.

The following morning highlighted exactly what Vic had said about one of Jolly's main fetishes. That was the one about seeing that everything had been seen to be properly and 'professionally' handled. It was yet another means of using as much paper as possible to cover the simplest of procedures. Jolly had sidled over to have a deliberately quiet and secretive few words with Rusty after the morning meeting. He then took him over to one side just in case some one overheard what he had to say. Rusty wondered what it was all about.

'I had thought,' Jolly said, almost whispering, 'that there might have been something on my desk this morning.'

Rusty dismissed a revolting thought but still didn't know what the hell he was talking about.

'I'm sorry Jol,… err, Headmaster,' he said. 'I'm not quite sure what you mean.'

Jolly became quite flustered but tried again, but this time whispering so low Rusty could hardly hear him.

'Your new position,' he said. 'I'm talking about your *'resignation'*.'

This last word he mouthed, without making a sound. Rusty thought he'd cracked altogether and couldn't understand why he was being so secretive.

'Oh, that!' Rusty said in a normal tone. 'Yes, I'll let you have that sometime today. By the way why are we whispering?'

'Well,' Jolly whispered again, looking round to make sure no one was listening. 'We don't want everyone to know until the normal procedure has been dealt with!'

'But it's not a secret!' Rusty said.

'What!' Jolly said, a look of sheer horror on his face. 'Does anyone else know?'

'Yes!'

'Who?'

'Everyone!'

'What!'

Now he knew Jolly was completely potty. It didn't matter who the hell knew.

'I really don't see the problem,' Rusty said.

'But there is a recognised procedure for this kind of situation which must be followed!' Jolly said, his eyebrows and mouth twitching all over the place.

'Why?' Rusty asked calmly, folding his arms.

That threw Jolly completely.

'Be... Because it must be!' he said. 'It is a straightforward professional procedure. You write to me, offering your resignation, and then I write back to you, accepting it. Then, and only then, we can go 'public'! You write to me, I write to you! That's the way it should be done!'

'But everybody knows,' Rusty said, leaning against the wall, arms still folded. 'Even you!'

Jolly stiffened at this, for him, outrageous attitude.

'I look forward to your letter!' he said haughtily and stomped off.

'I bet you do,' Rusty thought as he watched the silly sod leave the staff room.

He told the Escape Committee all of this during morning break.

'He's bloody crackers!' Chewy said.

'What actually pisses me off,' Rusty said, 'Is that he has to have yet another extended series of ridiculous bits of paper to deal with the simplest of situations!'

'That's his version,' Harry said, 'of being professional'. The silly bastard commits everything to paper for one reason and one reason only. To cover his bloody back!'

'True!' came the collective reply.

They dismissed the 'management' paranoia, again, and were discussing the joint trip to the theatre when Adolf and Harvey Sheasby came in. They were in the middle of a conversation about the Sixth Form. Both of them ignored the Escape Committee and sat down just beyond them, continuing their theme.

'Good idea Harvey,' Adolf said, 'something like this should have been done a long time ago. I'm right behind you!'

'Lucky old Harvey!' Compo said.

The rest of them couldn't help overhearing the rest of the conversation. Adolf was grinding on about the need for Sixth Form 'control', based on the suggestion which Harvey had made to him. How the Sixth Form could be made to use their study periods properly.

'It's just that I see the Sixth Form wandering around,' Harvey said, 'when I know they should be using their time to study.'

'Oh, how I agree with you!' Adolf said. 'When I was that age I was at it all the time!'

'Now, there's an admission!' Lil said.

Neither of them heard that and continued with their discussion.

'That's right,' Harvey said, 'and that's why I think we need to do something about it.'

'What exactly did you have in mind?' Adolf asked. 'What's the plan?'

'Well,' Harvey said, 'If we organise the whole of the Sixth Form in one place, at the beginning of the next term, and make sure they're all engaged in their various studies, we can, after say three weeks, allow them to go off by themselves. Once we see that they're doing something constructive we can allow them to continue, strictly on trust, but, if they abuse that trust then we bring them back to a highly supervised situation. That way they might realise we mean business.'

'I like it!' Adolf said. 'Great idea!'

The rest of them were appalled. They couldn't believe that Adolf and Harvey were serious. This had to be stopped, and right now.

'You two must be nuts to even think of such a bloody silly idea!' Chewy said. Never one to hold back was old Chewy.

'I beg your pardon!' Harvey said.

'You heard!' Chewy said. 'That's probably the worst idea I've ever heard about 'trusting' the Sixth Form!'

Adolf swung round in his direction.

'So what do you know about these things?' he demanded.

'A hell of a lot more than you do!' Chewy spat back.

'I'm not so sure about that!' Adolf said, a smirk forming on his manic features. 'When you've had as much experience as I've had ...'

'Don't pull that 'experience' crap!' Rusty said. 'You have no more than anyone else! And judging by your last remarks probably less!'

The conversation became a little heated after that. Harvey was just a pompous, naïve, little twit and he sat back, shrinking into his chair while the argument raged. Adolf, on the other hand, thought he knew it all, and stood, bringing up one foot and planting it on one of the chairs and then crooked an arm, the hand locked into his side. He stood there like an old style colonial plantation owner, attempting to give forth 'the word' to his workers and lesser beings. He couldn't have chosen a more aggressive set of opponents.

'When I was in Africa... ' he began, but didn't finish.

'When you were in Africa,' Chewy said, 'you and your kind planted the fucking seeds of racial stupidity and hatred which are still with us today!'

That seemed to strike a chord somewhere inside the doubtful area of a brain which Adolf infrequently used. He stood there, still with one foot up, still with an arm tucked into the side of his body, but he just stared ahead of him, directly at Chewy. Seconds passed. It was just as if he'd been frozen in time.

'Hello!' Chewy said. 'Is there anyone there?'

Still nothing.

'He'll be back soon,' Rusty said. 'It takes a bit of time sometimes but he'll be back.'

'Pity!' Chewy said.

This happened time and time again with Adolf. He would stop in mid conversation with anyone, immobile, and stare. It was his way of trying to intimidate. It always failed, but he was always unaware of that. Then he suddenly began to speak again.

'The trouble with you lot,' he said, taking his foot off the chair, 'Is that you'll never understand professional teaching attitudes!'

'Oh, good!' Rusty said. 'Then there's hope for us yet!'

Adolf marched out, leaving Harvey still sitting there.

'Well, then Harve,' Chewy said. 'And what have you to say about this?'

Harvey sat upright, trying to show he was more than just the Senior Master.

'I... I think there are certain things which need to be done,' he said, colouring slightly.

'Oh, yeah,' Harry said. 'Like what?'

'The 'chit' system needs to be looked at for a start, and then...' He didn't finish that.

'The 'chit' system is 'Shit'!' Compo said, calmly. 'The only thing it does is to humiliate near eighteen year old people into thinking they're not trusted. And they're right.'

The 'chit' system was used for the Sixth Form. If any of them wanted to go into town, in the evening after prep to one of the two pubs allowed to them, they had to have a 'chit' signed by their House Mistress or House Master. It was just another of the 'safe' systems which Jolly had imposed.

'This is not the time or the place to discuss such things!' Harvey complained.

'Why not!' Chewy snapped. 'You and your kind have never discussed it with the rest of the staff, have you?'

'The Headmaster,' Harvey countered, 'has always been fully aware of all suggestions!'

'Not the ones from us!' Harry said.

Harvey knew he wasn't going to get anywhere. He stood, shaking with pathetic rage and tried to glower at all of them. They all smiled sweetly at him. He ran out.

While this was going on a few 'hard core' members of the Upper Sixth were discussing their end of term plans. This centred on the Sixth Form Ball, which usually took place a day or so before the end of term itself. Counter to all expectations they were looking forward to it, setting something up which would provide all of them with a fitting end to their academic life in the school.

'Are you sure you can organise that?'

'Yeah, no problem!'

'It'll cost a bit!'

'But think of the effect!'

'True.'

'Well, we'd better start collecting. There's not much time!'

'O.K. I reckon a quid a head should do it!'

'Right!'

'Better get started now. You know what the rest of them are like.'

'That's right. We need to get this organised as quickly as possible. They need at least two weeks notice. If we don't get it together soon we'll blow the whole thing!'

'O.K. Let's get moving!'

They were off and running. The word rippled through all of the Upper Sixth and the money began to roll in slowly. The next few weeks would then see a more pressurised move to ensure they would collect as much money as they could from every member of the Sixth Form leaving body. Their final leaving statement to 'dear old Jolly' would be one they would all remember for a long, long time.

'Have you heard?'

'What?'

'He's leaving!'

'Is he?'

'When?'

'End of term!'

'Why?'

'Don't be silly!'

That was the kind of conversation which had whistled round the staff room and had produced a mixed reaction from surprise to relief, depending on the individual. The news was flashing round the kids that Rusty was leaving the school for another job. The same thing happened a few days later but this time it was for another member of staff. Wooden!

Jolly announced Wooden's good fortune with a smile on his face, always a doubtful expression as far as he was concerned. After a short, stunned silence, the whole of the staff room erupted into loud applause in recognition of another escapee! Wooden allowed a wide smile to take over his normally immobile features and more than a few staff realised for the first time that there might even be a human being lurking in there somewhere. Sadly, it didn't last. Jolly turned up the 'worry' level after that. With the two of them going, in so short a period of time, this left a few of the staff in a rather miserable state. Quite a number of them had been applying for all kinds of posts but there seemed to be something about Braumstate which held on to them like glue. It wasn't fair!

Unknown to all, poor old Wooden, had been trying to get out for years, but until now hadn't been able to get anywhere. It was just as the others felt. The School and Jolly seemed to act as a dual millstone, preventing any from escaping. But now he, of all people, had succeeded. The lucky sod had been offered, and accepted, a Headship just outside London in a small Independent prep school.

Unlike Rusty he wouldn't be able to get away until well into the following academic year but then, during that time, the slow change which took over, as far as his personality was concerned, was a joy to see. Before that change fully took over, Wooden was given the task of quizzing Rusty about the joint trip. Jolly wasn't happy about what he'd heard from Harvey who had overheard Chewy, Rusty and Compo talking about their additional plans for the trip.

'There seems to be slight problem here,' he said to the pair of them after one morning meeting.

'Oh, yes?' Chewy asked. 'What's that?'

They all sat at one of the tables.

'Well, it seems there are two trips going and not one,' Wooden read from his notebook. 'We don't seem to have any information about that.'

'No there's one trip,' Rusty said. 'That's all.'

'But you seem to be doing one thing in the morning,' Wooden said, 'and then something else in the afternoon at different places. That makes two trips.'

'How do you figure that out?' Chewy asked, but then wished he hadn't.

'Well,' Wooden said again, 'You seem to be doing one thing in the morning and then...'

'Hang on,' Chewy said. 'There's one trip. Right?'

'Right,' Wooden said.

'Right!' said Chewy, glad to have established that. 'We're all going to see the play, right?'

'Right,' Wooden repeated.

'Right.' Rusty said, 'But before that we're making use of the time to do others things.'

'Right,' Wooden said again. 'But that's two trips then, isn't it?'

'Wrong!' Chewy snapped. He was beginning to lose patience with this idiotic conversation.

'Look,' Rusty said, trying to keep the temperature down. 'We're all going to see the play, right?'

'Right,' said Wooden.

'But as we'll arrive quite early, we're splitting into three groups. One group will go to the Science Museum, another to Covent Garden and the other one to the Museum of the Moving Image, right? Then we'll all come back and see the play, right?'

Rusty thought he'd cracked it, but he was wrong.

Wooden absorbed this new information slowly and then suddenly said, 'So there's *four* trips going?'

'No!' Chewy and Rusty said together, 'One!'

'But you just said...'

'I don't think I can continue with this!' Rusty said to Chewy.

The few members of staff who had been in the room had quickly left before the argument got out of hand. Those who came in saw and heard what was going on and turned on their heel and left immediately.

'Hang on!' Chewy growled. 'Let's just get this straight for the last time. At seven thirty in the morning, after the half term break, we'll *all* climb on the bus. The bus will take us *all* to London. We might stop for a piss on the way but we'll have to let you know about that.'

Wooden tried to interrupt but Chewy kept going relentlessly.

'When we get to London we will still be *one* trip. We will then split into three groups and do three different things for about two hours. Then we'll *all* meet again, the *same single trip*, and see the play. Then we *all* come back here. The *same* bloody trip as left in the first place. Is that clear enough?'

'So there *are* four trips then?' Wooden said.

'That's it!' Chewy said. 'I'm gone!'

'Just a minute,' Rusty said. 'This is ridiculous! What the hell is going on? Has the Head asked you to ask these silly bloody questions?'

'It's not that,' Wooden said defensively. 'It's just that we didn't know you would be doing something else. You didn't write that down on the first application to the committee.'

'Bloody paper and bloody committee's again!' Chewy snarled. 'Does anything happen round here without bloody paper and bloody committee's?'

Wooden suddenly snapped. He shot to his feet, bright red and snapped back at the pair of them.

'I'm just trying to do my job!'

'Then fucking well *do it*!' Rusty snapped back.

'The head won't like this!' Wooden squeaked.

'How do you think we feel?' Chewy said. 'Why don't you just say you don't trust us and have done with it?'

'It's not a case of trust!' Wooden spat back. 'It's a case of procedure!'

'*Procedure*!' they both almost shouted at him.

'Yes, procedure,' Wooden said and sat down again, thinking they were going to sort it out finally and hopefully more calmly. He was wrong. Both Chewy and Rusty stood up and stormed out before either of them ended up thumping him. It had come very close to it. When they'd had a chance to calm down they realised that was probably the first time they'd ever seen Wooden lose his cool. It had been just like watching an elastic band being pulled and then snapping. There was hope for him yet. As for the so-called lack of 'procedure', there was still another scene to run for this little incident but that didn't happen until after the trip.

They were now in the last week before half term and, with all the marking and paperwork behind them, they were gearing up for the ten day break in 'grown up land', if only for a short time. A number of staff sat in small groups, huddled in tense discussion. The Escape Committee wondered about this but then realised what was going on. Speculation was high about who might apply for the position of Deputy Head. Now that Wooden was on his way it opened up a near certainty. If Jolly was right about money being tight then it could easily be an internal appointment. The intrigue gathered pace as the half term came to an end.

'Examination land' was now upon all of them when they returned after the ten day break. Not just GCSE and A Level, but all the school examinations for the younger ones as well. It was going to be a hectic time, but at least the sports hall was now earmarked for most of it. Because of the numbers of kids involved, six staff at a time were required to invigilate in the hall. It was an extremely boring occupation. Full attention needed to be given without the chance of reading a book, catching up on subject literature, doodling aimlessly, knitting or even the concentrated excavation of the nose.

There were strict guidelines for this task, prepared by every examination board and laid out in full, closely packed text, about how it should be done. Not every one followed those guidelines. The Wide Mouthed Frog was particularly 'naughty' about this. She would invariably sit, without moving for the whole of her time slot, either reading or writing some piece of educational crap, not taking a blind bit of notice about what might have been going on. This, coupled with her terrible habit of nose blowing, proved to be more than irritating to a number of staff, quite apart from the kids who needed to concentrate. Staff were allocated a forty minute session at a time but there were a few instances where some didn't turn up and there is nothing more frustrating than being stuck in an examination hall, invigilating, without the means to escape.

Patrolling up and down passed some of the time but more than once in the period of a few minutes would put the kids off, especially if hard shoes were being worn. The slow click, clacking of feet up and down the hall can be very irritating. The biggest problem for the staff was simply trying to stay awake. As luck would have it Chewy, Rusty, Compo were on together one afternoon with Harvey, Rollerball and the Wide Mouthed Frog. They had taken over smoothly from the last batch of staff and moved into position at either end of the hall where they could see all the kids easily. One or two of them stuck their hands up for more paper but apart from that it was, as usual, as boring as hell. Then Wide Mouth started blowing her bloody nose again. Chewy sidled over to Rusty and had a few words. Rusty grinned immediately, nodding his head. Chewy walked back to his position. Rusty then walked slowly over to Compo and, as Chewy had done, whispered a few words to him. Compo had to cover his mouth quickly to stop himself laughing out loud but then controlled it and, as

Rusty had done, nodded his head and waved a thumbs up signal over to Chewy.

The three of them were standing, facing down the hall and, after unbuttoning their jackets, waited for the right moment. Rollerball, Harvey and Wide Mouth were sitting at the other end, Wide Mouth in the middle. They were facing the kids and as Rollerball looked up he could see Chewy and the others standing looking down the hall towards them. He thought no more of it and got back to whatever he was doing. Then Harvey did the same and again got on with what ever he was doing. Then, the moment Chewy, Rusty and Compo had been waiting for came as the Wide Mouth Frog looked up. What she saw at the back of the hall made her look quickly away, spluttering slightly and turning bright red. She looked up again and saw the same thing. More splutterings. A few of the kids looked up wondering what was the matter with the old cow this time. Things settled again but Wide Mouth couldn't resist another look. Chewy, Rusty and Compo responded for her. They were holding their jackets, slowly opening and closing them, pretending to flash in unison! Wide Mouth had to leave. Rollerball and Harvey watched her go spluttering and coughing, quite unaware of what had happened.

There was only one incident throughout the examination period which raised the level from total boredom to partial farce. That, not surprisingly, was generated by Jolly Jack. Under examination conditions most kids scribble away, through the two or three hours of their allotted time on the paper provided. There are a few who don't have that staying power and become totally jammed up through either nerves or lack of answers. That's when the doodling starts and it sometimes develops into major graffiti. Only one, amongst the hundreds who were trapped, writing desperately for their future, committed, as far as Jolly was concerned, a major graffiti 'crime'. It happened to be a rather 'naughty' word. It was just one word but it was enough to launch a full-scale investigation. Not one single member of staff had noticed it before Jolly, on one of his, 'I just thought I'd pop in to see everything is running smoothly' visits, spotted it immediately.

His face drained of colour as his eyes fastened on 'the word'. A remarkable feat in itself as it was a good thirty yards away from him on the leading edge of one of the desks. It was written in white, upside down and drawn with the one of those correcting pens which exude white opaque, quick drying liquid. Four letters, describing the human procreative act, shone like a beacon in his direction. The morning meeting, the following day, took on inquisitorial proportions.

'I was rather disappointed,' Jolly said, without the standard, 'Good morning everyone', 'to find a rather distasteful example of graffiti on one of the desks in the sports hall yesterday.'

'Hey, this makes a change,' Chewy muttered.

'Watch it,' Rusty said sideways. 'He's got his dander up about this!'

'I intend to find the culprit,' Jolly continued, 'and deal with him, or indeed her, severely. There really is no excuse for this kind of deformation of school furniture!'

'He really has got his dander up!' Chewy said. 'What's he found?'

Nobody knew.

Ray Butcombe, a 'nice' man and the examinations officer, was called to account for every kid who had sat at that particular desk over the previous week since the examination began.

'That, Headmaster,' he said mournfully, 'will take a day or so to find out.'

'See to it then,' Jolly snapped. 'I must know who has committed this heinous act!'

Fortunately for Ray, every examination board insisted that each desk had to be allocated a number so that they could be cross-checked with candidate numbers. It was an 'anti-cheat' system should it be needed. Two days later, after spending all his spare time checking endless lists, he had drawn up a list of fifteen kids who had used that desk. During this time Jolly had examined every desk in the hall for other samples of graffiti 'outrage'. All he found was 'Percy loves Ariadne' pencilled in tiny script over a terrible drawing of a heart.

Jolly grilled every one of the fifteen but without result. He'd even taken the trouble of having 'the word' photographed so that he could confront them with it without having to say it. They all denied writing 'the word'. Stalemate. He bore down on their form teachers, tutors, Heads of Department and anyone who could shed any light on who had written 'the word'. Nothing.

'He's gone!' was the general reaction which floated round the staff room as all this nonsense was going on.

'Again?' was the reply.

Jolly was very frustrated. Someone had to be lying. But who? He didn't know it then but there was another agency at work while this whole farce was playing itself out. One late evening someone entered the hall and removed 'the word' but added several more, all of the four letter variety, ready for his inspection which was due the following day. Harry was one of the staff on duty this time when Jolly walked in, and gleefully told the rest of the Escape Committee what had happened. Jolly had tip-toed in, not wanting to disturb anyone, sending out his sickening grin to all the staff but then froze as he read the new four letter 'words' which were scattered around on the front edges of several desks. He skittered out, red in the face, but this time determined to capture the 'criminals' who were obviously, as far as he was concerned, still there in the hall.

It was minutes before the end of the last session of the day when Jolly shot off. Time was called, the kids trouped out and the examination papers were collected and taken through to the office for dispatch to the board. Jolly was trying to round up Wide Mouth and Wooden to take them with him to the hall as back up witnesses to this new outrage. Someone else had crept in when all the kids and staff had gone, wiping clean all the other new 'words'. When Jolly eventually arrived back, only with Wide Mouth, there wasn't a sign of anything anywhere.

'Is there a problem here, Headmaster?' Wooden asked, who was already there, a vague sign of a smile on his face.

Jolly couldn't speak. He couldn't understand what had happened.

'I think the best thing to do,' Wide Mouth said, 'would be to have a nice cup of tea and just relax.'

She led him away like a little boy. No more was said about 'words'. But Harry had actually seen the culprit 'in the act' so to speak. He'd walked back into the hall to collect a book he'd left behind and there was the 'criminal' at work. Their eyes met and a grin broke out on each face. Harry left him to it and said not a word to anyone, except the Escape Committee. After all, that person was leaving so he didn't want to 'blow' his cover. Besides, Wooden had probably been wanting to do something like this for years!

Apart from that there were other bits of graffiti which Jolly missed completely. Some wag had been round every examination warning sign in the School adding comments. These things were white boards with two words on them in black. They were straightforward and to the point. They simple read, 'Silence Examinations!' Someone had added, 'When?' or 'I agree!' or 'What about the Noisy ones?'

For some of the staff, one of the final stages of the examination process was almost over. That was 'Moderation Consensus'. This was hateful process where several schools would come together, in subjects, and re-mark each others work. It was a cheap way round the difficult problem of finding Moderators, external examiners, and stemmed from the simple fact that they were never paid enough for the chore of marking hundreds of pieces of work. This was a method which was hoped, by the examining boards, to be fair and evenhanded. They were wrong. Very few staff enjoyed having to do it. Chewy was one of them.

This time it was Braumstate Cathedral School which had been given the 'honour' of hosting the Moderation Consensus Meeting for Design and Technology.

'Oh, shit!' was Chewy's reaction.

The day arrived and so did all the other staff from six other schools. Chewy sat in the office looking out as they arrived.

'Just look at them!' he said to Howard Stokes, his second in command. 'What *do* they look like!'

The vehicles they arrived in were the first indication of the subject taught. A few 2Cv's, a VW 'beetle' and a couple of battered Bedford vans rolled past the window and parked on the forecourt. Out from most of them emerged anoraks, corduroy trousers and beards. A kind of standard uniform. Design and Technology suffered from one large and fundamental flaw. Most of the staff teaching had rarely experienced commercial practise or had any track record as designers of any kind. All their expertise came from books, so they tended to be a little 'black and white' in their approach, without any real understanding of how designers and manufacturers performed. Added to this they were mostly dyed in the wool 'artisans' and were only concerned with producing apprentices for trade rather than creative minds. Chewy sighed. It was not going to be a happy day.

'Come on then,' Chewy sighed. 'The 'good with their hands lads' have arrived!'

With all introductions complete and the work from all the schools spread out in the studio, they began the marking process. Chewy and Howard waded through their allocation. It was appalling.

'Typical bloody blacksmith at work here,' he said, referring to the staff responsible.

The next batch, almost an hour later was no better.

'You can tell a friggin' chippie's been busy here,' he muttered.

With their attempts at re-marking complete, Chewy and Howard sat back and waited for the others to catch up. The agonising which was going on was painful to watch. The absolute literal sense of the examination board's guidelines were being used by the rest of them to reduce marks to a level Chewy hadn't seen for some time.

'The finish on that's not so hot,' one would say.

'I wouldn't accept that as an adequate standard of construction,' another chipped in.

'How can kids not understand how to use a chisel?' came another comment.

Chewy held himself back. How could kids be expected to perform as craftsmen? The idea was ridiculous. What was much more important were their ideas! Without ideas the world wouldn't progress. Couldn't these silly buggers see that? The answer to that was no. These so called teachers were their own worst enemy. Design and Technology had so much to offer, providing teaching staff encouraged creativity. It didn't actually matter whether the things they made were perfectly constructed or not. How could they be with so little time available to them?

With staff like that around, the subject would never rise above the perceived status which it still struggled against. Woodwork, Metalwork and Technical Drawing still lived, perpetuated by these silly bastards who were supposed to be making kids aware of the much higher horizons of creative expertise.

'Blacksmith's and Chippies!' Chewy muttered as they left. 'What the hell would we do without them?'

-4-

'Hi, Mag!' Quentin called as he flounced in. 'How are you today?'

Maggie looked up from her desk and winced as he bounced toward her then flopped into the chair opposite. Of all the people she could easily have done without, it was him.

'Fine, Quentin,' she said, unenthusiastically, 'Fine.'

'Oh, good,' he grinned. 'Because, have I got something for you!'

'Have you now,' she said, trying to refocus again on what she'd been busy doing before he arrived. It was the final shooting script for the School video.

'Yes I have!' Quentin said, handing her a video cassette.

'What's this?' she asked.

'My personal contribution to the promotion of the school!' he said, beaming at her.

Maggie didn't like the sound of that. Where Quentin was concerned she knew that he was not exactly the best person to know how to handle a delicate promotional event.

'Oh, really?' she said, half heartedly.

'Yes!' he said. 'But do take your time and look at it when you can. I think you'll find it to be quite interesting.'

'I'll bet I will,' she thought to herself, but did have the simple courtesy to say, 'Thanks Quentin. I'll look at it later on.'

He pottered off happily; feeling quite smug about having produced what he thought was a rather fine video statement about the school. Maggie didn't know he'd already dropped a memo to Jolly about it. The memo lay in the Mad Hatter's 'in' tray. A number of others dropped on top of it before the day had ended and that was probably just as well. It would be a while before it surfaced and he would almost certainly come in to see her fretting about it. Maggie held Quentin's cassette and thought about it. She wondered what he'd committed to tape. Dismissing its importance she put it down on top of a few other blank ones on the side of her desk. They just happened to be the same type as Quentin's 'special'.

Rusty arrived, looking particularly laid back.

'So you're leaving,' Maggie said. 'So don't make it so obvious!'

'Who, me?' Rusty said.

'Yes, you!' she answered, knowing damned well he knew exactly what she meant.

'You cut me to the quick!' he said theatrically.

'That'll be the day!' she said.

'Hang on!' Rusty said defensively. 'I only wanted to scrounge a spare tape from you for a lesson tomorrow morning. Don't give me such a hard time!'

'Help yourself,' she said, waving a hand in the direction of the tapes on he desk.

He took the one from the top of the pile and stuck into his pocket.

'Thanks,' he said. 'I'll replace this tomorrow.'

'Fine,' she said, closing the file on the script of the School video. 'There's no hurry. Drop it in when you can.'

Rusty looked at his watch.

'Come on,' he said. 'Time's up. Work's over. Let's go and have a drink.'

'Good idea!' she said.

A couple of hours later Rusty pulled the tape he borrowed from its cover. Just before he loaded it into his recorder he noticed that it wasn't a blank tape at all. It was at least half way through. And it had 'Q.B' written on the label What could be on it?

'Interesting,' he thought. He rewound it and then pushed the 'play' button. This was Quentin's 'special'. His own presentation of the school, on video. Rusty couldn't believe what he was looking at and his luck at having it in his possession. It was a full half hour of the most terrible footage he'd ever seen but it gave Rusty an idea. If Quentin was seriously going to show this to Jolly then it might just be 'improved on' with a little bit added to it here and there. Finding a camcorder wouldn't be a problem. There was one in the Department. An editing rig would be the next step. He wondered who might have one.

During the next morning Rusty checked the camcorder, made sure the battery was fully charged and set off to take a few 'gems'. He used all of the morning break, lunchtime, afternoon break and another hour or so after school. He collected what he wanted without being noticed. With all of that 'in the can' so to speak, he was ready to splice the new footage into Quentin's tape but he still had the problem of editing. He wandered in to see Maggie at the end of the day and Quentin was there as well, fussing about another of his daft ideas. This one had something to do with flower arrangements for Open Day. Maggie was sitting trying not to listen to his mindless wittering as Rusty came in. She brightened up immediately seeing the opportunity of getting away from this latest piece of 'Quentinmania'.

'Rusty!' she said. 'What brings you over here?'

'Just wondered if you could help with a small problem,' he said, nodding politely to Quentin.

'Oh, yes,' she said. 'And what's that?'

'Well,' he said, leaning on the desk. 'I've just been taking a few shots for the department and wondered if you knew where I could get my hands on some editing gear.'

Quentin pricked up his ears at this.

'I know!' he said brightly.

'You do?' Rusty said. 'Where?'

'My place!' Quentin answered. 'I bought one a short while ago!'

He gave Maggie a knowing wink but Rusty had the good sense not to comment on that.

'Did you now,' Rusty said. 'I don't suppose I could use it, could I?'

'With pleasure!' Quentin beamed. 'When would you like to?'

'Well, there's no time like the present!' Rusty grinned.

This was incredible. Here he was with Quentin himself offering him the chance to sabotage his own video of the school. It was an opportunity not to be missed, but he would have to make very sure that Quentin didn't actually see what he was doing. That could prove rather tricky.

'Fine!' Quentin grinned. 'I'm off in a few minutes. I'll see you at the house in say, an hour?'

'Great!' Rusty said. 'I'll be there!'

An hour later Rusty pulled up in front of the Braumsley house. Ralph opened the door and showed him into the main drawing room.

'Master Quentin will be with you at any moment, sir,' he said, bowing and leaving Rusty there.

Rusty poked about looking at the family photographs on the huge mantle piece and then Quentin came bounding in.

'Oh, you're here!' he said. 'Glad to see you again. Can I offer you a drink? No? Well, let me show you my set up. This way.'

Rusty followed him upstairs and into his large bedroom. The editing desk was sitting against the far wall, complete with two monitors and twin recording decks.

'There it is!' Quentin said. 'I'll leave you to it. If you need anything just give Ralph a buzz.'

He pointed to a bell push on the wall.

'Thanks,' Rusty said, 'I'll be fine. I do appreciate this Quentin.'

'Not at all!' Quentin said. 'Not at all! Glad to be of help. I have to pop out for a while. Have to see one of the ancient relatives. Back in about two hours.'

'I might well be finished before then,' Rusty said.

'No problem!' Quentin grinned. 'See you later or tomorrow!'

Much relieved to see him go Rusty got down to work. He had finished what he was doing in less than an hour. The end result was much 'improved'. Now he had to get it back to Maggie and although he knew he could trust her he didn't want her implicated at all. He would have to get it back to her without her knowing about what he'd done, somehow.

The following day Jolly was wrestling with a problem. Computerisation. He'd been putting it off for a long time, mainly because he didn't know a great deal about it, but Maggie wouldn't let him off the hook. She was pushing him again for some kind of a decision.

'You did agree that we should go ahead,' she said, flipping through her notes. She had learned the power of paper.

'At our last meeting about this you agreed that we should go ahead, in the first instance, with five machines for the School.' she said, reading from the actual minutes which the Mad Hatter had taken. 'They should be organised in one building, the old disused stable behind the sports hall. Then, they would be added to, over the next academic year, until we have twenty operational units, some of those in as many departments as possible and probably networked.'

He couldn't deny it. It was there in black and white, on paper, irrefutable. She had him.

'Yes, yes, yes,' he said, slightly flustered. 'I just want to be quite clear that this is the right thing to do.'

'Here we go again,' Maggie thought to herself. 'I've been through this so many bloody times already!'

'What are other schools doing?' he asked weakly.

'Using computers all the time,' she answered flatly.

'Ah, yes,' he said, doodling frantically. 'Should we consult more of the staff about this first?'

'We have, several times,' Maggie said as evenly as she could.

'I, that is we, just need to be quite sure about this before we commit ourselves,' he said, not looking up from his doodlings. 'Don't you think?

Maggie didn't bother to answer that question. Instead she sat back in her chair and prepared her words carefully to use as a weapon which he could never cope with. This was the other 'P' factor. One was 'Paper' but this next one was even more powerful.

'Parents,' she said, calmly, 'expect their children to have the best in any Independent school. Without computers they may think twice about sending them here.'

That did it. That single word 'Parent' always worked. He wittered on about 'difficult financial times', 'addressing clear educational objectives', 'reassuring the Governors' and a catalogue of other worries but, eventually said, 'Very well. I think we should go ahead.'

'At last!' she thought to herself, but then had the wit to ask another question before he found some reason to change his mind.

'Will you inform the Financial Controller of you decision so we can make an immediate purchase?'

'Yes, of course,' he said, unhappily.

She sat staring pointedly at the phone.

'You mean now?' he asked, wide eyed.

'Well, there's not a lot of time before the end of term,' she said. 'Wouldn't it be nice to have them up and running for Open Day and the parents?'

'Oh, yes. Good thinking!' he said and picked up the phone.

She left him to it. Now she had to get moving. The ground staff, under her direction, had already prepared one of the buildings to house the 'Information Centre'. It was an old stable which hadn't been used for years. The lads had worked long and hard and now it was bright clean, carpeted and wired up ready to be used. There would be plenty of room for twenty machines and office space for staff. That last point, staff, had still to be resolved but first she needed to get the orders off for the first batch of equipment.

Howard Stokes was her next contact. With his help the best deal was found, the order dispatched and a few days later the machines arrived, neatly stacked in the middle of the floor of the new centre, waiting to be unpacked. All she had to do now was to find a member of staff competent enough to take the whole thing over. That wasn't going to be easy. Jolly had been following all of this closely, worrying about it as usual and then insisted on being fully involved in trying to decide who on the staff would be best qualified.

A little research though his files had brought up the name of one of the maths staff. Percy Hollingsworth, 'Holly' to the rest of them. He used a basic machine in his room and had even gone on a course for computer training! Jolly was beside himself with glee. He had found the right person for the job, or so he thought. Howard Stokes would have been the most suitable but that hadn't crossed Jolly's mind in that he'd only got to 'H' in his files.

'Me!' Percy wailed. 'Why me?'

'Oh, come, come!' Jolly said, beaming. 'How modest. You have, I think the expression is, 'hands on experience' don't you?'

'Well,' Percy said, still feeling a little dumbfounded, 'just a bit.'

'There you are then!' Jolly said. 'No more to be said!'

Howard was actually quite relieved that he hadn't been 'nobbled ' for this. He had plenty to do as it was. But he did give Percy a hand to unpack the stuff and it was then that the fun started and continued thereafter. Percy was rather nervous about the whole thing, and largely stayed that way. He wouldn't do anything without insisting that there was full back-up, guarantees for everything and instant service available from the supplier should anything go wrong.

'Percy!' Howard said. 'We haven't got the bloody things out of the boxes yet!'

'I just don't want to rush into these things,' he said, 'that's all!'

With all the packaging off the equipment they began to connect it all together. Howard picked up one of the processing units and heard a rattle. He shook it and it rattled some more.

'Don't do that!' Percy squeaked. 'You might break it and then we'll be out of guarantee!'

'Don't be daft!' Howard said. 'The damned things have been bouncing around on the back of a truck to get here. That's probably why there's a screw loose somewhere.'

'I'll phone for the engineer!' Percy said. 'Let them see to it!'

Howard sat down. 'It's not the only thing that has a screw loose round here,' he thought.

They eventually had the system together and switched it on. Everything worked perfectly.

'Right!' Howard said. 'Let's see what it can do!'

'Oh, no!' Percy said. 'We should leave it for a while to warm up and settle down!'

Howard gave up in disgust and left him to it.

The day of the joint departmental visit to London arrived and at seven thirty in the morning they were almost ready to leave. All the kids were on board, packed lunches and teas were stowed away and the staff gathered outside the bus while Rusty and Chewy performed a last head count, just to make sure they had everyone there. The weather was clear and they were all looking forward to the day away from the nuthouse, kids included. Lill and Harry had wangled the day off as 'volunteers' to help look after the kids and somehow Maggie had been able to persuade Jolly it would be a good idea for her to come along as well. That gave them six staff in all which was about right for the number of kids they had on the bus.

There was only one snag. They had the same driver from the tennis trip and he was even more twitchy than then. A bigger bus, a longer journey and more kids added up to pure misery for him. Why he ever drove the bloody things was a complete mystery to Chewy. After the standard threats had been issued by this character, backed up by Chewy, Rusty and Compo they set off. The kids settled down after the first few miles, the traffic was light and after a stop half way there, they eventually pulled into London by late morning. For some of the kids this was their first time in the 'big City' and rubber necking took over for the last few miles as they tried to pick out every main tourist sight. The coach dropped them off at the National Theatre and they organised themselves into three groups, two staff to each group, ready for their own 'diversions' before the play. The performance was due at two thirty.

'All right, you lot!' bellowed Chewy, much to the instant surprise of a few folk wandering past. 'It's just before eleven. We have to be back here for two, no later! So, let's go!'

And they were off. Chewy and Harry took their lot off to the tube at Waterloo Station and then on to the Science Museum. Rusty and Maggie led theirs across Waterloo Bridge to Covent Garden and Compo took his lot, with Lill, to the Museum of the Moving Image in the Festival Complex next door to the National. They all had a great time and arrived back in good time for the play. Chewy had a few bad moments on the tube, almost losing two of the kids who had taken a wrong turning in one of the pedestrian tunnels, but apart from that all went very well. The play itself was terrific, the kids really enjoyed themselves and the journey back was full of stories from one group to the other about where they'd been, what they'd seen and what they'd done. All of the staff were knackered. They'd had a full day but it had been one of the most successful trips the school had ever organised, until they turned up at the morning meeting.

Wooden wanted to see both of them. This was almost 'de ja vue' for them as they began the same discussion they'd had before.

'So I just want to get this right,' Wooden said eventually. 'There were four trips?'

'NO!' they both barked back at him.

During the morning Rusty was still spitting bullets about the mindless conversation with Wooden. Chewy was in the same state of mind and when they met at break they decided to do something about it. Within half an hour Maisie handed to Jolly, with a copy to Wooden, a carefully worded complaint about the harassment they'd both received about the trip, before and afterwards. They made great emphasis about appearing to be not trusted and questioning the need for such interrogation. That had the effect of a rather large dun coloured object coming into contact with a fast moving, circular, bladed device. The shit flew everywhere but most of it was to stick on Jolly's head. He was not 'jolly'.

During lunch time Jolly found the pair of them and, true to form, asked them to see him in his office but wouldn't say what for or why in front of the others. Chewy and Rusty were slightly mystified by this.

'We can talk about 'it' now if you like,' Rusty said, Chewy nodding his agreement.

Jolly became slightly flustered at this then shook his head. Before he turned on his heel and skittered away and, without looking at either of them, he had the gall to ask them to stand outside his study during the afternoon break and wait for his arrival.

'If he thinks I'm going to stand waiting for him outside his bloody door like a kid on detention,' Chewy said, 'he can go and bloody stuff himself!'

'You took the very words from my mouth,' Rusty said.

During the afternoon break, instead of following Jolly's 'instructions', they deliberately went in to see the Mad Hatter to pass the time of day.

'Hello you old bat!' Chewy said as they walked in.

'Oh, it's you, you furry old sod,' Maisie said.

'Nice to see you too,' he said.

'How's things?' Rusty asked.

'Don't ask,' Maisie said, 'He's in one of his sulky moods again.'

'Great!' Chewy said. 'Just what we want.'

Jolly had stepped out of his office through the side door to the hall and was standing there at that very moment, wondering where they both were. He came back into his office and tapped the top of his desk impatiently. Then he heard the sound of laughter coming from the outer office. He walked through and found Chewy and Rusty sharing some joke with Maisie. He didn't know it was about him.

'Ah,' he said testily. 'There you are. Would you come in.'

Chewy and Rusty followed him. Chewy closed the door behind him.

'No, no,' Jolly said. 'Leave that open. The Deputy Head will be with us in a moment.'

Chewy and Rusty looked at each other wondering what was going on. They were still completely in the dark as to what this was all about. Jolly didn't ask them to sit so they just stood there, arms folded, waiting.

'You wanted to see us,' Rusty said, as Jolly fidgeted, not saying anything.

'Yes,' Jolly said, 'but I wanted the Deputy here before I began.'

'Witness!' Chewy mouthed to Rusty. Rusty nodded.

Still no Wooden, and Jolly was becoming more agitated but then realised he couldn't just stand around with the two of them without saying something.

'I gather you have just been on a joint visit,' Jolly said, not looking either of them in the eye.

Both of them groaned inwardly. 'Here we bloody go again!' was the same thought from each of them.

'That's right,' Chewy said, 'London, the theatre.'

'But there were four trips in all, were there not?' Jolly asked.

Both of them sighed audibly.

Chewy leaned against the wall and Rusty sat on the edge of the large table.

'Is that right?' Jolly asked.

'No!' they both said.

Jolly was slightly taken aback at this but pressed on.

'But my Deputy has told me there were four visits, including the theatre itself, and I had not been informed of this prior to your leaving!'

Chewy and Rusty shook their heads slowly.

'Does that mean 'no' to the four visits or 'no' to my not being informed?' Jolly snapped.

He was becoming quite petulant now, which wasn't helped by the fact that Chewy had deliberately slouched against the wall and Rusty was still sitting happily on the table. Hardly the body language of the concerned. At that moment Wooden came in, looking wooden.

'Ah, now, good!' Jolly said. 'Will you please tell these gentlemen what the procedure is for educational visits!'

'The procedure for educational visits is...' Wooden began, but didn't finish.

'Just a minute,' Rusty cut in. 'We used a couple of hours to the best advantage for the kids before going to the play, that's all.'

'But the procedure for educational...' Wooden tried again.

'What you're really saying,' Chewy said, slightly changing his position against the wall, 'is that you don't trust us.'

'That is not the case at all!' Jolly said, going slight red.

'Then why are we here?' Rusty said calmly.

'The procedure for...' Wooden tried yet again. Jolly cut him off this time.

'The reason I asked you here has to do with this!'

He flourished the letter which Chewy and Rusty had sent to him earlier in the day.

'I take exception to the whole tone of this letter!' he said, now shaking with rage.

Chewy and Rusty said nothing but looked directly at him, unblinking. He couldn't cope with that. He turned to Wooden who was just standing there as if his motor had run down.

'Tell them what I mean!' he said.

Wooden came back to life, blinked twice and started the same statement again.

'The procedure...' He didn't get any further.

'To have actually published this is outrageous!' Jolly squeaked.

'Published?' Chewy and Rusty both said, nonplussed.

'That was an internal letter of justified complaint!' Rusty said. 'You talk about it as if it had appeared in the National press!'

'There was no need for this!' Jolly countered.

'I, we, think there was!' Chewy said. 'Besides, don't you think you're taking this whole thing a little too seriously?'

As he said this he leaned forward and patted Jolly's arm. Jolly flinched as he did this and almost went off with a bang in his frustration at the flagrant dismissal of his position as Headmaster. Bright red by now and searching for words he slapped his hands to his sides, crumpling the letter in his hand.

'So you have no remorse for taking this attitude!' he said.

'No!' they both said.

'Very well!' Jolly snapped. 'We shall leave it there!'

'Thank you,' Rusty said and, sliding off the table, left the office with Chewy.

Both of them had great difficulty not falling over with mirth at this crazy conversation.

'Jolly is not very 'jolly'!' Chewy cackled when they had cleared the corridor and were outside.

'When was he ever?' Rusty said.

On reflection that ridiculous confrontation was, in effect, the last straw which propelled both of them in a direction from which there was no return. They'd both had enough, and after a short while they had decided to do something about the whole sodding lot of the so-called management. The seeds of an idea began to form between them which bore very satisfactory fruit much later on. They were both fed up with this petty, picky, continuous crap which they had to wade through every day. There had to be a way of wreaking vengeance. It would take very careful planning and meticulous organisation but it could be done. It would just take a little time and that's exactly what they had.

In the few days after that 'meeting' Jolly went through a short period where he seemed to be reacting in the most peculiar and bizarre fashion to everything around him. The outright rejection of his authority by Chewy and Rusty had sent him off into the manic need to correspond with anybody on paper, it being his first and last love, and the means he used to 'organise' his little world. For a while it was just a little confusing for those around him.

He was, after all, at his happiest when he was churning the stuff out but some of the examples were, even for him, completely potty Over the period of one day several notices appeared on notice boards and in staff pigeon holes. The first one which appeared on the staff room notice board was backed up with copies to every member of the teaching staff. There were others but the following examples were the best of the crop. The first one was concise and to the point.

I will be obliged if all staff on duty in the dining room will pay particular attention to the plastic beakers.

Some of these have been damaged, quite deliberately, by the cutlery provided. Please ensure that pupils are denied the use of anything which will perpetuate this.

'I see the phantom beaker killer is on the loose again!' was the general response. There were other comments to follow this.

'It's going to be bloody messy in there for the next few days!'

'Why?'

'You try eating lunch without cutlery!'

Then the singularly stupid missive Chewy received was a cracker. It was a copy of a reply to a company who had written to the school on the chance of some business.

I am most grateful to you for writing to me and have passed on a copy of your letter and brochure to our Head of Design and Technology.

Chewy unfolded it and promptly fell about. The rest of the Escape Committee were intrigued.

'Just look at this!' he said, handing over the copy of Jolly's letter and the crap he'd bothered to reply to. A dreadful letter, extolling the virtues of a range of products was the preamble to the brochure which was stapled to it. This showed, in graphic detail, the most obnoxious examples of 'heavy metal art', and all in relief as badges and buckles. The examples were wonderfully awful. Grotesque heads, vaguely human, but mostly animal, glared from a full colour, glossy, multi-folded brochure. The names given to these things were incredible. 'Boogie Bum', 'Death Hound', 'Up it!' and 'Pig Head' were some of the least offensive. The rest were virtually obscene.

'And that is an example of how our esteemed Headmaster can recognise quality merchandise!' Chewy said. 'Why didn't he just chuck it in the bloody bin where it belongs? You only have to look at the name of the organisation to see!'

The name he was referring to was 'Billy Boggles Buckle Bonanza Company Limited.'

After this the next memo which all the staff received in their pigeon holes was another priceless statement which left a few of them wondering about Jolly's mental state.

I would like to remind all staff, with only three weeks left of the term, that we must be vigilant.

That was it. No more. No less. The question was, vigilant about what? So what did they all do? That's right. Nothing. What else was there to do?

Maggie was beyond all this, although she was given chapter and verse by the others. She was more concerned with her continued attempts to get a decision about the video of, and for, the School. Jolly still hadn't made his mind up, such as it was. She sat in her office mulling over the shooting script, wondering why she was still in this madhouse, when Rusty came in.

'Brought you back a blank tape,' he said, 'to replace the one I borrowed.'

'Oh, I'd forgotten all about that.' she said. 'Stick it over there.'

Rusty looked over to where she'd nodded. There were a few tapes stacked up on one of the shelves. He slid this one amongst them.

'So how are things in academic land?' Maggie asked, pushing her chair back.

'Two weeks, four days, three hours and...' looking at his watch again, 'fifty five seconds!'

'It's all right for some,' she said.

Jolly walked in and stiffened when he saw Rusty but then directed his next comment to Maggie.

'I've just had a memo from Quentin,' he said. 'Something about a video?'

'Oh, yes,' Maggie answered. 'He did drop something in. It's here somewhere.'

She walked over to the shelf and shuffled the pile of tapes around. Although they were all the same, she identified his by the 'Q.B.' scribbled over the front of the cover.

'Here it is,' she said, and handed it over.

'Excellent, excellent!' Jolly said. 'This might just save us a great deal of money!'

'But that's only Quentin's first attempt,' she said. 'I haven't looked at it yet.'

'Oh, I'm sure it will be perfectly all right,' Jolly beamed. 'I have a Governors meeting in the morning. I thought I'd show it to them then.'

'But is that really a good...' she began, but Jolly had turned and left. '...idea?' she finished saying.

'Not your problem,' Rusty said. 'Forget it.'

She did, and Rusty grinned to himself. His timing had been perfect. A minute earlier... But that didn't matter now. He wished he could be there in the morning to see the Governors reaction to the doctored tape.

Chewy and Rusty met by themselves later that evening.

'How're you getting on?' Chewy asked.

'O.K.' Rusty said. 'Take a look.'

'That's great,' Chewy said. 'That's all we need then. I'll get busy on the facsimiles. It shouldn't take too long.'

'I've got things set up in London,' Rusty said. 'All they need is the completed documentation. Then they can get going.'

'Right. I'll try and get these organised for the morning.' Chewy said. 'The sooner they get there the better.'

'Final check tomorrow?' Rusty suggested.

'Yep!' Chewy agreed.

They were in the final stages of a plan triggered by their level of blind frustration which had reached breaking point. Even though Rusty was leaving he was more than willing to set this operation in motion. It was to be the final 'coup' for the Escape Committee, at least for this year.

All the cones were out for the Governors meeting in front of the main building. This was done every time they met although many wondered why. Moving ten or more staff cars so that four rusty old bikes, two zimmer frames and a bubble car could park there didn't seem to justify the upheaval.

Inside the building the Governing body had now convened. They all sat round the big table in Jolly's study, some of them already on the point of nodding off. Jolly sat next to the Dean who took the head of the table. He sat there glaring down at the others, wondering which one would be the first to doze off. The rest were mostly clerics of one sort or another without a shred of knowledge about education. A couple of parents were included, recently appointed to placate the 'fifth column' which had grown amongst the parental body. The latest addition was one Hubert Sneddley, a 'Captain of Industry'. He was a complete buffoon and a recently retired director from a large international company. Jolly thought he had pulled a great coup at having him on board but he didn't know the background to the man. He'd been given the 'heave ho' from his directorship due to a take-over. They were glad to get rid of him. He'd been cocking the business up for years. Share prices in the city took off for the company when the word of his leaving had spread.

The two parents were complete opposites. First was Lorna Blomfield, a feisty lady who managed to intimidate Jolly most of the time. She had been the main opposition to him during parents' evenings and at any other time when she saw an opportunity to have a go at the School. Jolly's thinking had been to bring her onto the Governing body to spike her tendency to undermine him. He got that one completely wrong. She was even more inclined to upset things from this position. The other parent was Patrick Mannerham. He had the knack of saying the right thing at the right time, thereby keeping Jolly happy most of the time. A diplomat at all times, he would wax long and lyrical about various issues but, just like Jolly, would actually say nothing of any worth whenever he spoke. It sounded good though. So there they all were. Jolly stood to address them. He droned on at them for a good five minutes about how well they were doing but a nudge from the Dean stopped him and he finally got to the point of the meeting.

'And so,' Jolly said, slightly flustered, 'that brings me to the promotion of the School. We have looked long and hard into ways of demonstrating the excellence of the School. A great deal of work has already been done in this area and, at a great saving to the School, one of the staff has produced a video which we may well use as our main 'thrust' into potential parental interest.'

Mrs Blomfield didn't really like the sound of that. It sounded rather 'previous' as she might have said but this time didn't. Jolly picked up the tape and held it so they could all see it.

'This could be the answer to many of our problems. I'm given to understand that it shows the School in its best possible light and, if I may, I would like to show it to you now!'

If he'd only known what he and they were about to see... All chairs turned to the TV set in the corner. Jolly loaded the cassette and pushed the play button, standing well back, a wide smile on his face but that didn't last long.

Before any kind of image appeared on the screen, a blast of heavy 'schmaltzy' music washed over them. Three of the clerics woke up with a start. Then the screen filled with a shot of the Cathedral and a terrible commentary began.

Braumstate Cathedral School, wrapped in the mists of antiquity, set in the heart of the South West is the school for you!

The scene faded and changed to rolling lawns, the camera moving up to the mature tree line in front of the School but just catching one of the kids falling in the pond. Then there were several shots of the older buildings with the commentary still grinding on like an old style 'Look at life' of the fifties.

And here we can see the idyllic setting, the hallowed halls of academic life...

A few kids came into shot, stood like statues, grinning maniacally at the camera and one slowly brought up a hand written sign which had, "Hello Mum!' scrawled over it.

...but there are many other activities which are available to all the pupils....

The background music changed to 'Colonel Bogie' and the cadets, in full military, 'can't see me' gear flashed up and down. The speed of the tape had suddenly doubled. It was like watching a khaki version of the Keystone cops. Then Wooden's face appeared on the screen, but not looking at the camera. He began to say something but that had been dubbed to a staccato noise which sounded like the 'road-runner' cartoon character.

...'beep, beep! Beep, beeeeeep, beep!

The dreadful commentary continued as the scene changed again to shots of sport and then a rugby match taking place. In the background two of the opposing team were getting a good kicking from six of the Braumstate kids.

And the facilities for sport are second to none...

Inserted here was a quick shot of the rotting shed the school used as a pavilion, with two of the kids having a fag, just on the edge of the screen.

Then the Wide Mouth Frog appeared, dubbed with a 'Mae West' voice.

So as you can see we take every little 'problem' and see to it 'properly'. There are... 'ways'...

Jolly was up against the wall, his face white, hands clasped together. Two of the clerics had fainted, another was being given the kiss of life to revive him. The Dean was now standing, going a delightful shade of purple. The tape continued. More shots of ancient buildings, a slate falling off one as the camera panned sideways and then double speed took over again as the kids came out of lessons, streaking back and forth across the screen.

Then to his horror, Jolly himself appeared, standing in front of the main building and talking to one of the parents. Dubbed again, the voice of Liberace oozed from the set.

We are such a happy little bunch, don't you think? Nothing is too much trouble as long as you sign the cheque!

The final shot was of the Cathedral again with the commentary dripping with 'bon homie' and goodwill.

And so we say good-bye to Braumstate Cathedral School, that jewel of academic excellence and maybe, just maybe, say 'Hello' to YOU next term!

The tape ended, the screen went blank, and the room was totally silent. The Dean broke the silence.

'Headmaster!' he said, darkly. 'I think… we need… to talk!'

5

Speculation continued to bubble throughout the body of staff about who might apply for Wooden's job. Whoever got it would have to withstand the 'jolly' effect and that could prove to diminish the response from within. External candidates would be the ones at risk in that they wouldn't know what they were letting themselves in for but that, everyone agreed, would be their problem. Chewy and Rusty didn't give a stuff about any of that but with Wooden leaving it did reduce the plan they were hatching by a factor of one but that didn't matter.

A couple of weeks remained of the term and the kids were beginning to wind up to that. The Sixth Form were still trying to collect for a special 'event' but were having trouble with the actual amount they needed. Two of them sat talking in the D&T department before Chewy came up to start the lesson.

'We'll never get this organised!'

'Yes we will! It's just a case of a few more quid!'

'From where? We've been round everyone, there's no one left!'

'Then we'll just have to go round again. Another fifty pence per head will see us clear.'

'Don't be daft. You know how long it took to get this lot together. You can imagine the reaction if we have to do it all over again!'

'Well, what else can we do?'

'I don't know but if we don't get it together in the next couple of days, we'll be too late!'

'Too late for what?' Chewy said.

Both of them jerked their heads round to see him leaning against the doorframe. They didn't know how long he'd been standing there or what he might have overheard. This was going to be a bit tricky.

'Oh, nothing, sir.' one of them said.

'Nothing my backside!' Chewy said. 'What are you two sods planning?'

'Planning, sir?' they both said, trying to look as innocent as possible.

'Yes,' Chewy said, 'Planning, sir! Come on. What's up?'

The rest of the Sixth Form group shambled in and sat down, so Chewy decided to keep this conversation till later.

'I'll see you two after the lesson,' he said.

An hour or so later the group were on their way to their next subject, but Chewy stopped the two lads he'd been talking to.

'Not you two,' he said. 'We still need to talk.'

'But we'll be late!' they both said, urgently.

'Tough!' Chewy replied.

'But Adolf… err… that is… I mean… He'll go crackers if we come in late again!' one of them whined.

'Then you'd better tell me what you're planning, hadn't you?' Chewy grinned.

'Can we see you at lunchtime?' one of them asked.

'No. I want to know now!' Chewy demanded.

'Lunchtime, and we'll tell you everything, everything!' the other one said, looking at his watch desperately.

'Lunchtime it is then!' Chewy said. 'Make sure you turn up!'

'We will!' they said and shot off.

True to their word, they did come back and told Chewy what they'd been planning and the problem they had with it. Privately he thought the idea was fantastic, but being an upright responsible chap he had to suggest an alternative approach. Nonetheless he could just imagine the effect their idea would have had on Jolly.

'Well,' he said, 'I think the Headmaster will have some difficulty with two black, male strippers. His sense of humour is not what you could call 'sharp'. Besides the rest of us will still be here after you buggers have gone.'

They had to agree, but they still wanted to do something.

'What about this instead,' he said and gave them another idea.

'That's great!' they both said.

'But we're still short by about six quid!' said one of them.

'No you're not,' Chewy said, holding out a tenner. 'That should cover it!'

With great thanks they both shot off to finalise the 'special' for Jolly. Chewy was now really looking forward to the Sixth Form Ball.

End of term reports were due again and the usual scamper to complete these took place. Quite a few of the staff virtually repeated exactly what they'd said last time and after a few days of tedium they were complete, apart from the interference from the Fourth Reich who, this time, kept on sending back reports to some of the staff who had not, as far as she was concerned, given enough. The Escape Committee had their share of these and Compo, in particular, thought he'd sort her out, once and for all. He wrote all his out again in full Shakespearean, Elizabethan prose and dumped them in her pigeon hole. That slowed her down considerably as she read every one of them through, word by word, scratching her little Teutonic head, trying to work out the meaning of each sentence. Days later she had a bollocking from Jolly for being late with her reports!

In amongst all the other crap which continued to appear in pigeon holes, a few important letters had found their way to a few significant members of staff. They were a very select number. The Wide Mouth Frog and Harvey Sheasby weren't the only two of the teaching staff who found a rare invitation waiting for them. There were others. The Prick received one and the Fat Controller was another lucky recipient. Even Jolly received one. His was a surprise, to say the least. It had arrived from the same school in Pusan, Korea, where the two exchange teachers had come from last term. It was a glowing invitation for him to visit their school during the Summer holiday, with all expenses to be paid by them and even enclosed a first class air ticket. Jolly was totally 'gobsmacked'. He had only written to them, as a matter of courtesy, thanking them for the contribution the two staff had made to the School, that was all. The letter he was now reading implied much more. It was just as if he'd had further correspondence with them. Very strange indeed. He had to read their letter again before it began to sink in.

Dear Headmaster,

We are so happy to have had your kind words about our members of staff who were with you last term. They have also expressed their great delight in having had their time with you.

We share with you your feelings about 'bridging the gaps between our cultures' and, accordingly, we now invite you to stay with us for a few weeks, from July 20th until August 10th to study our methods and maybe advise us for the future.

It rambled on about educational trends and changes, nationally and internationally and then ended with a sentence which left Jolly wondering.

We look forward to seeing you and your suggestions for a greater link between us.

That sent him scuttling over to his filing cabinets, searching for his last letter to them. Eventually he found it, with Maisie's guidance, but it didn't help at all. His was a standard limp statement of 'an enjoyable experience' and 'worthwhile educational exchange' and he had stated the business of 'bridging the gaps between our cultures' as well. He re-read the thing and could only assume that they had taken his last words a little further than he had intended at the time. They were, *'I look forward to establishing greater links between us'*. That was it.

'But,' he thought. 'Did it matter? What an opportunity!'

He was hooked and sent off a letter of thanks to the address given. That was obviously a Korean Government office somewhere in London to help communications between countries. At least that's what Jolly thought. In fact it was just the beginning of Chewy's and Rusty's grand plan. Everything was now in motion. Both of them took great delight in watching the response from the next two in line, and were careful to take up position in the staff room before the Wide Mouthed Frog and Harvey Sheasby arrived. Both of them always sat in the common room opening their correspondence and reading everything rather than dumping most of it in the bin where it belonged.

Wide Mouth and Harvey opened their letters at the same time during morning break. Both of them sat there being observed closely by Chewy and Rusty. They pretended to read the papers but they were both looking over the tops of the opened pages as the letters were opened and absorbed by the other two. Wide Mouth's eyes widened and a huge grin slid across her pudgy features. The same thing was happening with Harvey. Wide Mouth's letter was a query about P.S.E. which appeared to have come from the Department of Education and Science. As with all communications from this central educational source, it was businesslike and to the point.

Dear Mrs Broadstead,

It has come to our attention that you have been endeavouring to establish a platform of knowledge and understanding, via the P.S.E. syllabus, which has been particularly useful to many pupils. We have received many letters of praise from parents, regarding the way you have handled the delicate nature of human relationships, and would like you to speak to an invited audience from several European educational centres.

We are now in the final stages of organising this major event and if you are able to be with us, we will be delighted to arrange all the necessary details, on your behalf, for a London venue.

July 20th has been chosen, as this is the only convenient date for a number of highly prestigious members of the Royal Family, who will be attending the conference at the same time. We do hope you will be able to attend. Please inform us of your decision within the next seven days.

Yours sincerely.

D.E.S.

Wide Mouth couldn't believe her luck. Recognition at last! She'd been at this for years and nobody, but nobody, had realised how right she'd been. Now she would show them! With such a prestigious gathering this would give her an international reputation! She couldn't wait to go. The letter of acceptance must be sent today! Getting up from the chair she waddled off with a smug expression on her face to write that letter in complete privacy. Chewy and Rusty exchanged glances and winked. The plan was working well. Harvey was going through the same process. His was a communication from the Meteorological Office.

Dear Mr Sheasby,

We understand that you have been demonstrating a remarkably high standard of weather forecasting. This has been brought to our attention by several people, including a number of parents at your school.

In view of this extraordinary record of achievement we would like to invite you to lecture to our trainee personnel, on the evening of July 20th, to allow them a different perspective for this highly technical service.

If you are available to perform this function for us we will be pleased to hear from you, in writing, to the above address.

Yours sincerely,

M.O.

Harvey's face was a picture. He was just like a little boy who'd been given a big sweety jar. As far as he was concerned this was a complete vindication of all he'd been trying to do. He couldn't wait! Rusty folded his paper and dropped it onto the table. Chewy did the same and they both grinned at each other as Harvey almost ran from the room clutching the letter.

'So far, so good!' Rusty said.

'Three down, two to go,' Chewy said.

Two other letters were for the Prick and the Fat Controller. Neither Chewy or Rusty were able to witness the effect they had, but judging by the reaction they'd seen from the Wide Mouth Frog and Harvey Sheasby, they reckoned they would be just as successful. They were right. The Prick opened his letter with great interest the following day. It was from the Ministry of Defence.

Dear Sir,

It is with reference to your long-standing service as former Captain of the Administrative Services of the Armed Forces of Her Majesty the Queen that we write to you.

Her Majesty has informed us that all previous personnel who have worked in this important section of her defence system should be recognised and rewarded for their exemplary service to the nation. Accordingly, we have been instructed to write to you to inform you of this important event and request that you should appear at the Palace to receive a token of Her Majesties appreciation.

Please inform us immediately of your acceptance of this honour so that we can make the necessary arrangements for the day, July 20th.

Yours faithfully,

M.O.D.

It wasn't until later that morning that the Fat Controller opened his. His eyed widened and he sat forward in his seat. It was a letter from the Independent Schools prestigious Head Masters Conference Group.

Dear Sir,

Your service in the Independent sector, as Financial Controller, has recently come to our attention. There are few instances when such sterling professional ability shines through an otherwise mundane world of accountancy.

For this reason we would think it an honour if you could find the time to advise a number of our colleagues on the finer principles of Independent Financial control.

This will be held in London on July 20th. We look forward to your reply for this important meeting of several National organisations.

yours sincerely,

H.M.C.G.

It took a few seconds for it to sink in, but then he shook himself, picked up a pen and began to write a reply. How could he possibly keep them waiting? This was going to be an important career move if he handled it properly.

And so, one by one, all the fish took every scrap of the bait. The date given to each one, July 20th, was in the second week of the Summer holiday so there would be no need for arranging cover for any of them or even the need for putting in for special leave to attend any one of the 'events'. Added to this, Chewy and Rusty were counting on the fact that none of them would let the others know. They would want to gain their glory first, then blab about it afterwards, at great length.

They had sussed that one perfectly. Not one of them said a single word to the others about their supposed good news. They just began to wear an even more smug expression than usual. Chewy and Rusty now had time to wait until each one of them had replied to the address given. They reckoned that probably wouldn't take too long. Their contacts were ready to dispatch replies. When the letters of confirmation came through to all of them the scene would be set for the final act. So far, things were going very well.

'There it is,' Harry said. 'In black and white.'

He was looking at the staff notice board and the notice about the Deputy Head's job.

Staff are invited to apply for the post of Deputy Head of Braumstate Cathedral School.

The successful candidate will need to take up the appointment from the beginning of the Lent Term in the next academic year.

'It'll be interesting to see who applies for that,' Lill said, sardonically. 'Can you imagine working with Jolly Jack? It would drive me up the wall!'

'At least!' Vic agreed. He'd had plenty of experience of the 'Jolly effect' as chaplain.

'Well,' Rusty asked. 'Who do you think will?'

'Difficult to say,' Chewy said. 'Can't think of anyone who has the guts.'

'You don't need either guts or brains for that job,' Compo said. 'All you need is a nodding head and a face like a door mat! Jolly's always wiping his verbal feet on Wooden!'

They all nodded sagely. Compo had it just right. It would be fascinating to see who would apply. Two days later Maggie heard the Mad Hatter shrieking and ran through to see what had happened. She found Maisie collapsed with laughter in her chair, a few letters opened on the desk in front of her.

'What's up?' she asked, surprised.

'Just look at this lot!' Maisie giggled. 'Of all people...!'

She continued laughing as Maggie picked them up and flicked through them. They were applications for the Deputy Head post. In amongst ten or more others there were three in particular which had set Maisie off. Rollerball, Deep Throat and the Head Boy! Maggie couldn't help joining Maisie. They both giggled together. Any one of those three would be an absolute disaster for the school. The problem was that Jolly might not see it the same way. He had a knack of identifying the worst possible personalities for any role of responsibility. The wonder was that there were no more dick heads on the staff than were already there. It had been the influence of others, such as the Dean, which had prevented that.

Both Maisie and Maggie hoped that there might be some of the external candidates who might just be more suitable. The deadline for applications was only a week away, the day after Open Day. There wasn't a lot of time left.

'Barbecue time' now advanced towards all of them and this was always a pain. Every boarding house, and some Departments, held end of year barbecues at this time in the term, every year. After they were over, and the barbecue stands had cooled, they were usually dumped in any convenient, dark corner, their role finished with, over and done with until the following summer.

That always gave the same problem the following year. Where the hell were they now? A mad scramble would then take over as staff and kids rooted around the site looking for the rusting stands, Where had they been left? How many did they have? Were there enough?

They were always eventually found, one by one, lying underneath overgrown shrubs, lurking behind various buildings, all in a rusting, falling apart state, requiring substantial restoration or repair. That's when Chewy found himself at the sharp end. Several staff crept around him, weedling at him for the prospect of repair or remaking their rotting metal structures so that the barbecues could emerge again like mini phoenixes from the ashes of the previous year.

His enthusiasm did not rise at all to these requests as there was never more than a day or so available to have the work done. Bribery came to the fore during this time with quite a few bottles of the amber liquid changing hands.

Some of the houses had the sense to organise themselves for this event, in that they recognised that the basic essence of the school was co-educational. It had been since 1969, although some of the older staff still thought that to be rather 'racy', and were not happy with joint barbecues for girls and boys houses. Wide Mouth and Harvey didn't like that. 'It was far too advanced', they said, but were promptly ignored by all.

On the morning of the joint barbecue which Chewy was involved with, as 'assistant house person', he walked round to the gardens at the back of the boarding houses and wondered what he could do to make the evening a little more suitable for the adults, the other staff who shared house duties with him. Usually, as the sun set over these events, the garden was still vibrating with heavy rock music, and as darkness fell it was almost impossible to find a way through without falling over horizontal bodies or kicking tinnies and plates of half eaten food.

He rooted around amongst the ground staff's store and found half a dozen hurricane lamps, ideal for hanging in the trees for the evening. They would add to the atmosphere and also help to lower the procreative urges of their charges. Darkness was always convenient for extra mural activity of all kinds during these 'knees ups' at the end of every Summer term.

Chewy checked the lamps over, topped them up with paraffin, but two of them had broken glasses. They'd be useless without them so he decided to see if he could replace them. He'd rather have another two than be without. There was only one shop in town that might have spares. That was Whottleys, an old style ironmonger come bric-a-brac merchant. If they didn't have them then nobody would. Whottleys was one of those places which stocked everything from kitchen equipment to garden tools to all kinds of hardware and obscure bits and pieces which had disappeared off the face of the commercial earth ten years before. It was still possible to buy one fuse for a plug instead of a sealed pack of ten. Even wooden clothes pegs still existed in their stock room and there was hardly a domestic item which was not available. Much of it hadn't been in stock anywhere else for the better part of twenty years. Chewy walked into the place and stood at the counter. A conversation was going on behind it between two of the assistants, who were just standing there but quite oblivious of his presence.

'Well, Oi dunno,' one was saying. 'Oi mean, you never know what's goin' t'happen next, d'you?'

'Oi know what y'meam m'dear,' the other said. 'Oi've never seen one o' they fer a long toime.'

'No,' said the other. 'You never have call frem these days.'

'Thass roight! You never see 'em these days, do ee?'

'No, thass true!' came the easy reply.

It was a slow motion kind of conversation which didn't seem to be going anywhere. Chewy was fascinated by it and just stood there listening, they didn't even notice him. Standing there, on the other side of the counter, vaguely male, one tall and skinny with a high pitched voice, the other short and squat, both of them 'communicating' in a thick south west accent. They stared ahead, not at each other at all, fixed, unmoving, but carrying on this weird exchange about something which was impossible to identify.

'So I says to 'im,' said the first one. 'Oi 'aven't seen one o' they f'years.'

'Ooh, ahh?' came the reply.

'Ahh,' said the first. 'Oi said, there's difficult, oi 'aven't seen one o' they fer a long toime.'

'Well, y'wouldn't would ee?' said the other.

Chewy was getting a little bored by this now and he attempted to interrupt.

'Excuse me,' he said.

Not a flicker. They kept on talking.

'Thass roight. Moind you oi did see one, once,' said one of them, 'but that were a long toime ago.'

'Ahh!' came the slow reply.

'Well,' said the first. 'Oi'd better be goin' now.'

'Ahh,' said the other and the short, squat one walked slowly away.

The one who remained didn't move, he just kept staring ahead. Chewy tried again.

'Hello?' he said hopefully.

'Hello, zurr,' came the reply, just as slow, just as immobile. 'An' what can oi do f'you, then?'

'Ah, roight, I mean right,' Chewy said. 'I've got a slight problem.'

'Ooh, ahh?' the other said.

'Yes,' Chewy continued. 'It's this,' and offered one of the broken glasses from the hurricane lamps. The other reached out slowly across the counter and took it, pulling it slowly back.

'Ooh, ahh,' said the other, slowly taking it. 'Oi 'aven't seen one o'they fer a long toime.'

'Oh, hell!' Chewy thought. 'Here we go again!'

'Do you think you might have one?' Chewy asked.

'Well,' the other said. 'Dunno 'bout that. Don't have a lot of people ask f'them these days.'

'Do you know where I might be able to get one then?' Chewy asked, slightly disappointed.

'Well,' said the other. 'Oim not sure. Lessee now.'

Without moving his body at all, one arm came slowly back from the counter top and disappeared over the edge to come back up with a brand new glass which he held out to Chewy. The assistant's face didn't follow it as if it didn't belong to him.

'Do y'think it moight be one o' they?' he asked.

Chewy was amazed at the way the glass had simply materialised. He took it anyway and compared it with the broken one. It wasn't quite the same.

'Thass a British one oive juss given ee,' the assistant drawled. 'Kwality that is.'

'Really?' Chewy said.

'Ooh, ahh, kwality that be,' said the assistant.

Looking closer at the old, broken one Chewy could see the country of origin stamped on the bottom edge.

'Ahh,' he said. 'That's a pity. The old one's Czechoslovakian.'

'Ahh,' the assistant said. He took the British one back, and slowly down over the edge of the counter while his other arm disappeared and came up with another glass. All this in one easy movement, his body being absolute still. He handed it to Chewy. This glass was a perfect match.

'Don't get much call fer they these days,' was all he said.

Chewy took it silently, even more amazed at the slow motion performance and the twin materialisation of hurricane glasses from, it seemed, nowhere. He leaned over to look on the assistant's side of the counter, wondering what the hell he had over there but couldn't see anything in particular. Chewy paid for it and left, the assistant still standing, immobile, behind the counter.

By the time he returned, the Barbecue had been lit and preparations were well underway for the evening. The dining room staff had equipped them with a range of goodies and the House staff had organised plenty of soft drinks for most of the kids and a barrel of beer from the local for some of the Sixth Form as well as the staff. There were quite a few bottles of wine standing ready as well. It looked as if the weather was going to stay clear so it seemed they were all in for a good night. Some of the kids had set up a sound system and the musicians amongst them were tuning up guitars and a synthesiser. Next to this, one of the TV sets had been rigged up for a karaoke 'knees up' later on so it all began to build nicely for a major end of term party. Two hours later most of the food had gone and the place was echoing with heavy rock music, the kids gyrating around all over the lawn. Then Jolly and the Wide Mouth Frog arrived and had the effect on everything of a balloon slowly deflating. They were carrying torches and both the staff and the kids knew what they were for, beating the bushes for smokers.

'I say,' Jolly yelled at Wide Mouth. 'Popular music, eh?'

'Eh?' she screeched back over the noise.

'Music!' he yelled back.

'What? More?' she shrieked at him.

He just shook his head and wandered round nodding and grinning at the kids. As he approached all of them they stopped dancing and stood back, as if he was a leper. Chewy came over and shouted something in his ear.

'Really!' Jolly yelled back.

Chewy just nodded. Jolly scuttled over to Wide Mouth who was standing with her fingers in her ears. He pulled her hands down and yelled something at her. Her face took on a startled expression and they both ran off across the lawn and into the bushes. Most of the staff had watched this and Vic ambled over to Chewy.

'What did you say to him!' he yelled over the music.

'Told him there were smokers next door in Wide Mouth's house!' Chewy shouted. 'That should keep them busy for a while!'

It did. Every now and then they could see the glimmer of torches as Jolly and Wide Mouth rushed around in the undergrowth looking for give away 'glows' in the dark. They didn't come back and that had saved the party from certain death. Chewy caught some of the comments from the kids as he walked round.

'Did you see that?'

'What?'

'Jolly and Wide Mouth in the bushes!'

'No!'

'Yeah!'

'Are they...you know?'

'Probably!'

'What? Those two?'

'Yeah!'

'Must have their bloody eyes shut then!'

'Difficult to know which one to feel sorry for!'

'Neither. They deserve each other!'

The aftermath of the barbeque took a couple of hours to clean and tidy up, but it had been a great night for both the kids and the staff. Amongst all the empty tinnies and fag ends in the bushes, one of the Sixth Form found a pair of knickers. The rumours which flashed around the place right until the end of term were ripe, to say the least. Wide Mouth wondered why she continued to be given funny looks for days afterwards.

The last week of the Summer term was always a complete waste of time as far as teaching was concerned and most of the staff gave up in the face of hyped up kids who could now see their 'imprisonment' coming to an end. 'Video land' took over completely again with practically every classroom blaring out the raucous sounds of the latest and most violent examples from the film industry. There were two exceptions. One was Wide Mouth and the other was Harvey Sheasby. Surprise, surprise!

The volume of paper rubbish had slowed but some important letters had turned up in the pigeon holes of a select few. These were the 'official' acknowledgements, confirming venues, timings and the date, July 20th, for five very special events. Jolly, The Prick, FC, the Wide Mouthed Frog and Harvery Sheasby were all privately ecstatic in anticipation of their 'big day' and began to count the days until then, brimming over with self satisfaction. It was awful to see and a number of staff wondered why but the Escape Committee knew.

Two events, outside the normal routine of the last week, were the Swimming Gala and Sports Day. The only bonus which this held for some of the staff was that they were never given anything to do with either event. They, the Escape Committee, had carefully cocked things up in the past to ensure that they would never be roped in again. That left the field open to all the other urgent nutters who were still trying to compete with the kids as a means of maintaining or boosting their pathetic little ego's. It was sickening to watch. The one event during the Swimming Gala which was to deflate every one of them was the staff freestyle, but that wasn't due to happen until the kids had done their stuff.

Parents were welcomed to both events and before the Swimming Gala began hundreds of them had lined the grass surrounding the open air pool. All of the kids not competing were sprinkled amongst them and the atmosphere had quite a party feel to it. A lot of folk had brought picnics with them and sat around on the grass munching, chatting and drinking. The events began and the cheering was deafening as friends and whole peer groups shouted encouragement. Jolly, Wooden and Wide Mouth sat, pride of place, at one end of the pool on a raised platform. A few of the Governors sat with them. At the other end, where all the events started, were the timekeepers and the P.E. oaf, supposedly in charge of the whole thing. He swaggered up and down dressed in shorts and T shirt, a whistle and stopwatch hanging round his neck. A right poser in front of the crowd. Waving his arms around and peeping his little whistle, he shepherded the kids into place, set them up and started them off with a small starting pistol, or tried to. After the first race the thing was soaked from the splashes as the kids hit the water and after that he stood there saying, 'Bang!', for every new race.

It was the relay races which provided the high point of the day. For some reason, unexplained to everyone, kids started at one end but then the second group was to take off from the other end, in front of Jolly and the rest. No one expected or foresaw what was to happen. Just before the race started a message came through to Wooden about a phone call, so off he toddled. As the second group waited for the first group to splash their way to them, Jolly, Wide Mouth and a couple of the Governors, instinctively moved forward on their seats. The second group took off as the first made contact with the pool edge and a wonderful tidal wave of water erupted from the surface, depositing itself all over Jolly and the rest of them. A huge roar of approval went up as they stood there, shocked, open mouthed, dripping and completely soaked to the skin. Couldn't have happened to a nicer bunch! They all squelched off to hoots and whistles from the kids and the stifled laughter of staff and parents alike. Then it was time for the staff relay.

A varied assortment of bodies lined up. First it was the women. Well, they just about qualified for that. Some of the parents had to look away as they stood there. Definitely a sight for a strong stomach. The PE Oaf shouted 'bang!' and they were off, splashing around like drowning turtles. Half way down the pool two of them lost their direction, not being able to see because of the water being whipped around, and promptly collided with each other, bounced away and smacked into the others. Not one of them reached the other end. It took another five minutes to drag them out where they lay panting like beached whales and wobbling jellyfish on the sides.

Then it was the turn of the men. Again it was an extraordinary sight. Mostly seven stone weaklings, one penguin-like shape and something which resembled a partially deflated beach ball. Action was there amongst them, flexing and stretching his muscles. The P.E. Oaf shouted 'bang!' and in they dived. Well, some of them did. The penguin look-a-like slithered off the edge very carefully while the beachball just seemed to roll off. Action was way ahead by this time and just before he reached the other end he looked round, saw the others floundering around behind him and smirked. Then he was ploughing through the water again, but he'd forgotten how close he was the pool edge and crunched straight into it, head first. It took the P.E. Oaf and four Sixth Formers to drag him up from the bottom, still unconscious. After the Gala the recounting of events gave the kids, staff and parents endless hours of amusement as they told others what had happened. The following day would provide another series of unfortunate, hilarious circumstances for them to relive. That was to be Sports Day.

6

Sports Day had none of the watery fun of the Gala, but there were a few moments of total farce, not that Jolly would have agreed. This was a much larger affair set on one of the extensive playing fields below the School. Again parents thronged the ground, picnics to the fore, and quite a number of the staff were ready to show their mettle as 'sports persons'. Aimit, the Head Boy, Adolph and even Harvey Sheasby as well as a few others had taken the day to heart. They were dressed in awful shell suits and looked like something out of the Beano. Each one had their own task to supervise from the Shot Put, Javelin, Long Jump, High Jump to the various distance races. All with stop watches and whistles. Chaos ensued. Every time a whistle blew, kids either started or stopped, threw something or put it down. The poor little buggers didn't know where they were half the time. Then Sheamus Gilpin, equally attired in a terribly garish green outfit, went almost 'ape shit' when a parent began walking down the lines of the running track with a pram. She didn't realise that the Sixth Form were charging towards her in the middle of the three thousand meter race.

'Look at the jolly green giant,' Chewy said, pointing at Sheamus haring across the grass, trying to attract the woman's attention and screaming his head off. He just managed to pull her off as the Sixth Form thundered past. She still hadn't noticed and went for Sheamus with her handbag, clouting him all over and chasing him off yelling, 'You dirty old bastard!'

The P.E. Oaf still hadn't fixed his little gun and was still shouting, 'bang!' at the beginning of every race. Down at the lean-to wooden hut, propped against one of the trees, which served as Pavilion, store and smokers' den, the first aid contingent were already in full swing as various kids began to arrive with their own personal trophies of the games. Twisted ankles, cuts, bruises, black eyes and various other physical maladies were being inflicted all over the ground. A few near misses with the Javelins and Discus had a few kids and parents in shock but this was about normal for the day so nobody was really worried.

As events came and went Wooden had been on the P.A. system. The set up had been thrown together too quickly by some of the Fifth Form and what with feed back and squeaks and grating noises, coupled with Wooden's incomprehensible words, it made a hell of a lot of noise but not a great deal of sense. By around three o'clock some of the staff were gasping for a cup of tea and made for the trestle tables set up next to the lean-to. It hadn't arrived. Twenty minutes later the ground staff turned up with a huge tea urn on the back of a tractor, but by the time they had bumped and slopped their way down to the lean-to, the thing was almost empty.

A thick impenetrable hedge ran round most of the ground with only one entrance. Harvey Sheasby, still in his hideous shell suit was standing guard, making sure none of the kids escaped. The Wide Mouthed Frog sat next to him on a deck chair, holding an umbrella against the sun and occasionally blowing her nose, as usual. The deck chair was fairly upright and the way she was sitting, legs apart, couldn't be missed by anyone foolish enough to look. With her sunglasses on she didn't notice the look of horror on some of the faces as they walked past. It was not a pretty sight. That alone accounted for at least three of the kids who had fainted.

By four o'clock the events were over and the time had come to award the prizes. The whole body of kids, parents and staff congregated round the trestles, which had been laid out with the

School prize cups. Jolly stood with Wooden and read out the winners as Wooden handed him the cups to be presented. Beyond them all, on the other side of the hedge, were a few houses, and while the presentation of cups was going on, a householder just happened to look out of her kitchen window to see smoke coming up from the lean-to. Some of the Fifth Form had been round the back for a few quick drags and hadn't put them out properly. That was half an hour before, and now the smouldering grass had caught the bottom of the lean-to and it was well away. She phoned the fire brigade immediately.

Minutes later the air was torn by the siren of a fire engine as it pulled onto the ground and roared towards them. Everyone scattered as it slid to a halt in front of the trestles, men jumping out and pulling out hoses. They had it out in a few minutes but it wasn't over for Jolly. It was the same Fire Chief he'd met last term. The Chief walked towards Jolly very slowly, then stopped, enticing Jolly to come over to him by crooking his index finger.

'I think you and I need to have a little talk, sir, don't we?' he said.

For all the manic activity up till now, there were still three main events to run. The first was the Sixth Form Ball and then, the following day would be Open Day followed by the Parents' Association Ball that evening. The marquee for all these events had been in place for a day or so, on the main lawn, much to the delight of the younger kids who were using it as a great playground. The ground staff chased them off eventually as the time came to set up for the Sixth Form Ball. Three hours of concentrated work brought in a temporary wooden floor, furniture, lighting, cases of red and white wine and the statutory two barrels of beer. Then the dining room staff took over. Table cloths, cutlery, and flowers were carefully placed and the venue was almost ready. A shift system had been organised in operation to guard the beer, just in case any of the Sixth Form, or anyone else wanted to 'sample' it. By the end of the two hours of Big Mac's stint, who couldn't resist 'testing' a few drops of it, he was pissed out of his head.

By seven o'clock the kids began to mass for the night, all of them dressed to kill. The girls were all wearing stunning evening dresses while the boys were looking very sharp in tuxedos. Some of them had already started their own liquid celebrations privately, consuming several tinnies in the houses, and there were a few wobbly footsteps as they entered the marquee. The band had arrived by then and the air vibrated as they blasted through an old 'Led Zeppelin' number on full amps. The party was now officially off and running. Over the next half hour staff and Sixth Form filled the marquee. Then Jolly arrived with his wife, Portia, who was wearing a ghastly puce coloured thing which looked like a nightie. They were followed by the Wide Mouthed Frog, dressed in a frothy black number.

'I see Dracula's daughter and the local Valkerie have arrived,' Vic said.

'No,' Rusty replied. 'That's really the rep for the Sunday Sport and the local chimney sweep in drag.'

All of the Escape Committee were there, mingling with the kids, swapping jokes and getting into the spirit of the evening. This was to be the last occasion when they would see them all together and it was an important, and sometimes a very emotional night for the kids. Any of the staff were welcome to come this but few of them ever bothered. Rollerball was one who had decided to come and he'd brought his spectacularly tarty wife, Sharon, with him. She was dressed like a 'Danny La Rue look-a-like' which had most of the Sixth Form creased up every time they looked at her.

'I see Dame Edna has arrived,' Chewy said to Rusty, nodding in Sharon's direction. He looked round and almost choked on his drink. Maggie found herself in deep conversation with the Head Girl, about 'women's problems', when Compo, Harry and Lill floated past, arm in arm, dancing along and singing at the tops of their voices the words to the song the band were busily bashing out. That was, 'I can't get no satisfaction!'

'How true!' Chewy said.

It was going to be one of those evenings. The kids thought that was great and joined in behind the three of them. Jolly saw this from the other side of the Marquee. He was not impressed. Just before they were due to sit for dinner, two of the Sixth Form were having a heated conversation outside. They were the same two Chewy had grilled about their 'special' for this evening.

'It's nearly seven forty! Have you phoned them?'

'Yes! I phoned them!'

'And?'

'They'll be here!'

'When?'

'In about an hour from now!'

'Are you sure?'

'Don't be bloody silly! Of course I am!'

'I bloody hope so! The timing for this is vital!'

'Will you relax. I know all about that!'

'We'll have to organise a look out for when they arrive, or the surprise element's gone.'

'O.K! Let's see to that now!'

Inside the Marquee the dining room staff were busily serving the first course. The band had taken the opportunity to partake of one of the barrels, and the sound system was now in the control of a Fifth Former, a disciple of forties and fifties 'swing music'. The strains of Glenn Miller filled the marquee. Above this, laughter filled the air from many of the tables except the ones where Jolly, Wide Mouth and Rollerball were sitting. Portia had helped herself to the wine just a little too much and at one point she and Sharon met on their way back from the ladies. A loud conversation was then heard by most of the assembled company as they both made their way through the tables and each of them quite pissed by this time.

'Does he? I wouldn't stand for that!'

'I don't as a rule, if you know what I mean!'

They both broke into filthy hysterical laughter and then carried on.

'But does he really do that?'

'Every time!'

'But that must be very tiring?'

'Yes it is. For him!'

They both almost fell over laughing, right in front of the bandstand, much to the delight of the kids, but not to either Jolly or Rollerball. As the crockery and cutlery were collected and the tables cleared, the band came back and the kids took over the floor in front of them, launching into a series of dance routines which left some of the staff at a complete loss. The Escape Committee jumped in with both feet, literally, and whether or not they had it right didn't really matter to them or the kids. Jolly and the rest of them faffed about trying to do the fox trot and other equally idiotic and totally inappropriate moves but gave up after a while under the thumping beat of rock standards. Vic staggered off, after leaping around like a maniac, followed by Chewy. Both of them walked out to get some fresh air. It was as hot as hell inside. Vic lit a cigarette and Chewy had his pipe going in the safety of the near darkness outside the marquee. Within seconds, a small gathering of the Sixth Form had surrounded them. They embarked on fatuous small talk until Chewy stopped them and asked a simple question.

'All right! Which one of you buggers wants a light?'

'Oh, great!' they all said.

'I'll keep an eye out,' Vic said, stubbing out his cigarette and walking back to the side of the Marquee. Chewy opened his matchbox and rattled out six matches. He held them out, but before he let them go he offered a few words of advice,

'Stay away from the Marquee!'

A few of the side openings were pulled up to allow some air into the interior and a number of the Sixth Form and staff took advantage of this, wandering around, in and out, while the band continued to pump out music. There was still a jumping, yelling mass of bodies on the floor jigging about to the music but now Jolly and Wide Mouth had their torches in their hands, yet again. The word spread like wildfire amongst the kids that they were on their way, and the shrubbery emptied of smokers as the beams from Jolly's and Wide Mouth's torches played around outside. They were all by themselves for quite a while, much to the amusement of everyone inside who knew exactly where they were. When they eventually returned they didn't notice the exit of several of the kids as the smokers took up residence again, with their relit fags and their renewed source of matches.

Then, a short time later, the time came for the formal speeches of the evening. An expectant lull settled as the Head Boy and Girl stood up at the top table. They had endured Jolly and Wide Mouth for the whole of the dinner and with great endurance had withstood the crap that both of them had been spouting. After this they would be able to escape with immense relief to the normality of being in the Sixth Form and, more important, on the point of leaving. They came to the microphone, in the centre of the top table, and gave a standard speech, sharing points between them about the school and the future for themselves and their peers. The statutory thanks to all the teaching staff were given and then it was Jolly's turn to say a few words. As the applause broke out and then died, Jolly prepared himself.

Just outside the Marquee the Sixth Form guard had a 'special guest' ready to go including two rather intimidating 'minders' complete with shades and stubble. They had found them wandering around, wondering where to go and had brought them over. Between them the 'special guest' walked calmly to the tent and waited for the signal to enter from the Sixth Former standing there. As Jolly pushed his chair back and rose to speak the signal was given. He didn't notice the figure which slid into the marquee and sidled round behind him as he stood to begin his speech. Before he could say a word he was engulfed by a mountain of a woman dressed in a thick, black fur coat. As she held him, taking the microphone at the same time, she peeled this off, revealing a vast, bloated, top heavy pink body with the flimsiest and scantiest of female top and bottom coverings, complete with suspenders, black stockings and singing into the mike, 'He's not heavy, he's my brother!'

A stunned silence held for only a second before a hundred cameras appeared and captured the scene for ever more, a photographic record which would last and be treasured by the whole of the Sixth Form as their remaining memory of Jolly Jack, their Headmaster.

It was here at last. Open Day. The one day of the year the staff had really been looking forward to, almost eight full hours of having parents bombarding them with questions, mindless conversations about their hateful brats and the simple fact that the stupid bastards were everywhere! The place would be thick with them all bloody day! But there was a lighter side. After enduring the minefield of aimless questions and forced politeness they would be free for a whole two, luxurious months. The only drawback was having to endure these cretins 'en masse'.

The ground staff had been hard at work, again, clearing up the aftermath of the Sixth Form Ball and now they were busily reorganising the furniture in the marquee for afternoon tea. Parents had been arriving since the night before and early morning and by eight o'clock the whole site was stuffed solid with coupes, 4 by 4s, limousines and just the occasional old 'banger'. A temporary car park was usually opened up on the playing field above the school and this was now filling up rapidly. By nine o'clock the school was effectively surrounded and looked like the M25 on a bad day.

Up in the staff room the last staff meeting had begun. It was just as inconsequential as any other but Jolly, being Jolly, always launched into various mindless concerns so that all the staff could go off and worry as much as possible during the holiday. Toadys nodded their heads at everything he said and Wide Mouth blew her bloody nose all the way through it. Eventually they were released. The weather was bright and clear but a few clouds began to form as everyone began to make their way to the Cathedral for the end of term service. By the time they all emerged, almost an hour later, it was raining. This did not bode well for the rest of the day.

'Hope you've got your wellies,' Chewy said, as he walked up with Rusty.

'Wellies?' Rusty asked.

'Wait till this afternoon,' Chewy replied. 'If this weather keeps up, the lawn round the Marquee will be like a quagmire!'

'Point taken!' Rusty said.

The next thing on the agenda for the day was the end of term speeches and academic prizes for the year. The Sports Hall was open and ready for them. Hundreds of chairs, taken from every available classroom, had been set out in two main blocks. One for the kids and the other for the parents and staff. In front of this sat a large, raised platform, steps on either side, a lectern at the front of it, with a line of chairs for Jolly, his 'mangement' team, the guest speaker and the Dean.

The hall filled up slowly and, as usual, by the time the Dean, the guest speaker, Jolly and the rest processed through the hushed congregation, the day was running well over an hour late. The dining room staff were not going to like this. The whole of the Escape Committee were wise enough to not join the main body in the hall but, instead, climbed up to one of the long balconies which ran along the inside of the building. Scanning the parental body was an education. This was much more interesting than seeing them arriving at the beginning of term. This was pure entertainment. Their conversation was just as much fun to listen to, and a few of the Sixth Form, who were up there with them, were doing just that.

'There she is!'

'Where?'

'Over there! She's the one wearing the flying saucer!'

'How can people walk around looking like that?'

'Good sense of humour?'

'Colour blind as well by the look of it!'

Many other comments were made but the temperature began to rise rapidly inside the hall and this only heightened the spectacle below them. Quite a number of the parents were peeling off various pieces of clothing, in an attempt to cool down and from where the Escape Committee were standing some of sights were incredible, particularly the women.

'Will you just look at the size of them!'

'Got a balance problem there, I'll bet!'

'You could crack nuts between them!'

As the heat continued to rise a number of heads began to nod,

'That one's gone! Spark out already!'

'There'll be more before too long!'

The Dean had welcomed all and rambled on about the need for 'high standards' a 'happy school' and 'caring staff'. The Escape Committee wondered who, where and what he was talking about. Then came the introduction of the main speaker and an extraordinarily small, wizened, 'ugly' stepped forward. This was Humphrey Netherbridge, a self made man in ceramics. Well, it said that in the programme but in fact he made toilet bowls. He'd specialised in them for years and now he'd cornered the market. There wasn't a bum in the South West he couldn't cope with.

'Came to the right place then,' Chewy muttered.

He began to speak in a halting, squeaky voice about the need for 'high standards' a 'happy school' and 'caring staff'.

'This is really interesting,' Rusty yawned.

'Fascinating,' said Harry.

'Riveting,' Lill said.

He droned on and on, oblivious of the low conversations which were breaking out all over the place. No one, except those on the platform, were taking a blind bit of notice. Quite a few other folk had dropped off in the heat of the hall and by the time he eventually finished, saying whatever he had been saying, most of the parents wanted to be somewhere else. The ones who were awake at any rate. Then the Dean stood, to a limp ripple of applause, and announced the presentation of prizes. Compo was appalled at the speech and said so loudly.

'That was the worst speech I've ever heard!' he said and his voice echoed round the top of the hall. A few people looked up wondering where the voice had come from. Humphrey Netherbridge, or 'the bog man', as Chewy had now nicknamed him, stepped forward again. As the Dean read out the list of names, Netherbridge handed out the cups, medals and diploma's but at such a rate of knots it was embarrassing to watch.

'I thought this was for the kids!' Lill grumbled. 'This is appalling!'

'It's like watching a bloody conveyor belt!' Chewy grunted.

The whole business was over in three minutes. That must have been a record but the assembled body didn't realise that the Dean was bursting for a pee and this was the only way he could get there without dragging the proceedings on for ever, as usually happened. As the last of the applause died away and sleeping bodies were dug in the ribs to wake, the multitude began to depart. Outside it was pissing down. The rain really didn't stop until well after midday by which time most of the parents were inside the marquee, all jammed up together. Most of the kids were outside, ambling round, soaked to the skin yet totally oblivious of being so wet. This is a true phenomenon, in that kids always walk and lazily stroll around in heavy rain, dripping, and seeming not to care. Must be something to do with their hormones, the lack of them or something.

The sky remained heavily overcast but the rain eventually stopped. It became very humid, and it took a strong stomach to enter the marquee half an hour later. Steaming bodies filled the place as most of the kids were now inside and the parents outside. This was the time which all the staff dreaded. It was 'hunt the teacher' time. All the petty problems, worries, paranoia and just plain stupidity came out during Open Day. It was like a 'mega' parents evening, where staff could be pursued, pounced on, pinned down and prattled at for hours. Chewy had a simple solution to this. He locked himself in his building. None of them got to him at all but there was another reason why he did this. There had been a time when he, like the rest, made himself available but circumstances had stopped that years ago. He summed it up to Wooden later when he was asked where he'd been.

'Is there some kind of problem here?' Wooden had said yet again.

'Not any more!' Chewy answered.

'So was there some kind of problem here?' Wooden had tried again.

'The problem,' Chewy said, 'if you want to put it that way, is theft!'

'Is that the problem then?' Wooden asked. Sharp as a razor, old Wooden.

'Every time!' said Chewy. 'Open Days are a bloody pain! I'm not opening up my place again! I've had so much of my gear in the department nicked during this day every year!'

'By the kids?'

'No! By the bloody parents!'

Apart from Chewy's problems there were a few parents who were able to talk sensibly to staff about their progeny, but quite a few of the others did not feel the same way. Some of the comments which flew around, parent to parent, were pointed, to say the least.

'How could he say that about little Christian?'

This was the result of one member of staff suggesting that their child needed more than just psychological therapy. He was a little shit of the first order.

'He said that to me as well!'

Same thing, same problem. A poisonous little shit.

'But what you're saying doesn't make sense!' was another standard line which was always offered to staff. Idleness, stupidity or ineptitude, as a comment upon their own child, invariably came as a shock to many parents. What they didn't realise was that some kids can show completely different personalities. There was the one who they knew and loved when they were at home but there was often another, less lovable, when that same child was at school. Some parents didn't like having that pointed out.

As the day ground on relentlessly, Jolly flitted amongst the throng smiling inanely, talking rubbish and hoping, not only that everything was going smoothly but that all the parents were happy. Maisie was watching him through the window as he performed for all.

'Oh, will you just look at him!' she muttered to herself. 'What does he look like. It's enough to make you throw up!'

The P.E. Oaf and Action, still with a headache from the Gala, were up on the playing field, setting up the stumps for the staff versus parents' cricket match but they were 'on a loser' there. Even with the heavy cloud, wet grass and the prospect of more rain at any moment, there were dozens of parents, with attendant offspring, all over the field. They were intent on having their picnic. Half a dozen or more had taken up residence on the pitch itself between the stumps and both the P.E. Oaf and Action had to give up. The match was doomed anyway as a few minutes later the rain came down again with a vengeance. Positive 'stair rods' this time and it didn't stop for the rest of the day. Inside the marquee the Dining Room staff, serving tea to the multitude, were on good form being highly appreciative of the parents who swarmed, pushing and shoving in their 'up market' demanding fashion, to be first to the front. The comments from the staff were succinct and accurate, but only to each other and from the corner of their mouths, while they retained a serene civility and a welcoming smile.

'Fat bitch!'

'Stuck up cow!'

'Stupid old shit!'

'Ugly old tart!'

'Hope they all fucking choke on it!'

Such a 'happy', 'caring' ancillary staff. These moneyed morons successfully continued to block any access to the tea even after they'd been served by standing around, unaware of anyone else who may have wanted refreshment. Vic was one of the waiting mass being jostled by others and, as he tried to inch nearer the tea table, he found himself being talked to by a particularly obnoxious and puerile worm of an individual, well known to many of the staff. He was not only a complete and utter snob and dilettante but, in short and common parlance, a total twat. This jumped up nematode was Mr Julian Stanton-Fantley, a self styled aristocrat with affected vowels and extremely limp with it.

'It's such a bore!' he began. 'What with this recession and having to tighten one's belt, life is becoming quite tragic these days!'

'Oh, really,' Vic answered in a totally uninterested monotone.

'I mean,' Stanton-Fantley continued, 'we've almost had to forget about the villa and the mountain chalet. We've only been four or five times to each of them this year and as for the houses over here, well, it's not the same with only six servants to look after one.'

'I can imagine,' Vic replied, feeling completely trapped by this fawning idiot.

'But, then again,' Stanton-Fantley grinned stupidly, 'We all have our cross to bear! Oh! Forgive the reference, Chaplain!'

'Not at all,' Vic smiled coldly. 'I was just thinking it must be rather hard being down to your last two million, a villa in Crete, a country house in Austria and two others over here. That's without the two Volvo's, of course, one B.M.W. and a fading one year old Rolls. Life must be absolute hell for you!'

Gradually, the Escape Committee had managed to negotiate their way to the staff room without being caught by any parents. They were all ready for the cupboard on the wall. It was a tricky kind of a day which needed some anaesthetic from time to time. The skill, which they'd all developed over the years, was in being seen but not stopped. Deft, deliberate footwork and careful manoeuvring through the crowd, perfected and honed during many events like this, kept them successfully free from the punters.

'I reckon we'll be free and clear in about another hour,' Harry said.

'With a bit of luck!' Vic agreed.

'I see Jolly Jack's still at it!' Lill said, pointing out of the window.

'He'll be going strong for hours yet,' Compo said. 'He's terrified not to!'

'I wonder what he finds to say, all bloody day long?' Rusty wondered.

'Bugger all,' Chewy said. 'But he's got a knack of being able to talk endless crap with about three thousand permutations to every line of it!'

The Wide Mouthed Frog and Harvey Sheasby were doing their bit at the same time. She was in the marquee, quacking on to some fright of a woman dressed in bright yellow and wearing a hat which looked just like a upside down dust bin lid. The whole effect took on the appearance of a giant walking, wrinkly daffodil. Wide Mouth was going on about her 'gels'.

'Of course,' she said. 'I do take a strong line on dress. I always insist on them being tidy.'

'Oh, yes,' said the daffodil, hanging on her every word.

'I do,' Wide Mouth said. 'For instance, there's the buttons!'

'Buttons?' asked the daffodil.

'Yes, buttons on the blouse!' Wide Mouth answered. 'One button undone is quite acceptable. Two buttons undone is simply untidy, but three buttons undone, well, that's just making themselves available!'

'Oh, how I do agree!' the daffodil said, the hat wobbling back and forth as she nodded. What she didn't realise was that Wide Mouth was referring to staff temptation, not other kids!

Harvey was only a few feet away, boring to death a frumpy fat couple who couldn't get away from him. He was banging on about his 'healthy body, healthy mind' routine and a few minutes later he was still at it. Their eyes had glazed over after the first few seconds.

'Mind you,' Harvey continued. 'Things have changed. Oh, yes, changed.'

'Really?' came the tired reply.

'Oh, yes!' Harvey said. 'It's not the same as it used to be. There's not enough thought for 'service' these days. No. I remember when I first came into the profession....'

The fat frumpy couple closed their eyes in despair, then looked at each other, nodded and walked away, leaving Harvey talking to himself.

The ground, as Chewy had predicted, was now like a quagmire, mud everywhere. Women were having a hell of a time trying to either keep their high heels on, or stopping themselves sinking into the mud. Some of the kids looked as if they'd been dipped in the stuff. It was even causing problems with the secret smokers sector, in that even in the bushes, under the dripping trees, they couldn't keep their fags going at all. Other problems developed as the nurse had a rash of injuries arrive, all caused by umbrellas being poked into eyes, up noses, ears and all other points lower from folk passing in and out from the marquee.

On her way from the main building, Maggie dived into the marquee to see if she could grab a cup of tea and as she squirmed her way through the mass of bodies inside, she spotted one of the staff, sitting all by herself in the far corner, crying her eyes out. It was Blodwin McPhee. She taught music. Her speciality was the zither. A huge mountain of a woman, she now sat there, wobbling with distress.

'Blodwin,' she said softly. 'Oh, Blodwin, whatever is wrong?'

Blodwin looked up dolefully, tears running down her face.

'It's over!' she sniffed. 'It's all over!' She promptly burst into more tears.

Maggie steered her out from the marquee and up to the staff room, and she sat her down under the pigeon holes where they'd have a little more privacy.

'Hey,' Maggie consoled her quietly. 'Come on. It's just the end of term. That's all.'

Blowin shook her head, the tears still running. 'I know,' she moaned. 'I know. It's so sad.'

'But you have all of the holidays,' Maggie soothed, 'and then you'll be back, refreshed, ready to start all over again.'

'I don't give a stuff for this rat hole!' she said suddenly.

'Then what is it?' Maggie asked.

'I've just had an awful, terrible phone call from my hubby,' warbled Blodwin.

Maggie immediately assumed there had been some awful accident, a sudden death or even the beginnings of a divorce. She didn't know what to say as Blodwin continued to sob, muttering,'It's over, it's… over.'

'Can I help in any way,' Maggie offered in desperation.

Blodwin looked at her, tears streaming down her cheeks with a slow shake of her head.

Maggie tried again. 'Would it help to talk about it?

'Well,' Blodwin blinked, mopping her tears.

'Yes?' Maggie said softly.

'Well…' Blodwin said again

'Yes?' encouraged Maggie.

'The cat's just died!'

Later in the afternoon parents began to leave, trailing crying kids who had to leave their friends behind. They climbed into their cars, parked on one side of the field, and then spent a good half hour playing 'dodgems' with each other on the soft and slippery ground. Most of them were rapidly bogged down to their axles after spinning wheels churned up gobs of soggy earth, mud being sprayed everywhere and slithering around totally out of control. A dozen or so had smacked into each other and now the only exit was well and truly blocked. It took the ground staff, with the two school tractors and their truck to pull them apart and off the field. The P.E. Oaf was not a happy man. His playing field and cricket square now looked like the aftermath of the Battle of the Somme. And so ended another glorious Open Day, but there was still the Parents' Association Ball that evening.

7

By six o'clock the rain had eased and the ground staff had found various bits of board to lay over the entrance to the marquee where the mud was worst and deepest. That at least would give the main access a reasonable surface. Parents began to arrive just after seven by which time both ground and dining room staff had transformed the interior for the dinner.

This was a much more sedate affair than the Sixth Form Ball. A small ensemble were churning out 'fox trotty' music and Jolly, although feeling much more relaxed at this kind of event, was still fussing about making sure everyone was happy. Very few of the staff were there but all the toadys had turned up with their pathetic spouses. The Wide Mouthed Frog, dressed again like a black galleon in full sail, Harvey Sheasby in his threadbare dinner suit and Rollerball, complete with white double breasted jacket and black, remarkably tight trousers, were busily boring various people, while big Sharon, Rollerball's wife, in a wafty, chiffon, livid orange number, was getting steadily pissed. She wasn't the only one either.

The parents were indulging themselves heavily of the wine, spirits and beer which the School had provided for the small sum of thirty five pounds a ticket to the Ball. On the face of things they were a true collection of caring, understanding, sensitive and, yes, fairly wealthy individuals, but they were now showing their true colours as grasping, mean bastards, intent on consuming as much as possible while they were there. By the time the dinner things had been cleared away there were quite a few of them who were barely able to stand up, never mind dance.

Some of their kids were there but they were no better than their parents. There were going to be quite a few headaches in the morning. The popular place to be, as far as the kids were concerned was round at the back of the bar where the main stock of booze was held. Eddie Domple, Chewy's technician, was running that and slid more than a few drinks in their direction as the evening progressed. Behind that another service access had been organised in the marquee so that the bar could be set up more easily. That turned out to be a magnet for the smokers amongst the kids who used it regularly throughout the whole evening.

Unfortunately for them it was also the main entry for the electrical cable which supplied power for the beer pumps, lighting and the P.A. system. The traffic from the smokers was heavy and one heavily inebriated sixteen year old, staggered through grabbing anything to stay upright. He caught the main cable, which had been raised to clear one side of the entrance, and brought it down as he steadied himself. Then, under its own weight, it placed a great strain on the main contacts which sat just inside the Marquee. The main feed had been rigged up to this from which ran all the other smaller cables to service the other outlets. A drum roll then brought the assembled company to look towards the stage area where Jolly was standing in front of the microphone.

He tapped the mike to gain attention and then began. 'Ladies and Gentlemen. Here we are again at the end of another term...'

The main electrical cable, where it linked to the contact board, fizzed as the terminals complained under the strain from it's own drooping weight. A few sparks spat at the marquee canvass and, as Jolly rambled on, more of them crackled off, drying out the damp fabric and creating tiny brown marks. None of this could be seen as it was well behind the bar. Even Eddie Domple, leaning across the bar and sipping a freshly pulled pint, didn't hear or notice the growing flickering behind him as Jolly continued to quack on to everyone.

The alarm was raised by a passing cyclist, taking an illicit short cut through the school on his way back from a basket weaving class. He spotted the flames coming up from the back of the marquee and stopped, skidding, dropping his bike, and ran into the marquee yelling, 'FIRE! FIRE!', at the top of his voice. Everything stopped, all eyes turned to him and then the whole marquee was engulfed with laughter at this nutcase shrieking his head off and dressed in black and fluorescent green lycra cycling gear, complete with a cycling helmet. They all thought it was a deliberate joke. All except Jolly.

Then the flames billowed out from the back of the bar, singing Eddies hair and total panic took over. People ran in all directions, diving under the canvas walls to get out, not even considering the main exit. By the time the Fire Brigade arrived the marquee was well away. It took over an hour to control the blaze, by which time there wasn't a great deal left of it. Jolly, stunned, singed and flecked with black smudges, from the bits of the marquee which had burnt and floated off, just stood there in the blue flashing light from the Fire Engine. The Fire Chief, yes the same one, walked slowly up to him.

'Well, well, well,' the Chief said. 'You and your little ways!'

Saturday morning dawned bright and clear. Not a rain cloud or any kind of cloud was in the sky. With the weather warm and sunny, the ground staff had been busy since just after seven o'clock clearing away the debris of the previous day but mainly the evening. A blackened, scorched patch was all that remained where the marquee had been. The remains of the canvas, supporting poles and furniture had been taken away by a special truck brought in by the local authority. That had left the ground staff with the rest. Two full skips of empty tinnies, left over food, paper plates and all manner of tacky rubbish, including a remarkable assortment of 'undergarments', from both sexes, stood groaning, waiting to be taken away. Parental activity had obviously been much more rampant than the Sixth Form Ball attendees, by a long way.

The lads had spent the whole morning on this clearing up and they didn't get the place tidied up properly until well after lunchtime. It was just as well that this was the last main 'do' of the term. If the kids had been here it would have been impossible, and without them the place had a definite 'Mary Celeste' feel to it, which on reflection was not a dissimilar situation to having Jolly in control.

He was now by himself in his study, poring over the applications for the Deputy's job, trying to forget about the previous evening. The final written warning from the Fire Chief lay on his desk. That had not been a pleasant experience. Three in a row was not a special recommendation for any Headmaster. With a great deal of effort he now applied himself and tried to concentrate on the task in hand, the vetting of all the applications for the post of Deputy Head. In total there had been fifty four responses to the advertisement, and now he had the onerous task of sifting through them to finalise a short list which, he hoped, would be around ten. That shouldn't be too difficult. It actually proved to be less than easy.

There were so many applications which simply terrified him. They would be far too 'pushy' as far as he was concerned. In truth he'd eliminated at least fifteen who would have been an asset to the school but, bless him, he would never have been able to cope with common sense, efficiency and that rare commodity, intelligence. They didn't know it but they were all better off for this. They would have resigned in the first week if he'd actually appointed any one of them. Eventually he had seven, a lower number than he would have liked, but at least they were 'safe', although he wasn't too happy about one of them at all.

He was in fact obliged to include that application, another internal one, so he stacked it with the others in a neat, small pile on his desk and brought the others through to Maisie's desk ready for the despatch of the, 'I regret to inform you' letters on Monday. He added the chosen list of the seven contenders, together with a short letter of invitation for interview, and went off home.

The interviews were now set for just over a week's time, which was perfect timing to allow him to appoint someone and then catch his plane to Korea. He was looking forward to that.

On the afternoon of the second Monday of the holiday, the candidates began to arrive, one by one. Jolly had shown the applications to the Dean before the letters of invitation were sent and tried to point out to him the one he wasn't happy with.

'He's on the staff, so we're obliged to interview, I'm afraid,' the Dean had said.

Well, at least Jolly had tried. He would just have to see him. Three of the seven were from other schools and four from Braumstate itself. One of these, a late entry, had taken everyone by surprise. Jolly now sat in his study. With him were the Dean, a couple of clergy Governors, the feisty Mrs Blomfield and the Prick, although some of them wondered why he was there at all. The Dean acted as chairman and in front of him were the seven letters of application with their CV's. The late entry was to be the last to be seen.

'Well. Headmaster!' the Dean said. 'I think we should begin!'

'Indeed, Mr Dean,' Jolly said. 'Indeed.'

He picked up the phone and buzzed the Mad Hatter.

'Fine, fine,' she answered and then walked through to collect the first victim.

They were all sitting around in the drawing room, pretending not to see or notice each other, but surreptitiously doing just that. A few light smirks began to form alongside a couple of deep depressions as the atmosphere thickened with the heavy emotions of expectation. Interviews of this kind, where all the candidates were lumped together, were always hateful experiences. It was always slightly unnerving for any normal person but as it was, very few qualified on that count.

'Mr Ashborne?' Maisie asked, and a spindly, weak scarecrow got to his feet.

'Would you come this way please?'

He followed her nervously into the study, as if the last trump had sounded. He was shown to the chair in the middle and the front of the long table, with the 'panel' on the other side. Directly opposite him sat the Dean, appearing to be three times normal size, which he was to most of the others. One of the clerics had dropped off already and the other one was well on his way. They both woke up with a start when the Dean spoke.

'Good afternoon, Mr Ashborne!' he boomed.

The little man became even more nervous than before. Fifteen minutes later he was back out, to Maisie's surprise. 'He should have been in there for at least half an hour,' she thought. 'It must have been a riveting experience!'

It had been. He'd hardly said a word.

'One down, and out. Six to go!' she muttered to herself and then the phone buzzed again.

Number two was another 'outsider', a Mr Bygglowe. He was a rotund, ball of a man with a distinct waddle, rather like a penguin, as he walked through following Maisie into the study. This one lasted a little longer. Half an hour later he emerged looking rather satisfied with himself. This didn't help the rest of them who were now beginning to run out of cracks in the wall to follow in their attempt to pass the time. What he didn't know was that the Dean had been singularly unimpressed.

'Rather smug and self important,' he said, with Jolly immediately nodding.

Without the Dean's agreement it would difficult, if not impossible, for him to argue for any of the candidates on offer. The next to go was Rollerball. He slid into the study and sat there confidently, crossing his legs to one side but accidentally kicking the table as he did so. That 'blew his cool' slightly but also jogged the clerics out of their doze. It took him a couple of seconds to compose himself and then sat, waiting for the questions. Jolly welcomed him this time then the Dean asked him a question.

'I understand you have some experience at leadership already?'

Rollerball smirked.

'Yes, Mr Dean,' he said. 'As a matter of fact I have. Outside school hours I run a club for youngsters.'

'Oh, yes,' Jolly said. He didn't know about this. 'Can you tell us about that?'

'Indeed,' Rollerball replied. 'The club is specifically organised for those who are particularly interested in the digestive systems of slugs. We have a rich variety in the soil around here, so there is a constant source of specimens available to us.'

'Fascinating,' said the Dean, wrinkling his nose. This didn't seem to him to be an important qualification for leadership.

'What could you bring to the role of Deputy Head?' the Prick suddenly asked.

Rollerball smirked slightly at this. He'd expected that one.

'Well,' he said, shifting his weight. 'There are many aspects of the job which could be easily expanded.'

'Oh, yes,' Mrs Blomfield said, expectantly. 'And what are they?'

'Discipline, Respect, Understanding and, above all else, Guidance,' oozed Rollerball. 'These are the important areas which need some, slight, reorganising.'

Anyone else would have thrown up on the spot but they all sat there listening to the garbage which continued to fall out of his mouth. He then droned on and on, and after a few more questions he thought he'd given all the 'right' answers and said all the 'right' things. Everything which Jolly would want to hear. As he left the room with a self satisfied smile on his face the Dean scratched a thick line through his name. Rollerball had got that one substantially wrong. Although he'd been in there for just over forty five minutes he had talked undiluted crap for most of it. He was the only one who didn't know it.

With three down and four to go it seemed right to take a break. Maisie organised coffee and served both the 'panel' and all the interviewees. The four whom remained to be seen were in various states which ranged from something near fear to smug expectation, except for one of them who was bored rigid and wished he'd never applied for the sodding job. Twenty minutes later they began again and the first candidate, Mr Brocklehurst, was asked in. This one was in there for a good hour and smarmed his way through all the questions appearing to be a real smoothy, knowing exactly what to say and even making partial sense. They were, for the first time, reasonably impressed. He ambled out feeling he had it in the bag and what was worse he gave that impression to the others as he confidently sat, crossed his legs and slowly smiled at all of them. Bastard.

That left three to go, all of them from the school. The first one of these was Deep Throat. He slowly walked to the chair and carefully placed his bum on it as if it were made of glass, his bum that is, not the chair. Jolly provided the welcome again and the Dean began with the first question. 'How do you see the school developing over the next ten years?'

It was probably the worst question he could have asked. Deep Throat took in a slow breath and began. After ten minutes he hadn't reached year two.

'...so... you... see.., it... has... to... be... taken... in... a... very... careful... step... by... step... slow... process.' he droned on, a forefinger waving to every slow word spoken.

The two clerics had dropped off again, minutes ago, the Prick was doodling something vile on his notepad, Jolly stared fixedly ahead, the Dean had dropped his head to his chest and Mrs Blomfield was becoming totally pissed off with the whole thing. She cut into what he was saying with another question.

'How would you react to the need for major changes in the National Curriculum,' she asked, testily. She meant well but that was the other question none of them should have asked Deep Throat. He was off again.

'I'm... glad... you... asked... me... that... because... it... raises... very... im.. por.. tant... ques.. tions... for... all... of... us... in... ed.. uca.. tion... today... That... is... to... say......'

And so it went on and on and on.

When he eventually left the room, an hour and a half later, they were none the wiser than before he'd arrived, and they all had to walk around with the windows wide open, just to wake themselves up. One of the two clerics, however, was now gone to the world and snoring loudly. Before the next sacrifice arrived, the Dean smacked the table to bring them back to the land of the living.

'When you're ready gentlemen!' he snarled at them.

Now it was the Head Boy's turn. He bounced in, full of the joys of spring, humming one of his re-written hymns. In fact, he was terrified but tried desperately not to show it. Mrs Blomfield wondered what he'd be like and was offered the first question.

'Do you have any interests which might be useful to the school?' she asked, benignly.

In his nervous state he didn't know what to say for a moment and then made the great mistake of pulling out his pile of hymn re-writes. It was all down hill from that point. He managed to bumble along for ten minutes but then gave up. So did they. He walked out, dejected, and the phone buzzed for the last candidate. Maisie walked through and nodded to him. He walked through, sat down, smiled at the panel and said, 'Good afternoon!'

Jolly stiffened visibly. He wasn't going to enjoy this interview at all. Just over an hour later that candidate walked back to the drawing room, not caring a shit whether he was in with a chance or not. Twenty agonising minutes dragged by for the others while the panel attempted to sort out their feelings and decisions about the people they'd seen. Rollerball sat on the edge of his seat, wringing his hands. Deep Throat stared blankly ahead, looking as if he'd just died and the Head Boy sat over in the corner sulking, knowing he'd blown it. Of the others only Brocklehurst had a smile on his smug face. Inside Jolly's study the discussion eventually came down to a difficult decision. There were only two from all seven of them who the 'panel' agreed could handle the job, but that wouldn't have happened if the Dean hadn't been adamant about it. Only Jolly wasn't quite as positive. Then Maisie's phone buzzed again and she walked back to the drawing room.

'Mr Brocklehurst,' she said.

Another self satisfied smirk flooded over his face as he followed her back to the study. That, for the rest of them, seemed to be that. A second 'call' usually meant the job had gone. Fifteen minutes later he was back, looking just as smug. But then Maisie followed him out and nodded again to the other one. He was just as surprised as anyone. Another fifteen minutes ticked by and then he came back and sat down. Brocklehurst forced a smile as their eyes met.

'Nice day,' he said.

'So far,' answered the other.

'You work here, don't you?' asked Brocklehurst.

'Sometimes,' grinned the other.

'It's seems a very pleasant place,' Brocklehurst said.

'For the moment,' said the other.

'Oh,' Brocklehurst said. 'Something about to happen?'

'Nothing really,' said the other. 'But the demolition gang should be here in a couple of days.'

'Demolition?' Brocklehurst asked, his face taking on a puzzled expression.

'Yes,' the other said. 'This place was condemned a couple of years ago. The local authority are insisting that it comes down now. Could go by itself at any time.'

Brocklehurst immediately looked round the room. The cracks on the wall took on a special significance for him. Two of the others, Mr

Ashborne, the scarecrow, and Mr Bygglowe, the round ball, stiffened, stood up and quickly left the room.

'Then there's the health checks,' said the other.

'Health checks?' Brocklehurst asked, looking even more worried.

'Mmm. There's been an outbreak of syphilis,' the other said, nonchalantly. 'Bit of an epidemic. They still don't know where that arrived from. Six kids and two of the staff went down with it. Still in hospital as yet.'

Brocklehurst was sitting bolt upright now, hanging on the settee. 'I knew nothing of this!' said Brocklehurst.

'Not exactly the thing to boast about, is it?' said the other. 'Just like the coven. Bet you didn't know anything about that either.'

That was enough to get Rollerball out the door as fast as he could go.

'Coven? What coven?' Brocklehurst was turning ashen.

'Well,' the other said, 'this is the headquarters of the South West. You know that woman on the panel?'

Brocklehurst nodded.

'Chief Witch,' the other said emphatically. 'And sitting next to her, the big fella in black?'

Another nod.

'Chief Warlock, Head Wizard,' said the other. 'Has been for years, although he manages to keep it pretty quiet.'

The Head Boy and even Deep Throat blinked at this, then they too departed quickly.

Brocklehurst was looking very unhappy.

'The bore is having to join in,' the other said.

'Join in!'

'Yep, but only once a week,' the other said. 'Usually on a Saturday night, midnight, stark naked round the burning cross. That goes on right through the year, all weathers, then we have a gang bang on New Year's Eve. Makes a change.'

Brocklehurst was on his feet and out the door in seconds. Maisie ran after him.

'Mr Brocklehurst, Mr Brocklehurst!' she called. 'Is there anything wrong?'

'Nothing!' he yelled over his shoulder. 'Nothing at all! I have to go! I'm pulling out! Good-bye!'

And he was off, legging it away and round the corner. When the Dean, Jolly and the others found out, when Maisie buzzed through on the intercom, there was only one thing to do.

'Well', said the Dean, 'that leaves us with a simple decision.'

The remaining candidate would have to be the new Deputy. Jolly was horrified and tried to reason with the Dean.

'I'm not sure we have the right person, sir,' he whined, miserably.

'He seemed quite forthright to me,' the Dean answered, pushing the application letters to one side, 'and that is exactly what we need.'

'But…' Jolly tried again but the Dean cut him short.

'Headmaster, we don't have the time to readvertise, this last candidate knows the school very well and although I share your apprehension, to a degree, I think he will rise to the position and bring with him a certain directness to the role.'

The Dean may have been a difficult and overbearing Head of Governors with a tendency to apply an 'Old Testament' attitude to all around him but he was no fool, unlike his Headmaster. He was anxious to inject something more than Jolly had provided over the years and would not brook any argument. Jolly wilted visibly as the Dean picked up the phone and asked Maisie to send in the last applicant. And so the new Deputy Head of Braumstate Cathedral School walked back in and sat down. Chewy!

Later, in the early evening, the Escape Committee gathered in the local to find out what had happened.

'You jammy sod!' Rusty said. 'How did you pull that off?'

'Best man for the job!' Chewy grinned.

'Here's to next term!' Lill said. 'I'm looking forward to just watching. This is going to be the best spectator sport for years!'

'Any plans?' Maggie asked.

'None at all, but I expect I'll think of a few!' he said, a wicked twinkle in his eye.

'I'll bet you will!' Vic said.

'That's for sure!' Harry agreed.

'Right!' Compo said. 'Time for another drink!'

He shot off to the bar while the others began to discuss the near future.

'There's only a few days to go now,' Chewy was saying when he returned with a fresh round.

'Let's keep our fingers crossed,' Rusty said. 'Everything's been done, phone calls made. We should all keep an eye on the morning papers on the twenty first.'

'How long did all this take to organise?' Maggie asked.

'Not long,' Chewy said. 'Some photocopies to duplicate official headed note paper, carefully written text, a bit of graphic work printed out and a few phone calls to a handful of friends in London who were happy to co-operate, and that was it.'

'I'd love to see it happening!' Compo said.

'We might just be able to if the TV news gets hold of it,' Harry said.

'Well, we'll soon know,' said Lill.

'Here's to all of them!' said Vic, raising his glass.

'The Management!' they all said together.

On the morning of the twentieth of July, their esteemed 'management' were getting themselves organised. Every one of them was looking forward to the day. Jolly and the Fat Controller would be driving to London, but by different routes, the rest were to travel by train. Not one of them knew the others were going as well. None of them had said a word to each other about their presumed and individual 'good fortune'.

Portia was fussing about packing an overnight bag. She was going with Jolly and then intended to spend the rest of the day shopping in London after dropping him at the Airport, Heathrow. Then she'd be staying with friends before travelling back by herself. She ordered him around, as usual, making sure he had everything he needed and then, with all the bags packed and checked, they loaded the whole lot into the car and set off. Neither of them noticed the transparent bag of white powder under the driving seat.

An uneventful three and a half hours later and they were pulling into the terminal car park. A few minutes later they were standing at the first class check-in desk and Jolly handed over his ticket. The woman behind the desk looked at it, then at Jolly, then back at the ticket.

'Excuse me one moment sir,' she said smiling, and walked over to another of the airline's staff, a great amazon of a woman, and showed her the ticket. They both looked back at Jolly. The big one nodded and walked away.

'What are they doing?' Portia said, irritably.

'I don't know dear,' Jolly said. 'Just some kind of check I imagine.'

He was right there, but he didn't know quite what. The first woman came back, smiled again, and began to go through the routine of seating positions, and the rest of it, although she seemed to be doing it very slowly. Jolly felt a tap on his shoulder, just as he was about to say something to her, and turned to find two large and burly Airport Police standing there.

The Prick had been busy since the early hours, pressing and brushing his uniform. Then he dressed and checked himself in the mirror.

'What a fine figure of a man!' he thought to himself.

He was now back in his previous role as Captain Wilfred O'Rouke, R.A.F., and feeling very proud. He was looking forward to the day and the Palace and, most of all, being presented to the Queen herself. He was in good time for the train, which he climbed on board, being careful not to wrinkle his uniform as he sat and tried to relax for the journey to London. His invitation and pass were safely tucked into his breast pocket and he spent the time composing himself for his audience with her Majesty. A couple of hours later he was in a taxi driving down the Mall. The taxi drove off and straightening his tunic, he then stepped briskly towards the ornate gates of the Palace, his invitation and pass clutched in his hand.

'Good day!' he said to the two Policemen standing there.

'Good day to you sir,' said one of them smiling. 'And what can I do for you?'

The Prick handed over the invitation and pass and stood to full attention, calmly waiting. One of the Policemen took his paperwork and scrutinised it slowly. Then he had a quiet word with his colleague who immediately took his intercom and mumbled a few words into it. The Prick waited uncomfortably as the two Policemen studied both pieces of paper.

'Won't keep you a moment sir,' one of them said, smiling.

Another few seconds ticked by and then an unmarked Police car pulled up behind the Prick, who was still standing to attention. The plain clothes officers climbed out and walked over to the two uniformed men, looked at the paper and then turned to the Prick.

'Would you care to step into the car sir?' one of them asked, taking his arm firmly.

The Prick became somewhat confused by this but went meekly with them. The car drove off at high speed down the Mall.

The Wide Mouthed Frog and Harvey Sheasby were just pulling in to Paddington while this was going on. They had boarded the train separately and then, by chance, had met in the buffet car.

'Hilda!' Harvey greeted her. 'Fancy seeing you! Off to London shopping, eh?'

'Harvey!' she said, 'This is a surprise. Off to London too?'

They then told each other a complete pack of lies about why they were going to London. Neither wanted the other to know what they were doing until they had returned and could then blab on an on about how wonderful it had been. With a cup of coffee each they took over some empty seats.

'D'y know I've been *so busy*,' she said. 'I haven't had a *moment* to rest for days. There's been *so much to do* and...'

She hardly stopped talking until the train pulled in. They walked to the tube and then found they were going the same way. Wide Mouth just happened to mention her destination.

'Well,' Harvey said. 'There's a coincidence!'

'What's that?' she asked.

'Well,' Harvey said, a slightly puzzled look on his face. 'It looks as though were going to the same address!'

They compared addresses and, sure enough, it was the same.

'It's probably one of those big office blocks,' she said, sniffing.

Out came the handkerchief and the nose blowing started. Some of the other folk on the tube looked round to see what was making the row. Once out of the tube they made their way through a few streets and found themselves deep in Soho, standing outside a garish, neon lit frontage. One huge word was mounted up above them, flashing on and off. It was 'SPANKARAMA!'

'That's a funny title!' Wide Mouth said. 'I suppose it's just some sort of temporary exhibition.'

'Do you think so?' Harvey asked.

'Probably,' she said. 'Let's just go and have a look.'

While they'd been standing there two men had been watching them from a car across the street. One of them brought up an intercom as they walked into the building.

'Suspects have entered,' he said. 'Let's go!'

Three streets away, in Wardour Street, a centre for film and TV production companies, the Fat Controller had been lucky enough to find a parking place. Not an easy task in this part of the city. He locked his car and wandered down the street, looking for the address on his letter. He didn't get very far. In front of him and behind car doors opened and he was surrounded by four men.

'Michael Farnsworth-Hunt?' one of them asked.

'Y,yes,' he said nervously.

'My name is Detective Inspector James,' the man said, holding up his warrant card. 'I arrest you for suspected terrorist activity, and warn you that anything you say may be taken down and used in evidence!'

He was bundled into the lead car, the siren blared out, and they were driving fast through the narrow streets. Minutes later they pulled up outside Bow Street Police Station. Handcuffed and terrified they led him inside, took him through to the charge room and as he was taken inside, his chin almost hit the floor. Sitting apart, on the other side of the room were Jolly, Portia, the Prick, Wide Mouth and Harvey Sheasby.

'Oh, no!' Jolly whined. 'Not you as well!'

'Another one?' the desk Sergeant said. 'This looks far bigger than we thought!'

Ten minutes later the Sergeant took all the paperwork in to his Superintendent. He wasn't happy. There were too many coincidences about the bunch outside.

'I see what you mean Sergeant,' the Super said. 'All from some peculiar, ancient school in the 'sticks'. Looks like a clever cover for a much bigger operation. We could be onto something here. They'll be the tip of the proverbial iceberg, I'd like to bet. We need to find any others they may be working with. I think I'd better have a word with them all first. Funny looking lot aren't they?'

The Sergeant followed him into the charge room where they all sat round, every one of them steeped in a mixture of misery, humiliation and indignation.

'Right then!' the Super said. 'I think we need some answers from you lot!'

They looked at each other in confusion and Jolly tried to speak.

'If I might say, officer...' he began.

'Just hang on you!' the Super snarled. 'There'll be plenty of time for talking when I've finished!'

Jolly shut up, terrified to say another word.

'We have a catalogue of crimes here,' the Super began again, waving the paperwork in the air. 'First we have you two,' pointing at Portia and Jolly. 'Forged airline tickets and a kilo of drugs in the car! Very tasty!'

Then he turned to the Prick.

'And you!' he said. 'Impersonating a Captain in the R.A.F. with a forged invitation to see the Queen, of all people; and very poor attempt at that!'

The Prick tried to speak but was silenced by one look from the Super.

'We've already checked on you and discovered, lo and behold, that you were only a Flight Sergeant in some God forsaken hole in Scunthorpe! What, I wonder was your intent, if you'd been able to get into the Palace, eh?'

'And then we have you two!' he said, glaring at the Wide Mouthed Frog and Harvey Sheasby. 'Apprehended entering a rather sleazy emporium and tipped to be involved in the production of obscene pornographic images! Very nice!'

Wide Mouth spluttered at this, her face purple with embarrassment. Harvey's mouth had dropped open and stayed that way.

'Last but not least we have you!' the Super said, pointing at the Fat Controller. 'Caught red handed with half a dozen guns and enough ammunition to start a minor war, all badly concealed under the back seat of your car! I wonder what you were going to do with that lot, eh?'

A stunned silence was his only response and then they all started protesting at once.

'Now look here!' said Jolly.

'How dare you suggest...!' Portia shrieked.

'It's a lie!' the Prick squeaked.

'I have *never* been so *insulted!*' Wide Mouth complained, blowing her nose.

'I don't believe this is happening!' Harvey moaned.

The Fat Controller just sagged, head forward and shaking from side to side saying, 'No! No! No!'

They were booked, under loud and long protestations of innocence and 'invited' to inspect the cells. After two days they were released, on bail, but the whole thing was eventually sorted out a few days later. The news made the National press but only as a minor skirmish and was written up as a 'silly season' joke. The local papers nearer and around Braumston were much more explicit. A detailed story broke before they arrived back and the front page headlines were a joy to behold.

BRAUMSTON'S STAFF SHOCK!

SCHOOL STAFF ACCUSED OF... EVERYTHING!

BRAUMSTON'S BUFFOONS!

The Escape Committee were ecstatic about what happened. It couldn't have been better. Now they could enjoy their holiday to the full. But they all knew that in less than two months they would all be back and they wondered what that first day of another academic year would bring for Braumstate Cathedral School.

THE CHIEF SYCOPHANTS

Harvey Sheasby

The Wide-Mouthed Frog

'Farce - a form of drama which seems to me often more true to the facts of life as we know them than many great tragedies.'

John Mortimer 1923-2009

EPILOGUE

Postscript

All that happened last year. Since then a great deal has changed at Braumstate Cathedral School. Jolly couldn't cope with Chewy as Deputy Head. Chewy laughed at him too much. Jolly didn't like that. Apart from that Chewy scared the shit out of all the toadys and the nutters on the staff and, one by one, they were lucky to find jobs where other schools didn't realise what arseholes they really were. Chewy was really, really sad to see them go, waving his hankie at each one as they left, but not as sad as Jolly Jack. He was now without his faithful creeps and servile headcases to bolster his minuscule ego.

Except for every Monday, the morning meetings have gone, torpedoed by Chewy as he either didn't turn up or arranged fire drills just before they were due to start. There are very few time wasting meetings left as well. Chewy and the staff talk through what they need to do as things happen so Jolly had little opportunity to say anything.

And all of the crap memoranda which used to fly around are things of the past. If staff don't talk then Chewy doesn't act. If he gets a memo he sends it back with a brick attached. They got the point fairly quickly. Decisions, which Jolly never did make, were pushed through by Chewy first and then argued over afterwards. Jolly couldn't cope with that. Just recently he threw in the towel and took early retirement. He may soon, if he's not careful, be residing at Her Majesties Pleasure for being found guilty of impersonating a human being. There should be an ad in the Times Educational supplement next week for his job.

Wooden, bless him, emerged just like a butterfly, into a first class Headmaster in his new school. He laughs a lot these days.

The Wide Mouth Frog and Harvey Sheasby resigned in confusion and embarrassment after they were caught in the bushes, in a more than compromising position, by the Dean. They argued that they were looking for smokers, but as it was during the holidays no one believed them.

She is now living in St Annes-on-Sea, just down from Blackpool, working in an Ann Summers shop, loving every product on sale and Harvey is a proud commissionairre outside one of the South West's largest cinemas. He always did like uniforms.

Rollerball was arrested for 'lewd trouser movements' in the High Street and his case comes up next month. Deep throat is still there.

Chewy demoted him to looking after difficult parents. That works quite well. He bores them to bloody death so they don't make a lot of fuss anymore. The Head Boy, Nigel bloody St John Burroughs, was a challenge, but Chewy managed that one quite well. He now looks after the seating arrangements for breakfast, lunchtime, teatime and the beginning and end of term services. As before, nobody takes a blind bit of notice of him but it does give the silly sod a sense of power and endless opportunities to re-write all the hymns. He's also on a part time base. The rest of his time he spends hawking alternative hymn sheets outside the Cathedral.

As for the Prick and the Fat Controller, their's is a sorry tale. The Prick was run over by a heavy, petrol driven, grass roller which ran out of control during a cricket match. There's probably no truth to the rumour that Big Mac just happened to be leaning on it, fingering with the start button, before it ran out of control. No one believed that he'd been looking for an excuse to 'murder the bastard' ever since the Prick reduced his wages for taking an extra half hour one lunch time in 1978.

The Fat Controller now runs a car boot sale in Grimsby but not for much longer. For years he'd been using the proceeds from the Entrance Test days, five thousand pounds each time, to run an illicit cannabis 'farm' in his back garden. He supplied most of the clergy and the local Boy Scouts with their 'grass'. Now everyone knew where the money had been going. He should only get a couple of years inside, if he's lucky

Maggie and the Mad Hatter started up a consultancy between them and are doing very well. They advise Independent schools up and down the country how to spot that insidious disease known as 'Paper' and how to control it. There's a lot of business there.

Lill, Compo, Harry and Vic are still there and act as an advisory body to Chewy, salary adjusted and raised of course. This body just happens to convene most Saturday nights in the local pub.

Lady Braumsley and Quentin have now found their true vocations. She had to sell most of her assets in the end to pay for the new building, which should be complete this year. Being virtually broke and near bankrupt she now runs a 'B&B' in the big house with Ralph the butler as a full partner in the business. He fronts the whole thing, she cooks, Quentin still dithers between making the beds and watering his pot plants. Bernie the Bin, bless him, was taken on as a gardener/handyman and, now feeling much closer to 'Mummy', still enjoys living in the little lodge, the old gatekeeper's house of the original estate.

And that's about that, really. Oh, yes. Rusty went from strength to strength and was appointed Deputy Head in his new school after only six months.

They say he might even apply for the vacant Headship at Braumstate Cathedral School!

PPS

In this tale, 'H. E. Roales', the Headmaster's name, is an anagram for something which is a very accurate description of the man he is based on. 'Braumstate', the name of the ficticious school and another anagram, sums up the general attitude which existed during my tenure in the actual school where this whole story took place. I leave you to work out what they are.

KD 2011

Lightning Source UK Ltd.
Milton Keynes UK
UKOW050537191212

203853UK00007B/329/P